TEACHING: WHAT IT'S ALL ABOUT

LEO W. ANGLIN
KENT STATE UNIVERSITY

RICHARD GOLDMAN
NOVA UNIVERSITY

JOYCE SHANAHAN ANGLIN

1817

HARPER & ROW, PUBLISHERS, New York
Cambridge, Philadelphia, San Francisco,
London, Mexico City, São Paulo, Sydney

Photo Credits

viii Lambert, Frederic Lewis; viii Franken, Stock, Boston; viii, 42, 53 Bayer, Monkmeyer; 9 Frederic Lewis; 14, 98, 105, 118 Granger; 17, 19 Culver; 49 Rogers, Monkmeyer; 70, 73 Brody, Stock, Boston; 73 Anderson, Woodfin Camp, 1981; 73, 169, 266 Strickler, Monkmeyer; 73 Schlack, Monkmeyer; 110 IGE; 145 Vannucci, DeWys; 165 M. Pickens, 1981; 160, 171 Franken, Stock, Boston; 175 Beckwith Studios; 211 J. A. Meadows; 214 Kent Record-Courier; 226, 229 Stone, Peter Arnold; 260, 271 Herwig, Stock, Boston; 267, 301 UPI; 286, 291 M. Pickens, 1981; 288 Anderson, Woodfin Camp, 1980; 295 American Airlines; 304 Forsyth, Monkmeyer; 336 Grimes, DeWys; 350 Ponds

Sponsoring Editor: George A. Middendorf
Project Editor: Jon Dash
Designer: Robert Sugar
Production Manager: Willie Lane
Photo Researcher: Mira Schachne
Compositor: Ruttle, Shaw & Wetherill, Inc.
Printer and Binder: Halliday Lithograph Corporation
Art Studio: Danmark & Michaels
Cover Photo: Leinwand, Monkmeyer

Teaching: What It's All About

Library of Congress Cataloging in Publication Data

Anglin, Leo W., 1946–
  Teaching: what it's all about.

  Includes bibliographies and index.
  1. Teaching.   I. Goldman, Richard, 1942–   II. Title.
LB1025.2.A73   371.1′02   81-13326
ISBN 0-397-47399-0   AACR2

CONTENTS

PREFACE

This book is an attempt to portray the real world of teachers: their professional roles, their responsibilities, their joys and frustrations. Throughout the ages, teachers have had as a common goal the preparation of youth to become active citizens in a society. Although this ultimate goal has remained constant, the manner in which it is pursued has been constantly evolving in response to the ever-shifting social and cultural milieu (industrialization, cultural pluralism, egalitarianism, etc.).

Today, an unprecedented percentage of the population receives a formal education. Never before in human history has formal education been as greatly needed. Current U.S. government figures show that more than $75 billion are being spent each year to support various aspects of education. Our educational system employs more people (teachers, administrators, and support personnel) than any other single profession. Today's teachers are better educated and better prepared to meet the instructional needs of youth than were teachers at any other time in our history. Likewise, an unparalleled amount of educational support is available for today's teachers in the form of curriculum materials, teaching aids, and social services for both students and teachers.

At the center of our educational system is the instructional process, and at the hub of all instructional activity is the classroom teacher. A teacher must assume the complex task of orchestrating all the diverse elements in the educational system into a whole that is meaningful and helpful to the students. Because each teacher, student, school, and community is different, it is impossible to predict exactly what should be done in every teaching situation. The teacher must decide, based on the information that is available at a particular time, the best way to handle each situation on an individual basis. In essence, a successful teacher must be an effective problem solver. That role is . . .

Rewarding,

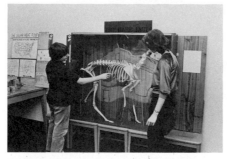

Exciting,

Complex,

Difficult at Times, but Always a Role in Which the Teacher Can Make the Difference.

Teaching is not new to you, even though this may be the first education textbook that you have encountered. In fact, it is very likely that you have had more contact with teachers than with any other occupational group. By the time the average student has finished high school, approximately 13,000 hours will have been spent in direct contact with classroom teachers. Looking back on this classroom experience, you can probably recall a teacher or two whom you highly respected and whom you now hold as an important personal model for the manner in which a teacher should perform. However, you view these past experiences from the point of view of a student judging an authority figure. Over the next few years you will find there is far more to teaching than meets the eye. The purpose of this book is to broaden your perspective about teaching by examing the teaching profession from the other side of the desk: from the teacher's perspective. Specifically, it should help you gain a better understanding of the following:

- *The major roles* (instructional and noninstructional) that teachers must play both within and outside their classrooms. The specific tasks, skills, and responsibilities that constitute these roles will be highlighted so that you can begin assessing the particular roles you wish to focus on in your teacher-preparation program.
- *The alternative patterns or models of teaching* that have evolved in an effort to carry out the various teaching roles. Since each child, teacher, school, and community is unique, and no single teaching style or technique can be expected to fit all situations, the teacher, as a professional, needs to develop and use a repertoire of alternative teaching styles, techniques, and activities.
- *The current issues* confronting teachers, such as the back-to-basics movement, the courts and the classroom, the teacher and the school community, unions and professional organizations, and mainstreaming. Each issue will be examined in terms of the conflicting theories underlying it, the educational alternatives that have evolved from it, and its implications for various teaching roles.
- Your own fitness for *a teaching or nonteaching career* in education. Each of you has a particular set of personal strengths and weaknesses with which you should become familiar and use as a primary criterion in your occupational choice. Consequently, *encounter activities* will punctuate the text in an attempt to relate the discussion of particular teaching roles, models, and issues to you as a potential practitioner.

The design of this book assumes that you will be visiting and participating in a variety of educational settings throughout your college experience. It provides tools and suggestions to assist you in your classroom observations. Since nothing is more boring than being a passive observer in the classroom, it is essential that as you observe in the classroom you react to and interact with the teaching situation in a systematic manner.

To the skilled observer, the classroom presents a plethora of activity that can only be fully understood with careful observation over extended periods of time. Consequently, Chapter 3 is devoted to the development of observational skills. In addition, there are suggested *encounter activities* at the end of each chapter that will help direct your observations in terms of the content of that chapter.

Our ultimate objective, once again, is to help you understand the real world of teachers — their roles, their responsibilities, their joys and frustrations — and to assess your own fitness for a career within this world. In order to develop a well-rounded view, each major role, model, and issue will be examined in terms of the author's perspective, the opinions of prominent educational leaders, the research findings, and, finally, your own observations. This four-part perspective is represented below.

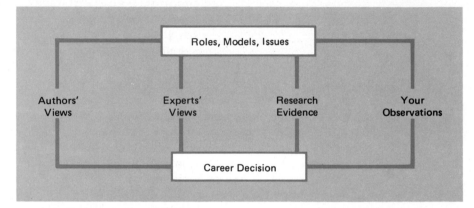

A "map" of your experiences.

Several special features that we hope will enrich and enliven our presentation have been built into the format of the book. These include:

- *Photo essays.* In addition to the usual array of individual photos, charts, and graphs, special photo essays appear, depicting teacher roles in a variety of settings. These essays enable you to analyze a small cross-section of diverse teaching situations and provide a point of comparison for the live situations you will be encountering in your field experiences.
- *Historical flashbacks.* These have been included to illustrate how today's classroom practices may or may not be different from the common instructional practices of 10, 20, 50, or even 200 years ago.
- *Research findings.* Since the turn of the century, the instructional activities of teachers have been extensively studied by educational researchers. Often, research techniques have been inadequate and the findings have not always been useful; occasionally, however, the research does provide useful insights. The findings of various re-

searchers have, therefore, been incorporated into the text of the chapters to help you become aware not only of what is presently known about teaching but also of what aspects of teaching are not, as yet, well understood.

- *Interviews.* These have been included to illustrate the widely differing interests and views of recognized experts in regard to the critical issues that teachers face. In addition to teachers, those interviewed concerning the roles of teachers and schools include superintendents, principals, school board members, janitors, and teacher aides.
- *Famous educator sections.* These include comments and thoughts of well-known educators concerning various issues discussed in the book. These sections illustrate the fact that there are many areas in which even the most respected educators do not agree.
- *Encounter activities.* These activities are designed to assist the reader in linking theory to practice. It is essential that you synthesize the relationship between theory and practice with regard to the classroom teacher if you are to develop your own unique perspective of teaching and the issues that surround it.

Finally, it is impossible to write a book of this nature without revealing one's personal assumptions and biases about teachers and the teaching profession. We have decided to handle this problem in a direct manner by stating our own assumptions and beliefs in this preface.

First and foremost, we believe that effective teachers must be enthusiastically child-oriented. Teachers must be for kids! That is, we feel that the primary reason for entering the teaching profession should be the desire to work with children and help them develop to their full potential. Excluding parenting, no other child-related occupation is charged with the total (physical, intellectual, social, emotional) development of the child. Teachers must not merely create an atmosphere that makes learning exciting; they must also contribute to the child's feelings of importance and self-worth and help the child relate to peers, parents, and other adults.

Next, we believe that effective teaching combines craftsmanship with science. It is a craft in that many of the activities that teachers perform cannot be predicted ahead of time and must vary, based on the learning situation, the instructional goals, and the needs of the individual children. The teacher, as an expert craftsman, draws upon personal experience as well as highly developed instructional skills to provide students with the highest quality educational experience. At times, circumstances and predilections require the teacher to modify, invent, or create new techniques and methods to fit a particular situation.

Teaching is also a science, however, in that there are some instructional techniques and methods that have been proven over time to be more effective than others. Teachers, we believe, must not only be aware of what practitioners, experts, and researchers have found as basic truths in education; they must also be confident about their own abilities to apply and adapt these truths in classroom practice.

We also believe that effective teachers must constantly be sensitive to human individuality. Much has been written about the need for teachers to plan for, interact with, and evaluate students as individuals rather than as nameless groups. Equally important but somewhat less publicized is the need to view teachers as unique individuals. Since every teacher has a unique combination of strengths and weaknesses that influence his or her teaching style, we do not assume that there is one model or ideal that should be used to prepare all teachers. Rather, there are many successful teaching models that both novices and experienced teachers should draw upon in developing their own individual styles.

We realize, of course, that teacher behavior is influenced by environmental considerations as well as by the personal characteristics of students and teachers. The other teachers down the hall, the principal's goals and objectives, the textbook materials that are present in the classroom, the general policies developed by central office personnel and the school board, and the nature of the community that is served by the school — variables like these have considerable influence on how teachers function. Many of these environmental variables will be examined as issues that surround and shape the way teachers function.

Finally, although our primary goal is to inform you about the world of teaching, our secondary goal is to present this information in a manner that simultaneously interests and intrigues you. The world of the teacher is at once demanding, complicated, exciting and rewarding, and we wish to create a portrait that reflects all these features, a portrait that penetrates beyond the obvious surface features of the profession and captures the spiritual and emotional depths that characterize the inner life, the quintessential core of what it is like to be a teacher.

Leo W. Anglin
Richard Goldman
Joyce Shanahan Anglin

Chapter 1

"My Kiddies"

1925 - 1926

Chapter 1

THE PAST
AS PROLOGUE

The institution of schooling that most of us take for granted today is a very recent phenomenon in terms of human history. For the greater part of human history the process of teaching children to survive and function in a particular culture belonged to another institution: the family. Within the bosom of an extended family network, children were taught the skills, norms, and values needed for survival in a premodern society. Because premodern cultures changed little from one generation to the next, parents and grandparents were able to pass on their accumulated knowledge concerning the culture to their children without any need for outside assistance in the form of schools and teachers.

As some societies, such as ancient Greece and China, gradually evolved into more complex and productive economic systems capable of supporting a variety of noneconomic pursuits (e.g., art, music, literature, science, and technology), there arose the need for educated persons outside the family to help teach this expanded culture. Tutors and, in some cases, small, informal schools like the academies of Socrates and Plato came into being to teach the children of the upper classes. In short, the cultural explosion within these ancient societies gave rise to a variety of new, more specialized institutions, among them the institution of schooling.

In the succeeding cultural erosion of the Dark Ages, the specialized institution that had arisen to meet the needs of rapidly advancing cultures (e.g., schools, commerce, and representative government) gradually faded from the scene. Had it not been for the tenacity of one institution born during the Roman Empire, the Roman Catholic Church, much of Western culture might have been lost forever. As in the case of the premodern family, the Roman Catholic Church became an all-encompassing institution that dispensed a broad array of human services—political, economic, educational, and emotional. Throughout the medieval period, teaching and formal education became almost synonymous with the Roman Catholic Church.

After more than a thousand years of dominance and relatively little cultural change, the Catholic empire, like those before it, began to erode. The forces of change—the Protestant Reformation, agricultural innovations, and the reemergence of national states—converged and set in motion another period of cultural explosion: the Renaissance. Once again, this cultural explosion brought forth an overlapping network of specialized institutions to replace the single dominant institution that had previously existed. Once again, the institution of schooling appeared—and, with it, the role of the professional teacher.

Teachers, Schools, and Society

As science and technology continue to quicken the pace of cultural change, the role of schools and teachers becomes increasingly complex. Modern schools are expected to provide a wide variety of social functions, some of which conflict with one another. Those entering the teaching profession must realize that to be successful and effective they must be willing continually to change, learn, and adapt. You are preparing to teach in the twenty-first century! Try to imagine what your role will be. You will not doubt be teaching facts and skills that do not yet exist, in many cases with instructional techniques that have not yet been devised. Your success will depend upon your flexibility and your ability to view teaching as an everchanging process that reflects the society in which it occurs.

Schools, in carrying out their "transmitter of the culture" role, can be viewed as a barometer that reflects the complexity of the surrounding culture. The curriculum of our early colonial schools was usually concerned with little more than basic literacy skills: reading, writing, and arithmetic. Since the economy required no advanced technological skills and most families in the community already shared a common culture, there was little need for more complex schooling. With the coming of the industrial revolution and the sudden surge of European immigrants into American cities in the nineteenth century, schools broadened their curricula to include a variety of technological skills and socialization programs. American culture had expanded and become more technological and pluralistic, and American schools reflected this new cultural complexity. The pluralistic, rapidly changing character of modern American culture has led to a continuing debate over what constitutes the legitimate goals of our present-day schools. This conflict over goals has led to a philosophy of allowing "alternatives" to accommodate various educational goals and teaching models.

In short, as cultures get more complex, schools also get more complex. Out of this complexity, conflict arises: conflict over goals, philosophies, organizational patterns, and teaching methods. One method of managing this conflict is by offering alternatives to the conflicting groups. Another method of conflict management involves the use of the courts. In fact, it is safe to say that the more conflict a society has, the more extensive and highly developed is its legal system. Since America has perhaps the most pluralistic, competitive, and complex society in the world today, it should be no surprise that we also have what may be the world's most legalistic society.

What does all this have to do with you as a prospective teacher? Simply, you must not imagine for a moment that your classroom walls will shut out the complexity, the conflict, and the resulting legalism that characterizes the larger society. American schools and classrooms, like the larger society they mirror, have become increasingly more complex and prone to conflict. But they have also become an increasingly important and an integral part of our society. The advances and changes experienced by our educational system during its short history serve as a prologue of things to come.

SOCIAL SYSTEM

It is reasonable to ask why schools are so dependent upon the moods and trends of society at large. Our educational system is only one of the many social systems that constitute our society; others include the family, political, economic, religious, and judicial systems. A system can be thought of as a set of interdependent units that interact to perform one or more functions. A car is a good example of a simple system. When a car is running, the motor, chassis, tires, brakes, transmission, etc. work in unison. If any one of these units malfunctions, the effectiveness of the total is affected. In other words, a change in one of the units affects not only the other units but the performance of the entire system. A social system is, no doubt, infinitely more complex than a simple mechanical system, but it does follow the same principle. A social system refers to a cluster of interrelated roles and objects that revolve around a certain type of activity. Each society contains a variety of social systems that are themselves interdependent (see Figure 1.1).

A good example of how one social system affects another can be seen in the action resulting from the launching of the first Soviet satellite. The launch had a direct impact upon the American political system, which reacted and provided the impetus, and economic support, to revise the curriculum of the educational system. This interrelatedness stems from the fact that each member of society participates in many social systems. To illustrate this point, look at a day in the life of Shirley Parsons.

> The day began as usual for Shirley as she and her husband prepared breakfast for the family and discussed their plans for the evening. After breakfast Shirley departed for Turner Junior High School, where she is a teacher. During the lunch hour she rushed out and cashed her check at the local bank. After school Shirley stopped at the Democratic party headquarters to pick up campaign posters that she promised to distribute in her neighborhood. At the end of the day the family met again and as usual said grace before the evening meal. Later, Shirley attended a meeting of the local historical society.

During this day Shirley participated in a number of social systems. First, she participated as a member of the family social system. Her work in-

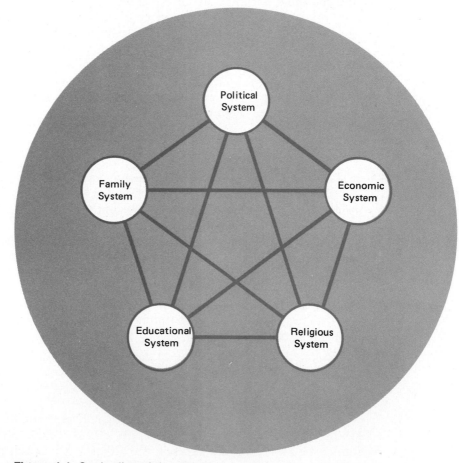

Figure 1.1 Societal social systems.

From Manuel G. Mendoza and Vince Napoli, *Systems of Society: An Introduction to Social Science,* 2nd ed. (Lexington, Mass.: D.C. Heath, 1977), p. 27. Reprinted by permission of the publisher.

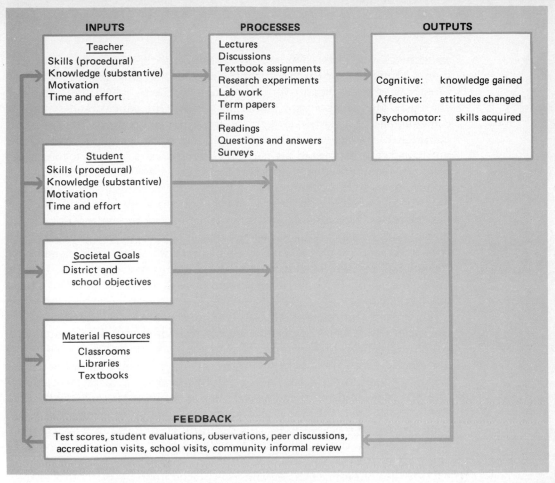

INPUTS	PROCESSES	OUTPUTS

Teacher
Skills (procedural)
Knowledge (substantive)
Motivation
Time and effort

Student
Skills (procedural)
Knowledge (substantive)
Motivation
Time and effort

Societal Goals
District and
    school objectives

Material Resources
    Classrooms
    Libraries
    Textbooks

Lectures
Discussions
Textbook assignments
Research experiments
Lab work
Term papers
Films
Readings
Questions and answers
Surveys

Cognitive: knowledge gained

Affective: attitudes changed

Psychomotor: skills acquired

FEEDBACK
Test scores, student evaluations, observations, peer discussions,
accreditation visits, school visits, community informal review

Figure 1.2. Structure of the educational system.

volved her directly in the educational system. As a Democrat she participated in the political system, and by saying grace at the evening meal she
and her family participated as members of the religious system. In the
evening she participated in a cultural system by attending the historical
society meeting.

Take a minute to identify the various social systems in which you participate during a typical day.

THE EDUCATIONAL SOCIAL SYSTEM

Every social system consists of inputs, processes, outcomes, and feedback
(see Figure 1.2). Inputs represent the base or starting point for our educational system and include the beginning knowledge and skills brought to
the system by both teachers and students, as well as their motivation and
effort, the goals and purposes of instruction set by society, and the
resources available to do the job. The process component includes the various methodologies that are applied in the teaching/learning situation to
achieve the stated goals. The processes used cover such diverse activities

as lectures and discussion, textbook assignments, and research experiments. Outcomes, or the results of the educational system, fall into three
broad categories: cognitive (knowledge gained), affective (attitudes
changed), and psychomotor (skills acquired). Our educational system is
continuously monitored through the feedback component. Teachers and
administrators receive feedback through test scores, student evaluations,
and observations regarding the effectiveness of student performance.
Students receive feedback from these sources as well as from peer discussions. Parents, the community at large, and regulatory agencies also
monitor and evaluate the progress of the schools through a variety of formal methods (report cards, test scores, accreditation visitations) and informal ones (school visits, back-fence chats). This feedback is used to con-
firm successful practices and to identify those areas that need to be
redesigned, revised, or eliminated from the educational system. The dynamic nature of our educational system is in part a result of this continuous feedback.

The primary purpose of schools is the preservation and continuation of
the society in which they exist. Schools provide a structured setting in
which individuals are socialized through the learning of the rules, roles,
and relationships that characterize the society. In this manner the educational system mirrors the society that supports it. Margaret Mead[1]
stressed that children in simple societies learn in order to survive; thus,
survival provides the impetus and motivation for seeking knowledge
from anyone who possesses it. This situation is reversed in more complex
societies, where the possessors of knowledge seek to organize knowledge
and present it to youth. Often children fail to grasp the value of much of
what is taught because the emphasis is placed upon teaching rather than
on learning.

As society becomes more complex, the educational process becomes
more formal and covers a longer time span, teachers are required to have
more training, and an increased number of special materials are
required. In this chapter we will see how the schools have become more
complex and have changed to correspond to the needs of society. We will
first look at the beginnings of the American educational system during
the colonial era; next, we will see the changes brought by society's
response to the industrial revolution; finally, we will look at the effect of
our fast-paced modern society on American education.

Colonial and Pre-Industrial Revolution Period (1700–1875)

Popular portrayals of schooling in early America usually depict a small
group of students clustered about their teacher dutifully reciting a lesson.
We visualize the students as obedient and attentive and the teacher as a

strict disciplinarian who manages all aspects of the schooling process. The curriculum is generally depicted as consisting of the "three R's," with little deviation from one community to another. In actuality, the role of early American teachers was not so simplistic nor so well established as this stereotype would indicate.

DeVault and Kriewall state that the function of our early schools was to "imitate the organization and purpose of schools in the motherland"; in short, the schools were to provide a link between the colonies and the Motherland as well as to continue "allegiance to God and King."[2] Consequently, each settlement in the "new world" established its own school with unique educational goals.

The idea of local control of schools was rooted in this era. Citizens' committees,* which evolved into our modern school boards, were organized to set policy for America's early schools. These committees usually consisted of prominent citizens in the community: wealthy businessmen, landowners, and members of the clergy. Their powers included certifying teachers (usually for one year at a time), providing instructional guidelines for classroom teachers, setting salaries, and developing strict codes of ethics to which classroom teachers were forced to adhere. Since the committees were responsible for hiring and certifying classroom teachers, they also assumed responsibility for evaluating the effectiveness of the classroom teacher. These evaluations were usually based upon unannounced school visitations. This practice gave rise to the term "snoopervision," which many administrators are still trying to overcome today.

The citizen committees were responsible for assessing local landown-

*See the section on the present-day school board member in Chapter 7.

ers with property taxes to support the schools. Since most of the committee members were landowners themselves, decisions concerning tax assessments were difficult to make, and taxes were usually kept relatively low. Property tax was based on the assumption that the wealthy owned land and were, therefore, best able to support the schools. Property taxes are still the primary means of support for modern schools.

In the early days of the American schools most teachers were men who had been educated in Europe. It was assumed that these men would provide a model after which the students could pattern their behavior. There was no special training required to become a classroom teacher; however, interestingly, many of the teachers had excellent credentials, including college degrees from prestigious schools. Cremin[3] asserts that this was true because many of the teachers at the time were planning to assume positions in the clergy, which required more extensive study. Moral standing and knowledge of the subjects to be taught in schools were the primary criteria for certifying classroom teachers.

Teachers were viewed as respected but not prestigious members of the community. Lortie[4] attributes this to their economic condition. Elsbree[5] states that the average salary of teachers at the time was similar to that earned by skilled artisans. Such a salary placed teachers in a wage bracket above that of common laborers but significantly below prestigious community members, such as leading businessmen, ministers, physicians, and lawyers.

Teaching was considered a seven-day-a-week job. During the week, in addition to preparing lessons, teaching students, and evaluating student progress, teachers were expected to maintain the school meeting place and make sure that water was available for the students to use during the day. In many cases teachers were also responsible for duties, such as sweeping out the church, ringing the school bell, and teaching Sunday School Bible classes. Above all, however, teachers were expected to be good models for their students.

Women did teach in colonial schools, but they made up a minority who taught mostly in dame schools held in their own homes. During this era, however, many men resigned their teaching positions to join the clergy or accept other community positions. As ministerial and business opportunities increased, it became more difficult to recruit men teachers. Consequently, community councils began to hire more and more women teachers until, by the end of the colonial period, there were more women teachers than men. In the year 1870 there were 123,000 women teachers, as compared to 78,000 men. Women teachers were treated differently from men during this period inasmuch as they were not allowed to marry and were paid lower salaries.

The code of ethics for the classroom at this time was extremely rigid. Figure 1.3 outlines the duties and code of ethics for teachers in Harrison, South Dakota, in 1872. Several historians note that the strict code of con-

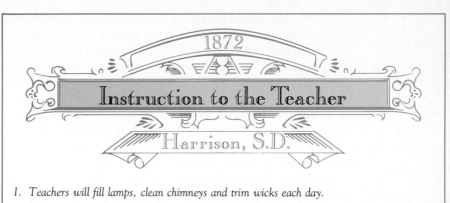

Figure 1.3. Instructions to the teacher.

duct may have resulted from the fact that many of the teachers, especially the women, were extremely young, sometimes only a year or two older than their students. In addition, the rigid code of ethics assured the parents of young women teachers that their daughters were engaged in a safe and respectable profession.

The students who attended the early schools represented a wide range of abilities and ages. Most teachers worked with all grades, one through eight, with class size ranging from 10 to 20 students. The ability to discipline was considered essential, and teachers were expected to use physical force when necessary to maintain an attentive, well-disciplined group.

When we think of the early American school building, we often visualize a little red schoolhouse in a rural setting surrounded by trees and a playground. The little red schoolhouse, however, did not appear until the latter part of this era. For the most part, school was held in homes and churches were teachers and students usually functioned alone except for an occasional visit from a member of the citizens' committee. This isolation afforded the classroom teacher much autonomy and encouraged the fragmented teaching practices that were common during this period.

One common element in most early American schools was religious instruction. Religious instruction was used as a basis for teaching reading, moral character, and moral education. The rest of the curriculum was built around the needs and interests of the local community. Instruction was often idiosyncratic inasmuch as it was based on the biases of the teacher and sometimes those of the citizens' committee. In some schools the classics were emphasized, while in others reading and writing were the focus. Occasionally, mathematics was considered to be the most important part of the curriculum. In such schools, working with money or learning to barter goods was a major part of the curriculum.

The Bible was often the primary textbook used. It was not uncommon for children to share books, and occasionally small schools had to share a classroom teacher; i.e., a teacher would travel around, spending a couple of weeks in one community, then moving on to another. Many of the early textbooks that accompanied the Bible were European imports. In the latter part of this era the Horn book and McGuffey's reader became very popular.

In the early part of this period, students were predominantly male and were usually from the wealthiest families. However, as increasing numbers of people began to view the schools as a means of upward social mobility, enrollments began to swell and to include many students from the working class. The school term was usually short; in fact, a three-month calendar was not unusual. The school calendar was developed to allow students to help on the farms during the planting and harvesting times, thereby leaving only the winter months for school. The historical tie to an agrarian economy is the primary reason for our present nine- to ten-month school year.

SUMMARY

Many of the ideas and practices of the colonial and pre-industrial Revolution periods are still prevalent in American schools. It was during this time that the idea of local control of the schools was established. Teachers still work under the supervision of community committees, now referred to as school boards. Teacher autonomy also emerged during this period because of the isolated settings in which teachers worked. This autonomy usually produced a curriculum and teaching style that reflected the teacher's personal talents and interests. The practice of supporting schools with property taxes also emerged from this era. The schools were then (and are still) primarily supported by the land-owning population. The nine-month school calendar, which had its roots in the agrarian culture of the time, is still with us, as is the stereotype of the teacher as someone of high moral character. Impeccable moral character was, in fact, one of the few requirements for teaching during this period when there was little specific training for teachers and very little emphasis on how to teach.

Industrial Revolution Period (1875–1950)

The latter part of the 1800's saw the spread of the industrial revolution across Europe and the United States. With it came significant changes in the institution of schooling and in the role of the classroom teacher. Schools were seen as the logical vehicle for transforming the immigrant masses who swarmed here into a source of productive manpower able to read, write, and speak English. In addition to this "Americanizing" function, the schools were also seen as a means of eradicating a variety of social ills and injustices that troubled American society. As education increasingly became identified with social advancement and the good life, enrollment in the public schools began to grow rapidly. It was not uncommon during the late 1800s to find classrooms with 60 pupils and one teacher.

Other factors that contributed to growing school enrollments were child labor laws, a major political topic of the day, and experimentation with mandatory school attendance laws. Massachusetts, under the direction of a young educator named Horace Mann, became a leader in school reform.

Many changes in the organization of American schools also took place during this period. The basic elementary school grade structure was changed from 1–8 to K–6, and four-year high schools became more prevalent. Many four-year colleges were also established during this period.

Although the Constitution of the United States gives control of the schools to the states, local school boards retained primary control of the schools in the early part of the century. Since membership on a school board was a prestigious role, it was not uncommon to find the boards populated with business and industrial leaders. These men were attuned to thinking in terms of efficiency, that is, producing products rapidly and cheaply. Therefore, it was not surprising that schools gradually adapted many of the practices common to American industry at the time. In fact, Frederick Taylor, the father of time and motion studies and an advocate of scientific management, also became a leading speaker for efficiency in schools. Consequently, schools became specialized, bureaucratic organizations where teachers were seen as laborers, and students as raw materials to be molded and shaped into finished (i.e., educated) products. Administrators (principals as well as superintendents) were viewed as supervisors whose role it was to guarantee efficient and effective results in schools.

Horace Mann
FAMOUS EDUCATOR

Many people recognize the name Horace Mann and associate it with education (after all, countless schools have borne his name), but relatively few people recall the extent or even the nature of Mann's contribution.

Horace Mann was born in Franklin, Massachusetts, in 1796. As a child he had little formal education, attending the village school only briefly when he was 14. However, as a child he did learn to read and write, and during his teenage years he learned Latin and Greek from an itinerant teacher. In 1816, at the age of 20, Mann passed the examination and entered Brown University at the sophomore level.

After graduating and spending four years as a successful lawyer in Dedham, Massachusetts, Mann was elected to the Massachusetts state legislature. His two greatest causes in the legislature were the development of a railway system and the building of insane asylums. In both of these he was persuasive enough to effect a great deal of progress. In fact, he was directly responsible for the first insane asylum built in Massachusetts, and while it was far from perfect, it was a vast improvement over the prison cells where the insane had previously been housed.

In 1836 he was elected president of the Massachusetts senate. By this time Mann had become interested in public education, and he supported a bill in 1837 to create a state board of education to investigate appropriation of funds for a seminary to train teachers for the state's common schools. Later that year, Mann accepted the position of secretary of the state Board of Education, and his love of law quickly became secondary to his dedication to the cause of education. He wrote, "The interests of a client are small compared to the interests of the next generation. Let the next generation be my client."[6]

Mann threw himself into his work immediately, studying extensively, writing for information, and finally touring the state, learning all he could about the schools and lecturing on the need for improved education. In 1838, $20,000 was raised, half as a gift and half from the state legislature, for the first state normal school to educate teachers. Plans for the school were closely supervised by Mann, and in July of 1839 the school opened in Lexington. Soon after this, two more normal schools were opened, one at Bridgewater and one at Barre. Mann was firm in his belief that the new schools could create a new kind of teacher: "Select schools for select children should be discarded. Instead of the old order of nobility, a new order should be created—an order of teachers, wise, benevolent, filled with Christian enthusiasm and rewarded and honored by all."[7]

He further believed that many of society's problems were due to the ignorance of the masses, and that such ignorance could be alleviated only through public education. In an 1837 address Mann said:

> The mobs, the riots, the burnings, and lynchings, perpetrated by the men of the present day, are perpetrated because of their tiger passions now, when they are full grown; but it was years ago when they were whelped and suckled. And so too, if we are derelict in our duty in this matter, our children in their turn will suffer. If we permit the vulture's eggs to be hatched, it will then be too late to take care of the lambs.[8]

In 1848 Mann was persuaded to run for the congressional seat left vacant by the death of John Quincy Adams. He took this step primarily in the hope of improving common school education throughout the country. His hopes for furthering quality education at the national level were lost, however, when he became embroiled in the Free Soil issue. Mann, who had long opposed slavery, fought hard for Free Soil, opposing none other than the powerful Daniel Webster. Mann did take time, however, for lecture tours in which he continued to speak out for the improvement of common schools.

In 1852 Mann, having lost the race for governor of Massachusetts on the Free Soil ticket, accepted the presidency of the new Antioch College in Yellow Springs, Ohio. There, Mann spent his remaining years working to build the college into a respected, and solvent, institution. Mann died in 1859, leaving behind a legacy of improved common schools and an improved system for educating teachers.

As a result of increased enrollments and the new bureaucratic philosophy of specialization, the old one-room schools, where a single teacher worked with a wide range of age and ability levels, were gradually replaced by larger schools featuring separate grade levels. The curriculum was subdivided into small segments of instruction, and each teacher became a specialist in working with children at a particular grade level: first-grade teachers, second-grade teachers, etc. This organization into grade levels was seen as a great breakthrough in education, one that allowed teachers to concentrate on a small segment of instruction and repeat it year after year, thereby creating a much more efficient mode of instruction.

As the demand for qualified teachers increased, administrators began finding it difficult to staff the rapidly growing school systems. Normal schools began offering programs to high school graduates that led to certification within three to twelve months. As a result, teachers often had little more education than their students, and the prestige level of classroom teachers dropped during this period. Fewer men began to enter the ranks of teaching, while more women were recruited. Those men who did teach generally stayed for a short period of time and viewed teaching as a stepping stone to administrative positions in the school system or to management positions in industry. Women stayed in schools because their salaries were sufficient as a second income for the family, and teaching provided a pleasant alternative to the factories that were the primary employers of women at the time. At the beginning of this era, women still had not entered the clerical occupations. In fact, typewriters were not even invented until 1868.

During this period, standard certification requirements for classroom teachers began to emerge in many states. Salaries were still low, but nonsexist pay scales were being developed based upon teaching experience and educational qualifications. It should be noted that elementary teachers during this time were considered inferior to secondary teachers, who were generally paid more than their counterparts in the elementary schools.

During the early part of the century, tenure was sought by many teacher organizations, especially in the city schools. The right of tenure means that teachers, after being certified and demonstrating teaching competence for a specified number of years, could be fired or replaced only by following due process procedures. This was particularly important since economy-minded school boards had a tendency to replace higher-salaried, experienced teachers with inexperienced teachers who worked for a much smaller salary. The National Education Association (NEA) was established in the early part of the twentieth century to represent teachers and to push for the development of teaching as a profession. Although the original membership was small, this was an articulate group whose influence was recognized by many of the leading educators of the time.*

Although teachers were still viewed as moral leaders and were expected to reflect outstanding moral character, the advent of mass education drastically changed their working conditions. Teachers were assigned to a single classroom within a large building that was organized into many self-contained classrooms. Since many teachers were poorly educated, supervisors were hired to monitor their work. This meant that teachers lost much of the privacy and independence they had enjoyed during earlier times. Teachers were still expected to demonstrate outstanding moral character and to be expert disciplinarians; however, physical force was increasingly frowned upon during this era and positive motivation became the goal to which most educators aspired.

Classrooms usually contained 25 to 45 students and followed rigid time schedules. Within a particular grade level a preset cirriculum meant that all students did the same thing at the same time throughout the school year. The curriculum emphasized the basic reading, writing, and arith-

*See Chapter 10 for an in-depth discussion of the teachers' associations.

Gary Indiana-
Innovative Schools

A HISTORICAL FLASHBACK

The year was 1908 when a 34-year-old man by the name of William A. Wirt assumed the position of superintendent of the Gary, Indiana, schools.[9] This unpublicized appointment would later bring national recognition, in the form of both praise and condemnation, to their educational system.

Although Wirt was coming into an infant community unburdened by traditional ideas of education, his road to educational success was complicated by the city's premature growth. The city was poor; a rough 1908 census showed that immigrants from 30 different countries constituted 56 percent of the city's total population. The school tax base was insufficient, since most of these people owned no taxable land, and the holdings of the wealthy United States Steel Corporation were consistently undervalued. The school system lacked sufficient facilities to meet the needs of its rapidly expanding enrollment.

Using the philosophy of John Dewey, Wirt designed a school system that represented the general life of the community. In addition to traditional classrooms where the usual academic subjects and skills were taught, his schools included gymnasiums, swimming pools, science laboratories, reading and drawing rooms and a variety of shops (machine, print, woodworking, dressmaking, and so on). In short, his schools were designed to educated the whole person: physically, socially, and vocationally, as well as intellectually.

Although the youngest children, up to and including third grade, stayed in their classrooms with a single teacher, all other students moved from teacher to teacher in a departmentalized structure. Wirt believed that if the school was to be run with emphasis on efficiency and quality, the teachers needed to be specialists in their fields. In addition to the trained teachers already present in the schools, Wirt brought in skilled craftsmen to teach in his newly added shops. Classes were scheduled to allow the school's physical plant to accomodate two identical schools (an arrangement referred to as the platoon system). Classes were arranged so that children in one platoon would be in regular classrooms receiving instruction in the fundamental subjects and skills while the pupils in the other platoon were participating in special activities such as workshops, application, auditorium, and play and physical skills. At a given signal the platoons would exchange places in the school plant. This system was facilitated by the lengthening of the school day to eight hours, a plan which also benefited the many families in which both parents worked.

The schools themselves were representative of community life: Students, under the supervision of teacher-craftsmen, maintained the school, prepared school lunches, built school furniture, worked in the school office, and ran a school store, print shop, pottery shop, and dressmaking shop. Then, at the end of the day, adult evening classes filled the schools. Community laborers came together with members of elite society to study topics ranging from foundry casting to French. All shops, auditoriums, gymnasiums, and special classes were also open for use by the community.

The Gary Plan was not without criticism. Some observers feared lack of supervision because of the large size of the groups and inaccuracies resulting from student-kept records, and they criticized manual-training classes in which many educators believed students were taught to work but not to think. Proponents of the system, however, characterized it as economic and realistic, and as providing a rich, diverse, well-balanced curriculum.

metic skills, and rote learning (memorization of facts) was the dominant mode of instruction.

By the early 1900s, and particularly after 1920, innovative buildings included, in addition to classrooms, large gymnasiums, community reading rooms, and libraries. Evening high school classes became prominent during the early 1900s, particularly in industrial areas, with enrollments often exceeding those of the daytime classes. Factory workers, many of whom were immigrants, eagerly participated in educational programs in the evenings.

With graded schools came graded textbooks. Publishing companies were eager to supply textbooks designed to meet the needs of students at each grade level. Schools quickly purchased such materials in order to standardize the curriculum and to assist poorly prepared teachers with their instructional programs. Even after World War II, the goal of many texts was to provide "teacher-proof" materials, i.e., materials that would prevent teachers from altering the school's predetermined curriculum.

Throughout this time various educational leaders were criticizing the instructional programs used in schools. One of the first educational critics, Joseph Rice, wrote searing criticisms of the American educational system after touring schools in the early 1900s. He was especially appalled by the inconsistent standards of American schools, and he eventually became a strong advocate of specific, set standards for each student to master before moving on to another grade level.

Another critic was John Dewey, whom some refer to as the "Father" of American education. Dewey was an innovator who believed that a school should be more than a place where students learn basic facts and skills.

John Dewey
FAMOUS EDUCATOR

John Dewey—who in education is not familiar with this much-lauded educator-philosopher? The man who has been labelled "The Father of Progressive Education" was born in Vermont in 1859. His father was an easy-going, reasonably successful grocer and tobacconist; his mother was an extremely devout Calvinist who constantly reminded her sons of their religious responsibilities. Although Dewey later renounced his religion's beliefs, his strict Calvinist upbringing affected his thoughts throughout his life.

At the age of 15 Dewey graduated from high school and entered the University of Vermont, then an institution comprised of only eight faculty members and about 100 students. Here he first entered into discussions concerning evolution and its implications for traditional religion, as well as the various branches of philosophy.

After graduating, he taught high school, first in Oil City, Pennsylvania,

and later in Burlington, Vermont. It appears that Dewey had many problems during this period. His intellectual approach was probably too advanced for his students, and his extreme shyness apparently made disciplining very difficult for him. Dewey's growing interest in philosophy eventually led to his decision to make it his life's work, and in 1882 he enrolled at Johns Hopkins University to study philosophy and psychology.

In 1884 Dewey became an instructor of philosophy at the University of Michigan, where he was later promoted to assistant professor. He left Michigan to teach for one year at the University of Minnesota, but he returned in 1889 as chairman of Michigan's Department of Philosophy. In 1894 Dewey left Michigan to become chairman of the Department of Philosophy, Psychology, and Pedagogy at the University of Chicago. During the next seven years, course offerings increased from 14 philosophy courses, 3 psychology courses, and 1 pedagogy course to 32 courses in philosophy, 12 in psychology, and 23 in pedagogy.[10] During this period he also established the University Elementary School, which functioned as a laboratory for educational demonstration and experimentation.

In 1902 Dewey was appointed director of the School of Education. While in this position, he appointed his wife principal of the University Elementary School, a poor diplomatic move that university president William Rainey Harper rescinded one year later. This, in addition to the many problems that Dewey, a poor administrator, faced as director of the School of Education led to his resignation in 1904. The reputation that Dewey had built while at the University of Chicago served him well, however, and he was immediately asked to join the faculty of Columbia University as a professor of philosophy. There he spent the remainder of his teaching years pursuing his goals in the fields of philosophy and education.

Students who attended Professor Dewey's classes invariably describe him as an outstanding educator, but many are hard pressed to articulate their reasons. Harold A. Larrabee describes Dewey as follows:

> His appearance was farmer-like, weather-beaten, and utterly unpretentious. . . . He remained seated throughout the hour and seldom seemed to be looking directly at his audience. Often he would turn in his chair and glance sideways, as if half-looking out the window and half-absorbed in his private thoughts. His facial expression was solemn, though it lighted up at times with something like a chuckle. . . . Questions from the floor were not exactly discouraged, but they were not invited.[11]

Larrabee goes on to say, however, that "one rarely left the classroom without the conviction that something intellectually *and* practically important had been said, no matter how uncertain one was about the precise steps in the argument."[12]

It is impossible to find a consensus of opinion when discussing John Dewey; he has alternatively been characterized as representing the best and worst of American education. However, whether one agrees or disagrees with his theories, one must acknowledge that his contribution has had a profound effect on both the theoretical and the pragmatic aspects of American education. Maxine Greene has attempted to summarize Dewey's contribution as follows:

> Those who seriously attempt to characterize Dewey's contribution agree, in general, that his influence was exerted in the broadening of the curriculum, the correlating of subjects, the development of a less rigid notion of discipline, and the relating of school studies to their application to life.[13]

He saw the school's role as one of social reconstruction, a place where children learned the skills and attitudes that would enable them to adjust to the problems and realities of an increasingly industrialized and urbanized society. He advocated an integrated curriculum, where real-life problems provided the motivation for learning and applying the skills and knowledge of the various subject areas. He also criticized the extreme attention to rote learning and advocated more attention to problem-solving skills. Dewey's philosophies were advocated by the Progressive Education Association, which helped many of Dewey's ideas gain acceptance in schools.

Another prominent educator of this period who helped bring about curriculum and instructional reforms was Edward Thorndike, a psychologist who did pioneering work in the area of animal and human learning. Through his experiments, Thorndike personally destroyed the long-held notion that the study of certain classical subjects, such as mathematics, science, philosophy, classical literature, and language, somehow produced a stronger, more disciplined mind than did the study of more vocationally oriented subjects. He showed that the transfer value of these classical subject areas was no greater than that of vocational subject areas, that is, that they did not have any special importance for producing general mental development.

Thorndike's experiments also opened up the field of operant learning theory, which has had a great impact on modern instructional procedures. His experiments demonstrated how, within a problem situation, the feedback or consequences produced by a subject's random responses gradually narrows down those responses to a few appropriate behaviors that are "instrumental" in solving the problem. Those behaviors that help resolve the situation are strengthened (i.e., learned), while the others are abandoned. These experiments into the consequences of behavior led to reinforcement theory, which in turn led to the many forms of programmed learning sometimes found in schools today.

SUMMARY

This era of American education is probably best remembered as a time when the bureaucratic model of industry was introduced into the schools in the form of grade-level distinctions and staff specialization. Students, curriculums, and teaching materials were all subdivided according to grade levels, while school staffs were enlarged and specialized according to function (principals, supervisors, and classroom teachers).

It was also a time when school curriculums were broadened to include more vocationally oriented subjects and to include a variety of nonacademic goals, such as socialization and physical development. Adult evening schools also spread during this era, as schooling increasingly became the road to advancement in an industrialized society.

This period also saw the beginning of standard teacher-certification requirements. Although they required little training beyond high school, they were a step in organizing minimum standards for the profession. Single pay scales that provided equal pay for equal work and tenure were also important innovations that emerged from this period.

Contemporary Period (1950 to the Present)

The 1950s signaled the beginning of the most vibrant, dynamic, and complex era in the history of American education. America had completed the transition from a war-time to a peace-time society. Education was a growth industry, and the ranks of those attending colleges and graduate schools were swelled by thousands of servicemen taking advantage of the G.I. benefits made available after World War II. Consequently there was a pool of mature, educated professionals who emerged from the universities that was unprecedented in American history. Elementary and secondary schools were also expanding to accommodate the children of the "baby boom" that followed the war. Not only was there a larger student population, but students were staying in school for longer periods of time. This growing student population, which required more schools and more teachers, provided an ideal setting for the introduction of many educational innovations. Several educational techniques that were originally developed for use with military personnel (for example, programmed learning, teaching machines, and mass testing) were used in the schools on an experimental basis. Teacher aides were incorporated into the schools in an attempt to relieve teachers of time-consuming clerical and administrative tasks. In addition, individualized instruction strategies were resurrected and incorporated into many schools, in some cases on a district-wide basis. This was a time to try new and different approaches to teaching; in fact, the refusal to try new ideas often led to one's being labeled as a stodgy and uncreative teacher. Although this was an exciting time for education, there was little organized direction to these innovations and many simply failed to move beyond the experimental stage.

The first major long-term change to take place during the contemporary era stemmed not from innovative educators but from the courts. In 1954 the United States Supreme Court, in the case of Brown vs. the Topeka Board of Education, ruled that it was unconstitutional to segregate black and white students in public schools. This ruling had an impact on a vast number of school districts in the United States, and even today many schools are involved in litigation concerning compliance with this judicial decision. This was only the first of several contemporary court rulings that have altered the direction and goals of our present-day schools. As educators were just beginning to understand the implications of the 1954 court ruling, another event took place that further shaped the direction of education.

In 1957 the Soviet Union launched Sputnik I; this event signaled the beginning of the space age. The impact that this first satellite had on education was immediate and profound. The general public, led by congressional critics and the news media, charged that the launching indicated that the United States was trailing the Soviet Union in scientific technology. Many critics pointed the finger of blame at the schools and charged that they were failing to provide the preparation necessary to educate scientists capable of maintaining our national defense. This criticism led to a complete revamping and modernization of school curricula, with a pronounced emphasis upon replacing "old" mathematics with "modern" mathematics and placing greater importance upon process-oriented science programs. An understanding of the processes underlying various concepts was emphasized in these programs, while the rote memorization of facts, a common instructional practice at the time, was deemphasized. Soon interest in school-curriculum revision spread to other subject areas, and a variety of new and innovative programs in all subject areas began to appear. The curriculum revolution had begun.

The 1960s was a decade marked by protests regarding a variety of social issues, such as U.S. involvement in Southeast Asia, civil rights, and womens' rights. A general feeling of dissatisfaction with the status quo prevailed, and the schools were no exception. During the 1960s a cadre of authors emerged who have been labeled as romantic educational critics. Paul Goodman, John Holt, Jonathan Kozol, James Herndon, and Herbert Kohl represent a group of teachers turned writers whose chilling exposés of life inside the school provided a startling view of what was taking place in American education. Their books, usually based on personal observations, described what they saw as oppressive authoritarianism pervading classrooms and schools in general. Students were directing similar criticism at college administrators throughout the country. At all levels the reformers stressed the need for humanistically organized classrooms and teaching techniques, and above all else they advocated the need for greater teacher autonomy and less outside control. Allan Fromme's introduction to John Holt's book, *How Children Fail,* provides a good example of the theme that was present in these books:

> Failure in a success-oriented culture is hard to take. We are failing and our children are failing in our schools at an alarming rate. Even children who achieve enviable grades are failing to learn much of what we hope to teach them: abstraction, curiosity, and, most of all, appreciation. The subject matter of a course is frequently little more than merely a vehicle for the achievement of these educational goals—yet, all too often, the subject matter becomes an end in itself.[14]

The romantic critics provided the impetus for the development of humanistic instructional techniques. Elementary schools patterned around the British primary-school model began to appear in communities across the country. At the secondary level storefront schools and schools without walls were developed to involve the students in planning the curriculum and the manner in which it would be taught. A. S. Neil, founder of Summerhill, a small, private residential school in England, became the philosophical leader for many of the people in this movement. His philosophy was that letting children do what they want to do, when they want to do it will eventually result in effective learning. This movement created much controversy among the supporters of the free schools, the humanists, and the technologists who wanted to put their resources into teaching machines and computers. There were also some less vocal groups who felt that the abandoment of the traditional curriculum was a fatal mistake. In essence, the 1960s entailed a long series of philosophical debates among educators that nurtured the development of alternative types of instructional programs.

Throughout the 1960s the courts continued to be involved in shaping the schools. State and district courts were spending large amounts of time interpreting the Brown vs. Topeka ruling as it applied to specific local situations, and desegregation became a major goal of schools. The courts also began to make rulings involving actual classroom procedures. In 1963, for example, the Supreme Court (Abington vs. Schempp) ruled that required prayer recitations in public schools were unconstitutional. This ruling created much controversy among the general public, and in some areas of the country this controversy is still simmering today.

Congress also became actively involved in shaping the schools during the 1960s by enacting the Elementary and Secondary Education Act (ESEA) under the Johnson administration. This act provided the means for dramatically increasing federal support of local educational programs. This act has been heralded as one of the most significant educational events in contemporary times. The primary impact of this program has been to improve educational opportunities for the poor, provide better-quality instructional resources for schools, and to improve the resources of state departments of education. This much-lauded program has been criticized by some for allowing greater federal control of local schools. That some federal control has become a fact of life for schools is reflected by the fact that those schools not conforming to federal guidelines are in danger of losing all federal support—a crippling measure for any school. Today, ESEA supports more than 120 different programs for schools and universities at a cost of more than $12 billion dollars per year.

By 1969 when Neil Armstrong took those first steps on the moon, interest in space exploration and national defense had begun to fade, and Americans were beginning to take stock of the domestic problems they were facing. With the memory of protests and riots painfully fresh, educators in the 1970s began concentraring on equal opportunities for all, regardless of race, religion, economic background, or physical or mental disabilities. The courts were still involved in controversial litigation, such as court-ordered busing to achieve racial integration in the nation's large city school districts. Court-ordered busing in Boston and Louisville led to outraged public criticism and protests. In a dramatic step toward equal educational opportunity for all, Congress in 1975 enacted legislation (Public Law 94-142) mandating that schools provide programs to accommodate the educational needs of all children, including those with mental and physical disabilities. This legislation at the national level encouraged additional legislation at the state level, and unparalleled amounts of educational dollars were earmarked for children who had previously been excluded from schools or assigned to special classes.

The expansion of school curricula that had begun in the 1960s was continued into the 1970s. In addition to basic reading, writing, and mathematics, subjects like career education, sex education, driver training, multiculture education, foreign languages, and physical education were added or expanded, and greater emphasis was placed on other basic areas, such as science, social studies, and health. Breakfast programs were added to hot-lunch programs in many schools, further crowding the already hectic schedule.

During the 1970s many teachers became politically active, and in some cases militant, regarding matters of teacher welfare and policy formulation. Much of this activism came in the form of collective bargaining efforts of the two professional organizations: the National Educational Association (NEA) and the American Federation of Teachers (AFT). The NEA currently has a membership of more than one million, while the AFT has approximately a half million members. The recent membership surge in these organizations is an indication that teachers are becoming increasingly active in virtually every aspect of education. By organizing, teachers have won the right to negotiate with school boards concerning salaries and various fringe benefits, such as reduced class loads, duty-free lunch periods, and "due process" protections in cases involving dismissal or demotion. One of the teachers' most powerful negotiating weapons has been the threat of strike, a tactic that has been used with increasing frequency in recent years. At present, more and more teacher organizations are seeking an expanded role in policy formulation regarding matters such as textbook selection, instructional procedures, insurance, professional development, and school staffing.

The media became active in appraising the progress, or lack of progress, of the schools in the 1970s. Published student-achievement scores and comparisons of school performance became a regular role of the newspapers. The public was informed that the modern schools of the 1970s were dealing with more society-related issues, e.g., drug education, sex education, and drivers education, than schools of any other time. Achievement-test scores demonstrated that students were learning more than their parents in both the basic skill areas and other curriculum areas. However, the schools were failing to meet the public's expectations for universal literacy, mass elementary and secondary education, racial and social integration, and higher-education opportunities for all who desire it. Newspapers, television, and radio carried reports that large numbers of students were failing. For example, a 1975 NEA conference report showed that nearly 33 percent of white students from middle-class communities and approximately 45 percent of black students from poor families were receiving less than passing grades at both the elementary and secondary levels. Other reports issued by the U.S. Office of Education stated that in the mid-1970s one million youths aged 12 to 17 could not read at the fourth-grade level and that almost half of all American adults were either incompetent or barely competent in the minimal skills necessary for survival in a contemporary society.

These revealing achievement data gave rise to many special-interest groups throughout the country. In response to the problem, state legislatures across the country began to draft laws that would require the demonstration of certain reading and mathematics competencies, often labeled as "survival skills," as a prerequisite for graduation. In short, this movement sparked a renewed emphasis on basic skills and marked the return to an earlier philosophy regarding the role of the American educational system.

Despite the reports of numerous educational critics, it is evident to the objective observer that American schools have made significant progress. During the colonial period schooling was out of reach for the common person. Today, nearly one of every three people in this country is enrolled in school; programs range from nursery school to the postgraduate level. In 1870 only about 56 percent of all children between the ages of 5 and 17 were enrolled in school, and only half of those enrolled attended school on a daily basis. Currently, 89 percent of children in this age group are enrolled in schools, with 90 percent of them attending on a daily basis.

The total number of instructional staff employed in the elementary and secondary schools of the United States has also grown dramatically. As recently as 1960 only a million people were employed as instructional staff (including principals), but that number has grown to approximately 2.5 million. This increase is particularly significant in light of the fact that the number of school-age children has stabilized, and even declined slightly, in recent years. This rapid growth can be attributed in part to the increasing popularity of specialization among educators in areas such as instructional supervision, art, music, physical education, speech therapy, school psychology, and guidance counseling. Another reason for the rapid increase in instructional staff is declining class size. Government figures indicate that in 1955 there were an average of 30.2 students per teacher in public elementary schools and 40.4 in nonpublic elementary schools.[15] By 1974 these figures had dropped to 22.7 in public schools and 23.1 in nonpublic schools. This trend has continued because of the decline in student enrollment and the pressure put on school boards by the general public and professional teachers organizations.

There have also been significant gains in teachers' salaries since the 1950s. For example, in 1953–54 the average teacher's salary was $3825, but by 1975–76 this figure had jumped to $13,400. Figure 1.4 illustrates the upward trend in teachers' salaries—a trend that is expected to continue throughout the 1980s.

One of the most drastic changes to have occurred in education has been the increased amount of financial support that schools receive. Long strides have been made since colonial days when a hat was passed among the grumbling city fathers to support their teacher and school. To be sure, the taxpayers still grumble a bit, but they support the schools to the tune of approximately $120 billion dollars each year. This is roughly 10 percent of the Gross National Product. The bulk of the support for schools comes from state governments, followed by local governments. In recent years the federal government has increased its support of the schools dramatically, while the local governments have gradually decreased their percentage of support.

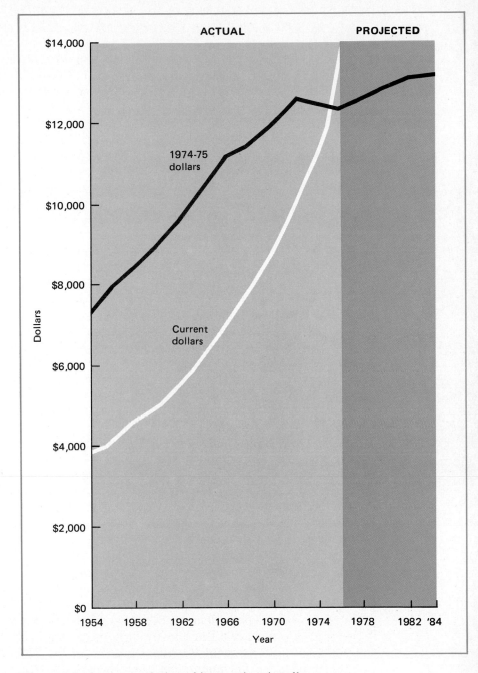

Figure 1.4. Average salaries of instructional staff.

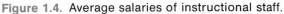

From Mary A. Golladay, *The Conditions of Education: A Statistical Report on the Condition of Education in the United States.* (Washington, D.C.: U.S. Department of Health, Education and Welfare/National Center for Education Statistics, 1976), p. 132.

Jamestown, Virginia, founded, 1607	1610	
Pilgrims land at Plymouth, 1620	1620	
Massachusetts Bay founded, 1628		
	1630	Public Latin school founded, 1635
		First college in colonial America, Harvard, founded, 1635
		First school supported by direct taxation established, 1639
	1640	
		First locally elected school board installed, 1642
		The Old Deluder Satan Act, first law providing for public education, passed, 1647
	1650	
	1700	
	1750	
French and Indian War, 1755–63		Benjamin Franklin opens his academy, 1751
	1760	
Stamp Act passed, 1765		
Boston Tea Party, 1773	1770	
First Continental Congress organized, 1774		
War of American Independence, 1775–83		Noah Webster publishes *The American Spelling Book,* 1778
American Declaration of Independence, 1776		
	1780	
Northwest Ordinance adopted, 1787		
U.S. Constitution signed by nine States, 1788	1790	
Eli Whitney invents the cotton gin, 1793		First State university opens, 1795
First spinning mill begins operation in United States, 1796		
	1800	
Purchase of Louisiana from France, 1803		
Fulton operates first steamboat, 1807		
	1810	
Purchase of Florida from Spain, 1819		First formal education for the handicapped (deaf), 1817
Missouri Compromise over slavery, 1820	1820	
		First public high school, English High School, founded in Boston, 1821
Monroe Doctrine set forth, 1823		Massachusetts passes law requiring establishment of public high schools in larger communities, 1827
Erie Canal completed, 1825		
Cyrus McCormick invents reaper, 1831	1830	Oberlin College is first to admit women to formerly all-male institution, 1833
Samuel F. B. Morse develops electric telegraph, 1832		Pennsylvania Public School law establishes free education, 1834
		First *McGuffey Reader* published, 1836
		Horace Mann becomes chairman of Massachusetts Board of Education, 1837
		Henry Barnard named first commissioner of education in Connecticut, 1838
		First teachers college established, 1839
Annexation of Texas, 1845	1840	
Gold discovered in California, 1848		
	1850	
		Massachusetts enacts first compulsory attendance law, 1852
Civil War, 1861–65	1860	
Homestead Act passed, 1862, encourages settlement of frontier lands		Morrill Act–Land Grant College Act, donates lands to encourage establishment of land-grant institutions, 1862
Emancipation Proclamation, 1863		

Figure 1.5. Schooling in the United States, an historical perspective.

Based and expanded upon by Mary A. Golladay, *The Condition of Education: A Statistical Report on the Condition of Education in the United States* (Washington, D.C.: U.S. Department of Health, Education, and Welfare/National Center for Education Statistics, 1976), pp. 4–5.

Atlantic Cable laid, 1866		Organic Act–Department of Education established, 1867
Typewriter invented, 1867		
Transcontinental Railroad completed, 1869		Office of Education placed within the Department of Interior, 1868
	1870	
Alexander G. Bell invents telephone, 1873		Stuart vs. School District of Kalamazoo establishes right of school authorities to levy taxes for the support of public schools, 1874
Joseph F. Glidden invents barbed wire, 1874		
Thomas A. Edison invents electric lamp, 1879	**1880**	
Edison perfects motion picture, 1889		
	1890	Second Morrill Act provides federal funds for land-grant colleges and universities, 1890
	1895	Plessy vs. Ferguson; Supreme Court permits racially separate but equal schools, 1896
First airplane flight, 1903	**1900**	
Major earthquake strikes San Francisco, 1906		
Ford places Model T in mass production, 1909	**1910**	
Panama Canal completed, 1914		
United States enters World War I, 1917		
Child Labor Act passed, 1916, and ruled unconstitutional in 1918		Smith-Hughes Act provides federal aid to States for vocational education, 1917
Prohibition and Woman Suffrage adopted by Constitutional amendment, 1920	**1920**	Smith-Bankhead Act provides funds for vocational rehabilitation for veterans, 1920
Stock market crashes, 1929		Scopes Trial tests the teaching of evolution in public schools, 1925
World War II begins, 1939	**1930**	First television is used in classroom, 1938
United States enters World War II, 1941	**1940**	Serviceman's Readjustment Act (G.I. Bill) passed, 1944
First self-sustaining nuclear chain reaction achieved, 1942		
World War II ends, 1945		Fulbright Act establishes Board of Foreign Scholarships, 1945
Charter of United Nations drawn up in San Francisco, 1945		Feinberg Law prohibits hiring communists in public schools, 1947
Eckert and Mauchley develop the electronic computer, 1946		
Korean War begins, 1950	**1950**	Congress provides funds for operation and maintenance of schools in federally affected areas, 1950
One family in eleven owns a television set, 1950		Congress requires Commission of Education to publish list of nationally recognized accrediting agencies, 1952
		Department of HEW created; Office of Education made a constituent unit, 1953
		Appointment of National Advisory Council on Education, 1954
		Cooperative Research Act authorizes Office of Education to conduct cooperative research with institutions of higher education and State education agencies, 1954
		Brown vs. Board of Education of Topeka; Supreme court outlaws racial segregation in public schools, 1954
Civil rights demonstrations begin, 1956		Library Service Act establishes five-year grant program to extend library services to rural areas, 1956
Space-age exploration begins with launch of Sputnik I by the Soviet Union, 1957		National Defense Education Act authorizes federal aid to all levels of education, 1958
		Congress authorizes expenditures of grant funds for scientific research, 1958
Peace Corps created by Executive Order, 1961	**1960**	Manpower Development and Training Act, part B, authorizes Office of Education to assist in retraining program, 1962
American aid is sent to Vietnam, 1961		
First manned space capsule orbits the earth, 1962		Congress authorizes grants to aid educational television, 1962
March on Washington demonstrates for a civil rights bill, 1963		School District of Abingdon Township vs. Schempp; Supreme Court rules unconstitutional laws requiring prayer recitation in public schools, 1963
Civil Rights Act passes, 1964		
		Congress passes Elementary and Secondary Education Act (ESEA) providing funds to improve education of special groups, 1964
Man lands on the moon, 1969		

	1970 Serrano vs. Priest; California Supreme Court rules that the quality of a child's education cannot be dependent on school-district wealth, 1970
	Pennsylvania Association for Retarded Citizens vs. Commonwealth rules that educational needs of mentally retarded may not be ignored, 1971
Fertility level drops to replacement level-threshold of zero population growth, 1972	Swann vs. Charlotte-Meckienberg, N.C.; Supreme Court rules that busing of students may be ordered to achieve racial desegregation, 1971
	Wisconsin vs. Yoder; Supreme Court exempts Amish from compulsory attendance based on First Amendment grounds, 1972
American combat forces leave Vietnam, 1973	Congress passes education amendments, 1974
	1972 Title IX Education Amendments Act authorizes the withdrawal of federal funds to institutions shown to be discriminating against women.
	1974 Congress passes bill that authorizes the withholding of federal funds to any educational institution or agency that refuses parents the right to inspect any official records or files which pertain to their child.
	1975 Congress enacts the Education for All Handicapped Children Act (Public Law 94-142), mandating a free public education for all children regardless of type or severity of handicap.
	1978 Schools become fully responsible for implementation of Public Law 94-142.
	1979 Congress approves the creation of a cabinet-level Department of Education with a budget of $14.1 billion.

We will discuss each of these landmark events, as well as others, in more depth in later chapters. Our primary purpose here is to illustrate some of the factors that have added to the increasing complexity of the role of the teacher.

SUMMARY

In introducing this section we described the contemporary era as one that has been both dynamic and vibrant. Contemporary schools are perceived as a starting point for solving many of the social problems of the day. In the 1950s the schools were charged with aiding the country's national defense position by preparing more mathematicians and scientists; in the 1960s they were assigned a major role in the racial integration of our society; in the 1970s they were charged with guaranteeing that students would leave the schools with at least the minimal skills necessary to "survive" in a complex and competitive society. Many of the responsibilities with which the schools have been charged have been incompatible, thus giving rise to ever-increasing disparity among school programs. Today, there are a wide variety of support services and instructional materials available, and teachers are constantly faced with difficult decisions regarding the materials to use and those to exclude.

The contemporary period has given rise to increased power for many groups that exert influence on the schools. During this period many teachers moved from passive acceptance to activism, sometimes to the point of militancy. This change has resulted in a greater voice for teachers in the policy decisions that affect their role in the schools. The judicial system has also become an active force in American schools; judicial decisions made in the past 30 years are very evident in the operation and organization of schools as well as in some of the instructional procedures that are carried out in the classrooms. The increased involvement of the federal legislature in the support of schools has done much to increase the quality of instructional programs that are now available for students. While federal control of the schools has increased, however, local control, long the mainstay of the public schools, has gradually been eroded. This has indeed been a period of dynamic and vibrant change.

Schools and the Community Setting

Thus far we have been discussing the vast impact that society at large has on the American educational system, but we would be negligent if we ignored the role of the smaller society — the community — in which schools exist. The community has always been an important determiner of educational practices as well as a valuable resource for the schools. In previous sections we saw how the rural communities of the colonial era did much to shape the American educational system. The industrial era brought greater emphasis on the educational needs of the growing cities, and school buildings that could accommodate hundreds of students became the norm. More recently, we have witnessed the emergence of suburban communities with their own unique characteristics. Today, all three types of communities exist and support community schools. There are many similarities among the three types of schools resulting from the influence of mass media and the ease of travel that has reduced much of the isolation of earlier times. Nevertheless, each type of school has retained many characteristics that are unique to the community it serves, and teachers and administrators must recognize and address these differences if schools are to be successful and effective.

RURAL COMMUNITY

Most schools in rural communities are every bit as modern and well equipped as their suburban counterparts. Rural communities have a history rich with a special feeling of neighborliness among community members, many of whom were born and raised in the community. Life in the rural areas of America is changing as many small farms are taken over by large corporation farms, and as small industry gradually moves away from the urban centers and into the rural communities. Although people may live miles apart, they do know their neighbors, and the schools frequently serve as the hub of community life and activity.

The family unit is still an important aspect of rural life, and parents are extremely interested in the educational progress of their children. Schools reflect the conservative attitudes that characterize most rural communities; while rural schools offer quality instructional programs, they are often slow to adopt "new" and "untested" programs. Special services are usually kept at a minimum unless supported by special federal grants. Generally, the curriculum offered in a rural school lacks the scope of those found in other types of communities, and the single textbook is the most commonly used instructional approach. Rural-based schools have been leaders in the development of comprehensive vocational and technical schools, a high priority for community members, even though a college preparatory curriculum is stressed here as it is in most schools.

Teachers in rural schools are as well prepared as are those in the suburban and urban communities. Professional teacher organizations are not as active, however, and wages and fringe benefits are often considerably lower. Teachers usually live in the same community in which they teach, and their dedication earns them the respect and support of parents in the community. Student mobility is generally lower in the rural schools, adding to the overall feeling of stability in both the community and the schools.

SUBURBAN COMMUNITY

Suburban communities usually exist on the fringes of large metropolitan areas and residents commonly commute to the city to work; thus, the frequent label of "bedroom" communities. These communities have many idiosyncratic features that affect the schools. Suburban communities tend to be segregated by income rather than by nationality, religion, or race. This has a sheltering effect on suburban community schools, where there is little opportunity to interact with people from different social and economic classes. Since many heads of households commute to the city, family life often tends to have a matriarchial structure. Even on weekends the father's time is often taken up with lawn care, activities in golf and tennis clubs, or service club activities. Single-parent families are not unusual in suburban communities, with babysitters, day care centers, and summer camps undertaking many of the child-care responsibilities. Suburban communities place heavy emphasis upon the importance of schools and are willing to pay for the latest curriculum materials and instructional tools geared to prepare the students for college. Parents generally want their children to be pushed and expect homework to be assigned despite the wealth of extracurricular activities in which they may participate. Special services such as counseling and speech therapy are normally comprehensive and of excellent quality.

The teachers in suburban schools are often described as the cream of the crop. They are well trained and most have or are working toward advanced degrees. Teachers are active in local, state, and national professional activities, and, as a result, salaries are usually high. Many teachers in suburban schools do not live in the community in which they teach. Teachers have to deal with a moderate amount of student turnover during the year, but the most difficult problem is the social and economic isolation of the community.

URBAN COMMUNITY

The problems and challenges facing the major urban centers of the country are far greater than those of any other type of community. The major problem has been the flight of the middle-class city dwellers to suburbia and the accompanying loss of economic security for the cities. Only recently have some major cities begun to reverse this phenomenon with urban renewal projects. Most children in urban communities, especially in the inner city, live in multifamily dwellings where they know few of their neighbors. The street is the most popular playground since parks are scarce and poorly maintained. These areas are comprised primarily of minority groups who face serious economic and social hardship.

The schools are usually old, large, multistory buildings that house a host of instructional materials and equipment supplied primarily by federal monies. Teaching is challenging in the urban schools, but rewarding in that it is an area where students have the greatest needs. One of the most severe problems has been inappropriateness of curricula and instructional materials that dominate the schools; both have been geared toward middle-class students and thus have little relevancy for children of the inner city. Only recently have some inroads been made in changing city schools to reflect the specific needs of their students.

In urban schools discipline problems are frequently severe, and teachers are required to deal with countless social problems in addition to their regular teaching loads. It is not surprising, therefore, that large cities tend to have the most active and militant teachers' associations. Neither is it surprising that the teacher turnover rate remains high despite the lure of generous salary schedules.

Teachers in Transition

Thus far we have discussed the changes taking place in schools in very general terms; we have not focused on the impact these changes have had on the individual classroom teacher. But as we talked with several teachers whose long careers spanned a number of significant changes in American education, we came to realize the magnitude of this impact. We would like to share with you the career of one such teacher, Lena Kuhn,

Lena Kuhn
MASTER TEACHER

Lena Kuhn is representative of the many distinguished educators who have devoted their professional lives to teaching. Mrs. Kuhn began her teaching career in 1925 in a little one-room school in northern Indiana; when she retired in 1971 she was teaching in a modern, well-equipped school not far from the site of her original one-room school. Prior to being hired, she had completed only one year of teacher-education courses at the nearby college. Mrs. Kuhn describes her first teaching position and the responsibility it entailed as follows:

> My first job was in a one-room [see photograph] school which had a cloakroom and one large room with a stove in the middle. There was a well in the school yard and the toilets were in back of the school. Besides teaching the 20 or so students in grades 1 to 8, it was my job to see that the janitorial work was done. I got 15¢ a day for doing that! In the winter I hired a boy out of that money to build a fire. I got $110 a month for eight months the first year that I taught. In 1946 the school year was extended to $8\frac{1}{2}$ months, and in 1949 we went to a nine-month school year which remained in effect for the rest of my teaching career.

In 1926 the curriculum used by Mrs. Kuhn emphasized the basic areas of reading and mathematics. Reading and mathematics recitations lasted until noon, with students grouped according to their appropriate grade levels. Afternoons were devoted to subjects like English, spelling, geography, and agriculture. Academic activities were not much different from those used in today's schools, but Mrs. Kuhn is quick to point out that "we didn't have many frills — we never had movies or field trips!"

During the early part of Mrs. Kuhn's teaching career, students were not the only ones to receive grades. Once or twice a year, the county superintendent would observe each teacher and assess that person's performance by assigning "success grades." These grades were based not only on teaching skills but also on personal characteristics such as dress and voice quality. Success grades ranged from 1 to 100, and sorry was the teacher whose grade fell below 90!

Aside from the occasional visits from the county superintendent, teachers in the one-room schools had little contact with other educators. Teachers were, however, frequently invited to the homes of their students for dinner and often to spend the night. Mrs. Kuhn laughingly says, "You might say these visits were intensive parent-teacher conferences!"

Mrs. Kuhn believes the greatest change she observed during her teaching career involved the dramatic increase in the quantity of textbooks and supplies and the ever-increasing sophistication of educational equipment. With a sigh (or was it a grimace?) she describes the first duplicating machine she ever used, known as the hectograph: "You needed a shallow cookie pan and gelatin which you purchased from a school supply house. You would melt the gelatin, put it in the pan, and let it harden. A master copy was made by writing on the hardened gelatin with a special pen, and then copies could be made."

When Mrs. Kuhn began teaching she was responsible for teaching all areas of the curriculum (can you imagine teaching agriculture?), as well as coordinating the administrative and custodial work. She did not have the luxury of sending the misbehaving student to the principal's office. As her career progressed, however, the role of the teacher changed dramatically. The transition from multiple-grade to single-grade classrooms was greeted with both pleasure and regret. It was a welcome change to work with students who were approximately the same age and in similar stages of social development. Lost, however, was the joy of watching a child grow and develop over a period of years and the special understanding of the child with which such a process endows a teacher. Lost, too,

was the advantage of carrying over particular instructional goals from one year to the next.

Larger, more sophisticated schools brought additional changes for teachers like Mrs. Kuhn. Custodians assumed responsibility for the care of the building, and the installation of a building principal relieved the teacher of many administrative tasks. Special teachers were added to work in areas such as music, art, physical education, and speech therapy. Such changes greatly reduced flexibility, since teachers and students were required to adhere to strict time schedules.

The complexity of Mrs. Kuhn's role increased constantly. She was expected to become a tests and measurement person responsible for administering, scoring, and interpreting IQ and achievement tests. Grading systems came and went, and "new, improved" teaching strategies quickly became as obsolete as the Model-T.

Mrs. Kuhn kept abreast of these educational changes by attending professional workshops and by taking courses at nearby colleges. In retrospect the changes don't seem particularly dramatic to Mrs. Kuhn: "As changes came along through the years, you just gradually changed with the times. It wasn't such a big step; if you are with the tide, you accept the changes and go on."

As time went on Mrs. Kuhn found herself devoting more and more time and energy to her teaching responsibilities. Teachers' meetings, night courses, in-service meetings, and professional association meetings also consumed vast amounts of out-of-class time. Indicative of the changes she observed during her more than 40-year teaching career was the evolution of the Indiana teacher certification requirements—from one year of normal school training to a master's degree!

The most challenging aspect of teaching, according to Mrs. Kuhn, is holding the childrens' attention. *"Since children have so much more today than they had in 1926, a teacher must work harder to keep the children interested."* Discipline is another area she describes as challenging: "They used to tell us that discipline comes first, and then you teach school. And there are always one or two in the class who keep you on your toes!"

Mrs. Kuhn believes that successful teaching depends on one's really wanting to teach: "There are many rewarding things about teaching, but there are many discouraging things, too. But if you really have a desire to be a good teacher, you will do the things that can make you successful."

who taught in elementary and junior high schools for 45 years. As you read this vignette we would like you to consider the following points:

1. What would you consider the most difficult change that Mrs. Kuhn had to face during her 45-year teaching career?
2 What advantages do you think a teacher in a one-room school might have over a teacher in a contemporary school?
3. Consider the gains contemporary teachers have made since 1926?
4. Project the types of changes that you might have to make if your own teaching career spans 45 years.

Summary

The central theme of this chapter is that education does indeed have a rich history, and an understanding of that history enhances our appreciation and respect for our own profession. To personalize this point, consider that if you do become a member of the education profession, either as a teacher or in a related role, it will be necessary for you to continue learning and changing throughout your career. Mrs. Kuhn's story is but one of thousands of stories that illustrate the dynamics of the teachers' role. Furthermore, in this chapter we have tried to point out that schools and teachers do not exist in isolation; they are part of the larger society made up of political, economic, religious, and family subsystems, all of which affect the educational subsystem. In order to have a complete understanding of teachers' roles, students' needs, and schools themselves, we must view them in terms of this complex society.

1. The year is 2001. (Would you believe that you will be less than halfway through your teaching career that year?) Predict the changes that will occur in schools and classrooms during the next two decades.
2. Interview a relative or acquaintance who immigrated to the United States during the early part of the twentieth century. Focus your questions on how the school tried to "Americanize" this person.
3. Citizens' committees (or school boards) have controlled education since colonial times. Interview a school board member. Focus on the member's perception of the job responsibilities and the information she or he has regarding the evolution of responsibilities over time.
4. Teachers' motivations for selecting their career have changed throughout history. Cremin notes that teachers in the early years of American history viewed teaching as a stepping stone to the ministry.[16] Today, many teachers choose education as a career because they feel it is a stepping stone to the middle class. Examine your reasons for choosing education. Share these reasons with your colleagues.
5. In Figure 1.3 the 1872 instructions to the teacher are outlined. Develop a list of "instructions" for the teacher of today.
6. Many communities have created their historical past by constructing a replica of life in the eighteenth or nineteenth centuries. If your community has such a village, visit its schoolhouse. Use your imagination in the schoolhouse; describe your feelings. Contrast these feelings with those you experienced during observations in a modern school.
7. Much has changed in the way of salary and benefits since the early days of American schools. Survey the local schools and determine average starting salaries and maximum salaries. Determine salaries for teachers with bachelors, masters, and beyond-masters degrees.
8. Times are changing. Survey the local paper and outline what the current local educational issues are that are receiving press coverage. Were these issues present in the early 1900s and late 1800s?
9. Discuss and outline the following types of teacher:
   a. The one who was really excellent and made you excited about teaching.
   b. The one whom you remember as not very exciting or effective.
   Based upon your schooling experiences, describe the characteristics a person would need to be an effective classroom teacher.
10. We have stated that graded classrooms were the innovation of the 1920s. What do you see as the innovation of the present day?

Notes

1. Margaret Mead, "Our Educational Emphasis in Primitive Perspective," in *Education and Culture: Anthropological Approaches,* ed. George D. Spindler (New York: Holt, Rinehart and Winston, 1963).

2. M. Vere DeVault and Thomas E. Kriewall, *Perspectives in Elementary School Mathematics* (Columbus, Ohio: Charles E. Merrill, 1969), p. 3.
3. Lawrence Cremin, *The Transformation of the School: Progressivism in American Education, 1876-1957* (New York: Vintage, 1964).
4. Dan C. Lortie, *School-Teacher: A Sociological Study* (Chicago: University of Chicago Press, 1975).
5. W. S. Elsbree, *The American Teacher* (New York: American Book, 1939).
6. Louise Tharp, *Until Victory: Horace Mann and Mary Peabody* (Boston: Little, Brown, 1953), p. 136.
7. *Ibid.*
8. *Ibid.,* p. 143.
9. Randolf S. Bourne, *The Gary Schools* (Cambridge: MIT Press, 1970).
10. Robert L. McCaul, "Dewey, Harper, and the University of Chicago: July, 1894–March, 1902," in *John Dewey: Master Educator* 2nd ed., eds. William W. Brickman and Stanley Lehrer (New York: Society for the Advancement of Education, 1961), p. 34.
11. Harold A. Larrabee, "John Dewey as Teacher," in *John Dewey . . . ,* eds. Brickman and Lehrer, p. 95.
12. *Ibid.,* p. 97.
13. Maxine Green, "Dewey and American Education, 1894–1920," in *John Dewey. . . ,* eds. Brickman and Lehrer, p. 82.
14. Allan Fromme, "Introduction," in *How Children Fail,* John Holt (New York: Dell, 1964), p. xi.
15. Mary A. Golladay, *The Condition of Education: A Statistical Report on the Condition of Education in the United States.* (Washington, D.C.: U.S. Department of Health, Education, and Welfare/National Center for Education Statistics, 1976), p. 247.
16. Cremin, *Transformation of the School: Progressivism in American Education* (New York: Vintage, 1964).

For More Information

JOURNALS

Brown, S. D., and Brown, D. E. "A Look at the Past." *Arithmetic Teacher, 27* (1980), 34–37.
Gores, Harold B. "The Future File: Schoolhouse 2000." *Phi Delta Kappan, 56* (1975), 310–313.
Hudgins, H. C. "Brown and Public School Segregation: 25 Years Ago." *NOLPE, School Law Journal, 8* (1979), 116–126.
Kliebard, H. M. "The Drive for Curriculum Change in the United States 1890–1958. I. The Ideological Roots of Curriculum as a Field of Specialization." *Journal of Curriculum Studies, 11* (1979), 191–202.
Leiberman, Ann. "Political and Economic Stress and the Social Realities of Schools." *Teachers College Record, 79* (1977), 259–267.
Lucas, C. J. "More things Change . . ." *Phi Delta Kappan, 61* (Fall, 1980), 414–416.
Muir, J. Douglas. "Teachers and their Right to Bargain: How Far Have They Come and Where Are They Going?" *Education Canada,* Spring, *16* (1976), 4–11.

Newman, Philip R. "The School: A Psychosocial Ecosystem. *Educational Horizons, 51* (W 72–73), 59–63.

Sinowitz, Betty E. "What About Teacher Tenure?" *Today's Education, 62* (1973), 43.

Steuer, L. O., and Steddom, S. S. "From McGuffy to the Eighties: American Basic Reading Programs." *Teacher, 96* (1969), 58, 63–64, 66.

Tyack, D., and Hansot, E. "From Social Movement to Professional Management: An Inquiry Into the Changing Character of Leadership in Public Education." *American Journal of Education, 88* (1980), 291–319.

Tyack, David B.; and others. "Educational Reform: Retrospect and Prospect." *Teachers College Record, 81* (1980), 253–269.

Van Every, Ivalyn. "Teacher Education Meeting the Needs of Society: Past-Present-Future." *Kappa Delta Pi Record, 15* (1979), 72–75.

BOOKS

Cremin, Lawrence. *Traditions of American Education.* New York: Basic Books, 1977.

Cremin, Lawrence. *The Transformation of the School.* New York: Knopf, 1961.

Dewey, John and Dewey, Evelyn. *Schools of Tomorrow.* New York: E. P. Dutton and Company, 1915.

Lemlich, Johanna and Marks, Merle. *The American Teacher:* 1776–1976. Bloomington, Ind.: Phi Delta Kappa Publications, 1978.

Lortie, Dan. *School Teacher: A Sociological Study.* Chicago: University of Chicago, 1975.

Sarason, Seymour B. *The Culture of the School and the Problem of Change.* Boston: Allyn and Bacon, Inc., 1971.

Toffler, Alvin. *Future Shock.* New York: Random House, 1970.

Van Til, William. *Education: A Beginning.* 2nd Ed. Boston: Houghton Mifflin, 1974.

MOVIES*

The Ascent of Man (Time-Life, 13 films, each 52 mins., 1976). Human development as seen through the history of science.

Civilization (Time-Life, 13 films, each 52 mins., 1974). Human history through culture—painting, architecture, music, poetry, prose. Perspective of humanities on learning and expression.

Horace Mann (E.B.E.C., 19 mins., 1951). Discusses his contributions as a teacher, lawyer, state senator, board of education member, and college president. Emphasizes Mann's work in pointing up the need for well-built schools, good textbooks, democratic methods of learning, schools for teachers, and universal education in the United States.

My Childhood (Benchmark, 51 min., 1977). Contrasts the recreated childhoods of Hubert Humphrey and James Baldwin. It shows the effect of parental influence and environment in the forming of a man.

* Addresses for film distributors found on page 367.

No Little Hope (Center for Urban Education, 28 min.) Deals with what education means to different people of N.Y.C. A point is made to show the importance of parents, the community, mass media, and the schools.

The Prime of Miss Jean Brodie (Films Incorporated, 116 min., color, 1969). Miss Brodie's personal view of world events clashes against the realities of the girl's experience in the era of the Spanish Civil War and the rise of Mussolini. The film illustrates the power a teacher can exercise over students and the dangers of importing too much personal attitude into the classroom.

Chapter 2

Chapter 2

WHAT GOES ON
IN THE CLASSROOM

Teachers do make a difference. A study of Project Follow Through* by Abt Associates[1] compared various curriculum approaches for children in grades K to 3 in diverse communities throughout the United States. A major finding of this study emphasizes the importance of the individual classroom teacher. It was found that a major determiner of both successful and unsuccessful classroom results was the quality of interactions that occurred between the teacher and the students.

We ask you to keep this major finding in mind—that teachers do make a difference—as we examine the processes that occur in the classroom. By *processes* we mean the "series of actions or operations" that occur in all classrooms: good and bad, effective and ineffective, humanistic- and academic-oriented, preschool and high school. As you begin to understand the processes, you will be able to make sense out of that very complex system called the classroom.

We will look into classrooms through the eyes of Philip Jackson, Barak Rosenshine, and Michael Dunkin and Bruce Biddle. These keen observers of this very complex environment present frameworks for understanding the literally thousands of interactions that occur each day in the classroom. Through the encounter activities at the end of the chapter, you will be able to apply their frameworks to those classrooms you visit as an observer, a participant-observer, and an active participant. Without the

*Project Follow Through is a federally funded program designed to serve primary-age students (K–3) and their families whose income falls at the official poverty line or below. In most cases the children in Project Follow Through have participated in preschool programs, such as Head Start.

frameworks you would have difficulty making sense of the beehive of activity found in all classrooms. Please keep in mind that we are presenting you with only three frameworks; numerous other frameworks do exist. We chose the viewpoints of the above observers because of the comprehensiveness of each of their frameworks.

The Classroom through the Eyes of Philip Jackson

In 1968 Jackson wrote *Life in the Classroom,* a book on the processes found in the classroom; it has become a classic. In it he states:

> This is not to say, of course, that all classrooms are identical, anymore than all churches are. Clearly there are differences, and sometimes very extreme ones, between two settings. One has only to think of the wooden benches and planked floor of the early American classroom as compared with the plastic chairs and tile flooring in today's suburban schools. *But the resemblance is still there despite the differences, and, more important, during any particular historical period the differences are not that great.* Also, whether the student moves from first to sixth grade on floors of vinyl tile or oiled wood, whether he spends his days in front of a blackboard or a green one, is not as important as the fact that the environment in which he spends these six or seven years is highly stable.[2] [Emphasis added]

Goldman, Friedman, and Bogin[3] observed classrooms in grades 1 through 12 in selected Israeli schools that had high percentages of school dropouts. Their major finding supports the statement of Jackson that the processes used in all classrooms vary little from one environment to another. For example, they found that the interactions in elementary, middle, and high school classrooms were very similar in regard to the following:

a. the large percentage of teacher talk;
b. the lack of involvement by students in the lessons (i.e., teachers talked and students listened);
c. the relatively few students who received positive comments from teachers.

Begin your analysis of classrooms by studying the adjacent photo essay.

Questions About the Photo Essay

1. Jackson has stated that despite the historical period, the differences among classrooms are relatively few. Is Jackson seeing the same classrooms that you are? As you view the photo essay, how are you reacting to Jackson's statement?
2. What are the common processes that are occurring in all of the classrooms in the photo essay?

1 2

5

3

6

4

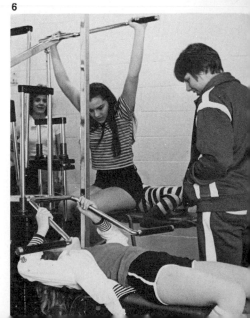

How would Jackson respond to the photo essay? Our best "guesstimate" is that he would present an analysis based on the following: If you presented the photo essay to persons who have experienced classroom life with the question, "What is happening to these pictures?" 99 percent of the respondents would state, "Those are all pictures of students and a teacher!" Why would the respondents concur in their responses, even though the classrooms differ so drastically from one another? Jackson would probably state that those who have experienced classroom life would recognize the roles assumed by the teachers and students in the photo essay, even with the contrasting classroom designs. Roses may be pink, yellow, or red, but "a rose is a rose is a rose." The classrooms in the photo essay, though significantly different from one another, can all be identified as classrooms—"a classroom is a classroom is a classroom."

ROLES IN THE CLASSROOM

In all classrooms students must adapt their behaviors to "crowds," "praise," and "power" if they are to experience school success. In Chapter 1 we discussed adoption by schools of an industrial model to school organization in the nineteenth century. The innovation of graded classrooms (as contrasted to the one-room school house) was felt to be more efficient— one teacher planned the same experiences for her 30, 40, or more students. To the present day, even with innovations in nongraded and family groupings, the mathematical concept of ratio of teacher to students is used to calculate classroom size. While most teachers desire smaller ratios (say, 20 students to a teacher, as contrasted to 40 students to a teacher), one can conclude that all classrooms, no matter what the teacher-student ratio, are crowded environments.

A second element to which students must adapt in the classroom is "praise" (and punishment). In no other part of our society does an individual receive as much evaluation as in the school. Evaluation, with its related praise and punishment, is not limited to the student's academic performance: How the student lines up, seeks the teacher's attention, passes out supplies, cooperates with others, and dresses are continually being evaluated in the classroom.

The third element, "power," is an important aspect of classroom life. Although many teachers feel they lack power over their destiny, they do have considerably more power than students in the classroom when it comes to issues such as what should be studied and what types of behaviors are acceptable.

"Crowds," "praise," and "power" have a direct influence on the roles assumed and assigned to teachers and students in the classroom. Jackson identifies four major roles that must be assumed by the teacher if chaos is to be avoided in the classroom: "traffic cop," "judge," "supply sergeant," and "timekeeper."

Teacher as Traffic Cop

"Bob, you can read next."

"Sue, when Barbara returns from the bathroom, it will be
your turn."

"When you finish your assignment, form a line at the
right side of my desk."

The teacher spends much of the day preventing "traffic jams" of students
and, when they do occur, trying to bring order out of the chaos. For example: "I told you at the beginning of the class, only three students can
work with the reading kit at one time. Bob, Carol, and Ted may remain at
the reading center. Alice, wait at your seat until one of the students
finishes the assigned task." For students, taking turns is not limited to
line-up type situations (lines for drinks, cafeteria, or boarding the school
bus); teachers also form psychological lines:

- One way is by calling on students to respond in a pattern based on seating assignments. For example, the first response is made by the first
  student in the first row. The pattern is followed until the last student
  in the last row responds. (An historical aside: One co-author re-
  members that in his high school Latin class, each student read one
  paragraph. The participation followed the pattern described above. As
  the third student in the fourth row, he was able to predict accurately,
  before class, his response for any given instructional period!)
- Another way is by informing the five students who have their hands up
  to respond in sequence: "Evan will answer first; Erin will be next. . . ."
- Lines are formed while assisting children at their desks, when the
  teacher's pattern of movement is based on the order in which students
  requested help by raising their hands.
- Finally, psychological lines are formed by telling a student who has already responded that it is necessary to wait a few minutes before
  responding again, since the other students have not had their turn
  (i.e., he must go to the "end of the line").

What effect does the "traffic cop" role have on the student? Perhaps the
most significant effect is the amount of time the child waits in lines, both
the physical "lines" (at the cafeteria, drinking fountain, and bus) and the
"lines" formed by the teacher in nonlinear situations (discussion or tutoring students). An analogy for this student "in waiting" situation is the
holding pattern of airplanes found at busy airports. Patience is needed,
and much time may be wasted. The holding-pattern analogy breaks down
for those students who do not receive their turn to "land." As a student,
how many times were you told by the teacher, "I'll be right with you,"
only to be forgotten because of other demands placed on the teacher? For
the quiet, passive student, landing rights may be bypassed numerous

times each day. Have you any guesses about the extent of psychological damage that may be done to this type of student over an extended period of time?

As the traffic cop, the effective teacher establishes routines that minimize the amount of time-wasting conflicts. However, in every class-room there are numerous interruptions that are difficult, if not impos-sible, to predict. Perhaps the most common such interruption is what we call collecting "milk money." For us, "milk money" is a generic name for money collections related to milk, athletic tickets, candy sales, lunch and snacks, overdue library books, and other sundry financial interruptions. We call "milk money" an interruption because invariably someone requests a count or a balance sheet right in the midst of the most interest-ing discussion on the workings of the brain or the death of a pet shell crab or the solution to a complex math problem. This instructional interrup-tion says to the teacher that the 15¢ carton of milk or the 27¢ overdue notice is now more important than the student, the teacher, and the con-tent. How can the teacher cope with the "milk money" interruption? The

best technique we have seen was used by a teacher who refused to spend the valuable instructional time of the students on figuring out the credits and debits of the milk bill. The teacher simply multiplied the number of milk drinkers by 15¢ and paid the total out of his own pocket. Students repaid him, using an honor system. After completing periodic accounting analyses, this teacher found that he was out very few pennies—in fact, no more than when he spent valuable moments asking, "Bobby, did you pay your 15¢ last Tuesday?" Can you think of other solutions to the "milk money" dilemma? Ask a competent (and trustworthy) math student to coordinate money collections. Arrange an honor system in which the entire group keeps track of payments. (We must apologize for spending your valuable time on milk money, instead of on one of the numerous substantive issues in this book, but we too often see teachers wasting valuable time on such trivial matters.)

It is your turn now. Look at the picture on the opposite page and describe the child's behavior. From the information you have read thus far in this chapter, what conclusions can you draw about this child's behavior? Share this picture with school-age children. How similar or different are their analyses from yours?

Make an analysis of the above photo. If you were the "traffic cop" in this picture, what would you do? Compare your response with those of your colleagues. Analyze the traffic cop behaviors of teachers in various open-style environments. Share this picture with school-age children. How similar or different are their analyses from yours?

Teacher as Judge

"I was pleased by the cooperation of the science club."

"Bobby, good try, This was your best effort."

"If I see the cigarettes again, you'll be sent to the office."

"Did you see the 100-percent spelling tests on the board?
Those five students did excellent work!"

From the moment the students walk into the classroom, evaluation begins. Evaluations of clothing, language patterns, completion of assignments, interaction among the students, study behaviors, entrance and exit behaviors getting into and out of the classroom, etc., etc. The list does not seem to end! Let us examine various categories of teacher judgmental behaviors.

Judge as Test Giver

> The most obvious difference between the way evaluation occurs in school and the way it occurs in other situations is that tests are given in school more frequently than elsewhere. Indeed with the exception of examinations related to military service or certain kinds of occupations, most people seldom encounter tests outside of their school experience. Tests are indigenous to the school environment as are textbooks or pieces of chalk.[4]

The formal use of tests begins as early as kindergarten. Many teachers in kindergartens that emphasize academic skills use formal tests in reading and math. Often the results of these kindergarten tests can be seen on charts labeled "I Know the Numbers" or "I Know My Words." On each chart, are listed the names of those students who have passed the test. Very early in their school experience, students learn that the taking of tests are private affairs, not to be shared with one's peers; test results on the other hand are often public information. Failure to work independently will often lead to punishment: a zero on the test, the paper being thrown away by the teacher, and punishment for the student.

In most testing situations there are a small number of "winners" and a much larger group of "losers." The winners, of course, will find their tests displayed on the bulletin board; the "losers" receive none of the spoils of the classroom. Many teachers have become sensitive to the "no-win" situation for the larger percentage of test takers. One solution to the "no-win" problem is the adaptation of Benjamin Bloom's idea that testing should not be a sorting process (i.e., the separation of the smart from the dumb):

> If students start each new learning task with the prerequisite knowledge and skills, they gradually need less additional correction time and help. *The major change for teachers is that they do less in the way of judging and grading*

students on what they had learned by a particular date and do more to see to it that each student learns what he or she needs as preparation for the next learning task.[5]

Judge as Evaluator of Students' Work-Related Behaviors. While the student's completed task (e.g., test, paper, worksheet), are of a large concern to the student, teacher, and parent, most of the teacher's evaluative comments are related to those student behaviors that are referred to as on- and off-task behaviors. On-task behaviors contribute to the student's successfully completing the task. These on-task behaviors differ slightly from one classroom to another, but typically they include holding pencil in hand, looking at the task, focusing on the teacher, listening to other students, writing, obtaining appropriate material, etc. You are probably able to predict off-task behaviors. Among those that receive the most attention from the teacher are shouting out, fighting, sleeping, not waiting for turn, unfinished work, etc. The teacher's task in this area must be to decide which behaviors deserve his attention and which should be ignored. Those teachers who use the principles of behavior modification will reinforce on-task behaviors with positive verbal and nonverbal comments and objects that may be of value to the students (e.g., stars, candy, opportunity to view a film); they will ignore off-task behaviors unless the student behavior is bothering other students or endangers the safety of either the student displaying the behavior or his peers. As the judge of students' work-related behaviors, the teacher will use the following processes for informing the students of their appropriate or inappropriate behaviors:

Verbal feedback:
   "I like your work."
   Johnny is working so quietly." (Bobby, who sits next to Johnny, is being disruptive; he changes his behavior as soon as he hears the teacher's comments.)
Nonverbal feedback:
   Smile, touch, point, change in volume and tone of the voice (nonverbal components of verbal behavior).

Many teachers reject the behavior-modification approach in their role as judge. They find the approach to be manipulative and a form of bribery. Those teachers who favor an intrinsic approach to their evaluator role feel that the student should do a task because it is perceived as being of value and that a significant portion of the reinforcement should come from the student rather than from the teacher (i.e., through self-evaluation and intrinsic reinforcement). As you observe teachers who favor a more intrinsic approach, an approach that gives more responsibility to the learner as evaluator, you will notice that the teacher uses many of the evaluation techniques of those teachers who use behavior modification (e.g., verbal and nonverbal praise, verbal feedback regarding appropriate behaviors). Those teachers who adopt the intrinsic approach, avoid the use of stars, points, and "pay-offs." While differences exist between the two approaches, the similarities are strong; in one way or another, the teacher evaluates the students' work-related behaviors.

Judge as Evaluator of Students' Attitudes. You may have said it (and may have been accused of it!): "You have a bad attitude." Typically, we infer this attitude in a student through nonverbal behavior: facial expression, movement of eyes and head, placement of hands, angle of body, clothes, voice intonation. Place yourself in the teacher's role in this situation, described by Russell L. French:*

> A white, male student, Billy Bigelow, comes running down the hall. There is a rule against running. So in your role as teacher, you call to him, motion him to you, and begin a brief lecture on why one can't run in the halls. A few years ago, Billy's response pattern during the lecture would have been predictable. Typically, he would have stood with hands thrust deep in his pockets, shoulders hunched, eyes on the floor. But, that was a long ago yesterday. Today, Billy "strolls" over to you when called and stands "insolently," head up but tilted slightly to one side, eyes forward but focused somewhere beyond you, body swaying slightly to an unheard rhythm, fingers silently snapping or pushed halfway into his pockets, body almost limp.
>
> Perhaps you end your lecture with a question, "What do you have to say for yourself, young man?" When we were teenagers confronted with that sort of unanswerable question, we responded with a shrug of our shoulders, eyes still fixed on the floor. If you have taught for some time, you remember students of seven or eight years ago who responded to the question as we did—humbly, contritely, with a shrug of the shoulders and lowered eyes. But Billy doesn't do that. He looks you in the eye for a moment, then rolls his eyes, turns on his heel and "strolls" off down the hall. It's maddening! It's frightening! "What's come over youth today? Must they always put me down? Conflict! Confrontation! Oh, I'd like to hit him!" Perhaps these thoughts flash through your mind as you stand there angry, confused, and helpless.

French feels educators must understand the nonverbal patterns that are acts of hostility and those that are part of the youth culture. Nonverbal behaviors and their associated meanings change over time; the evaluation of students' attitudes is a difficult process.

Let us now examine a photo essay that focuses on the teacher as a evaluator of students' attitudes. The photos on pages 53 and 54 focus on two perspectives: the students' and the teachers'. Your task is to interpret the meanings and possible inferences that can be derived from each photo.

*Russell L. French, "Nonverbal Patterns in Youth Culture," *Educational Leadership* 35 (April 1978): 542. Reprinted with the permission of the Association for Supervision and Curriculum Development and Russell L. French. Copyright © 1978 by the Association for Supervision and Curriculum Development. All rights reserved.

One final comment on the role of teacher as judge. We visited a school in a community that did not put a high value on academic achievement. In this particular school those student attributes that were valued highly by the "teachers as judges" conflicted with the values of the school and community. After each report-card period the student judged by the teachers as representing the best in academic achievement and attitude had his name placed on a large plaque in the school's main entrance. "Robert," the student selected for this honor, found that he was verbally and physically abused by a group of his peers after his name appeared on the "highest honor role." We came to the conclusion (and tested it out by interviewing a small sample of students) that Robert received punishment from his peers for his deviant behavior—the very same behavior that was valued in the culture of the teachers. Teachers have the primary responsibility for "judging." Apparently, students look to both their peers and teachers as evaluators of their performance in school.

Teacher as Supply Sergeant

STUDENT: Ms. Jones, I need another piece of paper for my work.

TEACHER: Katie, I'm so sorry. But I told you we will run out of paper by May if we waste the paper. Erase or scratch out what you have written.

TEACHER: Brent, give each student a pencil. Your pencil must last for the entire week.

STUDENT: Mr. Smith, I've been waiting for 20 minutes to use the microscope. It's my turn!

The current era of tight budgets has led many schools to limit the school supplies that were often taken for granted in the past. The end result of this paucity of materials is that teachers spend much of their valuable time "scrounging" materials and designing elaborate plans for materials distribution that often takes away from the teacher's planning and instructional time. One positive outcome from this current shortage is the creativity shown by many teachers in obtaining material and using material in ways in which the material was not originally designed: using computer cards for rulers and number lines; making flannel boards (display boards) out of remnants of cloth; asking parents to contribute household materials that have possible uses in the classroom; begging for material from commercial establishments that have a potential use for the classroom environment and instruction (e.g., carpet remnants for a reading area, nuts and bolts as counters for mathematics).

Teacher as Timekeeper

> . . . school is a place where things often happen not because students want them to, but because it is time for them to occur.[6]

STUDENT: But Ms. Jones, I'm not ready to begin algebra. I'm in the middle of my science experiment.

TEACHER: It's now 10:05. Put your literature books away and put your math books on top of the desk.

Time is an issue in all classrooms. One may assume that so-called traditional classrooms live by the clock; in reality, teachers in classrooms with more complex designs, such as Individually Guided Education, are more time conscious because of the elaborate teaming of teachers and students (see Chapter 4). As you observe in a variety of classrooms, you will begin to infer that students have a feeling that "time" is about to affect their lives. Notice the movement of bodies, papers, and purses a few minutes before the time to change classes or content areas. It seems that students can feel the upcoming change that is about to occur.

Summary

As you step back and examine the four roles described above, you may conclude that the critical teacher roles related to instruction have not been discussed. You are correct. We spent considerable time in this section on those roles of teacher and student that are unique to the social system of the school and classroom. The unique aspects of the school and classroom include:

- Compulsory nature of classroom attendance;
- Crowded conditions found in all classrooms (as compared to other environments in society);
- Continuous use of praise and punishment;
- Social conditions that require an imbalance of power between teacher and students.

The above conditions found in all classrooms do not occur in those learning environments outside the school and classroom.

In the home learning environment, attendance is not made compulsory by law. The infant acquiring language "studies" when she or he wants to, rather than by meeting the minimum state guidelines of 180 days of instruction. As contrasted to the school, the home is usually not a crowded environment. Because of the lack of crowds, the parent rarely assumes the roles of traffic cop and timekeeper. The parent is a source of praise, assuming a portion of the role of judge, but not nearly to the extent of the teacher in the classroom. What are possible reasons for not assuming the role of judge? The teacher often uses praise and punishment for crowd control (praising one child who is on-task to serve as a model for the children who are off-task). Unlike the teacher, the parent does not have specified objectives for each area of the child's development that require grades (and related praise and punishment).

In the community learning environment, e.g., music lessons at a community center, attendance is not compulsory. (A parent may force a child to attend two or three lessons. If the child's resistance continues, most parents will rescind the "compulsory" attendance order.) Crowded conditions can exist (group lessons), but the session lasts for a limited number of minutes as compared to the crowded conditions of the 300- to 400-minute school day. Judgment of the child tends to be personal and is not placed in a permanent file that follows the child to adulthood.

In the work learning environment, e.g., apprenticeship programs, compulsory attendance does exist; the violation of the attendance requirement is not a legal action, but a firing. The learner in this environment often works on a one-to-one basis with the instructor. The small ratio enables the instructor to abandon the role of traffic cop. The instructor as judge does exist. The use of the judge's praise and punishment differs from the classroom teacher; the praise is private and aimed at the learner.

The Classroom Through the Eyes of Barak Rosenshine

Philip Jackson viewed the classroom through a wide-angle lens as he tried to grasp an understanding of the entire picture of the classroom. In contrast to Jackson's wide angle, Barak Rosenshine limits his view primarily to the young learners (grades 1 to 5) and what the learner is able to learn in the academic areas, focusing primarily on reading and mathematics. Most research on the classroom has focused on the behaviors of the teacher (e.g., the questions asked, reinforcement used, movement, and leadership style). Currently, the focus is shifting to student behaviors, primarily to the concept of "academic engaged time." Rosenshine and his colleagues feel that there are two elements of academic engaged time: (1) content covered and (2) student attention or engagement on the learning material or learning situation.[7] From the observations Rosenshine has made and the reviews of research he has completed, one conclusion stands out: there is a strong positive relationship between the amount of time students spend studying a particular subject area and their achievement in that subject. To clarify this point we will review the conclusions drawn by Rosenshine concerning classrooms in which students tend to display high achievement (as measured by an achievement test).

1. The teacher uses a method of direct instruction. "[Direct] instruction refers to high levels of student engagement with *teacher directed classrooms* using *sequenced, structured materials*."[8] [Emphasis added]
   Your reaction may be a variation of "ugh!" to this first element of a successful classroom. You may have read a great deal concerning the need for democratic classrooms and learning material that is open-ended in format. We will return to your concern in the conclusion of this section.

2. The teacher limits student choice or activities. "Classrooms which were organized so that students have a great deal of choice about the activities they will pursue are usually ones with lower academic engaged time and lower achievement."[9]

What can we say to you about the money you just put out for the book on learning centers and the processes to facilitate student choice of alternative activities? Don't return your book yet. The learning-center design is alive and well, and we will discuss this issue in Chapter 4.

3. The teacher avoids working with one or two students. "[Time] spent working with only one or two students, was *negatively* related to class achievement gain, whereas time spent working with small groups (three to seven students) or with large groups was consistently positively related to achievement."[10] Close adult supervision leads to student achievement.
   We're sure you have much data that demonstrate that one-to-one interaction can be effective. A teacher, however, should spend little time with individual tutoring of students; this task should be the responsibility of classroom assistants, parent volunteers, and university students.

4. Effective teachers allocate sufficient amounts of time to academic areas and are *not* bound by the clock.[11]
   That is exactly the time schedule you just observed in an informal-type classroom. However, that informal classroom certainly was not what Rosenshine and his colleagues are describing as effective for students' achievement of academic skills. Are you confused? (We did promise you in Chapter 1 that teaching is a complex process.)

5. The use of factual single-answer questions is positively related to achievement gains.[12]
   You may be wondering whether he means that a question like "Which European first landed in America?" would be more effective than a more open question, such as "Why did Columbus risk his life to sail to an unknown land?" Perhaps one reason you decided to choose teaching as a career is your frustration with those many teachers who bored you to death with lower-level questions. Before you choose another career, read on for some possible explanations and alternatives to this phenomenon.

6. Students' self esteem tends to be higher in those classrooms that use a direct-instruction approach and a high level of academic engaged time.[13]
   You did *read the last point correctly: An emphasis on basic skills tends to be related to the student's positive feeling regarding self (see the Abt study on Project Follow Through). Perhaps we are involved in a "chicken and egg" issue: Does one have to feel good about oneself before effective academic work can be completed, or does one have to feel success with academic work before one feels good about oneself? This is a very complex issue that you will study throughout your career.*

Rosenshine pictures a successful classroom (success being measured by formal tests of academic achievement) as one that includes the following dimensions:

- Teacher uses direct instruction.
- Student's choice of activities is limited by the teacher.
- Teacher tries to work with large groups or the entire class.
- Teachers are not bound by the clock.
- Discussions tend to focus on factual-level questions.
- Students in direct-instruction-type classrooms tend to have higher self esteem.

You may picture the classroom with the above dimensions as having a cold, prison-like atmosphere. Rosenshine disagrees: "Teachers in more formal classrooms today are warm, concerned, flexible, and allow much more freedom of movement. But they are also task oriented and determined that children shall learn."[14] Research must be completed regarding the optimal amount of time that students can be engaged in academically related activities. This amount of time may vary according to age, ability, past experiences, and other variables. While Rosenshine does not have the data to recommend the optimal amount of time for direct instruction, he feels that there must be a balance between the direct-instruction classrooms that use structured, sequenced materials with an emphasis on academic engaged time *and* classrooms that focus on creativity, learner choice, and individualized assignments. One solution, according to Rosenshine is a classroom that:

> . . . uses both approaches, but separately in their instruction. Mornings in these schools are spent in structured programs in reading, writing and mathematics. The teachers make the assignments but the children complete them anywhere in the room in a relaxed and informal manner. These assignments are from the same sequential structured workbooks and readers that are used in traditional schools. Although each child works at his own task and at his own pace, no more than two activities, such as reading and writing, occur at the same time. Although the atmosphere is relaxed, informal, and respectful, the setting is large groups, teacher centered, and structured. Afternoons are given to projects, exploration, messing around, trips, and discussion. Fridays are for hobbies and crafts. Thus the school teaches didactic goals, such as reading and math, in a didactic way; and spends the remaining time on more open activities. This approach seems intuitively appealing and sensible.[15]

One of the themes that pervades this book is the availability of *alternatives*. We have tried to attach a neutral meaning to this term. Rosenshine, in our opinion, merges two diverse (and in the minds of many educators, conflicting) alternatives. Again, the issue returns to your analysis as you try to build a classroom that meshes well with your philosophy, the knowledge that we have about children and learning, and the goals of the school and community. It is a very difficult balancing act.

Before we leave Rosenshine's view of the classroom, we will keep the following issues in mind related to his findings:

1. Rosenshine limits his research to those student and teacher behaviors that tend to be related to student achievement on formal achievement tests. (Most achievement tests measure factual information rather than the higher-level tasks of problem solving, creativity, and comprehension.)
2. Rosenshine limits his research to children in grades 1 through 5. One can only make inferences about his findings as they relate to middle school and high school students.
3. Rosenshine's work is a pioneering effort. Future efforts may develop conclusions that conflict with his findings.

Even with the above caveats, Rosenshine presents us with a handle (a "model," if you don't mind the jargon) for a better understanding of what goes on in the classroom.

The Classroom Through the Eyes of Dunkin and Biddle

Keen observers of the classroom, Michael Dunkin and Bruce Biddle feel that the "truly wise teacher is one who views the classroom social system as an asset rather than a hinderance."[16] This so-called wise teacher, having acquired the knowledge of how the classroom functions, can design an environment that improves the opportunities for success by all students. The knowledge needed includes information from social psychology, sociology, anthropology, and other related disciplines. Much to the surprise of many beginning teachers, the world of the classroom is not limited to basal texts, chalk and chalkboard, questions and answers, and tests.

One of the major findings on classroom life is that the learner tends to be passive and the teacher to be active. A thread that passes through this book is an attempt to encourage the reader to be active rather than passive. *Your task here is to read each statement presented and decide whether you feel the statement is accurate (based on your knowledge, past experiences, and so on).* Following each statement we present the actual findings of Dunkin and Biddle that either support or repudiate the statement.

Statement: **Classroom activities constitute a "game." Since the game is so complex, the participants (teacher and students) do not understand the rules of the game.**

Think of your past classroom experiences that support your conclusion. Compare your response to that of Dunkin and Biddle.

Dunkin and Biddle summarized Arno Bellack's classroom interaction study in which he concluded that classroom activities do constitute a game-type situation whose rules are well understood by both students and teacher.[17] It is particularly interesting to note that the rules for the classroom game are usually unwritten but well understood by all participants. The typical student (or teacher) who violates the rule is often aware of the violation even without receiving direct feedback from the game's participants. The game, similar to chess or checkers, consists of a series of moves; each move "consists of one or more sentences uttered by a given speaker that have a common content and purpose."[18] The following is a sample of typical moves:

TEACHER MOVE: Who knows the origins of authoritarian ideologies?
STUDENT MOVE: A first example of an authoritarian government occurred
    during. . . .
TEACHER MOVE: Right.

Students are well aware that their moves tend to be ones of responding rather than initiating. Teachers know that their moves typically consist of questions and feedback to the students' responses. Who enjoys the game more, the students or the teacher? Since teachers tend to have the active and students the passive role, teachers tend to enjoy the classroom game more than the pupils. In addition, because of the rules of the game, teachers tend to have more power than the other participants.

Statement: The physical environment has little or no effect on the students' behaviors.

You have spent thousands of hours in classrooms. As your mind returns to the sights and sounds of your second-grade or tenth-grade classroom, do you remember whether the physical environments affected your social and academic behavior?

The co-authors did not attend school in the Dark Ages; however, we remember desks that were bolted to the floor, and there was the hole in the desk top for the ink and the dip pen! That environment was an integral part of our classrooms' social system: Talking to our neighbors was discouraged since our bolted down desks were situated in straight lines; left-handed students had a terrible time with the ink wells that were located on the right side of the desk (they tended to be in continual trouble because of difficulties with spilled ink). Dunkin and Biddle conclude:

> The physical environment of the classroom affects the behavior of classroom members. Pupils at the back of the room are likely to be treated somewhat differently by the teachers and to behave differently than those in the front. Doors, pencil sharpeners, the teacher's desk, cloak rooms, library shelves, maps, goldfish bowls — all potentially attract a unique pattern of pupil behaviors in their environments. Sunlight and bright colors are likely to encourage a lively classroom, while carpeting on the floor probably deadens sound, increases attention span, and reduces fatigue.[19]

Statement: Teachers who tend to move about the classroom and use nonverbal gestures tend to be more effective teachers.

Think of teacher *X,* who sat at a desk during most of the instructional time, compared to teacher *Y,* who moved continuously around the classroom. Did these different styles have an effect on your performance? What about the "actor" who used many gestures; did you feel more involved in this type of learning environment?

Dunkin and Biddle summarize a study completed by Rosenshine that found that movement and gestures improved the possibility for learning in the classroom.[20] If you reported this finding to B. F. Skinner, he would probably respond with a variation of "those findings are consistent with my findings on the effects of reinforcement on the learner." Assuming that Rosenshine's finding is correct, perhaps the shy, introverted teachers will have to adjust their behaviors.

Statement: The ideal teaching situation is not one in which students work individually but rather one that includes a set of small supervised groups.

Before you turn back to Rosenshine's section on the relationship between academic engaged time and group size, think a moment: Does this conclusion conflict with Rosenshine's? Basically, it does not. Rosenshine concludes that the most appropriate group size includes that number of students that enabled the teacher most effectively to supervise each student. Therefore, he rejects one-to-one tutoring as an ideal model and supports small group instruction (three to seven students) and large group instruction, since the teacher is better able to supervise those groupings.

Statement: Teachers' reactions toward students and the students' accomplishments tend to be positive.

An accurate statement? You're not too sure. You can think of teachers who fit into both the negative and positive categories. Please remember that the findings in this section are trends and patterns; there are always exceptions to any finding. Dunkin and Biddle concluded from their review of studies on teachers' use of reinforcement "that most teachers are predominantly, if not ritualistically, positive in tone."[21] Successful teachers differentiate their use of positive reinforcement through the tone of voice and the specificity of the comments. Those teachers who are ritualistically positive (e.g., basically the same positive reinforcement is given to all student behaviors, whatever the level of student response) are not as successful as those teachers who add emphasis to their reactions.

Statement: **Teachers spend about half their instructional time as "emitters."**

During a six-hour school day, teachers spend half their time talking.[22] (Based on a 180-day school year, that amounts to 540 hours of talking per school year.) Teachers tend to do more talking than a professional actor or TV talk-show host does during the same period of time. Does the number appear to be too high? Too high it may be, but it is an accurate description of the amount of "emitting" one hears from the typical teacher. Who talks more in the classroom, male or female teachers? You can throw out one stereotype: Male teachers talk more in the classroom than do their female colleagues.

Statement: **Students spend most of their time creating, problem solving, and actively "doing" tasks.**

In all likelihood, relatively few readers will report that the above finding typifies the types of student involvement in the schools they attended. In the words of Dunkin and Biddle:

> Pupils spend most of their time in *listening* and *watching* and *reading* and *writing*. Less time is spent in any activities that involve gross muscular effort or expressiveness or in talking with others. And when pupils speak at all, it is likely that they are addressing the teacher. All of these findings institute grist for critics who would find the classroom a dull, teacher-dominated environment, although whether pupils actually suffer from such practices or whether it would be possible to run a multipupil classroom effectively by other techniques is not yet established.[23]

Summary   In this chapter we have viewed classrooms from three perspectives: those of Philip Jackson, Barak Rosenshine, and Michael Dunkin and Bruce Biddle. Your task is a complex one. You must align these various perspectives with your own so that a clear picture begins to emerge of what goes on in the classroom. The diverse, and frequently conflicting findings presented are consistent with an important theme in this book: there are alternative classroom designs, alternative approaches for studying the classroom, alternative inferences that you can state from any set of teacher-student behaviors. A key for understanding the complexity of the classroom is to *begin* to build a framework from which you can obtain tentative answers to your questions. Your framework can contain elements from Jackson, Rosenshine, and Dunkin and Biddle. Other elements for the framework will come from your experiences, information from experienced teachers, and from those observers who try to develop a rational order from the complex interactions that occur in every classroom.

1. Complete the following chart that summarizes four different perceptions of the classroom.

Jackson's View	Rosenshine's View	Dunkin and Biddle's View	Your View

2. Ask a teacher whether you can take photographs in the classroom. Analyze the photographs, using the conclusions suggested by Jackson, Rosenshine, and Dunkin and Biddle.
3. One conclusion that was made by Jackson is that classrooms, when compared to one another, have more similarities than differences. Visit a wide variety of classrooms: day care, university, elementary, middle school, and high school. Note the similarities that you observe in the classrooms.
4. Prepare a brief, ten-minute lecture for your colleagues on the topic, "What Goes on in the Classroom."
5. Visit a classroom as a participant (i.e., a student) rather than as an observer. Do all the tasks assigned to the students. After the visit (the duration of the visit should be between one hour and the entire day), write a log of the events that occurred during the visit and your reactions to the events. Compare your reactions and conclusions to those stated by the experts in this chapter.
6. Creatures from outer space have landed their space vehicle in the playground of a local school. In their environment the concept of "school" does not exist. Try to explain to them the happenings in a classroom.
7. Nonverbal behaviors, according to the experts in this chapter, have an effect on students' behaviors. Visit a classroom; try to turn off the sounds of the classroom in your mind, and develop some conclusions about classroom interactions. You can do this activity by videotaping the classroom interaction without taping the sounds of the environment.
8. Verbal behaviors are also very important. Listen to an audiotape of a classroom activity and describe your conclusions about the classroom environment and interactions.

Notes

1. Linda B. Stebbins and Robert G. St. Pierre, *Education as Experimentation: A Planned Variation Model,* Vol. 4-A (Cambridge, Mass.: Abt Associates, 1977).
2. Philip W. Jackson, *Life in Classrooms* (New York: Holt, Rinehart and Winston, 1968), p. 6.

3. Richard M. Goldman, Robert Friedman, and Michael Bogin, "The School System and Its Relationship to Irregular Attendance," report funded by the Israeli Ministry of Education and the University of Haifa (Haifa, Israel: University of Haifa, 1971).
4. Jackson, *Life in Classrooms,* p. 19.
5. Benjamin S. Bloom, "New Views of the Learner: Instruction and Curriculum," *Educational Leadership 35* (April 1978): 563–76.
6. Jackson, *Life in Classrooms,* p. 13.
7. Barak V. Rosenshine, "Primary Grades Instruction and Student Achievement Gain," paper presented at the annual meeting of the American Educational Research Association, New York, April 1977.
8. *Ibid.,* p. 9a.
9. *Ibid.,* p. 11.
10. *Ibid.,* p. 12.
11. *Ibid.,* p. 14.
12. *Ibid.,* p. 16.
13. *Ibid.,* p. 22.
14. *Ibid.,* p. 22.
15. *Ibid.,* p. 24.
16. Michael J. Dunkin and Bruce J. Biddle, *The Study of Teaching* (New York: Holt, Rinehart and Winston, 1974), p. 29.
17. *Ibid.* pp. 283–85.
18. *Ibid.,* p. 194.
19. *Ibid.,* p. 200.
20. *Ibid.,* p. 228.
21. *Ibid.,* p. 225.
22. *Ibid.,* p. 217.
23. *Ibid.,* p. 218.

For More Information

JOURNALS

Brophy, Jere E. "Teacher Behavior and Its Effects," *Journal of Educational Psychology, 71* (1979) 733–750.

Goebel, Barbara L., and Cashen, Valjean M., "Age, Sex and Attractiveness as Factors in Student Ratings of Teachers: A Developmental Study," *Journal of Educational Psychology, 71* (1979) 546–553.

Gulley, Beverly, and Norwood, Elizabeth. "Critical Aspects of the Open Classroom," *Education, 96* (1976), 207–208.

Hughes, Marie. "What is Teaching? One Viewpoint," *Educational Leadership, 19* (1962), 251–259.

Hult, Richard E., Jr. "A Pedagogical Caring," *Educational Theory, 29* (1979), 237–243.

Kaplan-Sanoff, Margot. "In Search of Self: Teaching and Practice," *Educational Forum, 44* (1980), 339–347.

Marksberry, Mary Lee. "Student Questioning: An Instructional Strategy," *Educational Horizons, 57* (1979), 190–195.

Martin, L. S., and Pavin, B. N. "Current Research on Open Space, Non-grading, Vertical Grouping, and Team Teaching," *Phi Delta Kapan, 57* (1976).

Martin, William R. "Teacher Behaviors—Do They Make A Difference? A Review of the Research," *Kappa Delta Pi* Record, *16* (1979), 48–50, 63.

Morine-Dershimer, Greta. "Teacher Judgements and Pupil Observations: Beauty in the Eye of the Beholder," *Journal of Classroom Interaction, 12* (1976), 31–50.

Salek, Charles, "Helping Teachers vs. Evaluating Teachers," *NASSP Bulletin, 59* (1975), 34–38.

Turner, Richard L. "Good Teaching in Its Contexts," *Phi Delta Kappan, 52* (1970), 155–158.

Unks, Gerald. "The Front Line: Thou Shalt Not Think," *High School Journal, 62* (1979), 309–310.

Wright, Robert B., and Hosford, Philip. "Developing an Individual Teaching Style," *Clearing House, 48* (1974), 555–559.

Zahorik, John A. "Teacher Verbal Behavior: Perceived Value, Source of Aquisition, and Method of Justification," *Journal of Teacher Education, 28* (1977), 50–55.

BOOKS

Borton, Terry. *Read, Touch, and Teach.* New York: McGraw-Hill, 1970.

Dennison, George. *The Lives of Children.* New York: Random House, 1969.

Holt, John. *How Children Fail.* New York: Pitman, 1964.

Holt, John. *How Children Learn.* New York: Pitman, 1967.

Jackson, Philip W. *Life in Classrooms.* New York: Holt, Rinehart, and Winston, 1968.

Kaufman, Bel. *Up the Down Staircase.* Englewood Cliffs, New Jersey: Prentice-Hall, 1964.

Kohl, Herbert. *36 Children.* New York: New American Library, 1968.

Ryan, Kevin et al. *Biting the Apple: Accounts of First Year Teachers.* New York: Longman, 1980.

Ryan, Kevin, ed. *Don't Smile Until Christmas: Accounts of the First Year of Teaching.* Chicago: University of Chicago Press, 1970.

Seaberg, Dorothy I. *The Four Faces of Teaching.* Pacific Palisades, Calif.: Goodyear Publishing Company, 1974.

Silberman, Charles. *Crisis in the Classroom.* New York: Random House, 1970.

MOVIES

Behavior Modification in the Classroom (University of California, 24 min., 1970). Task oriented behavior shown through the use of operant conditioning. A before and after approach is used to show the results in attempting to create a positive classroom atmosphere.

The Best of the Real: Teaching in the Inner City Elementary School (Center for Urban Education, 1st film 28 min., 2nd film 22 min., 3rd film 40 min.). This film documents the teaching techniques of a fifth-grade teacher who was evaluated by his students as effective. The three films show him teaching a math class, reading a poem, and an analysis of his teaching.

Change-Training Teachers for Innovation (IDEA, 29 min. 1970.) Shows two techniques for involving the classroom teacher in making effective change. It helps education students to visualize the steps by which change in the classroom can win support from administrators and parents.

Critical Moments in Teaching Series (Holt, Rinehart and Winston, approx. 10 min. each, 1970). Series of 16 open-ended films shows children posing problems such as inattention, inability to do work, and withdrawal. The open-endedness allows for discussions for possible solutions.

Glasser on Discipline (Media Five, 28 min., 1972). Dr. William Glasser discusses five basic steps to achieving effective discipline in the school. Discipline according to Glasser is not punishment, but the learning of rules with natural consequences for violations.

No Reason to Stay: A Dropout Looks at Education (McGraw-Hill, 27 min., 1966). A look at the school drop-out and what he or she drops out from. Through the eyes of a student, we are shown both real incidents and fantasies about teachers who "bore to death thousands of innocent students."

To Sir, With Love (Columbia Cinematheque, 105 min.). Stars Sidney Poitier as a teacher in London's rough East End. The students are treated as adults and eventually show favorable results.

Chapter 3

Chapter 3

TECHNIQUES FOR OBSERVING WHAT GOES ON IN THE CLASSROOM

One trait common to all human beings is our constant observation of the environment in which we live. Since you have already developed some finely tuned observation skills over the past 20 (or 30 or 40 or more) years, you should begin this chapter with some confidence. Your past observations, however, have probably been formulated rather casually, as a kind of natural byproduct of your everyday interactions. In order to become a skilled observer, you must learn to observe the world as social scientists do: in a systematic manner. Anthropologists, for example, study a culture by looking at its artifacts (buildings, tools, religious objects, art work, etc.) and its social interactions (rituals at birth, death, marriage, prayer, etc.). You can borrow some of the anthropologists' techniques as you examine the artifacts of American schools in the 1980s. The artifacts from these schools are presented in the photo essay that follows on pages 72 and 73. Each picture (or set of pictures) is related to a set of questions; your task is to respond to the questions either on your own or with colleagues in your class.

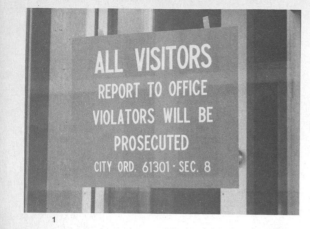

What is the underlying message of each sign in Photos 1 and 2? Visit a nearby school and read its bulletin board and chalkboard messages—how do you think they make the student, visitor, or parent feel?

What is happening in Photo 3? Look at the nonverbal behaviors: facial expressions, body movement, and dress. Would all teachers be comfortable in this role? Would you be comfortable in this role?

As an anthropologist, what type of social interaction do you feel is appropriate at a roundtable (see Photo 4)? What possible conflicts can you imagine between the behavior expectations implicit in the roundtable and the expectations stated and implied by the message on the chalkboard?

Teaching is described as a helping profession. What behaviors do you see in Photo 5 that support this description?

Is teaching really a helping profession (see Photo 6)?

You recognize the situations in Photos 6, 7, and 8 as "extracurricular activities" in elementary and middle schools. Would these situations be recognizable to anthropologists from other cultures?

5

6

7

8

9

As you discussed each of these photos with your colleagues, you may have found that your conclusions or inferences differed from theirs. To "conclude" or "infer" means that you made interpretations from the behaviors and artifacts you observed. Interpretation, by definition, means that both inference *A* (yours) and inference *B* (your colleague's) may be correct, even though they are not the same. As skilled observers, your next step is to do what other social scientists do: test your inferences with additional observations. The additional data (information and behaviors) collected through this testing will either support or conflict with your initial inferences. Presented below are data from school situations the co-authors have observed; each situation is followed by possible alternative inferences that one could test in subsequent observations.

SITUATION I

RICHARD: Leo, I'll present the first situation. You can suggest possible inferences for the situation. Here's an easy one:

After each question from the teacher, Bobby enthusiastically raises his hand.

What is your inference about Bobby's behavior?

LEO: That's an easy one. Bobby is bright and knows all the answers.

RICHARD: Your inference is the obvious one and the one I would have suggested. But I must tell you about my behavior as a student in a fourth-grade social studies class. After two weeks of studying the teacher's behavior (I've always been a social psychologist), I discovered that she called on only those students who did not raise their hands. You guessed it: I never listened to the question but always raised my hand enthusiastically. She inferred (incorrectly) that I was an exceptional student.

LEO: O.K., you've made your point. We must develop multiple inferences and then test them to discover which inference(s) is (are) the most correct. Before I present the next situation, I have question. How can we test the inferences in Bobby's situation?

RICHARD: We could (a) look at the quality of Bobby's written work, (b) observe his behavior in group situations when the teacher is not directly involved, (c) look at his test score, (d) talk with him after class regarding the content of the lesson, (e) . . .

LEO: O.K. I agree. The testing of the inferences can be done in many ways. Now it's my turn to present a situation.

SITUATION II

The teacher and Linda are standing within a foot of one another but away from the rest of the class. The teacher is doing all of the talking. As the teacher speaks, Linda looks at the floor.

LEO: What are some possible inferences for this situation?

RICHARD: Linda is embarrassed. Perhaps she did something wrong.

LEO: Other inferences?

RICHARD: Linda has no respect for the teacher and "tuned her out" by looking at the floor.

LEO: You're becoming a good observer! I have another inference. Linda comes from a culture where a child is not supposed to look "eye to eye" at an adult during a conversation. I can predict your next suggestion: Develop alternative observation systems that can be used to test each of the above inferences.

RICHARD: You read my mind.

Focusing your Observations

You may be saying something like this to yourself: "All right I've looked at the artifacts within the school and made some tentative inferences about each of them. I now appreciate the complexity of the school environment even before the arrival of the children in the morning. How in the world can I go about observing and analyzing this environment now that 200 to 2000 students have entered the building and dispersed into the various classrooms? It is physically impossible to monitor everything that is going on within the school. What do I do now?"

The answer to the bewildered observer is a simple one. Do not try to observe everything that is going on within this complex environment. Limit your observation to one or, at most, a few behaviors that you feel are most interesting or important. In short, focus your observation. The following list offers examples of a few behaviors that have been the object of study in recent years by students of classroom life, such as Philip Jackson, Barak Rosenshine, and Michael Dunkin and Bruce Biddle.

1. Teacher movement in the classroom. Dunkin and Biddle found that teacher movement throughout the class affects the social and academic behavior of children.[1]
2. Teacher's use of positive verbal and nonverbal reinforcement. See the studies by Bushell, Wrobel, and Michaelis on the effect of teacher reinforcement on the students' behavior.[2]
3. Teacher's ability to redirect a question to student B when student A does not know the answer. In many classrooms, students receive negative reinforcement for not knowing an answer. Dunkin and Biddle reported the most appropriate teacher response is to redirect the question to another pupil.[3]
4. Learning styles used by the student. Lehane and Goldman categorized students' learning styles into formal, informal, incidental, and imitative. They recommend that children should experience all of these styles.[4]
5. Types of questions asked by the teacher. Extensive research has been completed on the effects of teachers' questions on students' learning.

The questions are categorized as "open" or "closed," "high-" or "low-" level, "information seeking" or "synthesis."

6. Students' ability to manage their own time. Many teachers encourage children to manage their own schedules. See the study by Wang and Stiles, which analyzed students' abilities to manage their learning time.[5]

Our list of possible focuses for observations in the classroom is not meant to be exhaustive, merely indicative of the possibilities that await you. Your discussions with colleagues and instructors and your actual on-site observations will enable you to generate a more exhaustive list of areas, questions, and issues for observation in classrooms.

Observation Techniques

You are now ready to address the next question: how does one complete the observations? The observation technique you choose depends largely on the object of your focus. We will present five observation techniques in this chapter; your task at the end of the chapter will be to decide when to use each of them. These observation techniques are the tools you will use to decipher the complexities of the schools you visit. Jackson describes the problem one encounters when trying to understand the complex interactions which take place in the classroom:

> Anyone who has ever taught knows that the classroom is a busy place, even though it may not appear to be for the casual visitor. Indeed, recent data have proved surprising even to experienced teachers. For example, we have found that in one study of elementary classrooms that the teacher engages in as many as 1,000 interpersonal interchanges each day. An attempt to catalogue the interchanges among students of the physical movement of class members would doubtlessly add to the general impression that most classrooms, though seemingly placid when glimpsed through the windows in the hall door, are more like the proverbial beehive of activity.[6]

We will discuss five observation techniques in this section:

1. Anthropological analysis of "artifacts"
2. Counting specific behaviors
3. Time sampling
4. Verbatim data collection
5. Interviewing

OBSERVATION TECHNIQUE 1: ANTHROPOLOGICAL

We introduced the anthropological approach to observation with the photo essay earlier in this chapter. Our intent in the photo essay was to encourage you to examine various artifacts and situations within the school and to generate possible inferences (e.g., meanings and conclusions) about them. Listed below is a series of situations and artifacts typically found in the schools.

Try to generate at least three possible inferences for each situation or artifact. You may want to discuss this list with others in your class. After your discussion, compare your inferences with those that appear below. Hypothetical exercises such as this can do much to sharpen your skill with this technique before applying it in a real-life school situation.

Activity 1
1. Teachers and/or principal greet students with a smile and a "hello" as the students enter the building.
   Possible inferences:
   a.
   b.
   c.

2. The walls of the school are barren.
   Possible inferences:
   a.
   b.
   c.

3. The walls of the school have some artwork, but the art is placed above the children's eye level.
   Possible inferences:
   a.
   b.
   c.

4. During the seventh-grade study period, the teacher patrols the class with a paddle in hand.
   Possible inferences:
   a.
   b.
   c.

5. Teachers mingle and/or play with the children on the playground.
   Possible inferences:
   a.
   b.
   c.

6. Teachers send notes home to the parents when the children have done something well in school.
   Possible inferences:
   a.
   b.
   c.

7. Children are not allowed to talk in the lunchroom.
   Possible inferences:
   a.
   b.
   c.

8. The teachers' bulletin board contains brochures from neighboring colleges and universities that describe summer programs.
   Possible inferences:
   a.
   b.
   c.

9. Teachers punch a time clock upon entering the office in the morning.
   Possible inferences:
   a.
   b.
   c.

10. A large sign in the main corridor announces that the faculty will present a talent show to the children.
    Possible inferences:
    a.
    b.
    c.

11. The teachers and principal address one another by their first names.
    Possible inferences:
    a.
    b.
    c.

12. A note from the custodian is on the teachers' bulletin board: "Only those rooms that have their desks in rows will be cleaned!"
    Possible inferences:
    a.
    b.
    c.

Feedback for Activity 1

First, we want to give a word of caution. Our responses to Activity 1 are not the *right* answers; they represent a small sample of possible appropriate inferences. Remember, an observer must test each inference before deciding upon its appropriateness. With this caveat in mind, compare your responses with those of your fellow students and with ours.

1. Teachers and/or principal greet children with a smile and a "hello" as the children enter the building.

TECHNIQUES FOR OBSERVING WHAT GOES ON IN THE CLASSROOM

Possible inferences:

a. Teachers and/or principal feel that learning takes place in a supportive environment.

b. Teachers and/or principal recently completed a workshop on behavior modification; they are implementing an assignment from the workshop.

2. The walls of the school are barren.
   Possible inferences:
   a. The walls were just painted and are in the process of drying.
   b. The custodian is "in charge" of the building and will not allow children's art (or anyone else's) to be on the walls.

3. The walls of the school have some artwork, but the art is placed above the children's eye level.
   Possible inferences:
   a. Principal feels that the children will destroy anything that they can reach.
   b. Works of art have had the same placement for 25 years; no one has questioned the appropriateness of its placement.

4. During the seventh-grade study period, the teacher patrols the class with a paddle in hand.
   Possible inferences:
   a. Students are studying various approaches to leadership; the teacher is simulating an authoritarian leadership style.
   b. Teacher has acquired a limited number of approaches for dealing with classroom management.

5. Teachers mingle and/or play with the children on the playground.
   Possible inferences:
   a. Teachers want to use children's play activities in the language and social studies lessons in the classroom.
   b. Teachers are experiencing a role conflict: Are they social workers or teachers?

6. Teachers send notes home to the parents when the children have done something well in school.
   Possible inferences:
   a. Teachers want to develop a partnership with parents.
   b. This is another assigned activity from the behavior-modification workshop.

7. Children are not allowed to talk in the lunchroom.
   Possible inferences:
   a. Teachers feel that students and prisoners have much in common.
   b. The dietician read somewhere (she can't remember where) that talking while eating causes indigestion.

8. The teachers' bulletin board contains brochures from neighboring colleges and universities that describe summer programs.
   Possible inferences:
   a. Advanced training is valued by the school board.
   b. The colleges and universities have increased their recruitment because of decreasing enrollment.

9. Teachers punch a time clock upon entering the office in the morning.
   Possible inferences:
   a. Teachers are skilled craftsmen and not professionals.
   b. The principal does not trust the staff.

10. A large sign in the main corridor announces that the faculty will present a talent show to the children.
    Possible inferences:
    a. Teachers want to bridge the authority gap that exists between the faculty and students.
    b. The talent show is a traditional event at the school; no one questions the reasons for its existence.

11. The teachers and principal address one another by their first names.
    Possible inferences:
    a. The principal in this school wants a collegial rather than a superior-subordinate relationship.
    b. Most of the professional staff live in the same community and belong to the same social and religious organizations. These social contacts contributed to the informal interaction in the school.

12. A note from the custodian is on the teachers' bulletin board: "Only those rooms that have their desks in rows will be cleaned!"
    Possible inferences:
    a. The custodian was not included in the faculty meetings where the reasons for alternative classroom designs were discussed.
    b. Custodial concerns rather than educational issues have the higher priority in this school.

These artifacts/situations constitute only a small sample of the situations you will actually observe in schools. We suggest that you begin your anthropological expedition into a school before the arrival of the children. The quiet halls, offices, and classrooms will make it easier for you to observe the artifacts, for example, bulletin boards, seating arrangements, and textbooks. As you become a more experienced observer, your sensitivity to the environment will expand greatly. Artifacts and situations that formerly passed unnoticed will gradually become quite meaningful to you.

OBSERVATION TECHNIQUE 2: COUNTING SPECIFIC BEHAVIORS

A relatively simple observation technique consists of the observer counting behaviors that fit into a specific predetermined category. For example, the observation may focus on the teacher's use of positive and negative comments. You can place two columns on your paper and write *all* the observed behaviors that fit into the columns:

POSITIVE COMMENTS	NEGATIVE COMMENTS
Good.	Why is your work always sloppy?
I like your work.	
Nice try.	Stop it.
You both work well together.	Shut up.
Thanks for helping Bobby.	Do your own work.
That's a big improvement.	

Other categories for which you can count specific behaviors include the following:

- Short student responses (three words or less) vs. long responses (four words or more).
- Open questions asked by the teacher ("Why?" or "What do you think will happen next?") vs. closed questions ("What is the date of the treaty?").
- The number of times students ask for clarification on how to do a task.
- The number of students who complete assigned tasks.
- Percentage of time the teacher spends in each area of the classroom.
- How frequently teachers call on high-achieving students as opposed to low-achieving students and the average "wait time" for responses from the groups.

The specific behaviors "counted" do not always have to be listed. Assume, for example, that you want to observe a teacher's movement within the classroom. The observer's first task is to draw a map of the classroom. As the observer watches the teacher's movements, a continuous line is drawn on the map which coincides with the actual movement of the teacher (see Figure 3.1). At the conclusion of the observation, the observer can make tentative inferences regarding the teacher's and students' behaviors:

- Teacher walked to those children who had trouble with the task.
- Teacher had little interaction with the two rows on the right since these students were working on individual research projects.

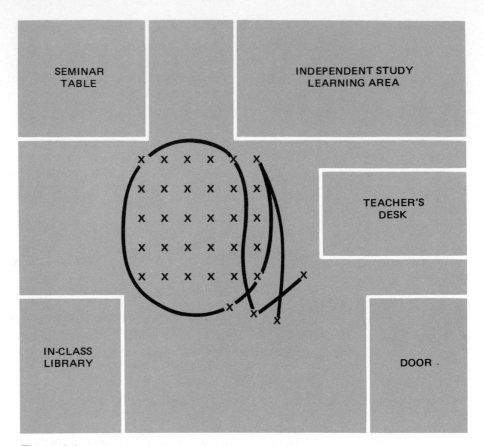

Figure 3.1. Sample map illustrating teacher movement.

- Teacher moved around the class in order to keep the interest of the students.

Each of the above inferences may need to be tested with additional observations. Moreover, the observation systems used may need to be more systematic and specific than the one described here. As we study the map of movement, we find that numerous problems exist. First, it is difficult to follow the direction of the teacher's movements, since the lines of movement become intertwined. A second problem relates to the time of the movement: Did it take place at the beginning or near the end of the class? A related problem is that the observer cannot tell how long the teacher spent in each area of the classroom.

A variation of this technique solves these problems. The observer again begins by drawing a map of the classroom; this time, dividing it into areas. The observer now times the number of seconds the teacher spends in each area. Whenever the teacher moves from one area to another, the observer times the duration of the stay within the new area, no matter how long. (See Figure 3.2.) The observer's sheet will now look like this:

AREA AND SEQUENCE OF MOVEMENT	TIME
I	40 seconds
III	20 seconds
V	2 seconds
VII	5 minutes, 15 seconds
VI	4 minutes, 30 seconds
IV	2 seconds
II	15 seconds
I	22 minutes, 45 seconds

At the conclusion of the observation, the observer can calculate the following:

1. The number of seconds and/or minutes and the percentage of time the teacher spent in each area of the classroom.

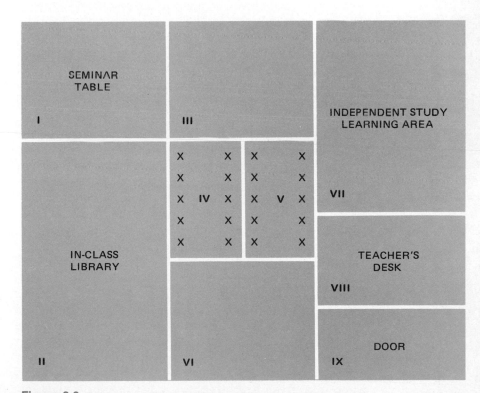

Figure 3.2. Sample map divided into areas to illustrate teacher movement.

2. The sequence and pattern of the teacher's movement (the teacher
moved in a counterclockwise direction around the room, spending extended time in areas I, VI, and VII and brief time in areas II, IV, and
V).

This technique enables the observer to make more accurate inferences
about the teacher's behavior since the sequence and timing of the movements can be followed.

OBSERVATION TECHNIQUE 3: TIME SAMPLING

A third type of observation technique, a time-sampling observation system, has many of the advantages of the technique just described and
others that we will discuss. The intent of this system is to select a sample
of the total interaction in the classroom. Since this sample is selected at
regular intervals (e.g., three, five, or ten seconds), we can infer that the
data collected represent an accurate picture of the total interaction in the
classroom. We will continue to use the teacher's movement in the classroom as the behavior to be observed. The observer's first step is to draw a
map of the classroom similar to the one illustrated by Figure 3.2. The
next task is to observe and place in the matrix of Figure 3.3 the number of
the area in which the teacher is located at the beginning of each five-
second interval. If the teacher is standing in area I when you begin your
observation, place a "1" in the first block. Five seconds later, you again
locate the teacher and write the area number in the next block in the matrix. With a little practice, you will become comfortable with the rhythm
of looking at your watch, locating the teacher, and writing the number of
the area in which the teacher is located on the matrix.

Let us assume that you have just completed a 15-minute observation
using the time-sampling system to focus on the teacher's movement. (You
may be slightly dizzy because of your constant head movement, but the
dizziness will disappear with practice!) We can anticipate your next question: "What is the advantage of the time-sampling system over the other
systems described?" One advantage is that the observer does not have to
follow and time every movement of the teacher; with this system, the observer focuses only on the teacher at given intervals of time (e.g., every
five seconds). A second advantage is that the observer can more easily see
the patterns of the teacher's movements (e.g., the teacher usually walks
from area IV to area II, or the teacher spends brief periods of time in
areas IV, VI, and VII and longer periods in areas I, II, and V). A third advantage of the sampling system is that the observer can use multiple
codes within each time interval. A concrete example may help to clarify
this last advantage.

Let us assume that you are interested in what the teacher is doing
when in a given area: Is the teacher asking a question *(q)*, praising a

MINUTES	SECONDS											
	5	10	15	20	25	30	35	40	45	50	55	60
1												
2												
3												
4												
5												
6												
7												
8												
9												

% 1 = _____   % 2 = _____   % 3 = _____

% 4 = _____   % 5 = _____   % 6 = _____

% 7 = _____   % 8 = _____   % 9 = _____

Figure 3.3. Time-sampling observation matrix.

student *(p)*, giving negative comments *(n)*, observing the students *(o)*, or giving information to the students *(i)*? The *q, p, n, o,* and *i* are the subcodes that you place next to the area number in the matrix. You may decide to code only the first teacher behavior observed in a given area. During the five seconds in area II, the teacher first praises one student and then gives information to another student; you write in the matrix "2p." As you become a more competent observer, you will be able to observe and code multiple behaviors for a given interval (e.g., "2pi"). The additional data provided by the codes will enable the observer to make more accurate inferences about the behaviors of the teacher and students.

OBSERVATION TECHNIQUE 4: VERBATIM TECHNIQUE

A complex system of observation—verbatim collection of data—can be used when you do not have a predetermined focus for your observation. Your goal with this system is to recreate, as closely as possible, the total picture of what happened in the classroom. Examine the transcript of classroom interaction below.

CATEGORIES

1. Open question, e.g., one that has many correct answers: "Why did we want to explore the moon?"
2. Closed question, e.g., one that has a limited number of answers: "Who first stepped on the moon?"
3. Positive comment: "That's right," "Good," "I like your work."
4. Negative comment: "This is poor work," "Shut up," "Is this the best that you can do?"
5. Long student response: four words or more.
6. Short student response: three words or less.

T: Look at the big picture on pages 10 and 11. What kind of a place do you see? **(2)**

S: A park. **(6)**

T: Where's Jim? **(2)**

S: With the policeman. **(6)**

T: What do you think the policeman might be telling Jim? **(1)**

S: He has to go to school. **(5)**

T: Is there anything else he could be telling him? **(1)**

S: That he couldn't go fishing, that he has to go to school. He was also telling him he couldn't go fishing at the park, 'cause there wasn't very many fish, and people might swim in it. Maybe there's no fish in it. **(5)**

T: Oh, that's possible. **(3)** Have you ever seen parks with pools that didn't have fish? **(2)**

S: Yes. **(6)**

T: Look at the title. It's in very dark letters at the top of the page.

S: Fishing on school days. **(5)**

T: This story is so long that it has been divided into parts. And when it's divided into parts, each part is often called a chapter. There are a couple of new words on this page. Look at the second line, the next-to-the-last word: H-O-M-E. When you come to that word, you think what word starts with "H" and ends with the "M" sound that would make sense with what the sentence is about. Try it out when you get there. Read the rest of the sentence to see what makes sense. Now look at the last line on page 10. The first word is "I." The word after that is a new one: T-A-K-E. You'll have to use the "T" and "K" sounds, but you also have to use the rest of the sentences to see what makes sense. Wait until you read it to see. Now you read this whole page and find out what the policeman said about going fishing. Go ahead and read the whole page, and maybe you can figure it out. Read it with your eyes.

That's a new one that you have to figure out. Use the letter sounds and the sense of the story. Well, let's read it both ways and see which makes sense: "I 'tick' the bus to school."*

s: No. **(6)**

т: "Took" would make sense, but that's not the word. "Took" has o's in it.

s: Take. **(6)**

т: Yes, all right. **(3)** When you came to the new word in the second line— HOME—did you have any trouble figuring it out? **(2)**

s: No. **(6)**

т: What is it? **(2)**

s: Home. **(6)**

т: Why can't this word be "hunt?" **(1)**

s: It wouldn't make any sense. **(5)**

т: Not with the rest of the story, right? **(3)** Who would like to be the police-man? Eric, you want to be the policeman? John, you want to be Jim? **(2)** We'll take turns; you'll all get a turn to read a part.

т: Where did the person tell Jim to go? **(2)**

s: School. **(6)**

т: No, look again. **(4)**

s: Home. **(6)**

т: Yes, he told him to go home, and he said he couldn't do something. **(3)** What couldn't he do? **(2)**

s: Go fishing. **(6)**

т: And why couldn't Jim go to school? **(1)**

s: Because he wanted to go fishing. **(5)**

т: But why couldn't Jim go fishing? **(1)**

s: Because the policeman wanted him to go to school instead—no, go home. **(5)**

т: Wanted him to go home, and he told Jim that there were special times when he couldn't fish at the park. Do you know when it was? **(2)**

s: On school days. **(6)**

As you analyze this transcript, your questions can focus on the following:

1. What percentage of the questions were open, and what percentage closed?
2. What percentage of the responses were short, and what percentage long?
3. Does there seem to be a relationship between open questions and long responses, and one between closed questions and short responses?
4. Compare the percentage of negative and positive comments.

*You may want to add a new category: "Teacher gives information."

You will notice that the observer had to develop the writing speed (and shorthand techniques) of a courtroom stenographer. In addition, the observer had to analyze the classroom interaction by looking for specific categories of behavior in the verbatim data collected. The categories used by the observer in the transcript are similar to the categories used in the observation systems described earlier (length of student response, positive and negative comments by the teacher, and types of questions asked by the teacher), but the observer need not be limited to these categories.

Modern technology — audio and video tape recorders — can be used as a verbatim technique. The advantages of this technology over written verbatim techniques are numerous. First, the observer is able to collect data on the behaviors often ignored with the written technique — the nonverbal behaviors. These behaviors, according to the research of Frymier, constitute up to 70 percent of the total interaction among persons.[7] For certain nonverbal behaviors, video recordings have an advantage over audio recordings: They can record facial expressions and body movements. Both the audio and video tapes record the nonverbal aspects of verbal behaviors: intonation, voice quality, and voice volume. Tape recordings allow the observer to have multiple viewings of the classroom interactions, which enables the observer to test out his inferences. Another advantage of the taped interactions includes the observer's ability to view the tape at a later time in order to compare present and past teacher/student behaviors.

Before you purchase an audio or video tape system, think about some of the disadvantages of taping as an observation technique. An obvious disadvantage is cost; paper and pencil are less expensive than audio and video tape equipment. In addition, the analysis of teacher/pupil interaction is sometimes difficult to complete on tapes. An observer searching for one short scene on the tape often feels like the child searching for "a needle in the haystack." The solutions to the above problems are not simple, but we do have a few suggestions. On the issue of cost, the audio tape recorder is now within the budgets of most college students (approximately $50.00); the video tape equipment is at present much more expensive. (Perhaps video tape technology will mirror the development of the hand calculators, which during the 1970s fell in price from $200.00 to less than $20.00!) On the issue of the "needle in the haystack," try these suggestions:

1. As you record the interaction, write a summary of the major events and activities in the classroom.
2. Next to each event, write the number on the recorder's indicator. Your summary may look like this:

Teacher asks for the students' attention. **(8)**
Teacher explains the tasks for the lesson. **(10–90)**
Students ask questions about the class. **(90–108)**

One group begins to work independently, and the other has a discussion with the teacher. **(108–175)**

Teacher asks both groups to summarize what they did. **(175–237)**

However, you now have a problem if you are using a video recording: on which group do you focus the camera?

OBSERVATION TECHNIQUE 5: INTERVIEW

Another method of collecting data on classroom interaction involves interviewing those involved in the interaction, e.g., students, teachers, and principal. Often, the seemingly logical inferences we develop from our systematic observations are simply erroneous. For example, since the child always completes her tasks quickly, we infer that she likes academic tasks; in reality, she loves to have free time for independent reading. Interviewing, therefore, is a technique for collecting additional data that can help the observer verify or reject his or her inferences. We are not suggesting that you develop a formal interview survey; you might simply ask students and teachers questions during their free time.

Only rarely do other adults—parents, principal, or teachers—enter a teacher's classroom. We remind you of this because you may find that some teachers are "uptight" about your presence and your questions. The teacher may be thinking, "Why is this college student here? Is the student going to tell his professor, fellow students, or my principal (ugh!) about what was observed? Did the students like my class? Why does the student want to talk to my pupils?" The following guidelines should make your interview less threatening and more efficient:

1. Be aware that the teacher may have just a few minutes to talk with you; therefore, focus your questions on one or more related issues.
2. In most cases, because of time limitations, do not attempt to discuss issues of deep philosophical or theoretical content. Either you or your college instructor can invite the teacher to a seminar if theoretical issues are being pursued.
3. If you are near the students when you interview the teacher, be sure that your questions do not focus on the students by name.
4. Inform the teacher of the questions you would like to ask the students and obtain the teacher's approval before you interact with them. The teacher is responsible for the management of a complex social system, the classroom. You do not want to upset this system.
5. Inform the teacher of the purpose (focus) of your observation. If your observation "agenda" is shared, the teacher may be less concerned about your presence since he or she knows your purpose. (An inability to convey your purpose to the teacher may mean you are there as an observer simply because "my instructor told me to be there," which is an unacceptable reason.)

6. Ask your college instructor to inform the teachers and principal that you will be writing while observing in the classroom. It is hoped that they will ask what you will be observing and writing. Your response is an opportunity to develop a colleagueship among the teacher, your instructor, and you.

7. Offer to share with the teacher the data you collect. Your openness about the data will lessen the concerns about "spying" that the teacher may have.

8. Be as inconspicuous as possible in the classroom. Sitting at the side of the classroom in a location that allows you to see the faces of both the teacher and pupils will enable you to have a clear view of the interaction without disrupting the classroom routine. Often a teacher will tell you where to sit. As the teacher begins to feel comfortable with your presence (since you have followed these guidelines), he or she may encourage you to move around the classroom so long as you do not disrupt the children.

9. Look at the total school environment and not just the classrooms. Study the halls, office, gym, walls, bulletin boards, etc. The messages in these locations, both written and unwritten, will help to give you a more complete picture of the school.

10. Walk through the community surrounding the school. Students' learning does not stop at the school's front door.

We have presented a brief introduction to several observation techniques. In order to digest these techniques, you must practice them in the schools, of course. However, once again, their real-life application will be easier if you first try your hand at the following encounters.

1. Explain to someone interested in education what you have learned about observation techniques: how observers record and make inferences from data and test their inferences.
2. The behaviors described below were collected by an observer. Once again, state multiple inferences for each set of behaviors and indicate how you might go about testing your inferences.
   a. The teacher made twelve positive comments and four negative comments during a 20-minute lesson.
      Possible inferences:
      1.
      2.
      3.
      How can you test your inferences?
   b. Eight students (out of a group of 27) asked that directions be repeated three times.
      Possible inferences:
      1.
      2.
      3.
      How can you test your inferences?
   c. The teacher spent 60 percent of the first class period in area I (near his or her desk), 30 percent in area II (near the math area), 5 percent in area III (near the quiet work area), and 5 percent in area IV (near the students' files).
      Possible inferences:
      1.
      2.
      3.
      How can you test your inferences?
3. In the table below, goals for observations are stated. Your task is to select the appropriate observation system(s) and state your reasons for selecting the system(s). (Here is a hint: There are no "right" or "wrong" responses; the important column is the "why" column in which you state your reasons for selecting one system or systems rather than others. After stating your reasons, compare them with the sample answers that appear in the box below.) You can choose the appropriate observation system(s) from the following list:
   a. Anthropological
   b. Counting behaviors
   c. Time sampling
   d. Verbatim
   e. Interview
   f. Other technique (one that you, your colleagues, and instructor design)

Goal for Observation	Observation Techniques Selected	Reasons for Selecting Techniques
a. Obtain a feeling for the total school environment.		
b. Obtain a feeling for the total classroom environment.		
c. Want to "test out" inferences.		
d. Analyze a specific behavior of teacher and/or students.		

Again, our responses to this encounter are not the "right" answers. When differences occur among your responses, your colleagues', and ours, discuss the possible reasons for the differences with your fellow students.

Goal for Observation	Observation Techniques Selected	Reasons for Selecting Techniques
a. Obtain a feeling for the total school environment.	Anthropological	The artifacts of the school often give an accurate picture of the entire school environment.
	Interview	Discussions with teachers, parents, pupils, and administrators will give you the perceptions of the primary "cast of characters" in a school. The agreement/disagreement in goals and methods of the school will become clear as one analyzes the interviews. (A cautionary note: Use this technique only after you have received the approval of your instructor and the school's administrator.)
b. Obtain a feeling for the total classroom environment.	Anthropological	See the discussion of technique 1 in this chapter.
	Verbatim	Both written transcripts and cassette tapes (audio or video) are appropriate for obtaining an overview of the classroom. Most teacher/pupil interactions can be recorded with this technique. Decisions can be made, after analyzing the total environment, about possible focuses for future observations.

Goal for Observation	Observation Techniques Selected	Reasons for Selecting Techniques
c. Want to "test out" inferences.	Interviewing, time sampling, counting behaviors	Frequently, when an observer tests out an inference, he or she is looking for the absence or presence of specific behaviors. The three observation systems selected are most appropriate for focusing on specific behaviors.
d. Analyze a specific behavior of teacher and/or student.	Time sampling or counting behaviors.	These two systems were designed specifically for this goal.

4. Ask two other college students to join you in practicing your interviewing skills. As a group, make up a hypothetical class and describe what happened in it during your observation session. As part of your description, create a teacher (perhaps one with whom you are familiar), and develop a list of questions that you intend to ask the teacher. Then role play the interview: you play the student interviewer, while your colleagues play the teacher and observer. Keep in mind the interview guidelines as you prepare for a five-minute interview. After the mock interview, discuss your performance with the observer, using the guidelines as the basis of your evaluation. Then switch roles and repeat the process until everyone has had a chance to play all three roles.

5. Researchers have been unable to make definite conclusions on the appropriate amount of positive and negative reinforcement needed for students' progress in a classroom. A bit of consensus does exist: In the long run, positive reinforcement may be more powerful (and humane) than negative reinforcement. Your task with this activity is to select an appropriate observation system and to calculate the percentage of positive and negative reinforcement in a variety of classrooms. From the data collected, generate a list of tentative inferences regarding the issue of reinforcement.

6. With the limited budget for learning materials, teachers must make creative use of the materials they have and develop strategies for obtaining materials from outside sources. From your numerous visits to the schools, select two or three teachers who seem to be creative "supply sergeants." Develop a questionnaire that asks them to describe how they are creative with limited resources. Listed below are possible focuses for the interview:
   a. Design of a materials-rationing system that does not infringe upon the students' learning
   b. Description of how you develop multiple uses for a specific piece of material
   c. Inexpensive sources for obtaining material from outside the school setting
   d. System for sharing materials with colleagues within the school.
   The data from these interviews may enable you to develop a system for dealing with a critical problem—a problem most beginning teachers know little about until their resources become depleted in March or April of their first year of teaching.

7. Observe in a classroom five to ten minutes before the end of the instructional period. During that segment of time, try to record the total interaction in the classroom. As you analyze the data collected, circle all the "teacher as timekeeper" statements (e.g., "It's spelling time; put your literature books away," or "I'm sorry we have to stop our science experiments in the middle, but we'll continue them tomorrow"). From the students' perspective, look for statements in your data that relate to students' frustration or resignation to the time demands. Were you able to develop any inferences regarding the effects of the timekeeper role on the students and teacher?

8. Visit numerous institutions: a hospital, a factory, a prison. Compare and contrast the timekeeping roles in the various institutions. Are bells/buzzers used? Are persons required to stop activities because of time restraints? Can you suggest alternative timekeeping systems for the various institutions?

Notes

1. Michael J. Dunkin and Bruce J. Biddle, *The Study of Teaching* (New York: Holt, Rinehart and Winston, 1974).
2. Don Bushell, Jr., Patricia A. Wrobel, and Mary L. Michaelis, "Applying 'Group' Contingencies to the Classroom Study Behavior of Pre-school Children," *Journal of Applied Behavior Analysis, 1* (Spring 1968), 55–61.
3. Dunkin and Biddle, *Study of Teaching,* p. 125.
4. Steven Lehane and Richard Goldman, "An Adaptive Model for Individualizing Learning in School and at Home," *Elementary School Journal, 76* (March 1976), 373–381.
5. Margaret C. Wang and Billie Stills, "An Investigation of Children's Concept of Self-Responsibility for Their School Learning," *American Educational Research Journal, 13* (Summer 1976), 159–179.
6. Philip W. Jackson, *Life in Classrooms* (New York: Holt, Rinehart and Winston, 1968), p. 11.
7. Jack R. Frymier (ed.), "The Challenge of Nonverbal Awareness," *Theory into Practice, 10* (October 1971), 227–314.

For More Information

JOURNALS

Calfee, Robert, and Calfee, Kathryn Hoover. "Reading and Mathematics Observation System: Description and Measurement of Time Usage in the Classroom," *Journal of Teacher Education, 27* (1976), 323–325.

Chatt, Mary Jo Puckett, "Play: The Window Into a Child's Life," *Childhood Education, 56* (1980), 218–220.

Edwards, Tony, and Furlong, Viv. "Time to Go Inside?," *Times Educational Supplement* (London), *3235* (1977). (no page given)

Elias, Patricia, and Wheeler, Patricia. "Instructional Activities as Reported by Teachers," *Journal of Teacher Education, 27* (1976), 326–238.

Emmer, Edmund. "Direct Observation of Classroom Behavior," *International Review of Education, 18* (1972), 473–490.

Fisher, Sue. "Revealing Students' Reasoning Practices," *Journal of Classroom Interaction, 15* (1979).

Goldman, Richard and Anglin, Leo. "Observation Tools for Administrators," *Day Care and Early Education* (Fall, 1979), 40–41.

Jacobs, Joseph H. "Insight Learning Through Structured Observations of Classroom Interaction," *Journal of Research in Science Teaching, 10* (1973), 213–220.

Keller, Harold. "Issues in the Use of Observational Assessment," *School Psychology Review, 9* (1980), 21–30.

King, Ina., "How do I Look as a Teacher?," *Teacher, 92* (1975), 45–47.

Koehler, Virginia. "Classroom Process Research: Present and Future," *Journal of Classroom Interaction, 13* (1978), 3–11.

Lambert, Nadine M., and Hartsough, Carolyn S. "APPLE Observation Variables as Measures of Teacher Performance," *Journal of Teacher Education, 27* (1976), 320–323.

Martin, Jack. "The Development and Use of Classroom Observation Instruments," *Canadian Journal of Education, 2* (1977), 43–55.

Nevjahr, James L. "Classroom Observational Research," *Educational Forum, 36* (1972), 221–228.

Nuthall, Graham, and Church, John. "Observation Systems Used with Recording Media," *International Review of Education, 18* (1972), 491–507.

Persons, W. Scott, Brassell, William R., and Rollins, Howard A. "A Practical Observation Procedure for Monitoring Four Behaviors Relevant to Classroom Management," *Psychology in the Schools, 13* (1976), 64–71.

Withall, John. "Research in Systematic Observation in the Classroom and Its Relevance to Teachers," *Journal of Teacher Education, 23* (1972), 330–332.

BOOKS

Allen, Paul M., et al. *Teacher Self-Appraisal: A Way of Looking Over Your Own Shoulder.* Worthington, Ohio: Charles A. Jones Publishing Company, 1970.

Bell, Donald R., and Low, Roberta M. *Observing and Recording Children's Behavior.* Richland, Washington: Performance Associates, 1977.

Boehm, Ann E., and Weinberg, Richard A. *The Classroom Observer.* New York: Teachers College Press, 1977.

Cartwright, Carol A., and Cartwright, Philip G. *Developing Observation Skills.* New York: McGraw-Hill, 1974.

Gronlund, N. E. *Measurement and Evaluation in Teaching.* New York: Macmillan, 1971.

Medinnus, Gene R. *Child Study and Observation Guide.* New York: John Wiley and Sons, Inc., 1976.

Sackett, Gene R., Ed. *Observing Behavior Volume II: Data Collection and Analysis Methods.* Baltimore: University Park Press, 1978.

Smith, M. D. *Educational Psychology and Its Classroom Applications.* Boston: Allyn and Bacon, 1975.

Stallings, Jane. *Learning to Look: A Handbook on Classroom Observation and Teaching Models.* Belmont, Calif.: Wadsworth, 1977.

Walker, Robt., and Adelman, Clem. *A Guide to Classroom Observation.* London: Methuen, 1975.

Weinberg, Richard A., and Wood, Frank H., Eds. *Observation of Pupils and Teachers in Mainstream and Special Education Settings: Alternative Strategies.* Minneapolis, Minnesota: Leadership Training Institute/Special Education, University of Minnesota, 1975.

MOVIES

For All My Students (Anti-Defamation League, 36 min., 1967). High school students from a ghetto evaluate their teachers. The teachers, in turn, reflect on their apparent successes and failures.

Learning About Thinking and Vice Versa (Film Bureau, 35 min., 1971). Illustrates methods including one-to-one interviews to encourage elementary children to think for themselves in helping to solve problems.

Sir! Sir! (McGraw-Hill, 20 min., 1970). Shows the positive effect of role reversal between teachers and students. Stereotyped teaching styles and cliches remind the teachers of how the students view them. This is a good observation technique for teacher attitude and performance.

Chapter 4

Chapter 4

LOOKING AT INSTRUCTION: MODELS AND MATERIALS

We human beings are forever trying to organize, simplify, and control our environment. Put another way, we are forever creating "models" that enable us to explain and control what is going on around us. These mental reconstructions of reality never account for all that is going on, but without them we could not comprehend and manipulate the myriad pieces of our environment. In short, as our ability to create analytical models improves, so does our ability to deal effectively with some aspect of our environment (physical, economic, educational, etc.).

The goal of this chapter is to describe four alternative instructional models that are commonly found in schools. Our use of the term *instructional model* refers to both the behavior patterns (i.e., the teaching style) and the classroom arrangements (including materials) that teachers adopt in order to implement the goals of the school. The term *alternative*, as we use it, is a value-free term that means "different," not "better" or "worse." It does not imply that existing practices are failing or that newer practices are somehow more promising. Rather, it implies that there are different techniques, each of which is potentially effective in certain kinds of situations.

The four alternative teaching models presented in this chapter are quite different; each has staunch supporters among both theorists and classroom teachers. There are, of course, other models in use, but you will find that most of them are built upon the same characteristics that constitute these four. It is our hope that an understanding of these four models will enable you to understand better the variety of instructional programs you will encounter in your classroom observations. It is your responsibility to study carefully the strengths and weaknesses of many instructional models before endorsing one over another.

Identifying Instructional Models

Instructional models can initially be categorized according to whether they focus on group or individualized instruction. In group-oriented instruction, it is assumed that all students share uniform instructional problems, and any variation that might exist among students is considered insignificant. Instruction commonly takes place in large, teacher-led groups. Two examples of group-oriented instruction are the *academic* and *traditional* models.

In contrast, individual-oriented instructional models are based on the assumption that each student is different and that individual differences must be addressed in planning an effective program. Rather than large group instruction, individual-oriented models present instruction to small groups or to individual students. Instead of planning one lesson for the entire group, teachers plan multiple lessons for each topic, taking into account the differences among the students. The two individual-oriented instructional models that will be discussed in this chapter are the *systems* and *open-classroom* models. The classrooms in which you observe will most likely be an adaptation of one of these four models.

Group-Oriented Instruction

THE TRADITIONAL MODEL

The "traditional model" is a label used to describe a wide variety of instructional programs organized around self-contained classrooms and grade-level distinctions. Typically, a teacher is assigned a classroom and a group of 20 to 35 children at the same grade level for an entire school year. The classrooms are described as self-contained because all basic instructional activities take place within the classroom under the direction of the classroom teacher. Chronological age is the primary determinant for placing a child in a particular classroom. Students progress through the school by completing the sequence of grade levels, each level being organized around a carefully preplanned set of instructional materials.

As was mentioned in Chapter 1, the traditional model of instruction was originally conceived in the early part of this century, when schools

were being organized along the lines of industry and mass production efficiencies were in vogue. Under this strategy, the school's entire instructional program is planned by a few select people—usually administrators—and then segmented into grade level objectives that teachers can implement with the aid of a standardized curriculum featuring carefully sequenced *basal* textbooks as the primary instructional resource. Graded texts eliminate overlapping teaching responsibilities between one grade level and another. This model guarantees a uniform instructional program for all children at each grade level and usually stresses the three "R's" (Readin', 'Ritin', and 'Rithmetic).

When the traditional strategy was first developed, students were expected to be passive learners, sitting quietly in their seats and listening intently to the lessons presented by the classroom teacher. Our familiar grading system (A, B, C, D, and F) was developed to record the extent to which students learned their lessons. In contemporary adaptations of the traditional model, students participate more actively in the learning process, and the teacher's lecture is normally augmented with a variety of mediated teaching methods (e.g., colorful textbooks, films, filmstrips, and various manipulative materials). Grades, however, are still the most common form of evaluation in the majority of traditional educational systems.

The teacher in the traditional classroom is seen as a conveyor of knowledge; one who translates the school district's goals and materials into daily lessons for the students. Policies are usually defined in school-district handbooks, and the teacher is expected to follow those guidelines with little deviation. A primary responsibility of the teacher is to cover during the school year whatever material is prerequisite to moving into the next grade level.

Teacher-Proof Education
HISTORICAL FLASHBACK

The traditional school, the most common form of schooling today, was considered an exciting educational experiment just 70 years ago.[1] At the turn of the twentieth century, the United States began to initiate mass education that required all children from the ages of seven to sixteen to attend formal schools. At this time, the population of the United States was growing by leaps and bounds because of an increasing birth rate and immigration. Furthermore, this was the time of the industrial revolution, and industrialists were preoccupied with efficiency and industrial production. Cremin, a famed educational historian, describes how the bureaucratic organizational scheme used for industrial mass production became influential in the organization of the traditional school. For example, the major reason that traditional schools were divided into grade levels was that it was a more efficient use of the teacher's time than the teaching of grades 1 through 8, which was the common practice in existing one-room schools. Furthermore, since many teachers had only slightly more education than their students, the grade-level distinction made it possible for educational experts to develop preplanned lessons in the form of textbooks, which were also an innovation. In this manner, it was felt that education could be made "teacher proof."

Although the traditional classroom is often disparaged, it is still the most prevalent model in use, one that has proved to be a workable alternative in situations that call for a high degree of structure and management. However, you will find in your observations that most of today's traditional classrooms are not as self-contained as they once were. In most cases today, they are supplemented by the work of special reading, mathematics, physical education, art, and music teachers. In addition, you may discover that many features discussed in connection with the other models have been adapted into the traditional model.

THE ACADEMIC MODEL

A variation of the traditional model is the academic model, which is also organized around self-contained classrooms and populated by small, homogenous groups of students who receive their instruction primarily through a lecture format. As in the traditional model, students are viewed in terms of uniform problems the teacher must address.

The primary differences between the two approaches involve (a) curriculum content and (b) the role of the teacher. The academic curriculum

focuses more heavily on history, philosophy, literature, art, and music and less heavily on the three R's than does the traditional curriculum. A primary goal of such schools is to nurture an appreciation and understanding of the classics, which are considered a crucial part of a good education.

The academy teacher, like a university professor, is expected to be an expert in a particular subject area and a gifted teacher who provides the highest-quality educational experience within that area. The academy teacher is quite autonomous in determining matters of instructional resources, content, and style. The student's role in the academy school is to explore and internalize the expertise of the classroom teacher.

Since the classroom teacher is expected to be an expert in only one or two subject areas, it is not uncommon for the students to change classrooms throughout the day to meet specialists in several different academic areas. The general organization of this strategy is based upon the university model of instruction in which each instructor determines what is important and what should be taught.

Mental Discipline and the Academy Model
HISTORICAL FLASHBACK

The academy model is the oldest one in existence. Lee dates this strategy back to the Jeffersonian era when schools were accessible only to the élite.[2] At that time, the arts were considered to have had top priority in the curriculum. Eisner and Vallance's description of the academy curriculum provides us some insight into this strategy:

> The curriculum, it is argued, should emphasize the classic disciplines through which man inquires, since these disciplines, almost by definition, provide concepts and criteria through which thought acquires precision, generality, and power; such disciplines exemplify intellectual activity at its best. To construct a curriculum that includes "practical" learning, such as drivers' training, homemaking, and vocational education dilutes the quality of education and robs students of the opportunity to study those subjects that reflect man's enduring quest for meaning. The wise schoolmaster knows that not all subject matters are created equal, and he selects the content of his educational program with this principle in mind.[3]

Individual-Oriented Instruction

Many educators have rejected the assumption that all children have roughly the same intellectual makeup, instructional needs, and learning styles. These people believe that each child is a unique individual with unique intellectual abilities and instructional needs. This latter assumption has led to the development of many individual-oriented instructional models over the past 70 years. In many cases, these models simply evolved as variations of traditional, group-oriented practices when master teachers began personalizing instruction through techniques such as differentiation of homework assignments, peer or teacher tutoring, and personalized reading and writing assignments.

One of the first attempts to organize an entire school district for individualized instruction began in Pueblo, Colorado, in 1888. The Pueblo plan was designed to present the same instructional material to all children, but each child was allowed to complete the assignments at his or her own rate. Thus, some students could complete the six-year elementary program in four or five years, while others might take as long as seven or eight years. The primary impetus for developing this early individualized teaching model was economics. Educators rationalized that if a child could receive a six-year program in five or even four years, that would offset the additional cost required to educate those students who "failed" or took seven or eight years to complete the program.

Another early individualized program, the Batavia System, was developed in 1898 to help overcome the problems caused by overcrowded schools. Although the rationale for the Batavia System was again economic, its plan was as sophisticated as many of the theoretically based models in existence today.

Today, most instructional models make some provision for individual differences among students. In fact, one of the major criteria by which strategies are differentiated is the emphasis placed on individualization in the classroom. As noted earlier, most attempts to individualize instruction have come from innovative master teachers who have experimented

The Batavia System
HISTORICAL FLASHBACK

The Batavia System resulted from a search for a more effective way of working with large classes of up to 60 or 70 students.[4] The superintendent of schools in Batavia, New York, was forced by a rapidly rising school population to house more students in large, old classrooms than had been planned originally. In order to cope with the overcrowded conditions, he employed a second teacher for each classroom whose job it was to work with individual children. This teacher was not to be of secondary importance; he or she was to be a fully qualified teacher who devoted full time to helping individual students work up to their full potential. Children were not expected to seek this help; rather, the teacher was to observe where help was needed and then to encourage the individual child to think out the solution.

Adaptations of the Batavia System found their way into many schools of the day. Although a second teacher was not always used, definite periods were set aside for individual instruction, and this instruction usually followed the principles used in the original site in Batavia, New York. Bagley states that the popularity of the system was based on the fact that it actually succeeded in the classroom: "Some good results may be found in almost every school, but in Batavia schools the results are *uniformly* good with *all pupils. . . .* [There] are practically no failures in promotion."[5] Bagley does, however, suggest that some serious drawbacks to the system should be recognized: "[In] one-teacher classrooms, the difficulty [is] of supplying independent work with the pupils who are not undergoing individual instruction."[6] Careful assignments for seatwork are important, and one must take care "not to overemphasize written work, which will be the line of least resistance in supplying independent tasks."[7]

with group-oriented strategies. Often, these uncoordinated efforts have resulted in haphazard procedures whose success depended solely on the ability and commitment of the classroom teacher. More recently, however, some instructional programs have attempted to treat individual differences in a systematic manner, i.e., by first diagnosing the instructional weaknesses of students and then prescribing instructional objectives and activities that are matched to those weaknesses.

THE SYSTEMS MODEL

Although several "systematic" instructional models were developed in the late 1960s, the three that are most widely used and imitated today are Individually Prescribed Instruction (IPI), Program for Learning in

Accordance with Needs (PLAN), and Individually Guided Education (IGE). IPI, PLAN, and IGE all offer a variety of prepackaged instructional activities that have been carefully developed by curriculum experts to accommodate a wide range of learner differences. Similar content is provided for all students, but the type and rate of instruction, the depth of coverage, and the types of instructional materials are manipulated to fit individual student differences. In each program, the teacher is responsible for fitting the curriculum to the diagnosed needs of the students. Note the similarity to the goals of the 1888 Pueblo program and the 1898 Batavia System for individualized instruction. The impact of these experimental programs has been extensive. The vast majority of individualized instructional programs in the United States has been developed by individual teachers or local school districts, and these three programs have exerted their greatest influence as models for those who would adapt or combine features of all three experimental programs. A brief overview that contrasts these three systematic instructional models follows.

IPI

IPI was developed at the Learning Research and Development Center at the University of Pittsburgh during the mid-1960s. This program consists of a carefully developed sequence of detailed learning objectives and related instructional activities that require a minimum of teacher-led instruction. Included in the IPI materials are tests designed to monitor each student's progress. When the tests diagnose a student as being deficient in a specific skill or concept, appropriate instructional materials are prescribed for the student to study independently to become proficient in that particular skill. Students progress individually through the carefully sequenced instructional materials. The rate at which a student progresses through the curriculum depends on the *mastery* of skills on the pre- and posttests.

The student receives a "prescription" from the teacher for each content area that identifies the activities the student is to complete in order to master a specific instructional objective. The student is responsible for obtaining his or her own tests and instructional materials, generally from an instructional-materials center. The most common form of instructional materials are worksheets that can be completed with very little direction from the teacher. Except for the pre- and postmastery tests, students score most of their own work, since one of the primary goals for the student in IPI is the development of self-reliance and independence. Occasionally, students participate in small group seminars led by the teacher, but this sort of activity occupies only a small portion of the student's time.

The IPI teacher is the primary person responsible for observing and evaluating the student's progress. The teacher diagnoses the student's in-

structional needs and determines which instructional prescriptions (objectives and activities) are appropriate for correcting problems. The teacher also works with individual students who need help with their prescriptions and frequently directs supplemental activities. Seldom, if ever, will the IPI teacher lecture or lead large group instruction.

PLAN

PLAN uses as its building blocks a series of instructional guides called teaching learning units (TLUs). These include instructional objectives, a set of recommended learning activities for each objective, and a set of pre- and postdiagnostic tests. Unlike the IPI program, the instructional materials used in PLAN classrooms are not included in the TLUs; in most cases they are commercial materials commonly found in classrooms.

Each PLAN student has an individualized program of study consisting of a list of objectives that the student is to master over a period of weeks or months. Ideally, each program is prepared cooperatively by the student and the teacher. After the course of study has been developed and appropriate TLUs assigned, the student assumes the major responsibility for completing the program. When beginning a TLU, the student completes a pretest over the material to be covered in the unit. After the pretest is completed, the test is scored and the results recorded by the computer. The computer also provides a list of recommended activities for each student based on the test items that were incorrect. If the pretest demonstrates mastery of some aspect of the unit, the student would not be assigned activities in that area. The student is encouraged to seek assistance from the teacher whenever a problem arises. Although most of the student's work is done independently, occasionally students do meet in small, teacher-led groups. After completing the recommended activities, the student takes a posttest. If mastery of the assigned skills and concepts is not demonstrated, the computer will provide suggestions for remedial instruction. This sequence of testing followed by instructional activities is contained until mastery is achieved.

A teacher working in a PLAN program is freed from many noninstructional roles since the computer assumes most test-grading and record-keeping functions, normally the bane of individualized instructional programs. The teacher guides instruction by approving the recommended activities, modifying them when necessary, and working with individual students or small groups as learning problems occur. However, the bulk of instruction is built around commercially prepared materials rather than teacher presentations.

IGE

Development of IGE began in the mid-1960s at the Wisconsin Research and Development Center for Cognitive Learning, but today IGE schools can be found throughout the country. The IGE concept attempts to individualize instruction by reorganizing the role of both teachers and principals as well as the school curriculum. Unlike the PLAN and IPI models, self-instructional material is just one of many available alternatives. The bulk of IGE instruction takes place in small, teacher-led groups of 5 to 20 students.

In the IGE plan, the self-contained classroom is replaced with a multiaged instructional group (unit) consisting of a team of teachers (a team leader, two or three staff teachers, a first-year teacher or an intern, and an instructional aide) and 90 to 150 students. The teaching team cooperatively plans instructional activities for the total group of children for whom they are responsible. Team teaching and multiage grouping of students permit a wide variety of grouping possibilities. At a given moment, one teacher might be conducting a large group activity, such as showing a film, while the other teachers are working with small groups of children, tutoring individuals, or planning activities for later periods of instruction. The IGE concept aims at professional staff development as well as improved instruction for the students.

IGE students will have 90 to 150 classmates, with an age range of three to four years. Although they occasionally receive large-group instruction, most activities are carried out in small groups. For the skill

areas, such as reading and mathematics, students are grouped on the basis of abilities. In other areas, such as social studies, they might be grouped on the basis of age; and in some academic areas, such as science or ecology, they might be grouped on the basis of common interests. Students share responsibility for planning with the teacher and, after receiving the teacher's individualized prescription, follow a pretest–activity–posttest system of instruction. Older students frequently assist younger ones with instructional activities and help orient them to the routine of the unit. Students can seek assistance from any member of the teaching team or from the many volunteers who often assist in an IGE program. The major difference between the role of IGE students and that of either IPI or PLAN students is the amount of time that is spent working as a group.

The role of the IGE teacher presents a decided alternative to that of the self-contained classroom teacher. The IGE teacher works as a member of a team that collectively plans instructional activities and, because of the use of both large- and small-group instruction, must perform a variety of instructional tasks. Therefore, different teachers on the team assume leadership roles according to their capabilities and interests. There is one teacher on each team, however, who is designated as the team leader (sometimes referred to as the unit leader). The team leader acts as a liaison between the team and the school principal and also represents the team in school-wide planning sessions. Although team leaders spend the bulk of their time teaching (70 to 80 percent), they are also responsible for coordinating the unit's instructional activities to insure the most efficient use of materials and personnel.

Summarizing the Systems Model

In nearly all variations of the systems model, instruction centers around diagnosis and prescription. It is assumed that children represent a wide range of abilities, interests, and learning styles; consequently, instruction is planned for individual children rather than for classroom groups. Continuous assessment of student progress along an individually designed instructional sequence is central to this model. Sometimes, as in the IPI program, learning objectives and instructional activities are segmented into carefully sequenced, self-instructional units that allow students to pass through the curriculum on an independent basis. Diagnostic tests are built into the curriculum to help teachers place students at the proper point in the curriculum sequence and to help determine when students are ready to move on to the next topic.

The systems curriculum specifies what should be taught and offers a variety of instructional paths designed to accommodate different learning rates, styles, and environments. In this strategy, the teacher is responsible for engineering the curriculum to fit the diagnosed needs of students. Students learn predominantly from the instructional materials, while the teacher is primarily responsible for working with individual children and creating an atmosphere conducive to learning. Advocates of the systems approach often describe their model using a medical metaphor:

> The teacher's main task in the classroom is to facilitate learning. It might be pointed out that students actually do not learn from teachers; they learn from materials in much the same way that sick people do not get well from doctors, but rather from medication. The doctor, however, is important in prescribing and facilitating the proper kind of medication, the same as the teacher is important in facilitating learning through the proper utilization of instructional materials in the classroom.[8]

Whatever systems model is used, students are expected to assume a major responsibility for their own learning. They must be able to use independent instructional materials and also keep a record of their daily progress. Study guides, ranging in sophistication from preprinted booklets that are used on a district-wide basis to a simple ditto format prepared by individual teachers, are popular as a means of directing students to available instructional materials.

At times, the students come together on a short-term basis for small group instruction aimed at remediating some commonly diagnosed learning problem. Occasionally, large groups of 30 to 120 students will come together for the showing of films or for introductory activities. Inherent in the successful systems program is an atmosphere in which the student can say to a teacher, "I just do not understand this concept."

IGE has contributed another dimension to this approach: team teaching. Often, teams of two to five teachers work together in planning and implementing an instructional program. In some cases, the teams incorporate a team-leader position similar to that found in the IGE program. It should be noted that the basic features of the systems model (objective-based curriculum, diagnostic tests, study guides, and team teaching) are not unique to the three experimental programs discussed here. These experimental programs have established the validity of these techniques, however, and, in so doing, they have helped establish the techniques in the educational community.

THE OPEN-CLASSROOM MODEL

Many persons agree that children should be treated as individuals in the schooling process but oppose what they label as mechanistic instructional techniques (e.g., behavioral objectives, checklists, and independent-study worksheets) that are an integral part of the systems strategy. An alternative strategy that has arisen from this conflict is often labeled the "informal" or "open-classroom" model of instruction. Although educators such as John Dewey have long recommended informal approaches to instruction, only in recent years has this concept became a viable alternative to other models.

In the open-classroom model, instruction is commonly organized around what is termed an "integrated day." This means that the day is not segmented into strict time periods, each one designated for a specific subject area or activity. Open-classroom teachers often open the day by listing different activities that are available to the children during the day and the times during which they will be taking place. The children then plan their own schedules, often with a teacher's assistance, selecting activities that are most appropriate. In an open classroom, one might see groups of children simultaneously participating in such diverse activities as reading, constructing a bird house, or having timed foot races and graphing the results.

In the open classroom, basic skill development (reading, writing, etc.) is integrated into the various projects that students voluntarily pursue; it is not taught as isolated academic subjects. Students are encouraged to work on projects and activities individually or in small groups for periods of time commensurate with their interests. This technique is based on the assumption that when a child has a need to read a book or to seek information, instruction is more relevant. Occasionally, students may devote an entire day to a single activity that encompasses a variety of areas of basic skill development. A unit of study usually ends with the completion of a personal goal set by the child in conjunction with the teacher.

The materials in an open classroom consist of a combination of teacher- and student-made materials in addition to commercially produced materials. A variety of textbooks are used and are normally found in sets of three to five copies, since only a few children would be using them at any one time. Students in open classrooms are usually grouped into instructional families of 20 to 40 youngsters of different ages. There usually are no specified seating arrangements. In fact, in many open classrooms, tables and learning centers have completely replaced the traditional one-seat desks. Since children are often free to move around the classroom, within the guidelines set by the teacher and class, the open classroom is usually noisier than any of the other models we have discussed. In the open classroom, the noise tends to be productive rather than intrusive, with children having an opportunity to learn from their teacher, their activities, and each other.

The informal conditions of the open classroom require that the teacher's role be broad and creative. Teachers must have expertise in many areas (e.g., psychology, pedagogy, curriculum planning, and school administration). In order to maintain a productive and stimulating learning environment, the teacher must be continually developing high-interest activities and must keep individualized records, usually in the form of diaries or anecdotal descriptions, of each child's daily activities. The children are also responsible for keeping many of their own records. Without a doubt, the teacher's role in the open classroom is more complex and challenging, but it has more chances for failure than any of the other instructional models discussed thus far. To be effective as an open-classroom teacher, one must be confident and prepared to plan spontaneous yet challenging and well-rounded instruction for each child.

Comparison of the Four Instructional Strategies

At this time, all of the research and experimentation that has accompanied these four instructional models has failed to identify any one as superior to the others. What does seem to make a difference in the effectiveness of a given model is the degree to which the teacher is committed to making it successful. That is, if you believe in the "systems" strategy and have the needed support in terms of high-quality materials and staff, you are likely to have an effective program. The same can be said of the open-classroom model. Tables 4.1 and 4.2 provides a capsule comparison of the four models based on student grouping, achievement standards, the teacher's role, school policy formulation, and instructional resources.

TABLE 4.1 Major Characteristics of the Instructional Strategies

TRADITIONAL	ACADEMY	SYSTEMS	OPEN
Student Grouping			
Students are placed in academic grade-level groups and progress through the school curriculum in a standardized manner, usually with whole-group instruction. Chronological age serves as the primary determinant for a child's placement.	Students are usually grouped into small, static, homogeneous classes with age-group determinant. Instruction takes place in these small groups with the total group often moving to various classrooms to meet with academic specialists.	Student grouping is handled in a variety of ways (e.g., multiage grouping or conventional classroom grouping), but instruction is conducted on an individual or small-group basis. Instructional grouping is determined by diagnostic instruments and techniques that relate the learner's competencies to a specified curriculum.	Students are usually grouped into multiage groups with instruction taking place individually or in small, short-term, flexible groups. Student interest and carefully conducted diagnosis are the primary determinants of student grouping.
Achievement Standards			
Minimum student achievement standards for grade levels are universally accepted. Maximum standards are seldom stated.	General achievement standards are cooperatively determined for the school via teacher and administrator conferences, but the teacher assumes autonomous control in translating these expectations for individual students.	Standard achievement expectations are generally provided by the instruction materials, but each student is expected to master the curriculum at his own rate and in the learning style most appropriate for him.	Unique achievement standards and performance levels are ideally determined by the teacher for each student. In determining achievement standards, teachers take into consideration individual abilities, general age, group achievement norm, and school and community goals.

TABLE 4.2 Major Characteristics of the Teaching Models

TRADITIONAL	ACADEMY	SYSTEMS	OPEN
Teacher's Role			
The teacher's role is clearly specified by the school organizational structure and is universally understood. For example, teachers are associated with grade levels (e.g., third-grade teachers), and the general nature of that role is understood by other teachers, parents, and students.	Teachers are regarded as professionals who, as academic specialists, retain authority in deciding matters of instructional and curricular policies in their classrooms.	The teacher is viewed as a highly skilled educator whose primary task is facilitating the proper classroom environment needed for children to interact properly with the curriculum.*	Teachers are viewed as professionals capable of making autonomous instructional and curricular decisions based on the unique needs and interests of their students.
School Policy Formulation			
Comprehensive school policies that stipulate school rules and regulations are provided for teachers by their supervisors (e.g., job descriptions, curriculum guides, and policy handbooks).	General school policies are formulated in a monocratic manner, but teachers and administrators are asked to revise and interpret those policies continuously.	School policies are usually determined in a centralized manner, but teachers are often asked to make recommendations and suggestions during the policy-formulation procedures.	School policies are continuously made via the cooperative efforts of the teachers and administrators.
Curriculum Materials			
Each traditional school uses a standardized curriculum, usually in the form of adopted textbooks or curriculum guides, to which teachers must adhere. This ensures that all students receive a proper and equitable education.	This curriculum reflects a combination of the school's global recommendations and expertise and the creativity of the individual teacher. As a result, the curriculum varies from one teacher to another, although all students within a classroom interact with the same curriculum.	The curriculum is a system consisting of small bits and pieces that can be rearranged to form a variety of instructional programs for students. This type of curriculum is predetermined and preplanned, generally by curriculum specialists, and normally requires teacher intervention only in exceptional situations.	The curriculum consists of a plethora of instructional materials (commercial and teacher-made); unique combinations of the materials are used to fit the individual needs and interests of students.

*This is taken from P. C. Lange, "Administrative and Curricular Considerations," in *Programmed Instruction: The Sixty-sixth Yearbook of the National Society for the Study of Education (Part II),* ed. P. C. Lange (Chicago: University of Chicago Press, 1967), p. 307.

Robert Gagné
COMMENTS ON INSTRUCTIONAL DESIGN

In an interview with the authors, Robert Gagné, a noted authority in the area of instructional design, summarized his career as "an attempt to interpret the result of learning research and learning theory and to bring this to bear on the problem of how to design and deliver instruction." Although interested in all kinds of learning (e.g., factual information, attitudes, and physical skills), he is particularly concerned with how people acquire intellectual skills such as the abililty to read, write, and perform mathematical calculations. Such skills, he feels, are at the heart of the educational process.

Gagné is particularly interested in how an intellectual skill such as reading can be broken down into what he terms a "learning hierarchy." He describes a learning hierarchy as the analytical scheme where some target skill is broken down into a sequence of prerequisite steps that go from simple to complex. In learning to read, for example, the ability to discriminate between letters normally precedes the ability to recognize words. Gagné is quick to point out, however, that while it is a fairly simple process to analyze the prerequisites involved in learning a mathematical skill, the process becomes considerably more complex when applied to a skill such as reading:

> As a matter of fact, nobody has done this very well, but I am convinced that it can be done. Reading, even in the sense of reading comprehension, can be represented in terms of a learning

hierarchy which represents successively simpler prerequisites of the intellectual skill which we know as reading.

In understanding learning hierarchies, Gagné emphasizes the distinction between verbal information and intellectual skills. Learning hierarchies are applicable *only* to intellectual skills:

> You get into trouble, as I and a number of other people have found out, if you try to make learning hierarchies that are simply organizations of information; that's not what they are. They are skills and not information.

Gagné stresses the importance of educators understanding this distinction:

> . . . every teacher is surely aware of the potential confusion that may arise when the teacher hopes that a student knows something in the sense of being able to do it, only to find that the student can only talk about it but can't really do it.

Gagné believes that the teacher's first job, as the manager of instruction, is to identify the learning outcomes that are desired. Teachers must ask themselves questions such as, "Do I expect the student to exhibit an intellectual skill, or do I expect him or her to show evidence of an attitude?" In the case of intellectual skills, prerequisite objectives should be formulated and used to diagnose where the learner stands in relation to that skill. Once this is done, the teacher can organize instruction to fit the students' current needs.

When asked whether he had any final suggestions for prospective teachers, Gagné summarized his beliefs in the following statement:

I think the functions of the teacher are to (1) find out what the students already know, (2) diagnose what they need in case they don't know something, and (3) give feedback to students concerning the results of their learning. These three things are exceedingly important for any teacher. I think these are the real core of teaching, and they are general; they apply to any subject matter.

Instructional Resources

The success of any instructional model depends upon a creative blend of teacher-centered and materials-centered instruction. Even the most dedicated teacher cannot singlehandedly cope with the various learning styles and rates of 30 to 40 students. Likewise, no set of preplanned learning materials, regardless of the care in designing, can foresee all of the learning difficulties that exist in the typical classroom. Consequently, in this section we will briefly examine some of the more important instructional materials found in today's classrooms. These materials are crucial to the successful operation of any instructional model. It is your responsibility to be aware of them and of the ways that they may be used most effectively.

TEXTBOOKS

Since Johannes Gutenberg first invented movable type in the mid-fourteenth century, the printed text has been the primary means of recording and transmitting information. Although today's schools are equipped with a variety of sophisticated instructional materials (movie and slide projectors, science equipment, and, in some cases, computer terminals), textbooks remain the most universal of instructional tools. They are found in all types of schools and in all types of communities.

In Chapter 1 we briefly traced the evolution of the textbooks, beginning with the Hornbook and the New England Primer of the Colonial Period. The content of these early texts, like the entire curriculum, was distinctly religious in orientation. It was not until 1836, when the McGuffey's Readers appeared, that this religious content was supplemented with poems, proverbs, and fables. Even this new material, however, was primarily concerned with moral development.

The McGuffey Readers were the first texts to use the concept of graduated reading levels. Until then, all students used the same textbook, regardless of age or ability. The McGuffey era also saw the introduction of informal language exercises to supplement formal drills and the use of instructional aids, such as clock faces and the abacus, in conjunction with the text.

During the Industrial Era, from 1870 to 1938, textbooks, like classrooms, began to be reorganized into distinct grade levels. This innovation was enthusiastically received by school officials, who were concerned about the abilities of many of the teachers recently pressed into service in overpopulated schools. These graded texts, together with their supplementary workbooks, provided a carefully sequenced "teacher-proof" program of instruction.

Today's textbooks, which have become quite elaborate and pedagogically sophisticated, are still the primary teaching tool of most classroom teachers. Covering all content areas from reading to sex education, they normally feature controlled reading vocabularies, high-interest stories, colorful illustrations, problems, and carefully sequenced content.

The Pros and Cons of Textbooks

To help you analyze the instructional pros and cons of textbooks, we offer the following balance sheet, juxtaposing the arguments of advocates and opponents. Based on your own learning experiences, in what direction do you see the balance tilting?

TEXTBOOK BALANCE SHEET

ADVOCATES

Textbooks constitute the most effective learning tool available to most teachers.

Textbooks have proved to be the most effective way of succinctly presenting a broad, up-to-date body of information in a reasonably interesting fashion. Given the budgetary constraints that limit the instructional materials available to most classroom teachers, textbooks are simply the best alternative available. If they were not effective, they would not have continued to be the primary tool of instruction for over 100 years.

OPPONENTS

They are for lazy teachers.

The widespread use of textbooks is more a matter of the convenience of lazy teachers than of instructional effectiveness. It is ridiculous to think that a single book can provide the breadth and timeliness of content coverage that can be achieved by using a variety of publications, such as, for example, books, newspapers, and periodicals. Because of the time it takes physically to produce and market a new text, the books' contents are at least 18 months old before reaching the first group of users. And since most schools use a text for four to five years, its content is quite dated by the time it reaches its last group of users. In addition, texts avoid important but controversial topics for fear of alienating potential users.

ADVOCATES

The use of textbooks provides curriculum continuity.

Modern textbooks provide a carefully sequenced core curriculum that permits instructional continuity from one teacher to another and between grade levels. If left to their own devices, nearly all teachers tend to emphasize those topics they are most knowledgeable about and deemphasize other equally important topics about which they are less interested or informed. This natural human tendency results in an unbalanced curriculum that leaves dangerous learning gaps in students' educations.

This problem is magnified at the next grade level when, for example, a fourth-grade teacher receives students from three different grade teachers, each of whom stressed different skills and concepts. Consider the curriculum and management problems facing this fourth-grade teacher, as opposed to another whose incoming students have all satisfactorily completed the work in the same third-grade math and reading texts.

OPPONENTS

Continuity is not the only educational concern.

Curriculum continuity is fine, but it should not become a school's primary focus. The best teaching flows from a teacher's unique personality. Academic freedom to teach according to one's personal style and interests and in accordance with the individual needs and abilities of one's students is more important than curriculum uniformity. Look back on your own career as a student, and ask yourself whether you profited more from the conventional teachers who dutifully taught the assigned text or from the highly motivated but unconventional teachers (if you had any) who taught according to their own personal dictates.

If the personal enthusiasm of the teacher is central to instructional success, as we are told, then isn't it counterproductive to organize instruction around an assigned text? In short, isn't it true that the more we center instruction around a core text, the more lazy, unmotivated, and "text dependent" our teachers are likely to become?

ADVOCATES

Textbook authors are experts.

Most textbook authors are experts in the particular subject area about which they are writing. Consequently, they are better prepared than classroom teachers to judge the relative importance of the topics within that field and emphasize those that deserve to be taught. Their expertise normally extends into the pedagogical realm, too, where they have learned to adapt the latest principles of instruction to the presentation of their materials. In addition, the editorial staffs of most publishers include a variety of specialists (researchers, writers, illustrators, etc.) whose job is to further refine the selection and presentation of content. As a result, almost all commercially produced texts feature graded vocabularies, high-interest stories, problems and exercises, elaborate illustration programs, graded student workbooks, and teachers' manuals rich in teaching suggestions and validated test items. So involved is the design of such texts that their development normally takes four to five years. Compare this with the typical preparation time for most classroom teachers.

OPPONENTS

Even experts are limited.

Even though most textbook authors are experts in the areas they are writing about, they are still limited by their individual point of view. Their selection and presentation of content is based on personal judgments that simply may not square with those of classroom teachers. Should teachers give up control of their classrooms to a so-called expert who writes for a national market and is totally removed from local situations? Aren't classroom teachers the experts when it comes to evaluating the instructional needs of their students, and isn't it their responsibility to personally assemble instructional materials that are well-matched to those needs and compatible with their own instructional philosophy?

However, it is dangerous to assume that textbook authors are somehow more expert than the people who write other kinds of books or who write for magazines and newspapers. Often these other materials are written by professional writers whose ability to organize and communicate difficult ideas far exceeds the writing skills of the professional educator. It is the classroom teachers' responsibility continually to search out those materials that are most applicable to the needs and interests of their students.

ADVOCATES

Textbooks are economical.

Given the increasingly frequent taxpayers' revolts these days, textbooks can be viewed as the budget-minded educator's best friend. The average textbook is adopted for a five-year period, and at least five different students use the text during that time. Moreover, given the carefully graded reading levels and the pedagogical care with which they are constructed, most texts can be read and understood by children with various learning styles and ability levels. Measured against the cost of teachers' salaries and the cost of high-priced instructional hardware, such as movie projectors, science equipment, and computer terminals, textbooks are probably the most cost-efficient of all educational investments.

OPPONENTS

Resourcefulness is even more economical.

Resourceful teachers can assemble a rich and diverse supply of instructional materials at very little cost. Printed materials (books, magazines, and newspapers) can be solicited from interested parents, friends, and educationally oriented organizations. In fact, the truly resourceful teacher can take the ordinary materials within almost any physical environment and use them to teach virtually any concept in the school's curriculum. In short, imagination and creativity are the keys to school economy, not any one type of resource, such as textbooks.

Tips for Using the Textbook

As you visit classrooms you will no doubt encounter a wide variety of textbooks and an even wider variety of ways in which those textbooks are being used. In order to bring some order into this diversity, we offer the following tips on how to get the most benefit from the texts you will, in all probability, be assigned.

1. *Never use the textbook as the sole teaching tool.* Textbooks are designed to provide a foundation or core of instructional content; to be effective they must be supplemented with other materials. The classroom teacher is the only person with a first-hand knowledge of the interests and abilities of individual students and, consequently, it is the teacher's responsibility to intervene and individualize lessons. The resourceful teacher will develop his or her own materials to complement the text, to emphasize or clarify important points or to address topics omitted altogether. Although teacher-made materials are usually of poorer quality than textual materials, they can be used on a limited basis and can add much interest and depth to the instruction. Most schools also have as part of their instructional resources commercially produced supplements that can be used in conjunction with the text. In fact, many textbooks now provide suggestions to the teacher regarding the most appropriate points at which to use a variety of supplementary materials.

2. *Decide what parts of the text to emphasize or deemphasize in accordance with the school's goals and philosophy.* Although most schools choose texts that are compatible with their own goals and philosophy, it must be remembered that commercial texts are designed to fit a wide variety of teaching situations, and consequently they do not adapt perfectly to the goals of any one school or school district. Therefore, the effective teacher will alter the text to meet the goals specified in the curriculum guide.

3. *Use the teacher's guide as an important instructional resource.* The effective teacher will not be dependent on the suggestions listed in the teacher's guide, but will use it as an important source of supplementary ideas. Often teachers will use several different teacher's guides as a small professional library. Many of the ideas and suggestions contained in these guides are quite effective, having been tried and tested by many teachers in a variety of teaching situations.

4. *Vary the use of the textbook.* All of us can recall the drudgery of using the same textbook day after day in the same old way. Perhaps you had a math teacher who always put an example on the board with a brief explanation, assigned a page or two or problems, and after 20 minutes or so spent the remainder of the period correcting papers. Although this technique may not be bad for a day or two, it becomes deadly if constantly repeated. The effective teacher will vary his or her instruc-

tional strategy, including the way the textbook is used. If, in your classroom observations, you see the students anticipating the teacher's next step, it is likely that the teacher is not using sufficient variety.

5. *Adapt the textbook to the needs of the students.* The effective classroom teacher will alter a textbook to fit the varying needs and dispositions of the students. This is absolutely necessary if the text is to be an effective curriculum tool. Some students will quickly move beyond the text while others will be able to master only a portion of its content. It is the teacher's job to provide additional outside material for the fast learners while helping the slower learners concentrate their efforts on certain key parts of the text.

OTHER INSTRUCTIONAL RESOURCES

Though textbooks serve as the basic instructional tool in most classrooms, other resources are available to add variety, depth, and excitement to the instructional routine. The effective teacher is forever searching—in the A-V center, in the library, in educational catalogs, in the old storeroom down the hall—for materials that will enhance the instructional process. In fact, the variety of instructional materials available today has gradually forced schools to broaden their libraries into "instructional resource centers." In many cases the librarian has either been replaced or joined by a media specialist who is trained to assist teachers in organizing and planning their instruction. These resource centers normally contain the following types of instructional materials.

Printed Materials

To supplement the basal textbooks currently in use, most resource centers stock the competing texts of other publishers. Thus, a teacher who is disenchanted with portions of the officially adopted text can direct students to other textual presentations that he or she feels are superior. Also, a wealth of non-text-oriented books and magazines dealing with common curriculum topics is normally available. These range all the way from high-interest trade books written by professional writers with an interest in a particular topic, to high-quality children's magazines, to educational comic books. And, of course, we must not forget to include the encyclopedias, dictionaries, and other reference materials that are used on a daily basis in the classroom.

Audio-Visual Materials

Thomas Edison often lamented the fact that motion pictures, which he visualized as an educational aid, were used primarily as an entertainment toy. Were he still alive, he would undoubtedly gain much satisfaction from visiting a well-equipped, modern school and seeing the variety of educational films, filmstrips, slides, and audio and video tapes that are a part of its instructional program. These and other audio-visual materials such as maps, globes, and physical models of humans and animals are available today in ever-increasing numbers. The instructional value of such materials is incontestable, and consequently it is the teacher's responsibility to keep abreast of these materials and the research that deals with their use.

Hardware

Mechanical and electronic devices are rapidly gaining in importance as instructional resources. The inexpensive hand calculator, once used only be engineers, is now used by elementary students all over the country. All types of visual projectors (e.g., overhead, opaque, and slide) fall into this category, as well as record and tape players. The computer has also moved into the instructional realm at both the elementary and high school levels. Students now use the computer to practice basic language and mathematical skills, to simulate real-life situations, to play educational games, and, naturally, to learn computer technology.

INSTRUCTIONAL RESOURCE QUALITY CONTROL

The recent flood of instructional resources has produced many valuable teaching materials, as well as others that could only be categorized as "junk." As a teacher you will want to select the highest-quality materials for the benefit of your students, but from an economic point of view it is also important that you invest the taxpayer's dollar wisely. As you begin to observe the instructional materials that are used in schools, inquire about the criteria used to select them, and find out who is responsible for making those decisions. Since teachers are rapidly assuming a greater voice in the difficult task of selecting instructional materials, there are a number of guidelines they should be aware of in making their decisions.

One readily available source of information is the publishing companies themselves. Most of them will readily provide information about how their materials were developed, where they are being used, and what results they have produced. Although admittedly biased, such information can be verified or contradicted by contacting actual users and getting their first-hand evaluations.

In addition, most state departments of education provide lists of recommended instructional materials that have been judged compatible with state-level goals and objectives. At the local level there are often review committees made up of teachers, administrators, and often parents who review materials with regard to the local school-district objectives. The most efficient way to select materials, however, is to compare the materials to a predetermined list of personal criteria or questions. The following is a sample of the types of questions that might be asked:

1. Is the content of the materials consistent with the aims and philosophy of the school?
2. Is the mode of presentation both forceful and flexible enough to adapt to a variety of instructional styles throughout the school or school district?
3. Is the content free of cultural, ethnic, religious, and sex bias?
4. Is the content and the mode of presentation appropriate to the abilities of the students for whom they are intended?
5. Is the material properly sequenced or graded so that it can be adapted to the needs of learners at various levels of development?
6. Is the material appropriate for its intended purpose, be it introduction, development, practice, or review?

Summary

The most important conclusion that can be drawn from this chapter is that there is no one instructional model or type of instructional material that will be appropriate for every student, teacher, or community. For some students and some teachers the structure provided by the traditional classroom will be best. For others the informality and spontaneous creativity inherent in the informal classroom will yield the best results. You may find some schools that are adapting or incorporating multiple models into their school programs and then attempting to match both teachers and students to whatever model is most compatible. Although we cannot predict the exact models that you will encounter in your teaching career, we are fairly sure they will be quite varied. Our advice to you is simply this: If you want to be marketable, be flexible.

1. Interview a classroom teacher to determine the predominant instructional model used and the specific tasks the teacher assumes within this model.
   a. Ask the teacher whether instruction is organized into whole-class instruction, small-group instruction, or individualized instruction. Who determines the mode of instruction (lecture, discussion, investigation, reading, etc.)? Does the mode of instruction vary from one subject area to another?
   b. What kinds of instructional materials are used in the classroom? Who selects them? (Include a guide for completing an instructional-resource inventory.)
   c. What kind of planning does the teacher do on a daily basis to prepare for the lessons? How much direction is the teacher given concerning what should be taught?
   d. How is the school organized (by grade levels, multiage groupings, etc.)? In what ways do the teachers in the buildings work together?
2. Discuss the differences or similarities you would expect to find in the traditional, academy, systems, and open-classroom models of instruction regarding the following factors:
   a. School announcements
   b. Student clubs
   c. Teacher responsibilities in lesson planning
   d. Textbooks
   e. Student seating arrangements
   f. Involvement of parents
   g. Bulletin boards
   h. Educational and socioeconomic background of teachers
3. Try to locate a school that uses team teaching. If possible, visit a team planning session and (a) identify the types of decisions that the team makes, (b) determine how much time team planning sessions require each week, and (c) discuss the advantages and disadvantages of being a team teacher.
4. Survey the local schools and determine to what extent the computer is being used for instructional purposes. Is it used at all? If so, is it being used for instructional and/or management purposes?
5. Select one of the four instructional models that were described in this chapter and identify the major strengths and weaknesses of that model. Document your position by interviewing and observing teachers using that model and by reviewing the professional literature dealing with that model.

Notes

1. Lawrence Cremin, *The Transformation of the School: Progressivism in American Education, 1876–1957* (New York: Vintage Books, 1964).
2. Gordon C. Lee, ed., *Crusade against Ignorance: Thomas Jefferson on Education* (New York: Teachers College Press, 1961).

3. Elliot W. Eisner and Elizabeth Vallance, "Five Conceptions of Curriculum: Their Roots and Implications for Curriculum Planning," in *Conflicting Conceptualizations of Curriculum,* eds. Elliot W. Eisner and Elizabeth Vallance (Berkeley, California: McCutchan, 1974), p. 12.
4. M. Vere DeVault and G. Thomas Fox, "An Historical Perspective on Individual Instruction," *Programmed Learning and Educational Technology, 15* (November 1978), 30–32.
5. W. C. Bagley, *Classroom Management: Its Principles and Technique* (New York: Macmillan, 1925), p. 218.
6. *Ibid.,* p. 221.
7. *Ibid.,* pp. 221–222.
8. John C. Flanagan, W. M. Shanner, H. J. Brudner, and R. W. Marker, "An Individualized Instructional System: PLAN," in *Systems of Individualized Education,* ed. Harriet Talmage (Berkeley, Calif.: McCutchan, 1975), pp. 151–152.

For More Information

JOURNALS

Barrall, Mary E., and Hill, David A. "A Survey of College Students' Exposure to and Preference for Eight Instructional Options," *Research in Higher Education, 7* (1977), 315–327.

Bork, Alfred. "Computer Graphics in Learning," *Journal of College Science Teaching, 9* (1980), 141–149.

Deshler, Donald D. and Graham, Steven. "Tape Recording Educational Materials for Secondary Handicapped Students," *Teaching Exceptional Children, 12* (1980), 52–54.

Doll, William E. "A Structural View of Curriculum," *Theory into Practice, 18* (1979), 336–348.

Edelfelt, Roy A. "Schools as Social Systems," *Theory into Practice, 18* (1979), 363–365.

Feldhusen, John, Rand, David and Crowe, Martin. "Designing Open and Individualized Instruction at the Elementary Level: A Guide for the Individual Teacher," *Educational Technology, 15* (1975), 17–21.

Frazier, Alexander. "Making a Curriculum for Children," *Childhood Education, 56* (1980), 258–263.

Gulley, Beverly, and Norwood, Elizabeth. "Critical Aspects of the Open Classroom." *Education, 96* (1976), 207–208.

Hedges, William D. "Computer-Assisted Instruction and the Schools." *Educational Leadership, 30* (1973), 361–365.

Henson, Kenneth T. "Questioning as a Mode of Instruction," *Clearing House, 53* (1979), 14–16.

Hull, Ronald E. "Selecting an Approach to Individualized Education," *Phi Delta Kappan, 55* (1973), 169–173.

Marksberry, Mary Lee. "Student Questioning: An Instructional Strategy," *Educational Horizons, 57* (1979), 190–195.

Marques, Todd E., Lane, David M., and Dorfman, Peter W. "Toward the Development of a System for Instructional Evaluation: Is There Consensus Regarding

What Constitutes Effective Teaching?," *Journal of Educational Psychology, 71* (1979), 840–849.

McGilvrey, M. J. "Television in Education," *Bulletin, XLII-2* (1976), 25–29.

Nash, Paul. "A Humanistic Perspective," *Theory into Practice, 18* (1979) 323–329.

Schneider, Donald O. "Guidelines for Selecting Media," *Social Education, 36* (1972), 799–802.

Sloan, Fred A. "Open Education American Style," *Peabody Journal of Education, 51* (1974), 140–146.

Turnbull, Ann P., Strickland, Bonnie, and Hammer, Susan E. "The Individualized Education Program — Part 2: Translating Law into Practice," *Journal of Learning Disabilities, 11* (1978), 67–72.

Vicary, Judith R., Swisher, John D., and Campbell, Robert C. "One School's Approach to Planning for Affective Education," *Humanist Educator, 15* (1977), 193–202.

Wright, Robert E., and Hosford, Philip. "Developing an Individual Teaching Style," *Clearing House, 48* (1974), 555–559.

BOOKS

Cooper, James M. et al. *Classroom Teaching Skills: A Handbook* and *Classroom Teaching Skills: A Workbook.* Lexington, Mass.: D.C. Heath, 1977.

Cuban, Larry. *To Make A Difference.* New York: Free Press, 1970.

Davies, R. A. *The School Library Media Center: A Force for Educational Excellence,* 2nd ed. New York: R. R. Bowker, 1974.

Fantini, Mario, and Weinstein, Gerald. *The Disadvantaged: Challenge to Education.* New York: Harper & Row, 1968.

Gage, N. L., ed. *The Psychology of Teaching Methods: The 75th Yearbook of the National Society for the Study of Education.* Part I. Chicago: University of Chicago Press, 1976.

Good, Thomas L., and Brophy, Jere E. *Looking in Classrooms.* 2nd ed. New York: Harper & Row, 1978.

Hertzberg, Alvin, and Stone, Edward. *Schools Are For Children: An American Approach to the Open Classroom.* New York: Schocken Books, 1971.

Joyce, Bruce, and Weill, Marsha. *Models of Teaching.* Englewood Cliffs, New Jersey: Prentice Hall, 1972.

Kemp, J. E. *Planning and Producing Audio-Visual Materials,* 3rd ed. New York: Thomas Y. Crowell, 1975.

Klasek, Charles B. *Instructional Media in the Modern School.* Lincoln, Neb: Professional Educators Publications, 1972.

Perrone, Vito. *Open Education: Promise and Problems.* Bloomington, Indiana: Phi Delta Kappan Educational Foundation, 1972.

Schaefer, Robert J. *The Schools as a Center of Inquiry.* New York: Harper & Row, 1967.

Silberman, Charles E. *Crisis in the Classroom.* New York: Random House, 1970.

Tesconi, Charles A., and Van Cleve, Morris. *The Anti-Man Culture; Bureautechnocracy and the Schools.* Urbana, Ill.: University of Illinois Press, 1971.

Travers, R.M.W., ed. *Second Handbook of Research on Teaching.* Chicago: Rand McNally, 1973.

MOVIES

The A, B, C's of Behavioral Education (Hallmark, 20 min., 1969). This behavior modification program for problem students uses positive reinforcement and individualized instruction to reach obtainable goals within the curriculum design.

A Class of Your Own: Instructional Technique (MLA, 25 min., 1965). Discusses the importance of planning ahead so the lesson will flow smoothly. Also shows that planned questions and media use are valuable.

How Children Learn (NBC, 23 min., 1972). Various trends in teaching are shown ranging from the traditional classroom to schools without walls. This is to show the change in attitudes towards the specific educational needs of the child.

I Am Here Today (EDC, 43 min., 1971). This film shows a Cambridge, Mass. school in which the integrated-day approach is used with five, six, and seven year olds. The children are shown planning their own work and helping their peers.

Inside Out (Jack Robertson, 56 min., 1971). Demonstrates the various resources available from the community that can be provided to urban high school students. This is exemplified by the Franklin Parkway Program.

IPI: Initiating, Planning and Implementing (Ralph Lopatin, 22 min.). Shows the implementation of a IPI (Individually Prescribed Instruction) program in an elementary school.

Learning How to Learn — The Open Classroom in America (IDEA, 22 min., 1970). Teacher-child relationships are examined in varying group sizes. All take place in an informal setting. The environments are prepared to meet the needs of the child.

My Name is Children (Indiana University Audio-Visual Center, 16 min., 1967). Shows one school using the "inquiry approach" to motivate student activity.

Open Classroom (Sherwin Rubin, 13 min., 1971). This open classroom situation shows children designing their own learning environments. Parents, community members, and older student volunteers are present in the room to provide additional resources. This film takes place in an actual classroom in California.

Somebody Special (IDEA, 22 min., 1972). Various aspects of the Individually Guided Education (IGE) program are presented in which the student is continually assessed and works closely with the advisor-teacher to develop individual learning strategies.

Summerhill (National Film Board of Canada, 28 min., 1967). The students at this experimental school in England are self-disciplining and are not required to attend classes. The school is looked at as a preparation for a life of learning.

Teach Me How I Can Do It Myself (IFB, 29 min., 1973). This film demonstrates the Montessori method of elementary education. Emphasis is placed on orderliness within a structured environment.

Chapter 5

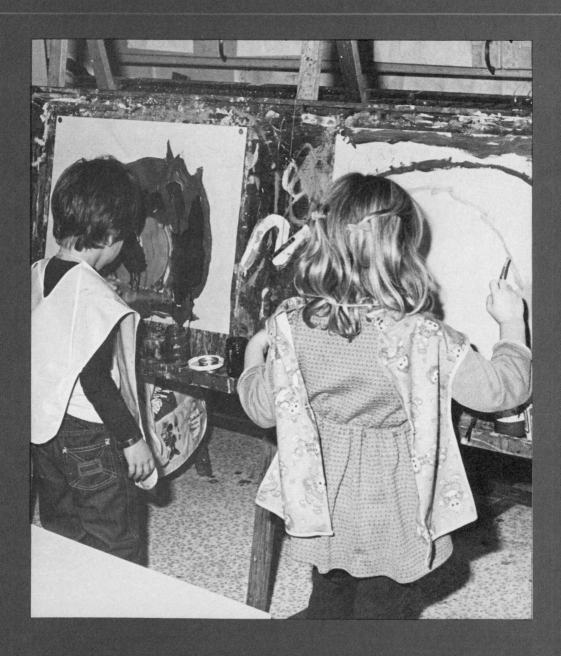

Chapter 5

CURRICULUM AND THE CLASSROOM TEACHER

Human beings need more than genetically programmed behaviors to cope with their environments. Humans, more than any other creature, are dependent on learning for their survival. This human dependence on learning is, however, a two-way street. While it is true that our condition at birth is a dependent one compared to creatures propelled by instinct, it is equally true that our ability to learn, i.e., to develop new, adaptive responses as a result of our experience, eventually makes us far freer and more flexible in responding to our environment. In short, the capacity to learn enables humans to modify their behavior quickly in order to cope with environmental demands, and therein lies our supremacy over other earthly creatures.

What people learn in order to survive as comfortably as possible is called *culture*. Culture is best thought of as the various products of human endeavor. These products are generally divided into two categories, according to whether they are material (artifacts) or nonmaterial (mentifacts) in nature. The nonmaterial, or knowledge, products are especially important, since their acquisition is normally prerequisite to the proper use of the material products. For example, what good is a typewriter to someone who is illiterate? The process of learning a culture can also be divided into two categories, according to whether the learning experiences are planned or unplanned. The earliest and, according to most psychologists, the most crucial learning experiences generally occur within a family setting and are the product of more or less spontaneous interaction between the child and the other family members, especially the parents. Family-based learning includes the fundamentals of self care, language acquisition, and social interaction.*

When culture—i.e., what is to be learned—reaches a certain level of complexity and change, the learning process must, of necessity, become more planned and less spontaneous. That is when the institution of schooling arises to assist the family with the learning process. Schools are simply places where trained specialists attempt to transmit the culture through planned learning experiences. These planned learning experiences are what most educators refer to when they use the term *curriculum,* and, as you will soon learn, they use the term often.

Modern Definitions of Curriculum

Working from the above discussion, we can now define *curriculum* as "the planned learning experiences that a school presents to its students in order to socialize them into the prevailing culture." As you will see, however, this definition does not satisfy all educators, nor does it answer two specific questions that tend to divide curriculum experts, namely:

- How encompassing should the formal plan of learning experiences be?
- What is the teacher's role in the curriculum-planning and implementation process?

As with most questions pertaining to education, the experts are divided in their answers to these questions. Regarding the first one, some experts maintain that all school-related learning experiences (planned and unplanned) should be included in the definition of curriculum. These people obviously would not agree with our definition, which limits the term to *planned* learning experiences.

A leading advocate of this viewpoint is Ronald Doll, who defines *curriculum* as "all the experiences which are offered to students under the auspices or direction of the school."[1] According to Doll, these experiences may occur in buses, on the playground, or in corridors, as well as in the classroom. They encompass such diverse, unplanned activities as lining up for lunch, organizing an after-school activity, and throwing paper wads, as well as traditional reading and writing activities.

People who use such an all-encompassing definition are, in effect, combining three subcategories of curriculum (the academic, the extra, and the hidden curricula) into one term. The "academic" curriculum, which is what most people think of when they hear the term *curriculum,* simply refers to the formal list of courses offered by a school. The "extra" curriculum refers to those planned but voluntary activities that are sponsored by a school, such as sports, drama, or social clubs. The "hidden" curriculum

*See Chapter 8 for a detailed discussion of parent-child instruction.

refers to those unplanned learning activities (e.g., learning how to cope with school bureaucracy and boredom, or learning how to gain popularity with ones peers) that are a natural by-product of school life.

Other curriculum experts, such as Mauritz Johnson and Thomas Romberg have defined *curriculum* more narrowly. Johnson refers to the curriculum as "a structured series of learning outcomes" that prescribe for the teacher the goals or expected results of instruction.[2] Romberg refers to the curriculum as "a set of intended learnings and the operational plan for achieving those learnings."[3] Such definitions explicitly confine the term *curriculum* to a school's planned, academic learning experiences.

As you might expect, just as much disagreement surrounds the second question, concerning the teacher's role in the curriculum-planning and implementation process. In general, the broader someone's definition of curriculum, the more likely that person is to advocate grassroots (i.e., teacher-student) control of the curriculum. For example, Doll, who included all school-related learning (planned and unplanned) in his definition, views the teacher as the person primarily responsible for planning the curriculum at all levels: classroom, school, district, and state. In his opinion the curriculum should reflect the characteristics and abilities of both teachers and students as well as the social dynamics of the particular school and community. The curriculum, in this view, is built from the bottom up in order to reflect the realities of the specific learning situation.

In contrast, Johnson's narrower view, which defines curriculum as "a structured series of learning outcomes," views the teacher as an interpreter and implementer of goals that are planned at a higher level. Although teachers do not, under his definition, become involved in curriculum planning, they are permitted discretion in interpreting curriculum goals and in planning, executing, and evaluating instruction aimed at implementing them. This view of shared control is not unlike the philosophy behind many federally sponsored programs, where broad guidelines are issued to local communities with the understanding that they will be adapted to local conditions.

The narrowest view of the teacher's role is supplied by Romberg. He views the curriculum as a sophisticated plan complete with goals, methods, and activities. Under his definition, teachers are confined to managing a rather detailed, preplanned curriculum. They are permitted little discretion in interpreting goals or in planning instruction. Programmed curricula, many of which pursue a "teacher-proof" ideal, are obvious examples of this viewpoint.

Figure 5.1 summarizes the degree of teacher involvement in the curriculum process as viewed by Doll, Johnson, and Romberg. It can be assumed that all teachers are involved in the final step in the curriculum process, executing and evaluating instruction. What varies is their involvement in the two preceding steps, planning broad curriculum goals

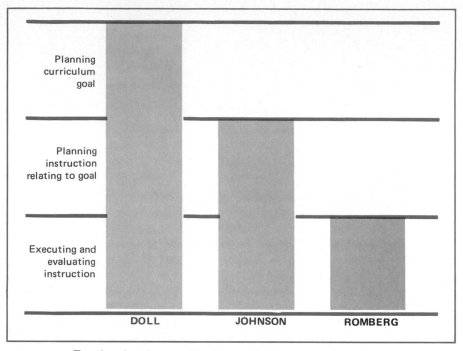

Figure 5.1. Teacher involvement in the curriculum process.

and planning instruction related to those goals. Whatever their planned involvement in the curriculum process, the actual impact of teachers on the curriculum is always considerable. We will examine the reasons for this in the following section.

Teachers and the Curriculum

The process of translating a curriculum plan into concrete learning experiences is the primary business of teachers. Inevitably, this transformation process is greatly influenced by the teacher's personality and abilities. For example, an elementary school teacher who likes mathematics is likely to emphasize mathematical topics, while a teacher with little interest or expertise in mathematics may treat the same topics very lightly. A common ploy used by many teachers, including the authors, to avoid teaching an uncomfortable topic is to schedule special events, such as outside visitors, field trips, or special films, to replace the undesirable topic.

In short, the success or lack of success of the curriculum, regardless of specificity, lies primarily in the hands of a classroom teacher. Louis Rubin suggests that a teacher's curriculum-translation role is the key to the effectiveness of any curriculum. If a teacher accurately interprets the goals of a curriculum and is sympathetic with those goals, the curriculum is likely to be even more effective than its planners anticipated.

Conversely, if a teacher misinterprets curriculum goals or is unsympathetic with them, it is unlikely that the goals will be achieved.[4]

Rubin investigated the power a teacher exerts in translating a curriculum into classroom practice. In this study Rubin and his associates provided teachers with an instructional unit dealing with World War II. The unit was complete with goals, objectives, suggested activities, and suggested sequence of instruction. Much more material was provided than the teachers could possibly complete in the time period set by Rubin and his associates. The teachers had to make choices about what to include, emphasize, or omit. Rubin was interested in determining whether teachers would emphasize facts or interpretations, or would strive for a combination of the two areas. His summarized findings follow:

> The cognitive elements (facts, principles, concepts, and the like) were given dominant emphasis by two-thirds of the teachers. Moreover, the degree of emphasis generally was extreme. In the tests they devised, for example, some teachers asked for as many as 30 to 40 dates, while others asked for none. Some teachers devoted a full week to the Nazi persecution of the Jews, whereas others ignored the matter completely. Of greater significance, however, we found in the end that there were almost as many different courses as there were teachers. Each, in effect, imbued the material with his own attitudes and values, using his classroom to act out his own motives and intentions.[5]

As you begin visiting schools and observing teachers in action, try using the content of the preceding two sections as a guide to your observation. Ask yourself the following:

- Does the curriculum role of the observed teacher conform most closely to the role advocated by Doll, Johnson, or Romberg? (See Figure 5.1)
- Does the teacher's unique personality and abilities tend to dominate the curriculum, as Rubin has suggested?

In the next section we will comment briefly on historical curriculum trends in American education before moving on to an analysis of the modern curriculum, its organization, and major trends.

Historical Curriculum Trends

As noted in Chapter 1, the culture of colonial America was closely tied to God and king. Most school curricula were, in fact, centered around religious and moral instruction. Bible reading was both the ends and means of formal school learning. Children were taught to read so that they might study the Bible and, thereby, live moral lives; their principle textbook was the Bible. In addition to developing literary skills through and for Bible reading, teachers were also expected to develop the moral character of their students by showing exemplary personal behavior at all times.

Aside from Bible-based moral education, there was little uniformity in school curriculums from one community to the next. Local needs and interests dictated the remainder of the curriculum. For example, there was more emphasis on mathematical and monetary skills in trading communities than in agrarian communities. Although curriculum goals during this period were theoretically determined by the local school council, the isolation and lack of supervision that characterized most schools gave real control of the curriculum to the classroom teacher.

Toward the end of the colonial era, political motives began replacing religious ones as the guiding force behind school curricula. Basic literacy skills still formed the core of most curricula, but the Jeffersonian vision of education for democracy rather than for salvation became increasingly dominant. Common schools, whose mission was to create a literate and well-informed citizenry across all levels of society, quickly spread across the country. Schools were increasingly seen as instruments of secular progress rather than personal salvation.

This secularization trend was intensified in the middle and latter part of the nineteenth century by the spread of the Industrial Revolution from Europe to America and by the mass immigrations that followed. Immigrants had to be transformed into skilled, "Americanized" workers. Thus, economic motives began to push aside religious and political motives in establishing curriculum goals. In addition to a continued emphasis on the "three R's," the industrial era saw the broadening of the curriculum to include vocational education, physical education, adult education, and a variety of community-oriented extracurricular activities. A complex, pluralistic culture demanded a broad, diversified curriculum.

At the same time that curricula were broadening and being divided for the sake of specialization into subject areas and grade levels, teacher qualification standards were sinking. The rapid spread of publicly supported common schools had greatly increased the demand for teachers at the very time that industrial opportunities were siphoning off many of the most qualified male teachers. The result was predictable. School administrators, influenced by the industrial philosophy of specialization and an awareness of teachers' declining competence, began pushing curriculum-development responsibilities to higher administrative levels. The teacher's role in the curriculum process began to shift from that advocated by Doll to that advocated by Romberg (see Figure 5.1). The idea of a "teacher-proof" curriculum had arrived.

Then came the progressive education era (1920s, 1930s, and 1940s) and the attempt to break away from the impersonal, efficiency-oriented industrial model of education that passed children, as products, through an assembly-line curriculum in which carefully sequenced units of knowledge were drilled one after another into their minds. The progressives, who viewed children as naturally active, inquisitive learners, called for a child-centered curriculum in which the teacher and child were invested with a considerable degree of control over what went on in the curriculum. Curriculum reform was now moving back in the direction of Doll's view.

The idea was to develop the total child, i.e., to see the child's social and emotional development as well as his or her more measurable intellectual development. Thus, personal and social development, crucial ingredients in a democratic society, took their place as legitimate curriculum goals alongside intellectual development. Teachers, once again, were given a prominent role in the first two stages of the curriculum process (see Figure 5.1).

Then, in fairly rapid succession, historically speaking, there occurred two events that once again swung the curriculum pendulum back in the direction of cognitive learning goals at the expense of social and emotional development. Both of these events, World War II and the Soviet launching of Sputnik I in 1957, were external threats to our society and, like all such events, produced a cry for technologists (not necessarily well-adjusted ones) who could defend us against aggression.

The decade following the launching of Sputnik can be characterized as the most intensive period of curriculum revision in our nation's history. Particularly in the skill-oriented subject areas, such as math and science, upon which our defense system rests, enormous sums of federal money were spent in an effort to develop more effective curricula. As might be expected, most of these new experimental curricula were developed at levels well above the classroom teacher, usually at the university level. In most cases they were extremely comprehensive and included a detailed statement of goals, methods, and even specific activities. The teacher's role in most instances was defined as the manager of a preset curriculum.

The intellectual focus in most of these new curricula was away from the teaching of existing factual knowledge and toward the teaching of problem-solving skills. Since problem solving depends upon mastering an intellectual process rather than a fixed body of knowledge, these new curricula came to be known as "process-oriented" curricula. Much of their emphasis was on the investigative processes through which relevant facts, principles, and theorems were discovered.

As students, many of you probably participated in these early "modern mathematics" and "process-oriented science" classes. These curriculum reforms were widely publicized, and most educators and parents had high expectations for their success. Disillusionment set in quickly, however, because of the great confusion and misunderstanding that accompanied the implementation of the new programs. The workshops, summer institutes, and community meetings that were organized to prepare teachers and parents for these new programs were often poorly planned and generally inadequate. Teachers felt unprepared to teach the new materials, and parents complained that they could not understand the work their children brought home from school. In short, there was a lack of grassroots preparation for these new programs, with the result that, before long, all sorts of unrelated school problems were being attributed to them.

The curricula found in today's schools often represent second- or third-generation descendants of the original programs introduced in the 1960s. Although most of the original programs were developed at the national level, many revisions have been the result of work done at the state and local levels. Consequently, the curriculum now being used in a given school is likely to represent an amalgamation of local and federally sponsored curricula.

Generally, the formal academic curricula currently found in most elementary and middle schools are organized into discrete subject areas (e.g., language arts, mathematics, science, social studies, art, music, etc.). In the elementary schools most subjects are taught by one teacher; the most notable exceptions are in the areas of art, music, and physical education. In the middle schools and high schools the various subjects are usually taught by specialists in the subject matter. There is great variety in the curriculum materials being used because of the many commercial curriculum packages offered by educational publishers, in addition to locally developed materials. The common element in all curriculum materials, however, seems to be the attempt to motivate students to learn.

The following section will provide a brief introduction to the structure of the formal academic curriculum found in most schools today.

The Formal Academic Curriculum

Whatever motives (religious, political, economic, etc.) have at different times guided curriculum development in our country, an ongoing concern of curriculum planners has been to transmit the basic ideas of the various academic disciplines. What follows is a brief survey of the current status of the formal academic curriculum in American schools.

MATHEMATICS

In most elementary and middle schools prior to 1960, the teaching of arithmetic focused almost exclusively on helping students sharpen their computational skills. The curriculum-reform movements of the 1960s deemphasized arithmetic skills in favor of theoretical concepts, such as set theory, that attempted to explain the "why" of mathematical operations. By enabling students to understand the logical processes behind mathematical calculations, curriculum revisionists hoped to broaden students' problem-solving abilities. Although the early programs virtually ignored computational skills, the pendulum of progress is swinging back, and both theory and practice are now emphasized in most mathematics programs. There are other changes coming that teachers of mathematics in the 1980s will need to address. One of the most difficult will be helping students through the transition to the metric system. Other changes will result from our rapidly increasing dependence upon hand-held calculators. Both of these changes will deemphasize the study of fractions and will increase the study of decimals.

SCIENCE

Prior to the curriculum-reform movement of the 1960s, science instruction was largely neglected in elementary schools. Those programs that did exist were usually textbook centered and emphasized learning the most practical, up-to-date scientific facts and principles. However, given the degree of change that characterizes our technological society, it is becoming increasingly difficult to predict either the problems that will confront us in the future or the knowledge base that will be available for application to those problems. In certain technical areas it has been estimated that the obsolescence factor for new knowledge is as high as 10 percent a year.

In view of this, science-education leaders began developing curricula that emphasized the basic skills of scientific inquiry, such as observing, classifying, using time-space relationships, using numbers, measuring, recording, and predicting. The purpose of such programs is to provide the student with general scientific skills that can be applied to the solution of any problem. Some of the most notable programs include the *Science Curriculum Improvement Study* (SCIS) materials; *Science: A Process Approach,* developed by the American Association for the Advancement of Science (AAAS); and the *Elementary Science Study* (ESS) materials.

As with current mathematical curricula, most science programs today appear to be a hybrid of the old knowledge-based programs and the newer process-oriented programs. It is felt that students must have a thorough grounding in the basic inquiry skills, but that it is unrealistic to expect them to rediscover through personal inquiry all the major scientific principles from which we currently operate. Finally, the science programs of many schools have expanded in recent years to include a variety of new topics such as ecology and the environment.

SOCIAL STUDIES

Social studies refers to that part of the curriculum that deals specifically with human beings, with their geographical and cultural environment, their social relationships, their values and achievements, and their ability to make rational decisions. Social studies should not be thought of as a distinct discipline built upon its own unique concepts and methods of inquiry. Rather, it should be thought of as an amalgamation of several disciplines (history, political science, economics, sociology, and anthropology) all tied together by the common focus: human beings. Each of these disciplines does have its own unique concepts and methods of inquiry, but, like a camera, each one has a limited angle of vision that analyzes certain aspects of the human condition better than others. In order to develop a comprehensive understanding of some social problem it is necessary to integrate the views of all these disciplines. This, of course, is what the "new" social studies of the 1960s attempted to do. To promote integration of the various disciplines, the National Council for Social Studies advocates the study of "enduring and pervasive social issues," such as the distribution of foods, reduction of poverty, and proper land use.[6]

Consistent with this issue- or problem-centered orientation, most of the curriculum revisionists of the 1960s also advocated a shift away from a fact-oriented curriculum and toward a process-oriented one. As with mathematics and science, many of the revised social studies curricula seek to implant in the student a set of basic inquiry skills that can be applied to the solution of any social problem, current or future.

Not all of these new curricula were integrative, however; some used only a single discipline such as anthropology or geography as their investigative base. To date some 50 new social studies curricula have appeared since 1960, making it difficult for any one of them to gain a foothold equivalent to some of the major new programs in mathematics and science. Despite this diversity, however, it does appear that the general trend in social studies, at least at the elementary and middle school levels, is toward curricula that are integrative, issue- or problem-centered, and inquiry-oriented.

LANGUAGE ARTS

Throughout the elementary and middle school years, language arts receive greater emphasis than any other curriculum area. This is not surprising since language arts instruction encompasses all the fundamental communication skills: reading, writing, speaking, and listening. Their prominence is based upon the realization that communication skills are the basis of most human learning and, consequently, lie at the heart of the human condition. Young animals learn mainly by observation and imitation of older animals, but, as we have seen, most human learning is conducted through verbal interaction in the home, school, and neighborhood. In fact, researchers have discovered a strong correlation between the amount of verbal interaction between infants and parents, particularly the mother, and the child's IQ and school success.

As with other curriculum areas, there have been numerous attempts to revise the language arts curriculum, particularly at the secondary level, but none seems to have had widespread acceptance. Several of these new programs have featured an increased emphasis on the oral aspects of language instruction, that is, speaking and listening. Several others have sought to introduce greater flexibility into the study of grammar by looking at language usage in terms of its communication "effectiveness" rather than by some fixed standard that had arbitrarily been designated as "proper."

Even though curriculum revisionists in the language arts have been less successful than their counterparts in mathematics and science, their work has had the effect of steadily broadening the scope of their field. Skill in listening, once considered a frill, is now considered to be a major component of the language arts curriculum. Writing skills range from letter writing to creative writing, and creative dramatics is receiving renewed

emphasis. Reading instruction, always a major curriculum goal, has been given both legislative and financial boosts at all levels of schooling by state and federal governments. In fact, some states consider reading skills to be of such overriding importance that they have designated it a separate subject area and, in some instances, have installed competency tests to insure that students acquire certain minimum levels of reading skill.

FOREIGN LANGUAGE

America's geographical isolation and economic self-sufficiency have combined throughout most of its history to give foreign-language instruction a relatively low priority in terms of school curriculum. However, World War II not only created a need for people who could speak a foreign language with fluency, it also led to some radical changes in the methods of foreign-language instruction.

Prior to World War II foreign-language instruction traditionally emphasized learning to read and write the target language and included extensive study of grammatical structure. Military needs, however, ran in the direction of verbal interaction skills and, consequently, military language schools developed what came to be known as the "audiolingual" approach to language instruction. In effect, it reversed the traditional emphasis and sequence of language instruction.

Under this new method, students first received practice in listening to and speaking the language and then were gradually introduced into the reading and writing aspects. Repetitious verbal drills and short dialogues were staple features of this approach. Pure audiolingual schools often

employed a "direct" language-learning technique in which little or no English was spoken. The idea was to simulate, as closely as possible, the natural language-learning environment in which a child first learns its native tongue.

It soon became evident, however, that the isolation a military language school could impose on its students could not be duplicated in public schools. English continued to be the dominant language 24 hours a day and, consequently, the audiolingual approach met with only limited success in school curricula. Today most foreign-language programs seem to employ an eclectic approach, one which borrows elements from both the traditional and the audiolingual approaches. Students are generally introduced to all four modes of communication (listening, speaking, reading, and writing) rather quickly and are given ongoing practice in them all. Although some English translation may be permitted, it is usually far less than the amount that characterized traditional programs. Finally, a good deal of verbal drill and dialogue is usually present in most language programs.

THE ARTS

The position of the arts (music, art, dance, and drama) in the curriculum of most schools can only be described as tenuous. Since the primary goal of schools is to insure the transmission of survival-related knowledge and skills, those cultural products like music and art, that have more to do with the enrichment than the protection of life, get relegated to a secondary status in school curriculums. In times of relative peace and prosperity, they tend to appear and flourish, but when war or economic troubles threaten, they tend to be pushed aside in favor of more "essential" curricula. This emphasizes the importance that all classroom teachers, especially elementary and middle school teachers, understand how to incorporate the arts into ongoing classroom activities.

Beyond the Academic Curriculum

If you were asked to list the most meaningful learning experiences that you underwent during your school career, what would that list look like? The chances are it would be heavily weighted toward those school-related experiences that occurred outside the classroom: sports competition, social relationships with peers and teachers, and social events, such as school dances or theatrical productions. The memory of these events probably still produces strong feelings of exhilaration, embarrassment, or anger, and undoubtedly influences the way you presently react in certain situations.

It is ironic that so much of our *meaningful* school learning occurs outside the classroom. As we have seen, some of these out-of-class learnings are deliberately planned by schools; we call them the "extra curriculum." Others are simply the inevitable by-product of school life, incidental learnings that sometimes do more to shape our lives than all of a school's deliberately planned experiences; we call them the "hidden curriculum." In the next two sections we take a quick look at each of these two powerful but often ignored aspects of school curriculum.

THE EXTRA CURRICULUM

The extra curriculum resembles the academic curriculum in two respects; otherwise, there is no similarity between them. First, both are planned. Second, the content of the extra curriculum often parallels the subject-matter division of the academic curriculum; for example:

- *Language arts:* creative writing, dramatic and debate clubs
- *Science:* science, science fiction, and ecology groups
- *Social studies:* current-affairs discussion groups, student government
- *Foreign language:* cultural study groups
- *The arts:* music, dance, and art groups
- *Physical education:* athletic teams, intramural sports, physical fitness

Of course, the extra curriculum contains many other activities that have no parallel in the academic curriculum, such as automobile mechanics, magic, yoga, or photography groups.

It is through its contrasts with the academic curriculum, however, that the extra curriculum is best described. Most important is the fact that attendance is entirely voluntary. Since they can "vote with their feet," students who participate in the extra curriculum ultimately have control over its content. This tendency toward grassroots control has prompted some to refer to the extra curriculum as the student's curriculum. This, of course, is in sharp contrast to the academic curriculum where course attendance is normally compulsory and course content is usually preset and resistant to change.

Two other contrasting features that stem from the voluntary aspect of

the extra curriculum are its nonthreatening, test-free atmosphere and its close link to the life of the surrounding community. Although extra-curricular activities are often competitive (e.g., sports and debating), the fact that competition is voluntary gives it a positive rather than a negative flavor. Also, far more than the passive, subject-oriented academic curriculum, the extra curriculum is active and centered around common community interests; this gives it an integration with community life much like that sought by proponents of progressive education (see Chapter 1).

Whatever its theoretical justification, there can be little doubt that the extra curriculum represents an important and positive source of learning experiences for students and teachers alike. In the next section we will look briefly at the last but certainly not the least important category of school learning experience, the hidden curriculum.

THE HIDDEN CURRICULUM

Thus far we have focused on the planned or targeted aspects of school learning, the formal academic curriculum and its support system, the extra curriculum. However, no matter how broadly the curriculum is defined or how comprehensively it is written, it will include only a fraction of what a child actually learns during the total school experience. In school children learn a great deal about themselves and about how to interact with their environment. Some learn that they are bright or athletic or popular, while others learn that they are slow or awkward or unpopular. They also learn how to wait, how to escape unwanted attention, and how to circumvent distasteful rules. Such aspects of school learning are so pervasive and ongoing a part of school life that they often have been totally ignored.

The hidden curriculum, as we have already noted, refers to such unplanned learning experiences that children have as a natural byproduct of their interaction with peers, teachers, and school ritual. Although not told to do so, children do, in fact, learn these things as they more or less successfully adapt to school life. In their book *Sexism in School and Society,* Nancy Frazier and Myra Sadker give some specific examples of situations which comprise the hidden curriculum:

1. From 8:30 to 9:15, the class studies English; from 9:15 to 10:00, science; from 10:00 to 10:45, social studies. . . . As a student in this class, you may learn that English has nothing to do with science, neither one has anything to do with social studies; and play time is totally unrelated to all three. Moreover, you may learn that all children learn the same thing at the same time and it takes forty-five minutes to do this learning.
2. In your class texts, there is only one picture of a black person. It is of a porter lugging baggage in a railway station. As a student in this class you may learn that black people do not fill many important roles in society.
3. Whenever your class elects officers, you are never nominated. When the teacher assigns work to be done by partners, it seems that nobody wants to work with you. When teams are chosen on the playground at recess, you are often the last one to be selected. In these situations you may learn that you are not a very likeable or worthwhile person.
4. In your class, the teacher gets very angry and yells at students when they don't know the right answer. You may learn that being unaware of knowledge is equivalent to being bad or naughty. You may also learn that being wrong is frightening and humiliating and that learning can be a pretty miserable affair.[7]

Among the most crucial topics that are generally found within the hidden curriculum are the following.

Sex Roles

For decades schools have been subtly programming children into stereotyped sex roles. Teachers, like parents, have admonished children to "act ladylike" or to "act like a man." Girls have been permitted to cry in school whereas boys have been discouraged from doing so. Boys have been urged into athletic competition and girls into cheerleading. Textbooks have depicted girls as gentle, passive homemakers and boys as worldly adventurers. Girls have been tracked into English and home economics and boys into science and shop.

In recent years the women's rights movement, acting through the courts and Congress, has begun to change this situation, but much still remains to be done. On a more personal plane, much change can be effected if teachers are willing to drag the issue of sexual equality out of the closet and into the light of the formal academic curriculum. Perhaps even more important, they must themselves demonstrate sexual neutrality when discussing various social roles.

Racial Bias

Although most teachers would be offended by the suggestion that they permitted "white supremacy" to enter the curriculum of their classroom, the fact is that most teachers come from middle class, white backgrounds and consequently draw most heavily from that part of our culture in their teaching. Ethnocentrism, the unconscious attachment to one's own values, attitudes, and beliefs, is a natural human tendency that must be consciously contained by teachers in a pluralistic society. By ignoring the culture and contributions of black, brown, red, and yellow Americans, the image of these groups and the self-esteem of their children can be unintentionally impaired. Conversely, by devoting a proportionate share of the formal academic curriculum to the study of the various subcultures in America, teachers can help minimize the destructive effect of hidden bias.

Rewards and Punishments

Every culture has its own system of rewards and punishments through which it seeks to guide behavior in desired directions. In schools both the type of reward and punishment used and the way in which they are used have a considerable impact on children's moral development. For example, by punishing tardy or sloppy work or by rewarding behaviors such as silence or walking in single file from one place to another, students are taught the value of such things as silence, punctuality, and conformity. Furthermore, the things used to reward or punish students (material objects, praise or blame, free time or its withdrawal, etc.) come to acquire a value consistent with their use.

In a pluralistic culture where it is increasingly difficult to overtly teach moral values through traditional channels such as daily Bible reading or the Pledge of Allegiance, the system of rewards and punishments used by teachers may become even more important in shaping the values of students. It is important, therefore, that teachers monitor their personal system of rewards and punishments in terms of the values that are communicated, a task easier said than done.

Competition

There seems to be an unending debate about the desirability of fostering a competitive atmosphere within our schools. Reformists point out the harmful consequences of a competitive grading system where only a few students, usually those from privileged backgrounds, have much chance of being labelled successful. Whatever evidence these reformists might muster in favor of reducing school competition, there is little likelihood that their efforts will succeed as long as schools continue to reflect the larger society.

The fact is that American society is pervaded through and through with a competitive spirit. Both our economic and legal systems are based on competition, among firms in one case and lawyers in the other. Even our leisure culture is dominated by competitive sports. In short, students and teachers each bring with them a well-developed sense of competition into the school, and there it is further sharpened by the use of competitive grading practices. Those who excel relative to group norms are rewarded, and those who fail are punished and drop out.

As with other aspects of the hidden curriculum, the teacher's role is to recognize the existence of these unintended learning experiences and, wherever possible, to control their direction. In effect, this amounts to removing them from hiding so that they can be consciously directed. To the really alert teacher there is no such thing as the hidden curriculum.

Current Curriculum Issues

Having contrasted several definitions of curriculum, reviewed historical curriculum trends, and taken a look at current curriculum structure, we will devote the remainder of the chapter to an examination of two contemporary issues in American school curriculum. Although our list is by no means exhaustive, these issues are among the most important and controversial of those currently being debated. The first of these, curriculum accountability, is perhaps the most widely publicized of all.

CURRICULUM ACCOUNTABILITY

How many times have you heard the following: "mastering the basics," "coping skills," "adult literacy," "survival skills," and "competency-based education"? If any of these are familiar, the chances are that you have been hearing about "back to basics."

This particular curriculum reform movement was initiated in the mid-1970s as a result of the public's disenchantment with the performance of our schools. Newspaper accounts of dropping Scholastic Aptitude Tests (SAT) scores among college freshmen, Office of Education studies reporting that more than 23 million Americans cannot perform so basic a task as reading a menu, and university research reports stating that one out of five American adults could not pass a minimum basic skills test—these provided fuel for the public disenchantment. Gallup Poll surveys conducted each year since 1974 have shown an increasing disapproval of public-school practices. In some cases parents of students who have received high school diplomas despite the fact that they cannot read at the sixth-grade level have sued the schools for negligence and fraud. As a result of such publicity and the resulting public pressure, many state legislatures, state boards of education, and local school boards responded by mandating minimum performance standards that must be demonstrated by students before they are allowed to graduate.

Defining the Basics

At this point you may well be wondering exactly what is meant by "back to basics." In a recent Gallup Poll, members of a randomly selected group were asked whether they had heard of "back to basics," and if so, to describe what it meant. More than 50 percent of those interviewed had not heard of the term. Those who had heard of the movement overwhelmingly endorsed the concept. Follow-up questions revealed, however, that "back to basics" can mean many different things.

To most people, "back to basics" means that the curriculum should focus upon factual knowledge. "The schools today should teach the basic facts that I had to learn in school" is a commonly heard statement. These people believe school programs should stress such things at the memorization of addition and multiplication tables in mathematics, the memorization of lists in reading, and the memorization of the 50 states and capitals—spelled correctly, of course—in social studies. The primary instructional strategies would be memorization and drill.

Others interpret the phrase "back to basics" as meaning codes of acceptable student behavior. These people feel that schools, primarily in response to recent court decisions, have become too lenient and permissive. They envision the ideal school as one in which all students are orderly, well dressed, and neatly groomed. Respect for teachers and other adults, good manners, politeness, and obedience would be the primary curriculum goals. Many people who fall into this category also believe that "frills," such as movable desks, carpeting, and air conditioning, are a waste of the taxpayers' money.

A third interpretation of the phrase "back to basics" involves emphasis on basic skills. This means that schools should be the place where children learn those skills, particularly in mathematics and reading, that provide the foundation for daily living. According to these people, the curriculum should focus upon skills such as handling a checking account and completing a job application form. It is this interpretation that has been used by most states and school districts that have legislated minimal performance standards for high school graduates.

Clearly, the public is stressing the need for quality instruction in the areas of mathematics, reading, and writing. They want to be informed about existing standards and about the effectiveness of the schools in meeting those standards. In short, they want schools and teachers to be acountable for what children have or have not learned. Such public concern is not new, nor is it necessarily unhealthy, since the schools were designed to reflect community concern and interest.

The Greensville Program

CURRICULUM ACCOUNTABILITY IN ACTION*

Countless school districts throughout the United States have to some degree moved "back to basics." The approaches used have been nearly as numerous as the school systems using them, so it is impossible to analyze them all. Instead, we will look at one school district whose approach seems to be working well.[9]

When students in the Greensville County, Virginia, school system took the Science Research Associates Achievement Tests in 1973, they ranked only in the thirtieth percentile when compared to national norms. Alarmed educators within the system felt that the time for action had come: They needed to develop a new program that would assure improved performance on such measures of achievement.

For years the Greensville County Schools had used the practice of social promotions, and evaluation procedures had varied widely depending upon the individual teacher's own theories. No general achievement criteria were required for promotion. Under their revised curriculum, basic skills in all subject areas became the target of instruction. Extensive testing was done to determine each student's present level of achievement relative to those skills, and students who were achieving below grade level were retained, but not demoted, until they had caught up. Intensive instructional programs were designed to benefit these slower students, and no one was permitted to graduate until he or she had demonstrated a twelfth-grade mastery of the basic skills. At the end of the first year of the new program, 800 of the school system's 3750 students were retained.

Efforts were also undertaken to make grading and evaluation more consistent. Teachers were responsible for evaluating student performance through various means, e.g., standardized tests, teacher-made tests, teacher observations, reports, recitations, and so forth. Grades now specifically reflected the student's mastery of basic skills. Principals were made responsible for directing evaluation practices in the schools in order to encourage consistency.

In the Greensville County program students who had been retained were grouped with others of their own age and placed in classrooms where the program was designed to meet their special needs. Partial promotions were given to students who mastered only part of the required skills at a given grade level.

At the secondary level, "01" courses were offered for college students, while "02" courses were available for those who were slower and/or had academic deficiencies. It is important to note, however, that students were permitted to take various combinations of "01" and "02" courses. An Occupational Training Program (OTP) was also available for students who were behind by two or more grade levels. Students who completed the OTP program received a certificate of occupational proficiency in their specific fields, and those who also met the general academic requirements were able to earn a general diploma.

Educators in Greensville County are pleased with the results of their new program. The number of retentions has been steadily dropping, standardized test scores have risen dramatically, and the dropout rate is declining. They also cite increased satisfaction among students, teachers, and parents as evidence that their goals are being met.

*Information for this section has been based on Samuel A. Owen and Deborah L. Ranick, "The Greensville Program: A Commonsense Approach to Basics," *Phi Delta Kappan* 58 (March 1977): 531–33.

Goals of the Curriculum-Accountability Movement

The overall goals of those stressing curriculum accountability are (1) to require school districts to state their curriculum standards explicitly in order that their programs and teachers may be evaluated against those standards and (2) to focus the curriculum more around basic reading, writing, and mathematical skills. The following school practices have all risen to prominence in support of the accountability philosophy.

Competencies. Minimum performance standards would be specified for basic literacy skills. In addition to completing academic course requirements, the student would be required to demonstrate specified levels of competency in these targeted skill areas in order to graduate. To date, this has been the most successful aspect of the curriculum-accountability movement. At present, several states and many individual school districts have adopted minimum competency standards at both the elementary and secondary school levels.

Criterion-Referenced Testing Programs. The concept of minimum competency standards implies the need for tests that will measure exactly what each student does and does not know relative to these standards. Criterion-referenced tests, as they are called, measure student performance in relation to a prescribed set of learning objectives. In contrast, standardized tests indicate where a student, school, or school district stands in respect to the average score of some representative group that has taken the test. While standardized tests are useful for measuring where a student stands in terms of "average" or "below-average" scores, criterion-referenced tests identify specifically what a student does or does not know in relation to some fixed objective.

Abolish Social Promotions. One of the most drastic goals of the "back-to-basics" movement has been the attempt to replace social promotions with achievement-based promotions. During the past 20 years, educators have been retaining or "failing" fewer and fewer students because they believed that such retentions stigmatized the student as "dumb" or "slow" and thereby impeded further development. By keeping all students of similar chronological ages together regardless of their academic performance, differences in academic achievement could be addressed at each grade level without stigmatizing the student. For example, it is not uncommon for a fifth-grade teacher to have students with ability levels ranging from three grade levels below fifth grade to three grade levels above.

In contrast to this view, back-to-basics advocates believe that social promotion encourages poor performance on the part of both students and teachers. Achievement-based promotions would require that students achieve satisfactory levels of competence before being assigned to a higher grade level. Students who did not demonstrate mastery would be retained until they were able to catch up. Promotion under such a system, they argue, would restore meaning and value to the concept of promotion.

Accountability in Salary Schedules. Many back-to-basics advocates would like to replace the standardized salary schedules of schools with a merit system. Under a merit system all school personnel (teachers, administrators, custodians, etc.) would be evaluated on the basis of student achievement gains. This would, in effect, make every employee accountable for what happens in the schools. The specifics of this goal have been outlined by James Wellington:

1. Establish educational goals and measurements and hold all school district employees accountable for meeting these goals.
2. Extend accountability beyond teachers. It should also include principals, superintendents, and everyone whose income is paid by taxes for the purpose of providing quality education.
3. Establish merit pay for all school district employees, especially teachers and administrators. This emphasizes the need for setting standards. Without them, how can you determine whether you are receiving effective teaching and administration? Poor teachers and administrators now are paid the same as good teachers and administrators.[8]

Curriculum Accountability: Problems and Concerns

According to an old saying, there are two or more sides to every story, and the curriculum-accountability, or back-to-basics, movement is no exception. Many educators who agree with the general goals of this movement suggest nonetheless that communities should understand that increasing the emphasis on certain targeted skills means cutting back or eliminating certain other programs. In short, the public must be made to understand that they are playing the game of "tradeoff": more of "X" means less of "Y."

Another concern centers around those children who are simply not capable of meeting the minimum competencies. Critics of the back-to-basics movement feel that the entire movement is based upon the performance of the weakest 15 to 20 percent of the student population. These critics believe that the time spent bringing these low achievers up to standards will detract from the educational experience of the majority of students who can master the competencies without special programs. To alleviate this problem, critics emphasize that multiple standards should be set, based on the ability of students.

The greatest outcry from critics of the back-to-basics movement, however, has centered around the return to academic promotions and the retentions that will result from such a practice. Gordon Cawelti summarizes the viewpoint of the critics regarding this issue:

> Those educators who retain pupils in a grade do so without valid research evidence to indicate such treatment will provide greater benefits to students with academic or adjustment difficulties than will promotion to the next grade. Thus, although the assumption is that retention will increase motivation for academic work, this does not bear up under close scrutiny. . . . The studies of nonpromotion show that it does not have a positive effect on achievement and it often has harmful consequences from the social standpoint.[9]

CAREER EDUCATION

As knowledge becomes obsolete at an ever faster rate in our technological society, so do the occupations that are based upon this knowledge and the curriculums designed to serve those occupations. When school curricula fail to keep pace with changes in the world of work, the charge of "curriculum irrelevance" inevitably follows. This was the case in the late 1960s when many persons began to criticize the schools for failing to adapt the traditional academic curriculum to the occupational needs of our society. One result of this criticism has been the movement known as "career education," which, by 1974, had spread, in one form or another, to some 5000 school districts in this country.

Defining Career Education

Career education is best thought of as a theme that pervades all areas and levels of the curriculum in an attempt to orient it to the world of work. Beginning in the primary grades and continuing throughout the entire school experience, career education seeks to provide students successively with:

1. A positive attitude toward work and toward oneself as a potentially productive worker;
2. A realistic knowledge of current and future work options and how to prepare for them;

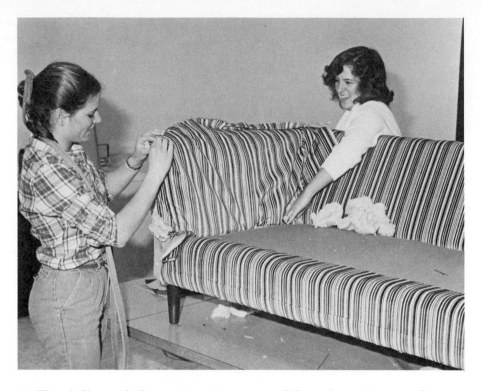

3. The skills needed to enter one or more of these occupations or the professional programs that lead into them.

To achieve these goals requires ongoing coordination among teachers at all grade levels and among parents and community leaders. In short, career education is an effort to create continuity between the school curriculum and the demands of community life, just as John Dewey recommended.

Structuring Career Education

The three goals of career education just listed correspond roughly to the three organizational levels found in most American school systems. At the elementary school level, career education focuses primarily on creating a positive attitude toward work and toward oneself as a potentially productive worker. At this level, the child's perspective is limited to home and school experiences, so any attempt to deal realistically with the career world of work would be futile. Work at this level is usually defined as accepting responsibility for completing a specified task. By stressing and rewarding task completion, the dignity of a good effort, and pride of accomplishment, the value of work and productivity are implanted in the child along with a sense of achievement motivation and self-worth.

As students approach the middle school level, the focus of career education begins to shift toward the second goal, that is, toward career orientation. At this level, the student's experience is broad enough to begin dealing realistically with a wide range of potential occupations. Job and worker characteristics, educational and training requirements, the relevance of academic subjects to various occupations, and self-evaluation in terms of interests and abilities are all touched upon. The purpose at this point is not to determine career choices or even preferences, but merely to help students learn the steps to be taken when they are ready to make career decisions.

At the secondary school level, the final goal, that of specific training, comes into focus. Whatever the student's aspirations, whether it be immediate employment (as a result of dropping out or graduation) or continuing education toward some professional career, it should be supported at this level by the acquisition of specific vocational and educational skills.

Summary   There are a variety of ways in which the term *curriculum* can be defined. These range from very broad definitions that include everything that occurs in connection with school activities to narrow definitions that include only the specified goals of the educational process and the activities planned to achieve those goals. This variation in perception regarding curriculum leads in turn to differences in teachers' roles and expectations.

The formal academic curriculum used in most schools in the United States includes mathematics, science, social studies, language arts, foreign language, and the arts. In addition to this, most school programs include a wide range of extracurricular activities including, for example, photography, theater, athletics, and science clubs. Also inherent in every educational program is the hidden curriculum, which encompasses a variety of subtle socialization processes and through which discriminatory stereotypes are frequently perpetuated.

The final section of this chapter dealt with two current curriculum issues: curriculum accountability and career education. The curriculum accountability movement, which began in the mid-1970s, stems primarily from public disenchantment with the schools. The result has been a variety of "back-to-basics" programs and the implementation of a great deal of minimum competency testing. Career education programs have resulted from the feeling that school curricula are often irrelevant — a feeling that began with the student activism of the late 1960s. Both movements have added a new dimension to curriculum planning and have distinctly altered the course of American education.

Encounters

1. In this chapter we have presented differing definitions of a school curriculum. We would like to have you form your own definition for curriculum. Form a committee of three or more persons and do the following:
   a. Form a working definition of curriculum.
   b. Describe the teacher's role that is implied in your ideal curriculum for planning, teaching, and evaluating student activities.
   c. Compare and contrast the teacher's role in *b* with the way you remember your teachers' roles in elementary and secondary schools.
2. Your university or college library has sets of textbooks that are commonly used in schools. Select two sets in an academic area (mathematics, reading, science, social studies, etc.). One set should be contemporary (a copyright date not more than two or three years old) and the other set should be at least ten years old. List five similarities found in the old and new texts and five differences.
3. In a group, identify the two most meaningful learning experiences that you encountered in school. Classify each experience as part of the (a) formal curriculum, (b) extracurriculum, or (c) hidden curriculum.
4. Interview five students (any age level) and determine what they consider as the most meaningful learning experiences they have had in school. Classify them as part of the (a) formal curriculum, (b) extracurriculum, or (c) hidden curriculum.
5. Identify strategies that you as a teacher can use to transfer the most meaningful learning experiences that you and students you interviewed had to use with students that you might have in the classroom.
6. Through research concerning television and newspaper coverage of educational issues, identify the most prevalent curriculum issues of today.
7. Describe what you believe to be the impact of these issues on the classroom teacher.
8. Review a curriculum guide from a local school district and list all programs that are included in the school curriculum. Many schools have been criticized for suffering from "curriculum obesity." This means that there are so many extra curriculum topics that teachers cannot adequately teach the basics. Does the school curriculum you reviewed suffer from curriculum obesity? If so, what would you as the classroom teacher do about it?

Notes

1. Ronald C. Doll, *Curriculum Improvement: Decision-making and Process* (Boston: Allyn and Bacon, 1964), pp. 15–18.
2. See Mauritz Johnson, "Definitions and Models in Curriculum Theory," *Educational Theory* 17 (April 1967): 127–40; *idem,* "The Translation of Curriculum into Instruction," *Journal of Curriculum Studies, 1* (1969), 113–31; *idem,* "Appropriate Research Directions in Curriculum and Instruction," *Curriculum Theory Network* (Winter 1970–71), 24–37.
3. Thomas A. Romberg, "Curriculum, Development, and Research," in the *Thirty-third Yearbook of the National Council of Teachers of Mathematics* (Washington, D.C.: National Council of Teachers of Mathematics, 1970), p. 57.

4. Louis J. Rubin, *Curriculum Development: A Study Guide for Educational Administrators* (Ft. Lauderdale, Fl.: Nova University, 1972).

5. *Ibid.,* p. 110.

6. James A. Banks with Ambrose A. Clegg, Jr., *Teaching Strategies for the Social Studies: Inquiry, Valuing, and Decision-Making,* 2nd ed. (Reading, Mass.: Addison-Wesley, 1977).

7. Nancy Frazier and Myra Sadker, *Sexism in School and Society* (New York: Harper & Row, 1973), p. 81.

8. James K. Wellington, "American Education: Its Failure and Its Future," *Phi Delta Kappan 58* (March 1977), 529.

9. Gordon Cawelti, "Requiring Competencies for Graduation—Some Curricular Issues," *Educational Leadership, 35* (November 1977), 90.

For More Information

JOURNALS

Allan, John A. B. "Training in Caring: A Practical Program for Sixth and Seventh Graders with Pre-Schoolers," *Canadian Counsellor, 14* (1980), 146–150.

Dunn, Rita, and Dunn, Kenneth. "Educational Accountability in Our Schools," *Momentum, 59* (1977), 10–16.

Garner, Arthur E., and Acklen, Leila M. "Involving Students in Curriculum Planning," *Clearing House, 53* (1979), 36–39.

Gross, Richard E., and Dynneson, Thomas L. "Regenerating the Social Studies: From Old Dirges to New Directions," *Social Education, 44* (1980), 370–374.

Helm, Estelle Bailey. "Developing a Curriculum to Enhance Self-Concept," *Tennessee Education, 10* (1980), 10–18.

Mussio, J. J. "The School Curriculum: A National Cancer?" *Education Canada, 20* (1980), 11–15.

Ornstein, Allen C., and Talmage, Harriet. "The Rhetoric and the Realties of Accountability, *Today's Education, 62* (1973), 70–80.

Saunders, Malcolm. "The School Curriculum for Ethnic Minority Pupils: A Contribution to a Debate," *International Review of Education, 26* (1980), 31–47.

Simmons, Daniel I. "Beware! The Three R's Cometh," *Phi Delta Kappan, 54* (1973), 492–495.

Storey, John. "'Dick Does' and 'Jane Watches': Sex-role Stereotyping in the Curriculum," *Interchange on Educational Policy, 10* (1979–80), 15–19.

Sullivan, Paul J., and Sullivan, Mary Dockstader. "Establishing Moral Education Programs: A Priority for Guidance," *Personnel and Guidance Journal, 58* (1980). 622–626.

Wagschal, Harry. "Towards a New Pedagogy for the Humanities and Social Sciences," *Roeper Review, 2* (1980), 7–9.

Wees, W. R. "Values in the Curriculum," *Education Canada, 20* (1980), 23–27.

Woal, S. Theodore. "Room to Grow: Educating for a Total Life Experience," *Journal of Career Education, 6* (1980), 217–224.

Wood, Leslie A. "Expanding Global Education," *Viewpoints in Teaching and Learning, 55* (1979), 11–26.

Yates, Daniel S. "Beyond Computational Skills," *Curriculum Review, 18* (1979), 417–421.

BOOKS

Bank, James, et al. *Curriculum Guidelines for Multiethnic Education.* Arlington, Va.: National Council for the Social Studies, 1976.

Borton, Terry. *Reach, Touch, and Teach.* New York: McGraw-Hill, 1970.

Combs, Arthur W. *Educational Accountability: Beyond Behavioral Objectives.* Washington, D.C.: Association for Supervision and Curriculum Development, 1972.

Davis, O. L. *Perspectives on Curriculum Development, 1776-1976.* Washington, D.C.: Association for Supervision and Curriculum Development, 1976.

Dyer, Henry. *How to Achieve Accountability in the Public Schools.* Bloomington, Ind.: Phi Delta Kappa Educational Foundation, 1973.

Eisner, Elliot W., ed. *Confronting Curriculum Reform.* Boston: Little, Brown, 1971.

Eisner, Elliot, and Vallance, Elizabeth, eds. *Conflicting Conceptions of Curriculum.* Chicago: The National Society for the Study of Education, 1974.

McNeil, John D. *Curriculum: A Comprehensive Introduction.* Boston: Little, Brown, 1977.

Oliver, Albert. *Curriculum Improvement.* 2nd ed. New York: Harper & Row, 1977.

Peddiwell, J. Abner. (Harold Benjamin) *The Saber-Toothed Curriculum.* New York: McGraw-Hill, 1939.

Steeves, Frank L., and English, Fenwick W. *Secondary Curriculum for a Changing World.* Columbus: Charles E. Merrill, 1978.

Tanner, Daniel, and Tanner, Laurel. *Curriculum Development: Theory into Practice.* New York: MacMillan, 1975.

Zais, Robert. *Curriculum: Principles and Foundations.* New York: Crowell, 1976.

MOVIES

The A, B, C's of Behavioral Education (Hallmark, 20 min., 1969). The behavior modification program for problem students uses positive reinforcement and individualized instruction to reach obtainable goals within the curriculum design.

Choosing to Learn (EDC, 26 min., 1970). Children of varying backgrounds are free to choose what and when they will learn. These children are involved in many of the decision-making processes.

The Individualized Education Program (Instructional Media Services, 22 min., 1977). In accordance with Public Law 94–142, all handicapped children receiving educational services must be given an I.E.P. This film shows the development of an I.E.P. from the multifactored assessment to the placement. Stress is placed on the importance of parental involvement for the child's supportive needs.

Open Classroom (Sherwin Rubin, 13 min., 1971). This open classroom situation shows children designing their own learning environments. Parents, community members, and older student volunteers are present in the room to provide additional resources. This film takes place in an actual classroom in California.

Summerhill (National Film Board of Canada, 28 min., 1967). The students at this experimental school in England are self-disciplining and are not required to attend classes. The school is looked at as a preparation for a life of learning.

Teach Me How I Can Do It Myself (IFB, 29 min., 1973). This film demonstrates the Montessori method of elementary education. Emphasis is placed on orderliness within a structured environment.

Chapter 6

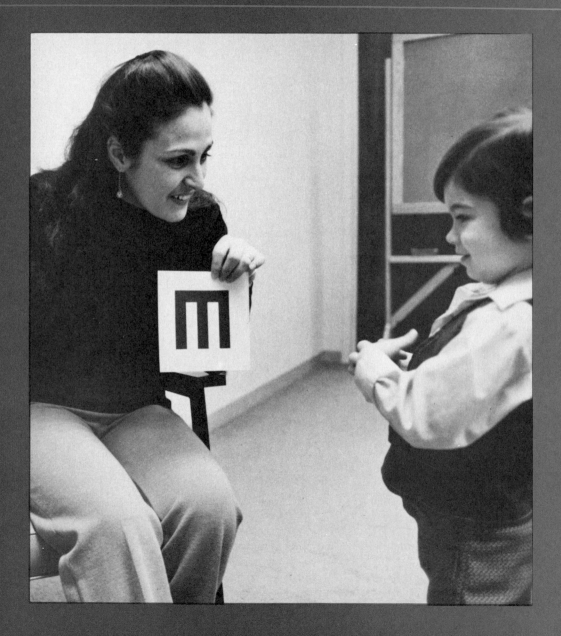

Chapter 6

THE TEACHER, THE EXCEPTIONAL STUDENT, AND THE MAINSTREAMING MOVEMENT

"Take the child where he is."

"Teach the whole child."

"Value the individual differences of children."

"Meet the individual needs of every child."

Those were the maxims with which a previous generation of teachers entered the profession. Who can argue with them? Of course they are truisms of good teaching, at any time and in any school. The problem was not that they were wrong, but that those principles were difficult to translate into practice. What do they mean, and how does one actually center one's teaching around the individual and his or her unique needs?

That same generation of teachers-in-preparation also learned that "normal" six-year-olds had certain developmental characteristics, as did sevens, eights, nines, and so on through the years of middle childhood and early, middle, and late adolescence. One was supposed to become aware of and to understand the characteristics of the age group one was preparing to teach: the way they think, the things they worry about, the incentives that motivate them.

---

* Philip L. Safford was the primary author of this chapter. Dr. Safford is chairman of the Special Education Department at Kent State University.

Whether teachers ever really internalized this normative developmental perspective is uncertain. The realities of what Philip Jackson called "life in classrooms" probably soon disabused most of us of our belief that children and adolescents of a certain age are more alike than they are different.[1] Unfortunately, many teachers probably found it difficult to reconcile the developmental perspective with the philosophy of individual differences, and even more difficult to apply either approach when confronted with the reality of individual differences, the expectations of adherence to curriculum guides, the need to evaluate and to be evaluated, and—most influential of all—what a beginning teacher once called "that *counter* teacher training institution": the teachers' lounge.

For in spite of the lip service given to "individual differences," "individual needs," and "the whole child," it soon became apparent to the novice teacher that the educational system operated on the basis of an assumption of homogeneity. All members of a given instructional group were expected to learn in the same way and at the same pace. It almost seemed that those "individual differences," especially if they were very pronounced, were to be eliminated rather than capitalized upon.

For those who deviated greatly—in learning rate or style, in social behavior, or in physical characteristics—there were special classes. Teachers have probably always been most troubled by their lack of success in providing for the individual needs of all their students. It was a relief to learn that one need not feel guilty about this, since there were specialists to do the job. All one had to worry about, at least in schools that had good special-education programs, was the teaching of normal students.

The Mainstreaming Movement

To some it may seem odd that, after many years of attempting to convince regular teachers and administrators of the need for special education for students with special needs, special educators now seem to be saying just the opposite: these students need to be "mainstreamed" in regular classes and taught by regular teachers. Actually, however, the recent legislation concerning handicapped students by no means denies the need on the part of these students for "special education." What this legislation has done is to define special education in a different way, a way more likely to insure that the special individual needs of handicapped students can be met as effectively as possible while helping them to experience as much normalcy as possible.

With all of its merits, the prevailing special education model of the past could be thought of as implying a "two-box theory" of education.[2] According to this theory, most students are normal and require no special educational adaptations to function quite well with "regular" teachers. However, for the 10 to 12 percent of the school-age population that is in some way exceptional, special education is required. Special education, according to the two-box theory, means placement in a self-contained special classroom (possibly within a segregated special school) and instruction by a special-education teacher. One need only establish that a student qualifies as exceptional and then determine the appropriate category of exceptionality. In addition to these two alternatives, there is a third: the determination that the child could not benefit from an education in public school and that he or she therefore should be excluded from school (this alternative has now been eliminated by law). There were certainly many exceptions to the two-box division. This "theory" was never universally accepted because of its obvious flaws. In addition, limited resources required the maintenance of perhaps half the identified handicapped children in regular programs. A great many children with "low-incidence" handicaps, such as visual impairments, because of both their geographic dispersion and their observed ability to adjust to most of the demands of "regular education" (with some program modifications and with periodic support of specially trained itinerant/consultant specialists), remained in the regular classroom setting with their age peers.[3]

Perhaps the greatest challenge to the self-contained, segregated special-class approach, however, was posed by a series of *efficacy studies* comparing the achievement and social adjustment of exceptional students taught in special classes with others of comparable characteristics who

were taught in regular classes, in most cases *without* supportive assistance of resource specialists. Most of these studies (with some noteworthy
exceptions[4]) point convincingly to advantages of the special-class approach. Furthermore, growing evidence indicated that the approach of
labeling, categorizing, and placing exceptional learners may be a very
dangerous one. Labels, such as *mentally retarded* (although perhaps not
as inherently disparaging as formerly used labels such as *feeble-minded*),
could potentially have very negative effects when applied to children
because of the expectancies and attitudes implied. It may be that the use
of labels in schooling and in other social institutions is inevitable to and
even necessary for the successful delivery of needed services, but labels
must be employed cautiously and wisely.[5] Labeling a child as having a
certain sort of disability or as being "deviant" in some way does not determine what the child's educational needs are.

It has also become increasingly clear that it is very difficult to label
children accurately as candidates for special-education programs. In
American education, probably more than in most other cultures, standardized tests of learning ability (usually referred to as "IQ tests") have
played a very important role in this regard. Because of the inherent cultural bias of most, if not all, of these tests, this practice has resulted in the
erroneous labeling of great numbers of quite normal Hispanic, black, Native American (American Indian), second-generation European and
Asian, Appalachian, and other minority members as mentally retarded.[6]
If such labeling and "sorting" resulted in segregated placement and in
lowered achievement expectations placed upon the pupil, it clearly represented educational practices that were inherently discriminatory and
even racist in effect, though not in intent.

If what was formerly regarded as exclusively the realm of specialists is
now to involve the "regular" teacher, does this mean that one must really
be "all things to all people"? A number of years ago, writing about the
mental health of teachers, Fritz Redl and William Wattenberg cau-
tioned against the "omnicompetence demand."[7] They pointed out that
teachers often feel that they are expected to be equally effective with all
students, regardless of the special needs and problems many students
may present. If this were the expectation, it would certainly be an unrealistic and unfair one. Furthermore, it would be a dangerous one, for in
defending against feelings of guilt and inadequacy caused by recognition
of one's inability to help some children, one might actually come to resent
these children: to displace one's frustration and project the blame onto
them. This is precisely what occurs in the social phenomenon that has
been called "blaming the victim."[8]

There are undoubtedly still some who interpret "mainstreaming" to
mean the indiscriminate "dumping" of students with special needs and
problems into regular classrooms, rather than providing them with the
specialized educational services that have evolved in public education. If

this were intended, it would surely be a big step backward! Initially, also, there were probably those who believed that the mainstreaming movement would have the effect of reducing the high cost of special education. (Special-education services *are* costly!) However, the financial provisions of Public Law 94-142 make it clear that new and emerging practices in educating the handicapped pupil are expected to be more expensive than was special education "before the revolution." To understand why this is so, and why the classroom teacher is not expected to cope unassisted with the truly perplexing problems presented by some students, we must look more closely both at the law itself and the practices it implies.

Basic Requirements of Public Law 94-142

This law, called The Education for All Handicapped Children Act, was enacted in 1975 by the 94th Congress of the United States. It is historic legislation, mainly because it affirms the right of every handicapped child, regardless of severity of handicap, to a free, appropriate education, based upon an individualized education plan. The Congress noted that vast numbers of handicapped children in the United States had not been served at all by public education, and that many more did not receive the kinds of educational services they needed in order to achieve their full potential. Often, special education was available only at great cost to the child's family (through private facilities).

The law makes explicit provisions for accountability, based on three types of special-education plans. First, every state, in order to comply with the law and to receive federal assistance, must submit annually a plan for special education. This must include a report of the total number of handicapped children, by age and by handicapping condition, who live in the state. They must note the numbers "served" and "unserved"; the law specifies a time-line for states to achieve a full service goal. The state agency responsible for compiling this information, using it to develop a plan for providing full services to all handicapped children, and submitting this plan as an application for federal funds is called the State Education Agency (SEA), that is, the department of education of each state. This is important to note, because, even though there may be many state governmental agencies concerned with helping children and youth who have special needs, there is one agency in each state that is completely accountable for their being appropriately educated.

The state agency does not, however, serve each child directly. That is done by local public schools (the local education agency, or LEA), each of which must submit to the state agency its local plan for special education. This plan is based on an accurate count of the children residing in the community who need special education services, with clear statements of the kinds of services that are to be provided. Based on this plan, the LEA is eligible to receive the financial assistance necessary to provide certain types of services related to special educational needs. The financial mechanisms and structure for basic support of special education programs depend upon the laws and standards established by the particular state.

The third, and most basic, level of accountability is that of the Individual Education Plan or Individualized Education Program (IEP). This plan is really the basic unit of special education; each handicapped student's IEP determines what, for that student, constitutes "special education":

> The term "individualized education program" means a written statement for each handicapped child developed in any meeting by a representative of the local educational agency or an intermediate educational unit who shall be

qualified to provide, or supervise the provision of, specially designed instruction to meet the unique needs of handicapped children, the teacher, the parents or guardian of such child, and, whenever appropriate, such child, which statement shall include (A) a statement of the present levels of educational performance of such child, (B) a statement of annual goals, including short-term instructional objectives, (C) a statement of the specific educational services to be provided to such child, and the extent to which such child will be able to participate in regular educational programs, (D) the projected date for initiation and anticipated duration of such services, and appropriate objective criteria and evaluation procedures and schedules for determining, on at least an annual basis, whether instructional objectives are being achieved.[9]

It is necessary at this point to examine closely three very important concepts set forth in the law and in its immediate predecessor, Public Law 93-380 of 1974: due process and procedural safeguards, multifactored and nonbiased assessment, and least restrictive alternative.

DUE PROCESS AND PROCEDURAL SAFEGUARDS

The U.S. Congress had had ample evidence that, in a great many instances in the past (documented by a growing body of court decisions), children had been "labeled and placed" in special education programs—or excluded from school altogether—without parental awareness or informed consent. The law details the steps that must be followed once a child is identified who may be handicapped and who may, therefore, require special education services of any kind. Before any special assessment is done (that is, any assessment that is not conducted for all children in a child's classroom or grade grouping), informed parental consent must be secured. If parents do not agree that there is a need for special assessment or, ultimately, for the kind of educational plan favored by school personnel, an impartial hearing may be necessary. The basic goal is to resolve disagreements among the presumed advocates for the child—the parents and the school—so that the child's best interests are served. It is the spirit and intent of the law that planning and decision making affecting the child's education is conducted jointly by parents and educators. The due process provisions are necessary in part, however, to insure that the letter of the law is followed.

MULTIFACTORED AND NONBIASED ASSESSMENT

We scarcely need more evidence than has already been documented that standardized tests are not infallible. Although it is possible to measure with absolute accuracy the height, weight, or girth of every person, the same cannot be said for those human characteristics that are not directly observable. One of the best examples we have is the twentieth-century American fascination with the measurement of the ability to learn. However, even learning itself cannot be directly measured with absolute reliability; it can only be inferred. But measurement of the ability to learn is, at best, a probabilistic estimate of future achievement based on measurement of the individual's present knowledge (including vocabulary), which is in turn the result of past learning. The concept of the intelligence quotient (IQ) is certainly a fascinating one, at least to many people. But it is simply an artifact, based on scores on a test that attempts to sample certain areas of thinking, reasoning, and knowledge believed to imply "intelligent behavior."

Such a procedure as an attempt to measure a person's ability to learn is certainly subject to error. In fact, all standardized tests assume some degree of error in measurement. For the general population, tests that have been carefully developed and are appropriately normed are reasonably good predictors of success in school learning (assuming there has been no tailoring of the school program to fit the individual student's learning characteristics and needs). For individuals, however, we must remember the inherent weaknesses of the measurement instruments.

These problems and weaknesses are compounded whenever an individual differing to a significant degree in background experience from the dominant, majority culture is compared to norms that are derived from members of that majority culture. As Lloyd Dunn pointed out, segregated self-contained special classes for the "educable mentally retarded" contained disproportionately large number of Hispanic, black, Native American, and other racial or ethnic minorities who were later found not to be retarded at all.[10] They were identified as "retarded" and consequently placed in a segregated educational setting because of the discriminatory nature of the tests (especially intelligence or ability tests) used to determine eligibility.

This is far too complex an issue to be dealt with thoroughly here. Our legislators, however, have recognized that test data have been inappropriately used in the past, with the effect of discriminating against whole population groups within our society. For this reason, the law requires that testing used to determine the possible need for special-education services must be nonbiased. This is certainly a tall order, since, almost by definition, any standardized test will inevitably contain elements that make it discriminatory against some people.

Partly as a safeguard against this bias, and partly to insure that assessment data are truly relevant to planning an individualized educational program, the law requires that assessment be multifactored. This means two things: (1) no single test, and no single test criterion (such as IQ), can be used as the sole basis for determining the need for special education placement; (2) a variety of assessment procedures are needed to obtain information about the student that can be directly applied to planning an appropriate, individualized education program, including accurate descriptions of current educational functioning and meaningful, measurable educational goals.

LEAST RESTRICTIVE ALTERNATIVE

The educational plan for an individual child, then, must be appropriate. The child must receive the needed services. But there is another very important criterion that must be met: the child must participate as much as possible in "regular" education programs and have the opportunity to interact as much as possible with nonhandicapped peers. This is essentially what is meant by the doctrine of least restrictive alternative (LRA).

Does LRA mean the same thing as mainstreaming? In the sense that mainstreaming suggests being as much as possible and as much as appropriate in contact with nonhandicapped age-mates in "regular" school programs, that is exactly what LRA means. Although the entire text of P.L. 94-142 can be understood as an elaboration of the doctrine of least-restrictive-alternative education, since it sets forth in detail the provisions that assure the handicapped child his or her right to an appropriate education, the specific reference to mainstreaming is quite brief:

> . . . procedures [are required] to assure that, to the maximum extent appropriate, handicapped children, including children in public or private institutions or other care facilities, are educated with children who are not handicapped, and that special classes, separate schooling, or other removal of handicapped children from the regular educational environment occurs only when the nature or severity of the handicap is such that education in regular classes with the use of supplementary aids and services cannot be achieved satisfactorily. . . .[11]

Why was this sort of legislation necessary? Why do many people have "restrictive" attitudes about handicapped persons? These attitudes are really not so surprising. For one thing, our media culture and the world of advertising have tended to reinforce the idea of the prime importance of physical beauty, as well as certain standards of physical beauty. Deviance from these standards is often met, if not with revulsion or fear, then with an attitude of pity. Persons who deviate in visible ways—such as through differences in facial features, or in means of moving about, or in the absence of a limb—have probably been the victims of the most blatant discrimination, since they are more obviously "deviant" and hence devalued.[12] An important aspect of the required educational integration is that it will provide opportunities for nonhandicapped children to develop positive attitudes through contact and association.

By no means, however, are all students who have special needs and are provided special services considered to be handicapped. This term has a specific definition, based on provisions in law, and the need for special education is determined on the basis of criteria specified in federal and state law and state standards.

But as we have already seen, this does not necessarily mean that the student is to be taught exclusively by a special teacher in a self-contained special class. There are various placement alternatives that may be considered for any student who is determined to require special education. Processes are detailed in law, state standards, and school-district policy for making these decisions, but the first need is to identify the student.

Referral of Students with Special Needs

Increasingly, with the impact of the law, school districts are able to carry out extensive, effective screening programs in order to identify all handicapped children living in the communities they serve. Since many handicapped children can be most effectively helped if they are provided services early in life, during the crucial periods of physical and psychological development, many have already been identified before they enter school. The massive national effort to identify all handicapped children is referred to as *child find*.

For children whose problems were either not present or identifiable during the years before school, the classroom teacher serves a critically important role. Despite regular in-school screening efforts involving testing for problems in vision, hearing, and other physical or health problems, even these kinds of disabilities may be first suspected by the child's teacher. This is, of course, especially true during the beginning years of school attendance. However, these forms of handicap, like learning and behavior problems, conceivably may have their onset at any time.

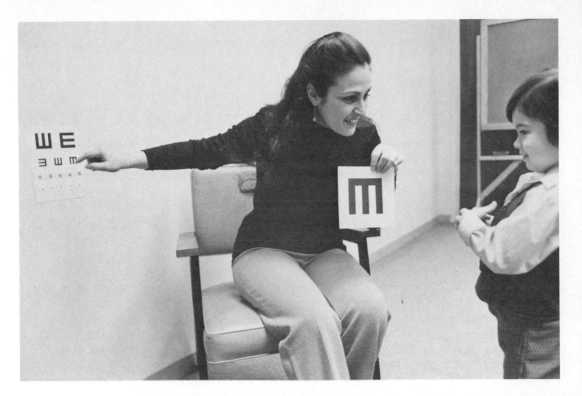

The teacher's role is not to diagnose specific maladies; it is to observe and report accurately and objectively unusual patterns of behavior or problems encountered in academic learning. Since teacher-parent communication is perhaps the most vital dimension of effective teaching and guidance of all children, we can assume that, before a referral is initiated, there have been discussions with the child's parents. The teacher should never say, "I believe your child is emotionally disturbed," or "Perhaps Johnny should be in a special class," or "Mary seems to have a learning disability." In the words of a one-time TV police detective, "Just the facts, Ma'am!"

Eventually, the teacher should have a very important role, together with other team members, in carrying out a comprehensive diagnostic child study if such a study is warranted. At this point, however, the child does not have a "suspected handicap." There is insufficient basis for the teacher to express his or her belief that the child may be in need of special education.

A school district should have a written policy concerning referral, but it is possible that this will not be the case. Generally, whether or not expressed in written form, the expectation is that the building principal should be aware of a referral made by a teacher for any reason. In most

The Cooperative School Staff and the Exceptional Child

In one school, the building principal has taken the leadership in fostering a school environment in which mildly mentally retarded students, previously served exclusively within self-contained special classes, are members in full standing of a school community. Every classroom teacher has regular experience within the special classroom, sharing instructional leadership with the special class teachers. During these times, the principal himself substitutes, giving him an opportunity to interact closely with all the pupils. Students who have been identified (through the required multifactored assessment, and in cooperation with their parents) as being eligible for special-education services, participate in "regular" programs as much as possible. The dual criteria for each child are the two principles of most appropriate program and least restrictive alternatives. Some of the "special" community activities, previously developed especially for the retarded youngsters, such as using community recreational facilities for swimming and roller skating, are now experienced by all students, in groups that include both the educably mentally retarded and the nonretarded youngsters. This has helped greatly to remove not only the "stigma of being special" but also the resentment other children had had about these "special privileges." For the most part, name calling and ostracism are things of the past. The special skills of the educable mental retardation (EMR) teachers are respected and used, but school planning for the EMR pupils is always carried out through the joint efforts of regular and special education personnel, together with parents.

cases, the teacher will initiate a referral by consulting with the principal (unless he or she has specifically identified someone else). The principal may then advise the teacher to prepare a written statement that describes the basis for concern. Once again, the teacher is not recommending special education at this point. A team makes the decision that special education services may be indicated, following suitable individualized diagnostic study, if informed parental consent has been secured. The teacher's referral may lead to the determination that interventions other than those associated with special education may be helpful to the student.

By no means do all students who require special services need the services associated with special education. A wide variety of resources exist in many schools expressly to provide for special needs presented by many students who are not "handicapped." These include remedial reading, individual and group counseling, programs related to vocational needs, supplementary academic tutoring, enrichment programs, and the like. Some schools have extensive community-participation programs. Many have developed exciting approaches involving parents, community-resource persons, "foster grandparents," and peer tutoring. These, in addition to the use of specially trained professionals who have specific technical knowledge and skill, support the ongoing work of the classroom teacher. Besides the reading specialist (who is not usually identified as a special educator, although his or her skills and services are indeed "special"), there is the very important school nurse, and possibly the guidance counselor, school social worker or home-school liaison person, and career-education specialist. The speech clinician (speech therapist, speech pathologist, speech and language specialist, communication specialist) is usually regarded as a major component of the special education program, as is the school psychologist. However, these professionals are likely to be involved in helping nonhandicapped as well as handicapped students. Increasingly, school staffs are found to include other specialists, as well, such as a physical therapist, occupational therapist, adaptive physical-education specialist, and audiologist. Although these specialists work primarily in areas relating to special education (identification through screening programs, diagnostic evaluation of children's special learning needs associated with a disability, and direct therapeutic and rehabilitative work with exceptional children), they can also be very valuable resources to the "regular" educational program.

Disability vs. Handicap

What determines whether a pupil has an educational handicap? It is clear that the characteristics of the individual is an important consideration, but they are not the only determinants. A wide variety of environmental factors can be even more important: the physical characteristics of the school and the classroom setting, such as the presence or absence of architectural barriers; the availability of transportation, as well as other provisions for accessibility;* the social milieu of the classroom and the school, including the social acceptance of the handicapped pupil by his or her peers; and the attitudes of adults who are important in the child's life, especially parents and teachers.

---

*Section 504 of the Rehabilitation Act of 1973 prohibits denial to otherwise qualified handicapped persons of the benefits of any program or service receiving federal financial assistance; it also prohibits any other form of discrimination against the handicapped. Inaccessibility of educational facilities, because of a person's handicap, would constitute an illegal denial of educational services to that person.

Teaching Mildly Educationally Handicapped Students

The issue really is not what *kind* of student we happen to be dealing with, that is, what category or label has been applied to him or her. Nor is it what "disabling condition" the student has. The real need on the part of the teacher is to know how best to teach the student. This knowledge is based primarily on accurate observation and careful analysis of what the student does within the context of school. This clearly implies a different usage of the term *diagnosis* than that associated with the practice of medicine, although even in medical diagnosis treatment is based upon sound analysis of symptoms.

For purposes of effective instruction, however, it is not necessarily so important to arrive at conclusions concerning the "underlying cause" of a problem in learning. These underlying causes may include a number of factors over which the teacher has no control at all, such as less-than-optimal stimulation during the early years, certain deviations from the norm with respect to central nervous system functions, or current difficulties at home. What the teacher *can* control are the various interactions that occur within the classroom, observing carefully the effects that modifications in the physical environment, in the sequence and pattern of instructional activities, and in the teacher's own manner, style, voice quality, etc. have on the student's learning behavior. In a very real sense, the teacher assumes the role of a scientist, systematically manipulating the conditions of learning and studying the effects of these manipulations.

Of course, it is often essential that causes of problems in learning or in social adjustment in the classroom be correctly identified. Perhaps the best examples would be disabilities in hearing or in vision, which, in far too many cases, have gone undetected. Determination that a problem exists in either of these processes is essential in order for corrective measures to be initiated. Other examples would be serious problems in physical or mental health. If the source of the student's difficulties is determined, help can be provided.

The form of "mild" educational handicap with which teachers will have the most frequent experience (excepting speech-articulation problems in the primary grades) is referred to by the term *specific learning disabilities:*

"Specific learning disability" means a disorder in one or more of the basic psychological processes involved in understanding or in using language, spoken or written, which may manifest itself in an imperfect ability to listen, think, speak, read, write, spell, or to do mathematical calculations. The term includes such conditions as perceptual handicaps, brain injury, minimal brain dysfunction, dyslexia, and developmental aphasia. The term does not include children who have learning problems which are primarily the result of visual, hearing,

or motor handicaps, of mental retardation, of emotional disturbance, or of environmental, cultural, or economic disadvantage.[13]

As a category of exceptionality, *learning disabilities,* has been unique. Whereas other labels applied to exceptional children refer only indirectly, if at all, to teaching and learning, the idea of a learning disability is based on the practical realities of learning and teaching in school. The relatively recent "discovery" of learning disabilities* has constituted a major breakthrough in the field of special education for several reasons:

1. A child with a learning disability is considered to be essentially "normal."
2. Children within this group now are believed to have highly individualized needs and unique profiles of strengths and weaknesses (the same could be said about any of us!), rather than common characteristics indicating the need for instruction in homogenous groups.
3. This is truly an educational category, rather than a medical or psychological one.

---

*This "invisible" handicap has probably always existed. The extent to which its prevalence has been influenced by historical or specific cultural factors is uncertain, however. Some writers have implicated ecological factors, nutritional considerations, or the rise of a media culture, with attendant demise of the influence of books. In any case, a number of prominent figures, some of them geniuses or great leaders, are often cited as having had learning disabilities: Winston Churchill, Albert Einstein, and Nelson Rockefeller are examples. This does not imply that all those with learning disabilities are potential geniuses.

The Sensitive Teacher
and the Exceptional Child

Jerry Starchey's American Problems student, Bill Osborne, is considered severely hearing impaired. Bill wears hearing aids, but Mr. Starchey has been told by the speech and hearing supervisor for the school district that since these amplify *all* sounds, Bill will continue to have difficulty understanding speech and will have to rely heavily on visual cues. Since Mr. Starchey tends to move about quite a bit when addressing the class (he is known for his ability to make discussions about government, politics, and societal problems "come alive" and admits unashamedly to being "a bit of a ham"), he has had to be conscious of a few of his own mannerisms that might make it difficult for Bill to understand him. He is surprised at how easy it was for him to adopt the supervisor's suggestions, and they are now second-nature to him. He no longer speaks while writing on the board or strokes his moustache or leans against the window ledge while speaking. Although still frequently "in motion," he has adopted a sort of rhythm for pausing and facing his listeners (in class, and outside as well) that seems to enhance the effect of his words.

Not all students who have trouble mastering academic skills in school "qualify" to be designated as learning disabled. If this were the case, we would have a situation in which perhaps one-third to one-half of the student population would be considered exceptional. The course of learning is not smooth for a great many youngsters, but that does not make them "learning disabled."[14]

Disabilities affecting the sensory abilities of sight and hearing present very special problems and needs. However, with optimally effective intervention—educational as well as medical—and the opportunity to experience normal living and learning experiences, these forms of impairment, in many if not most instances, need not adversely affect the child's achievement and adjustment. Because of the very important role that vision and hearing have in early development, especially within the first year or two of life, the help that the child and his or her family receive then may be the most important determinant. Even though our society has been very slow in demonstrating its recognition of the importance of early intervention for handicapped children by mandating infant and preschool programs, such programs for congenitally deaf and blind children have been in effect for many years.

Generally, these same principles also apply in the case of children who are physically handicapped or who have a chronic medical condition. However, in many instances there is a continuing need for close coopera- tion and teamwork among many professionals besides the teacher, such as an occupational therapist, physical therapist, audiologist, and speech pathologist. A child with a physical disability or sensory disorder, how- ever, is not necessarily one who is educationally handicapped. These con- ditions may coexist with problems in academic learning and/or social be- havior, of course, but they are by no means necessarily related.

In the case of mental retardation, however, the child's principal problems, almost by definition, relate to academic skill learning and mas- tery of behavior that is adaptive to the demands of life. Although mental retardation has traditionally been classified according to degree of sub- normality, there is tremendous variability within these classifications (as is the case with all children). The issue now is really not to determine that the child is "mentally retarded" or how retarded the child is; rather, the need is to determine for each child, on an individual basis, what his or her specific learning characteristics and needs are, what specific in- structional objectives and methods are appropriate, what special services may be needed, and how to serve the child, to the maximum extent pos- sible, in educational settings with children who are not retarded.

With respect to emotional problems in children and youth, terminology and standards for providing services vary from state to state. It is impor- tant to distinguish severe emotional disturbance, which probably in- volves the need for specialized treatment, from mild and moderate behav- ior disorders. Probably more teacher referrals have involved children's behavior problems than any other factor. However, inappropriate or even disruptive classroom behavior does not necessarily indicate the need for special education. Such problems may or may not coexist with academic learning difficulties, and a great many students with emotional or behav- ioral problems do not, of course, "act out" through aggressive, disruptive, destructive, or bizarre behavior.

Among those students thought of as exceptional is one very diverse group not usually thought of as handicapped: the gifted and talented. The teaching of gifted/talented students is regarded as an area of special edu- cation, although most of them are and have always been served in regu- lar programs. The same error of applying a one-dimensional criterion that has characterized approaches with other exceptional populations has characterized education of the gifted. In general, the IQ has been regarded as the most convenient, if not the best, index. Those schools that have established special programs of any kind for the very capable have sought to identify those to be served on the basis of high IQ. However, the specific score criterion has varied: it is sometimes 120, sometimes 130, and sometimes even higher. Obviously, giftedness, defined according to this standard, is a relative, rather than absolute, quality. It should also be obvious that use of this criterion alone fails to take into account the many ways in which students may be gifted, the inadequacy of measures of "intelligence," and the lack of a one-to-one correspondence between measured intelligence (IQ) and achievement. Most authors recommend that at least the following areas of giftedness and talent be considered when planning special educational programs: academic talent, special talent (e.g., in music or dramatics), social abilities, and creativity.[15]

What types of special programs have been provided? Usually, these have taken any of three general forms:[16]

- *Acceleration,* including early school entrance, early graduation, advanced placement in college-credit courses taken in high school, and grade skipping.
- *Special classes or programs,* including ability grouping, sometimes in the form of a special-class approach paralleling that which had served many mildly mentally retarded students.
- *Enrichment,* including individualized modifications within the regular class designed to permit the very capable student to learn at his or her own pace and to pursue individual interests.

The provisions of Public Law 94-142 do not apply to the gifted and talented, since the law addresses the educational needs and rights of the handicapped. It is probably safe to say that the very able, individually and collectively, have generally been neglected. Society seems to have assumed that they will learn and achieve success under any conditions, but there is much evidence to the contrary.

If it is likely that a "typical" classroom group will include students who are very creative, bright, or otherwise unusually able, as well as students who can succeed only at a slower pace, they cannot all be approached as though they were the same. But this is true even when only the "normal" range of learning ability is considered. Even without the inclusion of pupils who deviate significantly from the "average," a uniform instructional approach is likely to result in optimum achievement for only about one-third of any group of students.[17] The challenge is to provide for *all* students' special needs effectively, not only those of the "exceptional" student.

One of the most effective "resources" for exceptional students, and for regular classroom teachers, is called the resource room. The idea of a resource room suggests several alternatives to the regular vs. special education dichotomy. Basically, a child's participation in a resource-room program is determined entirely on the basis of his or her specific individual needs, rather than on the basis of a categorical label, such as *educable mental retardation* (EMR), *learning disability* (LD), *emotionally handicapped* (EH), *behavior disorder* (BD), *orthopedically handicapped,* or *hearing impaired.* The precise services a child may need will, of course, vary, as will the amount of time the child actually spends in the resource room.* Generally, however, the resource teacher will be skilled in the following:

1. The use of formal diagnostic tests relevant to academic skill areas, as well as informal, criterion-referenced assessment techniques.
2. The development of specially adapted instructional materials and teaching techniques.
3. The expert use of motivational strategies and behavior-management and change techniques.
4. Counseling and consultation methods for supportive work with the pupil and his parents.
5. Developing alternative ways of structuring the physical learning environment and sequence of learning activities in order to optimize the pupil's motivation, achievement, and social adjustment.

In a school in which many students (perhaps all) move from one area of a building to another for specific activities, the child who leaves to see the resource teacher is not stigmatized. Basically, this child is "just like everyone else." This is certainly one of the principal advantages of the resource-room approach.

The relationship between the resource room, specialized support services, and the regular classroom is best illustrated through the well-known Cascade Model (Figure 6.1). This model illustrates the principle that most handicapped children can and should be served in normal settings, while still receiving whatever specialized services they may need. It also emphasizes that movement out of or away from normal classroom settings should be done only when it is absolutely necessary, and that the child should be "moved" in the direction of the normal classroom setting as soon as it is feasible.

The two later modifications of the "original" Cascade Model reflect the belief that special education and related services should become decentralized, that is, that there should be fewer specialized settings, but more diverse, individualized regular classroom settings (Figures 6.2 and 6.3).

When we talk about organizational systems and "models," it may seem as though the classroom teacher has little to say about how to provide for exceptional learners. The school in which you teach may or may not be following the Cascade Model, emphasizing the resource-room concept,

---

*Depending upon special education rules and standards in individual states, the resource teacher may give greater emphasis either to direct work with the pupil within the regular classroom or to guiding and advising the classroom teacher, who will actually carry out the procedures that have been jointly developed. In any case, the secret to success is teamwork between them in actually implementing the IEP.

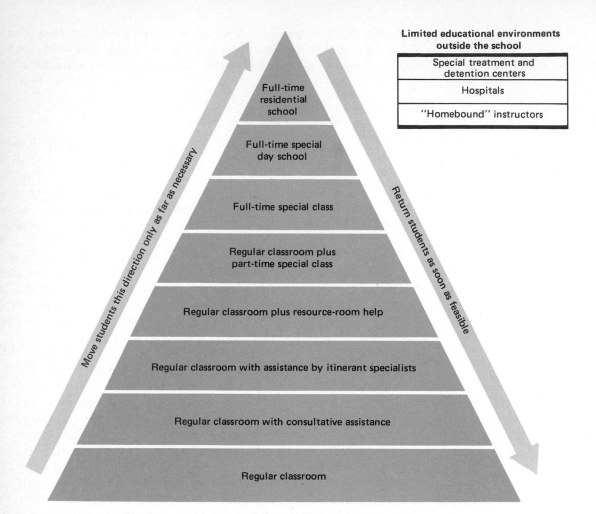

Figure 6.1. The original Special Education Cascade.

From Maynard C. Reynolds and Jack. W. Birch, *Teaching Exceptional Children in All America's Schools* (Reston, Va.: Council for Exceptional Children, 1977), p. 32.

may or may not have a standing committee to deal with planning and placement decisions, etc. Whatever the structure is, however, in the last analysis, successful work with exceptional students depends to a great extent upon the ability of the teacher in the following:

1. Coordinating team recommendations and translating them into practice.
2. Maintaining communication and close cooperation with parents.
3. Being skilled at objectively reporting the student's responses to variations in the classroom program.

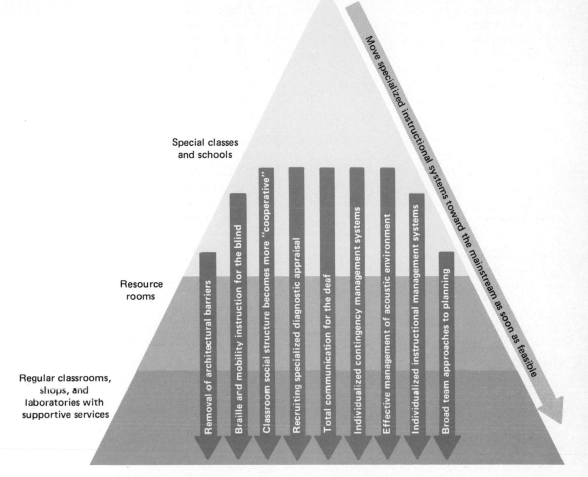

Figure 6.2. Changes occurring in the Cascade. There are fewer specialized places and more diverse "regular" places.

From Maynard C. Reynolds and Jack W. Birch, *Teaching Exceptional Children in All America's Schools* (Reston, Va.: Council for Exceptional Children, 1977), p. 34.

4. Being open and responsive to suggestions from resource colleagues, as well as parents, without defensiveness.
5. Being flexible both in planning and in carrying out instructional plans.
6. Providing the student with regular and consistent opportunities to work at tasks at which he or she can succeed and feel good about his or her success.
7. Being willing to seek assistance.

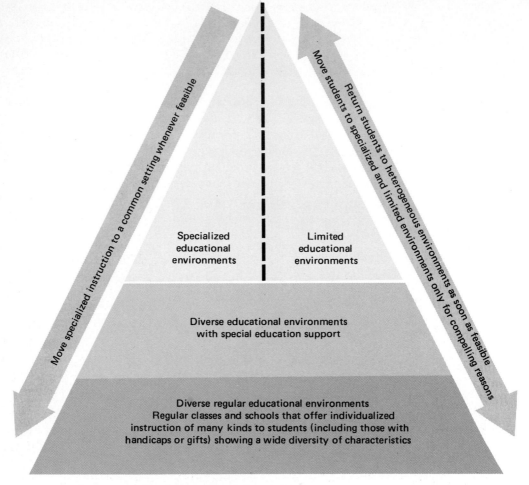

Figure 6.3. The Instructional Cascade.

From Maynard C. Reynolds and Jack W. Birch, *Teaching Exceptional Children in All America's Schools* (Reston, Va.: Council for Exceptional Children, 1977), p. 36.

8. Being thoroughly familiar with school policies and procedures concerning referral, assessment, placement, related services, and the like.

9. Being thoroughly familiar with the particular student's IEP, and especially with one's own responsibilities for implementation, evaluation, monitoring, and reporting.

10. Regarding the exceptional student as, first of all, a child or young person who, like all of his or her age-mates, needs to feel competent, valued, and worthy of respect.

A number of "interventions" are possible, and one needs to approach instructional planning with flexibility and resourcefulness. Generally, in order to accommodate students with mild educational handicapping conditions and to provide effectively for their unique (and ever-changing) needs, adaptations in areas such as the following may be required.

Provide Alternatives. Text materials written at varying levels of difficulty can and should be employed for independent, small group, or tutorial use within any regular classroom. Similarly, the availability and use within the classroom of cassette tape recorders, single-loop projectors, an overhead projector, and other media equipment can make it possible for both "visual learners" and "auditory learners" to master skills and concepts. It is unrealistic to expect all members of a group of "normal" students to perform initially at the same level, to learn at the same rate, and to manifest the same style and preference.

Tap into the Student's Motivational System. It is never accurate to say that a student is "not motivated." Since all behavior is motivated, and (by definition) behavior is exhibited by everyone who is living, the problem is one of altering behavior. Inappropriate behavior (maladaptive, off-task, antisocial, etc.) is altered when the motivating conditions that serve to reinforce (that is, reward and consequently maintain it) no longer do so to the same degree. How does one most effectively get a student to reduce inappropriate or undesirable behavior patterns? The basic strategy is as follows:

1. Identify as specifically as possible the behavior.
2. Chart the frequency (and possibly the circumstances) of its occurrence.*
3. Identify the reinforcing consequence of the behavior and, therefore, what may account for its occurrence.
4. Intervene educationally, by making incompatible behaviors more rewarding and/or by making the undesirable behavior less rewarding.

Be student-conscious, not self-conscious. It is understandable that some teachers—especially beginning teachers, perhaps—may interpret a student's misbehavior as being directed at the teacher. It is easy to think of a rebellious or disruptive student as posing a threat to you, or testing you, placing you in a situation in which your authority is challenged. Asserting your "power" through the threat of punishment or with verbal aggression (through, for example, using sarcasm to "put down" the student) is almost always counterproductive. It may even be difficult to achieve the short-term gain of a momentarily orderly classroom this way. Help the student to manage his or her problem.

*See Chapter 3 for a description of useful observation techniques.

The Impact of the "Regular" Teacher with the Exceptional Student

When Peter was 18 months old, he and his mother entered a special parent-child program for physically handicapped toddlers, conducted by a community agency. With a medical diagnosis of mild cerebral palsy, Peter was not able to stand or walk, and had little use of one arm. Ultimately, however, with ongoing physical and occupational therapy, and following orthopedic ("heel cord") surgery, Peter could walk unassisted, although with a pronounced gait, and learned to use his involved arm as a "helper." Obviously bright and outgoing, Peter adapted readily to the toddler group, and later to a nursery school group in the same agency. His speech and language functioning were not affected by his disability, and he also mastered the developmental tasks of social play, communication, self-care, concept learning, and developing a positive self-concept.

Although psychological testing for young children, especially those with disabilities such as motor impairments, is notoriously subject to error, test results (and staff observations) suggested that, as a learner, Peter was not only "normal," he was quite possibly gifted.

Parents and school personnel were in agreement concerning school placement planning: he was to enter a regular kindergarten. His successes continued there, and by the end of the year, he was reading with enjoyment. Well accepted by peers, he developed several friendships and participated actively in all classroom activities, as well as field trips. Although physically handicapped, Peter was psychologically, socially, and educationally normal.

All did not go so well the following year. Peter frequently came home from school in dejection. His teacher complained to Peter's mother that he was "slow" and that attending to him required neglecting his classmates.

There were many teacher-parent conferences—so many, in fact, that his mother, whose husband had left the family, nearly lost her job because of her frequent absences from work. Finally, in some desperation, she suggested to the principal that Peter's teacher seemed angry about having Peter in her class, seemed actually to resent his being there. There was, after all, a special school for physically handicapped children in the system, but Peter's mother (and the agency nursery school staff) had felt Peter should be in a regular classroom. With difficulty, the first-grade teacher—and Peter and his mother—survived the year, but his progress was disappointing and he was becoming rather shy, almost withdrawn.

This year, things have changed. His enjoyment of school and enthusiasm for learning have returned. He also occasionally displays a little mischievousness, but this has not become a problem; the same classroom rules apply to him as to his classmates who are not handicapped. His second-grade teacher apparently does not think him "too slow" or requiring undue attention, although she has a large and diverse group with which to work. Furthermore, he seems to be realizing the promise that had been shown earlier: his work in some areas is truly exceptional.

As the end of the year approaches, Peter's mother is optimistic but, at the same time, a little anxious about the future. She has requested a conference with the teacher he will have in the fall, Peter's present teacher, and the principal.

Summary Teaching exceptional students, that is, handicapped or gifted/talented ones, is not simply a matter of assigning them to "special education." But neither is it simply a matter of assigning them to "regular education." These students do have individual characteristics and needs that may require highly specialized, individualized interventions. We have come increasingly to see, however, that even such specialized needs can be expertly served while still allowing the student the experience of normalcy. But this requires the cooperative efforts of many people; it is not a sink-or-swim situation, either for the student or the teacher. Effective teaching of exceptional students requires the application of our greatest efforts, our best technology, and our most responsible use of resources to do what education in our society aspires to do for all children and youth: to help the individual student become what he or she is capable of becoming, as a learner, a contributing citizen, and a human being.

Encounters

1. Interview a school administrator regarding the steps that have been taken by the school system to comply with Public Law 94-142. Are most handicapped children handled in that system or sent to another? How much mainstreaming has been done?
2. Talk with a special-education teacher who has been teaching for several years. How has his or her job been affected by Public Law 94-142? Are the changes perceived as having improved the special-education program?
3. Spend some time in a classroom into which handicapped children have been mainstreamed. What is the attitude of the "normal" children toward their "exceptional" peers? Do the handicapped children seem to receive a greater than average amount of the teacher's time and attention? Talk with the teacher regarding his or her attitude toward the mainstreamed children and the amount of help being received from a special-education teacher.
4. Interview the parents of a handicapped child. Do the parents believe their child is receiving an adequate public school education? Are the parents familiar with their rights and the rights of their child as described by Public Law 94-142? Do they understand mainstreaming? Have they seen an IEP for their child?
5. Interview a school psychologist or a special education teacher regarding the methods used for providing nonbiased and multifactored assessment of handicapped children. What specific tests are used for children with various handicaps? What steps are taken to insure nondiscriminatory assessment? Reach your own conclusions as to whether the assessment program is truly nonbiased and multifactored.

Notes

1. Philip W. Jackson, *Life in Classrooms* (New York: Holt, Rinehart and Winston, 1968).
2. Maynard C. Reynolds and Jack W. Birch, *Teaching Exceptional Children in All America's Schools: A First Course for Teachers and Principals* (Reston, Va.: Council for Exceptional Children, 1977).
3. Samuel A. Kirk, *Educating Exceptional Children* (New York: Houghton Mifflin, 1972).
4. See Thomas Noffsinger, *Observation of EMR Students in Special Class and Mainstream Studies* (Mentor, Ohio: Mentor Exempted Village School District, 1973); Nicholas A. Vacc, "A Study of Emotionally Disturbed Children in Regular and Special Classes," *Exceptional Children, 35* (November 1968), 197–206.
5. Nicholas Hobbs, *The Futures of Children* (San Francisco: Jossey-Bass, 1975).
6. Lloyd M. Dunn, "Special Education for the Mildly Retarded—Is Much of It Justified?" *Exceptional Children, 35* (September 1968), 5–24.
7. Fritz Redl and William W. Wattenberg, *Mental Hygiene in Teaching* (New York: Harcourt, Brace & World, 1959).
8. William Ryan, *Blaming the Victim* (New York: Random House, 1971).
9. Public Law 94-142, Section 4 (19).

10. Dunn, "Special Education for the Mildly Retarded."
11. Public Law 94-142, Part B, Section 612, 5, B.
12. Wolf Wolfensberger, "The Origin and Nature of Our Institutional Models," in *Changing Patterns in Residential Services for the Retarded,* eds. R. Kugel and Wolf Wolfensberger (Washington, D.C.: President's Committee on Mental Retardation, 1969).
13. "Education of Handicapped Children: Implementation of Part B of the Education of the Handicapped Act," *Federal Register, 42,* no. 250, 23 August 1977, 65083.
14. Gerald Wallace and James A. McLoughlin, *Learning Disabilities: Concepts and Characteristics* (Columbus, Ohio: Merrill, 1975).
15. Philip L. Safford, *Teaching Young Children with Special Needs* (St. Louis: Mosby, 1978).
16. James Payne, "The Gifted," in *Behavior of Exceptional Children: An Introduction to Special Education,* ed. N. G. Haring (Columbus, Ohio: Merrill, 1974).
17. Benjamin S. Bloom, *Learning for Mastery,* Vol. 1, (Los Angeles: University of California, Los Angeles, Center for the Study of Evaluation of Instructional Programs, May 1968).

For More Information

JOURNALS

Allen, K. Eileen. "The Least Restrictive Environment: Implications for Early Childhood Education," *Educational Horizons, 56* (1977), 34–41.

Barclay, James R., and Kehle, Thomas J. "The Impact of Handicapped Students on Other Students in the Classroom," *Journal of Research and Development in Education, 12* (1979), 80–92.

Bergman, Jerry. "The Tragic Story of Two Highly Gifted Genius-level Boys," *Creative Child and Adult Quarterly, 4* (1979), 222–233.

Chapman, Robert B., Larsen, Stephen C., and Parker, Randall M. "Interactions of First-Grade Teachers with Learning Disordered Children," *Journal of Learning Disabilities, 12* (1979), 223–230.

Cox, Ann. The Gifted Student: A Neglected Presence? *Teachers, 97* (1979), 75–76.

Gale, Jill. "I Was Always the Last One," *Teachers, 95* (1977), 56–58.

Masoodi, Bashir, and Ban, John R. "Teaching the Visually Handicapped in Regular Classes," *Educational Leadership, 37* (1980) 351–355.

McLain, Charles, "Five Stages Parents Go Through in Gifted/Talented Education," *Roeper Review, 2* (1980), 46–47.

Miller, Bernard, and Miller, Betty. "Reorganizing the Gifted: Is Differentiation Undemocratic?" *College Board Review,* n. 115 (1980), 2–7.

Mori, Allen A. "The Handicapped Child in the Mainstream—New Roles for the Regular Educator," *Education, 99* (1979), 243–249.

Renzulli, J. S., and Smith, C. H. "Two Approaches to Identification of Gifted Students," *Exceptional Children, 43* (1977), 512–518.

Robinson, Michael A. "SEAGULL: A Project for Releasing the Potential of the Gifted," *Childhood Education, 56* (1980), 268–273.

Sapon-Shevin, Mara. "Another Look at Mainstreaming: Exceptionality, Normality, and the Nature of Difference," *Phi Delta Kappan, 60* (1978), 119–121.

Stroud, Marion B. "Do Students Sink or Swim in the Mainstream?" *Phi Delta Kappan, 60* (1978), 316.

Turnbull III, H. Rutherford. "The Past and Future Impact of Court Decisions in Special Education," *Phi Delta Kappan, 59* (1978).

Wolf, Joan and Stephen, Thomas. "Individualized Educational Planning for the Gifted," *Roeper Review, 2* (1979), 11–12.

Yaffe, Elaine. "Experienced Mainstreamers Speak Out," *Teachers, 96* (1979), 61–63.

BOOKS

Clendening, Corinne P., and Davies, Ruth Ann. *Creating Programs for the Gifted: A Guide for Teachers, Librarians, and Students.* New York: R. R. Bowker Co., 1980.

DeHaan, Robert Frank, and Havighurst, Robert J. *Educating Gifted Children.* Chicago: University of Chicago Press, 1957.

Dunn, Lloyd. *Exceptional Children in the Schools.* New York: Holt, Rinehart, and Winston, 1973.

Hallahan, Daniel, and Kauffman, James. *Exceptional Children.* Englewood Cliffs, N.J.: Prentice-Hall, 1978.

Hank, Barbara B., and Freehill, Maurice F. *The Gifted—Case Studies.* Dubuque, Iowa: W. C. Brown Co., 1972.

Hodgkin, C. G. *Creativity and the Advanced Student.* Nedlands, Australia: Secondary Teachers College, 1970.

Khatena, Joe. *The Creatively Gifted Child: Suggestions for Parents and Teachers.* New York: Vantage Press, 1978.

Kird, Samuel, and Gallagher, James J. *Educating Exceptional Children,* 3rd ed. Boston: Houghton Mifflin, 1979.

Mann, Philip, ed. *Shared Responsibility for Handicapped Students: Advocacy and Programming.* Miami: University of Miami Training and Technical Assistance Center, 1976.

Passow, A. Harry, ed. *The Gifted and the Talented: Their Education and Development.* Chicago: National Society for the Study of Education, 1979.

Pickard, Phyllis M. *If You Think Your Child is Gifted.* Hamden, Conn.: Linnet Books, 1976.

Turnbull, Ann P., and Schulz, Jane B. *Mainstreaming Handicapped Students: A Guide for Classroom Teachers.* Rockleigh, N.J.: Longwood Division, Allyn and Bacon, 1979.

Tuttle, Frederick B., Jr. and Becker, Lawrence A. *Characteristics and Identification of Gifted and Talented Students.* Washington: National Education Association, 1980.

Weintraub, Fredrick, et al., eds. *Public Policy and the Education of Exceptional Children.* Reston, Va.: The Council for Exceptional Children, 1976.

MOVIES

Am I Being Unrealistic? (Media Guild, 25 min., 1974). Tells the story of a cerebral palsy victim and his struggle to become independent in society. This film gives solid testimony on the positive results of mainstreaming.

Assessing a Young Child (Media Guild, 24 min., 1974). Shows the importance of a multifactored assessment which includes the child's physical, behavioral, and developmental capacities. These assessments and periodic reevaluations are the foundations of the mainstreaming policy.

The Evaluation by the School Psychologist (Instructional Media Services, 20 min., 1977). Explains the process of a student evaluation by a school psychologist. Traces the steps from the teacher referral to the acquisition of remedial strategies.

A Film on Early Intervention (Instructional Media Services, 30 min., 1979). Focuses on the need for early intervention strategies of handicapped children in the first five years of development. Home-based, center-based, and parent involvement programs are shown using actual settings.

The Individualized Education Program (Instructional Media Services, 22 min., 1977). In accordance with Public Law 94-142, all handicapped children receiving education services must be given an LEP. This film shows the development of an IEP from the multifactored assessment to the placement. Stress is placed on the importance of parental involvement for the child's supportive needs.

In the Mainstream (CBS: Carousel, 14 min., 1979). Examines some of the successes and failures of Public Law 94-142 on placing handicapped children in the least restrictive environment. Some ramifications previously unseen by lawmakers, educators, and parents are presented.

Public Law 94-142: Equality of Opportunity (Instructional Media Services, 21 min., 1977). Explains the law and shows the steps involved in placing a child in the least restrictive environment. An IEP is described as the child is moved from a special education class to a regular class.

Sit Down, Shut Up, or Get Out (Films, Inc., 59 mins., 1971). Shows the plight of a twelve-year-old boy who experiences behavior problems, frustration, and peer harassment due to his high intellect. Teachers and peers do not understand why he does things his own way as opposed to following established patterns.

Chapter 7

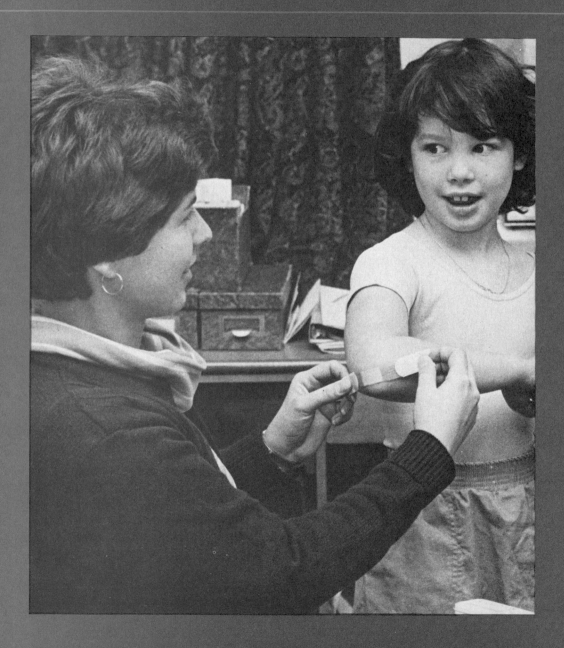

Chapter 7

THOSE WHO MAKE
THE SCHOOL WORK

The social structure of most modern institutions resembles a pyramid-shaped iceberg: a relatively small but visible cone supported by a large, invisible base. At the institution's top or point position are a few highly visible roles that, because of their visibility, gradually come to symbolize the entire organization of which they are a part. A few obvious examples of such roles are the presidency of a nation or large corporation, the starring role in a movie or theatrical production, and the quarterback or running back position on a football team. In every case these highly visible roles owe their prominence to a broad, invisible strata of supporting roles that actually constitute the main body of the institution. Presidents are supported by a coordinated network of interacting specialists (a bureaucracy); theatrical stars are supported by other actors, technical specialists, writers, and directors; quarterbacks and running backs are no better than the linemen who block for them.

Within the institution of education the featured roles are those of teacher and student. Most of this text and the general literature on education focuses on these two front-line groups. As with other modern institutions, however, modern school systems simply could not function without the coordinated efforts of a large, supporting cast of specialists that ranges all the way from the school board president to the school custodian and volunteer.

As a prospective teacher you should be aware of the various roles played by your supporting cast because, in many instances, your success in the classroom will depend on how well they carry out their assigned (official) and assumed (unofficial) roles. In short, education is a team effort where success depends on mutual knowledge and cooperation among the various team members.

Education was not always such a complex affair involving the coordinated efforts of a large team of specialists. In the eighteenth and nineteenth centuries, the teacher was responsible for all the roles found in present-day schools. It is reported of D. S. Domer, a teacher in the 1880s: that "His contract provided that he be compensated $28 a month for a period of six months. He was also required to be his own janitor."[1] A sample of a teacher's contract from 1922 follows. You will notice that the teacher was expected to assume many roles beyond that of classroom instructor. The contract reads that for $75 per month, the teacher agrees:

1. Not to get married. The contract becomes null and void immediately if the teacher marries.
2. Not to have company with men.
3. To be at home between the hours of 8 P.M. and 6 A.M. unless in attendance at a school function.
4. Not to loiter downtown in ice cream stores.
5. Not to leave town at any time without permission of the chairman of the school board.
6. Not to smoke cigarettes. This contract becomes null and void immediately if the teacher is found smoking.
7. Not to ride in a carriage or automobile with any man except her brother or father.
8. Not to dress in bright colors.
9. Not to dye her hair.
10. To wear at least two petticoats.
11. Not to wear dresses more than two inches above the ankles.
12. To keep the schoolroom clean:
    a. to sweep the classroom floor at least once daily.
    b. to scrub the classroom floor at least once weekly with soap and hot water.
    c. to clean the blackboard at least once daily.
    d. to start the fire at 7 A.M. so that the room will be warm at 8 A.M. when the children arrive.
13. Not wear face powder, mascara or to paint the lips.[2]

The remainder of this chapter will introduce you, through a series of short, biographical sketches, to various nonteaching members of the educational cast. Although their backgrounds and roles are diverse, their primary mission is the same as your own: to help students learn and develop to their full potential. These biographies, which are developed from personal interviews, should not only provide you with background information on these diverse roles but should suggest ways that you can use the services provided by these people in carrying out your own future teaching role.

School Board Member

"For most cities in the mid-nineteenth century, state legislatures and city councils chartered local school boards to hire teachers, buy books, build schools, and supervise instruction."[3] The tasks of school boards in the twentieth century remain basically the same. The major change in school boards is not in what they do but who is appointed/elected to the board. W. E. Chancellor suggested in 1904 the types of men who should and should not be included on school boards (he assumed that women should be excluded no matter what their background and level of competency). The "shoulds" included manufacturers, merchants, bankers, physicians, and college graduates. The "should nots" included inexperienced men, unsuccessful men, old men, politicians, newspaper men, uneducated men, and men in subordinate positions.[4]

George Counts disagreed with Chancellor and felt that all segments of the community should be represented on the school boards, not only the élite. His 1927 argument for total community representation is similar to the argument used in the 1970s and 1980s by various minorities who want (and demand) to be represented on boards of education. Counts argued: "No longer is the ordinary community homogeneous as regards interest, philosophy, and ideals. Hence the need of guarding the integrity of the various minority groups. In the absence of a board of education, which in its membership represents the various groups and points of view of the community, provision for such protection can hardly be assured."[5]

Our first sketch is of James Myers who has been a school board member in a small midwestern community for 13 years. Twice during the 13 years he has been school board president. We recommend that you focus on the following questions while reading his biography:

1. What are Myers' assigned (official) responsibilities?
2. What are his assumed (unofficial) responsibilities?
3. Why does he want to be a school board member?
4. How could the classroom teacher use the services of a person in Myers' role?
5. Do teachers in your neighboring communities know the functions and philosophies of their school board members?

You should not be surprised that Jim Myers is willing to listen to citizens' concerns and is willing to put his heart into an unpaid and often highly pressured position. Although a few school board members may be antiteacher or more concerned about educational costs than educational quality, our own experiences with school boards throughout the United States indicates that Jim Myers' behaviors are typical of most school board members. Test our assumption by attending a school board meeting and interviewing its members.

Jim Myers
SCHOOL BOARD MEMBER

Vestiges of participatory democracy still exist in the United States. In one small, midwestern town as parents purchase their aspirin and toothpaste, they can comment and/or complain about the public schools and know that they will get a fair hearing from the "establishment." The establishment in this case is represented by Jim Myers, the proprietor of the local drugstore and a school board member for the past 13 years. Myers affirms:

> I think the public expects a school board member to listen to their comments—even in the drugstore. I feel that it's my obligation to pass on the comments that I hear to the superintendent although I seldom try to get involved in discussing a specific issue. If an issue is going to take time to explain, I tell the citizen to call me at home in the evening. I've even made house calls to people who wanted to talk about issues.

Often, parents question a board member about a specific curriculum or activity under the mistaken impression that the board members are aware of every activity in the schools: "The public thinks that we make every decision that goes on in this school system—no way. Sometimes we're the last to find out about something."

Jim Myers' role, which he describes as community liaison, is an unofficial one that he assumed in addition to the official roles that are assigned him by state law. His official responsibilities include the following:

- Approving all teacher appointments
- Ratifying or vetoing the superintendent's recommendations
- Signing all contracts (completed by the president of the board)
- Establishing salary scales
- Giving authority to the school board clerk to invest, and borrow money
- Interpreting the desires of the public

The school superintendent is responsible for implementing the policies of the school board. Myers feels that the relationship between the board and the superintendent should be one of cooperation and trust rather than conflict. Myers explains:

> We elect the superintendent to do a job. If you want to have a well-run school system, you must allow him to have a free hand. They've appreciated our openness and historically they have been willing to share their ideas and problems with us. They use us as a sounding board of public opinion since we are representatives of the public!

What should any teacher, especially those who are just beginning their careers, know about the school system? Myers recommends that teachers develop an awareness of how the entire school system operates, along with a knowledge of pedagogy and learning theories. Too often, he feels, teachers lack an understanding of the larger school issues outside the classroom. Myers' recommendation is a simple one: attend a board of education meeting.

> Recently we've had a few candidates for teaching positions who have attended board meetings. If I were beginning a career in the school system, the attendance at a board meeting would be my first "must." Learn who the school board members are; see what they do in the meeting; see what types of questions are discussed. Often teachers don't get the full picture of the school system; they don't realize how complex the school system really is.

In regard to pedagogical issues, Myers feels that beginning teachers "are not finished products upon graduation from the university. They must be willing to change and learn new techniques." They should not be cast adrift to sink or swim; they should be given ongoing support in the form of advice from the school principal and in-service education programs funded by the school board.

We concluded our interview with Jim Myers by focusing on a current issue in education: "back to basics." He differentiated between a good basic education and the "back to basics" movement:

> Everyone should have a good basic education, but I get frightened by the "back to basics" label. What I fear is that there will be so great an emphasis on drilling the basic skills (reading, arithmetic, etc.) that the child who is able to advance will become bored to death. We're definitely concerned about those few children who lack basic skills and have developed a program for them, but I hope we never adopt a simplistic philosophy of "back to basics."

Superintendent

"The position [of superintendent] has been described as the worst job in the world and as the position which offers the greatest opportunity to influence, through the schools, the development of the attitudes, interests, and capacities of the succeeding generations."[6] The complexity of the superintendent's role in the 1980s—educational leader, implementer of desegregation, negotiator in teacher contracts, interpreter of community goals—has led to both health and professional problems for its occupants. One superintendent has been murdered, others have suffered heart attacks and ulcers, and hundreds have been fired. Cuban found that, in 1953, the average term in office for superintendents in the largest school systems was six and one-half years; this decreased to five and one-half years in 1963 and to slightly more than four years in 1971.[7]

Gross completed a study of the behaviors of superintendents in the state of Massachusetts and found that many superintendents suffer from extreme anxiety because of the pressures of the position:

> Many superintendents are more anxious, more insecure, more self-commiserating than they would be if it were not for the pressures and cross-pressures they face, and a number of them indicated that they had conscience problems because they did conform to some pressures that carried with them the threat of losing their job.[8]

Our next biography is of Dr. Pat Crisci, one of the very few women who is a superintendent of schools. As you read the biography focus on the following:

1. How have the pressures and cross-pressures of the position affected her?
2. What are her assigned and assumed responsibilities?
3. How might you, as a beginning teacher, learn about the responsibilities of the superintendent?
4. How can you meet the superintendent on a personal level?
5. What relationships do teachers in nearby communities have with their superintendent: colleague, adversary, or boss?

This particular superintendent involves herself in curriculum matters, visits classrooms, and urges teachers to visit her without a prearranged appointment. Unusual behaviors for a superintendent? Test them out by asking teachers in various districts about their superintendents. Go one step further and call the offices of two or three superintendents, asking for an appointment to discuss your concern regarding education. You may be surprised (or should we say shocked?) when one or more of them respond positively. Remember our suggestion in Chapter 3: test your inferences by interviewing those who can best clarify the issues that are of importance to you.

Security Guard

Violence and vandalism have become "big business" in American schools. No region of the country and no grade level seems to be exempt from these problems. Consequently, new industries and new school roles have been developed in the past 10 years to deal with them: "The Senate subcommittee on Juvenile Delinquency has focused national attention on the alarming incidence of school violence. Senator Birch Bayh reports 70,000 serious assaults on teachers this year, school vandalism costing half a billion dollars, increasing gang warfare, extortion, bribery, drug pushing, prostitution, rape, and murder."[9]

Pat Crisci
SUPERINTENDENT

As a female school superintendent, Pat Crisci is a member of a very élite group that includes less than 1 percent of all superintendents in the United States. During a community meeting early in her career as superintendent, one of her assistants overheard the following coments: "I wonder who she thinks she is? Now she is playing with her hair, now she is crossing her legs." They focused on picky things rather than on her performance as superintendent.

Our society often assumes that a female in a powerful position must be authoritarian or at least a "witch." One mother informed Crisci: "I always wanted to meet you, but in a way I didn't want to meet you because I was told that you were such a witch. Now I'm really glad that I did meet you because you really aren't a witch!" Crisci now feels that after her first few months in the position, her minority status had little effect on her performance.

Superintendents, whether from a large or small district, male or female, have assigned responsibilities that are similar to Crisci's:

> I'm responsible for anything and everything that happens in the school system. Let me give you some specific details. I'm responsible for making recommendations to the board about hiring and releasing personnel; responsible for spending the community's money in keeping the school system going; responsible for seeing that transportation is conducted properly; responsible for academic programs which encourage each child to learn to the best of his or her ability; responsible for providing information to the community — this is a very big responsibility.

Pat Crisci has established her own style for working with the community. Her first task was the establishment of a voluntary group of parents, the Citizens Advisory Council. The basic goal of this council was "to get as much information out to the community as we possibly could and also to bring the community into the school system. One of the things our council did was to conduct a survey on the community perception of the school system."

Crisci extended her community activities beyond the parents of school-age children. She became a member of the board of the YMCA and frequently spoke to the Lions Club, Kiwanis, and the Chamber of Commerce. Crisci even infiltrated a group of senior citizens:

> I was able to infiltrate, and I say this word in its positive sense, a group of senior citizens who had no children in the school. This group, referred to as the "brown baggers," has met every Tuesday for ten or fifteen years in the local church. They bring their lunch and sit around a large table and talk about any topic that they feel is important. I tried to explain to them the importance of a strong school system. This definitely is not the kind of group that you would normally expect to be supportive of the school system and of school levies, but we need the support of this group.

Involvement with the professional staff has a high priority with Pat Crisci. She tries to visit all of the classrooms in her district within a period of two years. The goal of these visits is to compliment teachers: "They rarely receive reinforcement from colleagues." When asked why she enjoyed the position of superintendent, Crisci cited the power and authority of the position to effect needed changes. After learning that high school social studies test results were close to or below the national norm, she became involved with the professional staff in revising the social studies curriculum: "Before I could have changed the curriculum as a psychologist or supervisor, I would have had to write several reports, attend nu-

merous meetings, and spend several years on the task; as superintendent, I facilitated the curriculum change in six months."

What should an inexperienced teacher know about the school system? Crisci's advice to the beginning teacher is to learn about the whole system—not only the classroom, not only how the children learn or about a particular content area, but the entire educational system. She becomes more specific when she suggests: "I don't know if there is any change lately over what existed when I took my teacher certification course, but we learned absolutely nothing about where the money comes from, how it's spent, who has the power to do what, and what problems exist in the school district." To learn about the educational system, Dr. Crisci recommends that a teacher should:

- Attend board of education meetings
- Read what the teacher's contract has to say about the teacher's role (Crisci stated that "in all the time that I have been in education, I have only met one teacher who has ever said, 'Could I see this section of the code so that I can understand what I'm signing?'")
- Talk to parents regarding their interests and aspirations for their children
- "Knock at the superintendent's door and say, 'Hi'."

The solutions to the problems of vandalism and violence range from techniques that seem to be adapted from guerilla warfare to those that would be recommended by humanistic psychologists. Proposed solutions include:

- Police helicopters hovering over schools in a large metropolitan school district
- Armed and unarmed school guards
- Safety corridors through tough neighborhoods that are patrolled by parents and school security guards
- Staggered night shifts for cleaning personnel so that someone is always in the school
- Having school personnel carry a nonelectronic ultrasonic transmitter that can be used to send emergency messages to the central security office
- More student involvement in the curriculum process

The second technique, the use of armed and unarmed school guards, tends to be an approach used by many school districts. The role of the school guard seems to vary all the way from that of a prison guard to that of a counselor and helper. Often the school guard is a resident of the community and, consequently, many administrators feel that the guard can interact with the students and their parents as a neighbor rather than a policeman. Our interviewee, Connie Wellons, was among the first security guards hired in the Pittsburgh public schools. According to an administrator who worked with Wellons, she was the most effective school counselor in his building. This administrator often sent students to this "security guard" for help, support, and love. As you read Wellons' biography focus on the following:

1. Does she see a conflict between her guard duties and counseling responsibilities?
2. What is her relationship with the "professional" counseling staff in the school?
3. Can school guards solve the problem of school violence, or is the problem embedded in the fabric of American society?
4. How can you, as a teacher, use the services of the school guard for the benefit of your students?
5. As you visit nearby schools, observe the interactions among the security guards, teachers, and pupils.

Connie Wellons helps provide security in the best possible way: by helping prevent situations that are likely to spawn disruptive behavior. Observe other school guards who are effective, that is, who obtain positive results with students without using authoritarian techniques. How do they do it? What techniques could you borrow or adopt from the guards as you work with students in the classrooms?

Connie Wellons
SECURITY GUARD

After having helped to quell a racial riot in her community's high school in 1969, Connie Wellons was asked by the area superintendent of schools to become one of the first security guards in her community's high schools. The criteria for selecting Wellons were not based on physical strength and authoritarian behavior but on her understanding of the school community, an ability to deal with conflict using nonauthoritarian techniques, and a concern for all students and their parents.

Most positions in the public schools have clear role descriptions (e.g., you are to do *a, b, c, . . . x, y, z*). Wellons informed the area superintendent that she would accept the position if she could develop her own role description: "If they wanted me to go in there and squeal on kids, then forget it! I spent my first day walking through the halls,

introducing myself to kids I didn't know and informing all of the kids that they could come to me with any problems." When asked why she began her first day with a caring, counselor approach rather than an authoritarian, police approach, Wellons explained:

> I don't work that way; it never occurred to me to work that way. I was only interested in changing some racial attitudes in whatever way I could. I wanted to show the black kids that blacks could be friendly with whites without being "tomish." I wanted to show the white kids who have stereotypes, that most blacks aren't the way you've been taught.

As Wellons defined her role, a major responsibility that she assumed was to be a liaison between students, teachers, principal, and parents. One example she cited involved a teacher who had difficulty differentiating "spunk" from "insubordination" in a student's behavior. The principal, after hearing the teacher's report on the student, recommended that the student be suspended. Wellons objected:

> When I met with the vice principal and the teacher, I said, "Hey, you suspended that girl for the very thing that helped her survive: a spunky attitude. Her mother died when she was a kid and she's taking care of two others, one of whom is a deaf mute. If she didn't have the spunk, she wouldn't have survived to the twelfth grade, and you suspended her for that."

Teachers became aware of Wellons' ability to act as a liaison between school and community. Often, teachers requested Wellons' assistance with a problem that required information about the home and community:

> Teachers will come to me and say, "Do you know so and so?" They'll inform me that the student is not acting appropriately. I may know the child and his home life and recommend that the teacher does *a, b,* or *c*. I know if a kid is very poor or hungry or embarrassed by the way he is dressed. Some of the teachers are surprised to learn that I know, really know, the white kids and their parents.

Another of Connie Wellons' major responsibilities fits into the category of counseling: she makes a point of coordinating her counseling efforts with the school social worker. Often a student is more comfortable talking to a security aide or a teacher than the social worker. A high-level skill of Ms. Wellons is her ability to decide whether or not she has the ability to handle a situation with a child: "I will do counseling until I think it is over my head. I counsel them just like I would counsel my own kids. If the situation involves child abuse or running away from home, I make sure to get the social worker involved."

"Discipline," the major area of responsibility for the security guard, is often the major concern of beginning teachers. Wellons advises new teachers to maintain a balance between the two extreme forms of discipline ("love them" or "beat them"):

> Some new teachers have credited me with helping them develop effective discipline techniques. (I could not, of course, tell them what to do about the subject matter or even how to teach it.) I tell new teachers to go in with a strong attitude and accept only a minimum amount of disruptive behavior. But admit that you're wrong when you're wrong. A real cog in the wheels is when teachers refuse to admit they're wrong in front of the class.

She also counsels young teachers not to rely too heavily on IQ and achievement test scores:

> In talking with teachers, I found that if they expect a high standard of work from the students, they often get it. Their knowledge of test scores (especially low ones!) gets in the way of what can be expected from students. I would like to tell them not to push for or depend on corporal punishment, but to use this brain up here. You're all supposed to be students of psychology—use your knowledge!

School Volunteer

The school volunteer is part of the American tradition of volunterism that many feel forms the backbone of democracy in the United States. Today 2 million school volunteers perform numerous tasks in the school: tutor, materials designer, member of parents advisory committee and/or parents-teachers association, assistant on field trips, and classroom parent. Wilson Riles, Superintendent of Public Instruction in California and a national leader in the movement for involving parents in their children's education, states succinctly: "The teacher needs to know all he can about the child and the parents need to know all they can about the school. Parents and teachers need to work together as a team."[10]

Various events in the past ten years have influenced the growth of volunteerism in the schools. In many instances, especially in the cases of Florida and California, parental participation in the schools has been mandated by law. Additionally, professional educators realize that volunteers can sometimes save ancillary programs, such as tutoring of children with special needs, counseling, music, and art, that might otherwise be cut because of a lack of funds. Enrollment decreases in the late 1970s typically led to cutbacks in such programs rather than to a lowering of the teacher-pupil ratios. As Schindler-Reinman, and Lippitt put it: "[The] teacher-to-student ratio will tend to remain at 1 to 25 or 30. At the same time, there is a need for more development of teams of volunteers and para-professionals working with professionals to extend services."[11]

It is quite possible that in the not too distant future the primary role of professional educators may shift from one of giving direct service (i.e., teaching and counseling) to the client (i.e., student) to one that involves leading a team of volunteers and paid paraprofessionals who dispense most of the direct service to clients.

Ann Gargan is one of the 2 million school volunteers in American schools. She is tutoring individuals and small groups of students who are labelled as "autistic" and "learning disabled." The biography that follows focuses on Gargan's motivation for volunteering, her assigned and assumed roles in the classroom, her training, and her advice for beginning teachers. As you read the biography, focus on the following:

1. Why do volunteers volunteer?
2. Compare Ann Gargan's role in the classroom with other volunteers with whom you are familiar.
3. How can you as a teacher use the services of school volunteers?

Despite the use of 2 million school volunteers, most schools and teachers still fail to capitalize on the human resources available to them: the talented tutors, artists, and materials designers within the community. For numerous reasons (fear of meddling, lack of experiences with parents, lack of awareness of available talent), volunteer programs are still not used enough in the schools. Make a point of observing in a school where volunteers are used and contrast its program and environment with another school that does not use volunteers. Will the inclusion of volunteers in a school influence your decision to seek or not to seek a teaching position in that particular school?

Ann Gargan
SCHOOL VOLUNTEER

Ann Gargan is one of the 2 million volunteers in the public schools. Her multiple roles have included classroom parent, lunchroom parent, PTA officer, field-trip parent, and now tutor in a special-education classroom for autistic children. This parent of three school-age children was able to become deeply involved in the schools even though she had her own career, operating an informal day care center in her home. A combination of circumstances led Gargan to discontinue her home day care and to begin a full-time position as a tutor with exceptional children. One circumstance was the recognition by school faculty and administrators that she had developed exceptional teaching competencies from her day care experience; the other was an awareness by school personnel that she had a deep concern for her community's schools. "In my case, the director of special education asked some of his teachers if they knew of anyone who would be good at working with exceptional children. The teacher contacted me."

Her jobs in the classroom are many and varied. Gargan's responsibilities include:

- *Helping on field trips.* "Watching out for children and making sure they are all where they are supposed to be. I try to ask individual children questions about what we are doing; in this way they can better understand the purpose of the trip."
- *Tutoring children in math and reading.* "As the children work in learning centers, I decide who needs attention and go to that student. I ask questions, give praise, and focus the child on the task if necessary."
- *Assisting the teacher during formal instruction involving the entire class.* "If a child becomes distracted, I try to refocus his attention. I'll work with this child on a one-to-one basis if he can't function in a group."

The in-service training for Ann Gargan is primarily informal, on-the-job experiences. Each day the certified teachers spend ten to fifteen minutes with her, reviewing the schedule for the day and discussing specific children. Ann has designed her own "formal" training by borrowing books on instruction and exceptional children from the professional staff. After ten years of observing parent-teacher interactions, Ann has concluded that the direction of the relationship between parent and teacher must be changed. Typically, the relationship consists of the school professional asking (and hoping) that the parent comes to school for the open house, conference, and special events. Parent participation is often poor at these events. Ann believes that the teachers must get out into the community to meet the children and the parents. This community contact can, in Ann's words: "lead to a human-to-human interaction rather than a professional talking 'at' or 'down to' a parent." A second advantage of this changed direction in teacher-parent-child contact is that the teacher will have information about the home/community that can be used in classroom discussion: "If you're familiar with what's happening in the child's home/community you can make a better connection with the child, too."

Ann's advice to beginning teachers is to emulate one of her daughter's teachers who genuinely cared for all of her students, even the bad ones: "Now this woman may be unique. She never had to raise her voice, and every one of those kids felt that she truly cared about them." Ann's second area of advice concerns the need for providing individual attention for every child, even if the teacher has 25, 30, or 35 children. Ann's advice: develop a parent volunteer program.

Teacher Assistant

Pearl and Riessman, in their classic book, *New Careers for the Poor,* argue that the role of teacher encompasses too many diverse activities.[12] They propose splitting a teacher's role into a hierarchy of five more specialized positions as follows:

- *Teacher aide.* Functions would range from supervision of recess and lunch time activities to operating audiovisual equipment. Training requirements would include workshops but no formal college or university training.
- *Teacher assistant.* Functions would include preparation of teaching materials, correction of student assignments, and tutoring of individuals and small groups. Training requirements would include two years of college or university study in addition to a level of teaching competence acquired as an aide.
- *Teacher associate.* Responsibilities would be similar to those performed by the classroom teacher: tutoring, designing learning materials, evaluating students' progress. The associate would be under the direct supervision of a supervising teacher. Advancement to this level would occur with two additional years of work and university studies.
- *Certified teacher.* Responsibilities would focus almost totally on the instructional process: short- and long-range planning, designing instructional activities, and coordinating the teaching of the other professionals on the team.
- *Supervising teacher.* Responsibility is focused on the supervision of

those at the beginning steps of the career ladder. The career ladder developed by Pearl and Riessman meets numerous objectives. First, students will receive more individual attention from adults in the classroom. Second, certified teachers will be able to assume the role of professional by delegating to others the more menial tasks. Third (and perhaps the major objective of Pearl and Riessman), career opportunities will be opened up for those who have been excluded from roles in the schools: the poor. They write: "These five teaching roles would exist along a continuum in which advancement from entry position to full-fledged professional could be negotiable on the basis of talent and motivation, rather than economic means."[13]

The first large-scale experiment in the use of teaching aides occurred in the 1950s in Bay City, Michigan.[14] These aides, most of whom were from the middle-class, had little aspiration to climb the professional ladder of education from aide to teacher. Their objective was a limited one: to free the professional teacher from the menial jobs in the classroom. As late as 1960, only 19 states reported the use of aides in the classroom.

Then came the Kennedy–Johnson War on Poverty, with its extensive development of human-service programs. This led to the use of aides (often called "paraprofessionals") in numerous helping professions: education, social work, and health care. These new paraprofessionals differed greatly from the pioneers in the Bay City experiment. They tended to be economically poor, came from minority backgrounds, and desired the opportunity to climb the "career ladder," that is, not to be stuck in a low-paying, dead-end position.

Minneapolis, in 1964, was one of the first cities to initiate the widespread use of paraprofessionals in the schools. This program grew to 200 paraprofessionals by 1965 and, unlike most cities, Minneapolis initiated a career ladder for its participants. Increased pay and responsibility could be attained with the acquisition of teaching competencies and college credit.[15]

Statistics exemplify the growth of the new careers in education. In 1966 there were approximately 80,000 classroom paraprofessionals; by 1970 this figure increased to 200,000; three years later, 300,000 paraprofessionals were employed in the public schools. George Kaplan estimates that 1.5 million paraprofessionals will be working in the schools in the 1980s.[16] Between 1970 and 1975 the Career Opportunities Program (COP), funded by the U.S. Office of Education, developed a model for career development of paraprofessionals. The model encouraged cooperation among the public schools, community colleges, and four-year colleges that eventually led to a bachelor's degree and teacher certification. During the life of the program, 14,000 persons climbed to the top of the career ladder through this program; more importantly, it led to new teacher-training procedures, such as field-based training, open admissions, and life-experience credit.

Joanne Jackson
ASSISTANT TEACHER

1960 is an important year in modern education history. It was the year that public education, with the financial support of the Ford Foundation, began to bring other adults into the schools to assist teachers and children. Joanne Jackson was among the first assistant teachers hired in the United States when she began the 1960 school year with a group of 20 other assistants in the Pittsburgh public schools. The assistants (given the title "team mothers") were identified as mothers from the community who had a deep concern for children and the schools. Jackson's primary tasks were clerical: typing, preparing dittos, and operating and repairing audiovisual aids. It was also expected that the team mothers would assume a liaison role between the school and community, but this role was not specifically defined by the school administration. Jackson assumed numerous liaison responsibilities. A major responsibility was to in-form the teachers in her school about situations in the community and in specific families that might have affected a child's social or academic performance. She did not "spy" or "snoop" on the community; she simply tried to help the middle-class teachers in the school understand why a child was performing in a particular way.

"We become mothers to the children," Jackson reports. This mothering role might involve sewing a split in a boy's pants or replacing a missing button: "I always kept a needle and thread for emergencies!" Because of her previous career in nursing, she sometimes assumed the role of school nurse:

> It's really funny, the things that can happen in school. With my R.N. background, when the regular school nurse wasn't there, I had to ride in the ambulance when a child had an accident. Of course, it wasn't my job; I wasn't paid for this. And then if the child had a rash, the teacher brought him to me for an examination. This nursing responsibility was just something that came about.

Assuming a role that "was just something that came about" also occurred in another area. Jackson became the advisor, consultant, and the shoulder to cry on for new teachers in her school. As stated, a co-author of this book regularly went to her for advice about a child, a suggestion for a discipline technique, and information about the community. When asked why she helped beginning teachers who were paid twice her salary, Jackson replied: "We felt as if we were all one family.

You were taught this beautiful theory, experience is worth a thousand words, so I had to show the new people how to get along." She compared her induction of inexperienced teachers in the school to the induction inexperienced doctors with whom she had worked in hospitals received: "An intern straight out of medical school is dumb, and the doctor doesn't want to teach him the fundamental things; it's the nurse who teaches him the hospital routine. It's the same sort of thing in education with inexperienced teachers."

During the late 1960s, Jackson's title changed from "team mother" to "team aide." The assistant teachers began to be assigned more time for tutoring tasks and less time for clerical tasks. Later, the title was changed to "learning modality aide" to signify the added tutoring responsibilities. Presently, she spends 50 percent of her time tutoring individuals and small groups of children in reading and mathematics, 25 percent of her time preparing learning materials, and 25 percent assisting teachers in their classrooms. Jackson was asked how she liked the change in role from clerical to teaching during the past 20 years:

> I like it. The teachers think of you more as an assistant. The government decided that there's no use paying all these people all this money if they didn't work directly with the children. This year, each child has gone up at least a level in reading, so we felt it was a success.

We concluded our interview by asking Mrs. Jackson to give advice to those individuals who are considering teaching as a career:

> I first say to someone that they have to like the job. I don't believe in taking a job for money. You are there to do a job. The money to me may be basic, but it's not the reason for taking a job. You want to find out what you can do for this child or what you can do for this group of children.

Our interviewee, Joanne Jackson, was in the first group of teacher assistants hired by a public school system when she began her employment with the Pittsburgh public schools in 1960. In 1964 she was a teacher assistant with one of the co-authors of this book (Goldman). As you study her biography focus on the following issues:

- How does Jackson feel when she works with a certified teacher who has less skills than she has (as was the case with Goldman in 1964)?
- How does she feel that the services of teacher aides and assistants should be used in school?
- How would you like to use the services of a teacher assistant in your classroom?

In her job as an assistant teacher, Jackson is a liaison to the community, a tutor of children with learning problems, and a guide for new teachers. Do you think these roles are too complex for a teacher assistant who typically lacks a BA degree and specialized training in education? We think not. As Kaplan and Pearl and Reissman have documented, people with the competencies mentioned above exist in every community in the United States. We challenge you to visit urban, suburban, and rural communities in your region that make extensive use of teacher assistants and try to identify the teachers and the assistants. More often than not, you will have difficulty making the correct identification. Observe a formal teaching situation; does the assistant lack complex teaching techniques? You may be surprised at what you see.

Custodian

"The custodian's chief responsibility is to keep the school environment a pleasant, safe, healthful, and satisfying place in which to learn and work."[17] Although both custodians and professionals would agree with the above role description, they might not agree on how the role should be implemented. For example, you have probably heard stories about how teachers design their rooms to suit the custodian rather than to produce the best possible learning environment for children. One reason for this is the principal's failure to supervise the custodians adequately, a situation that allows the custodians to have complete freedom for determining what they should do and how they should do it.

Another reason for the above problem is the typical faculty's reluctance to include the custodian (and other nonprofessional personnel) in meetings where curriculum, classroom design, and specific children are discussed. Such involvement could lead to the custodian's understanding of why children's projects are on the floor, why the desks are not in neat rows, and why desks (for tutoring) are located in the halls. Interaction between custodian and faculty can also lead to improved faculty decision making. For example:

> In some situations the custodian knows the parents better than the teachers or principal know them, and if he has worked in the building over a period of years, he has information about the community, the neighborhood, and the youngsters to which the professional staff is not privy. It is quite natural for teachers and administrators to seek information from the custodian, so in addition to fulfilling the more technical aspects of his position, he becomes a communications center, a focal point of interaction within the school building.[18]

Herb Reed is a custodian who is involved with children, who knows what is happening in the school, and who should be involved in school decision making along with the professional staff. As you read his biography, think about the following:

- Why does he take time to be with children?
- How could Reed be a resource for the teachers?
- Should his interactions with children be formalized (e.g., assisting the counselor, tutoring children with problems)? Why do you think so—why not?

Herb Reed
SCHOOL CUSTODIAN

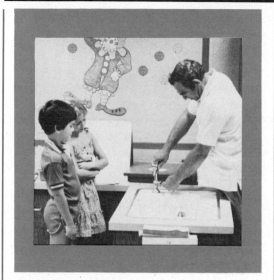

He orients kindergarten children to the school. He cuddles children who are in tears. He suggests strategies to teachers for children who have difficulty with school. We just met the school counselor? Wrong. He's the school's custodian! Herbert Reed is responsible for the physical operation of a new, open space school that has a student body of 843 and an adult staff of 50. His major assigned responsibilities include cleaning, general maintenance, and "fixing anything that goes wrong" in a large, modern school building.

Why does this custodian take time from a busy schedule to interact and care for "his" children? Reed's response to the question of why he wanted to become a custodian clarifies the reason he assumes responsibilities beyond his maintenance tasks: "Well, first of all, I like the kids, and second, I like to fix and maintain things." Reed chose the position of school custodian rather than that of an industrial custodian because the school environment enables him to do what he enjoys best:

> The kindergarten kids are new and so little, so you kind of have to help them a little bit. A hug, tying a shoe, helping them to find their class. First, I always try to make them smile when I see them in the morning. This helps them to begin their day on the right foot.

Fifth graders, Herb Reed feels, often have different needs from those of the younger children. The needs relate to the reasons why a child wants to interact with the custodian: "This fifth grader wanted a ramp built for his skate board. He doesn't have a dad at home; I guess that he felt that I was the best substitute he could find. So together, we built a ramp."

At the conclusion of the interview, Reed asked the interviewer to join him as he walked through the lunchroom. "I want to show you something with the kids," he said. We quietly entered the lunchroom. Within seconds, Reed was spotted by the children and was invited to visit each table. "I finished my vegetables," "Look at my new shirt," "Can I help you this afternoon?" were a few of the many comments addressed to the custodian.

Reed's special help is not limited to children. Daily, this custodian receives requests from teachers for tasks that are not within the assigned role description:

> One teacher came down here and

wanted holes drilled in her sea shells so that she could hang them from the ceiling. Teachers asked me to help decorate the main entranceway for the holidays. The job is mine now. At Christmas time, we make a fireplace and have pictures of Santa Claus coming down. For Halloween, we get an old dead tree and hang Halloween things on it.

Pressure is not placed on Reed to limit his role to the traditional custodial tasks performed by his colleagues in other buildings: "They are not going to do the same thing. No, they don't do nothing with the children. They ask, 'What do you do that for?'" The reaction of the people "downtown" (his supervisors in the central administration) is clear: "As far as the people downtown are concerned, they want the windows and floors cleaned. The other stuff is up to me."

The "other stuff" is the positive working/helping relationship Herb Reed has developed with students and staff: "I try to be good to them, and they are good to me. It's like a family. That's what I like."

Principal

Nineteenth-century urbanization led to the expansion of schools from one room to eight or more rooms. This increased size placed demands on the school that could best be accomplished by a part-time or full-time administrator. As early as 1838, Cincinnati established a "principal-teacher" in each school. This administrative layer spread to Boston in 1847 and later to St. Louis in 1859. Initially, the principals' tasks were clerical in nature, for example, keeping track of enrollment and placing students in the appropriate grades. Eventually, the principal was relieved of his or her teaching duties so that he or she could work full-time at management responsibilities. Marian Dogherty, a teacher in the Cambridge, Massachusetts schools in the late 1800s, described the "awe" (or should we say "fear"?) that teachers had for their principals during this time:

"But one day I became aware that a teacher was subservient to higher authority," Marian Dogherty observed. One day in came Mr. Dutton [the principal] to take his seat on the platform next to her and to hear the recitations. "Our principal was a stickler for the proprieties, and the proper way to read in the public school in the year 1899 was to say, 'Page 35, Chapter 4,' and holding the book in the right hand, with toes pointing at an angle of forty-five degrees, the head held straight and high, the eyes looking directly ahead, the pupil would lift up his voice and struggle in loud, unnatural tones." Miss Dogherty had properly trained the toes and arms, but she thought reciting chapter and page "a cold douche on the interest of the story." The principal was not amused by the childrens' prodigious ignorance of the proprieties. As he left, disconcerted, the children chorused: "Good afternoon Mr. Dutton." "As for me," recalled the teacher, "only centuries of the civilization process kept me safe. Had I followed my primitive instincts—but it is no matter." For the rest of the day, stretching to twilight, she coached the children on how to address the august principal, impersonating his mannerisms with an earnestness born of her own respect for the "benign but awful" power of the system.[19]

The principals' management style in the nineteenth century matched the administrative styles of large businesses or industries: authority rather than praise. Conversely, principals in the 1980s generally want to view themselves as instructional leaders who help design programs, lead in-service training, and establish a school environment conducive for students' social and academic growth. Dr. Donna Lightel, an elementary school principal, pursues the lofty goals associated with the role of instructional leader. As you read her biography think about the following:

- Why does Lightel stress both social and academic growth in children?
- How does this principal help teachers with their personal problems? Should this be a role of the principal?
- Unlike "Mr. Dutton," the principal described above, Lightel does not "put the fear of God" in the faculty and students. Has this principal's style moved too far from the authoritarian style that principals used to have?
- Do you agree that a teacher should try to develop a colleagueship with the principal?
- How would you use Lightel's skills if you worked with her?

Although Donna Lightel is a special principal with unique talents, remember that she works in a typical public school in a typical midwestern community. If you look around we feel that you will find other principals in your region with equivalent, if somewhat different, skills. Whatever the style, the principal functions as captain of the ship. As you visit schools look for data in the total school environment that indicate the type of leadership style assumed by the "captain."

School Counselor

The origins of the school counselor's role are somewhat obscure. Historically, teachers have felt that their close contact with students made them the best person to counsel students on their personal and vocational problems. Gradually, as schools increased in size and complexity, school administrators began to hire specialists in counseling. Their titles varied depending on the emphasis of the school districts: guidance officer, guidance counselor, guidance worker, placement counselor, or school counselor. The school counselor's approach also varied according to the school district's goals and the counselor's training: vocational guidance, clinical psychology, psychological testing, ego psychology, group or case work.[20]

Donna Lightel
PRINCIPAL

A person who invites children to her office for lunch and helps teachers solve personal problems that may interfere with their teaching—these are two of the roles assumed by Donna Lightel, an elementary school principal. Her concern for the emotional health of children and teachers stems from her background as a school counselor and from her own family where "caring" for others was the accepted philosophy:

> My parents are "people" kind of people. The philosophy that I was raised under stressed that you are on this earth to help other people. It has been drilled into me for years that you never do enough for other people. If you are not helping then you are not doing what you should be doing. My family's philosophy may help you understand why I like to work in schools with children and teachers.

This philosophy of "caring" can be seen in her relationships with students and teachers. She reacted to the statement, "So you look at the teaching staff as your colleagues rather than as subordinates," by stating: "Oh definitely. They are my colleagues. We often talk in small groups during lunch or after school about important issues; we problem solve together." Her concern for the faculty goes beyond their direct interaction with children. Most teachers feel comfortable talking to Lightel about personal problems that may have a direct or indirect effect on their teaching performance: "A teacher arrives at school in the morning and I read a real uptight situation; I would rather move in and listen with the hope of alleviating the problem so that when the teacher goes into the classroom, she can give it all to the kids."

Lightel's caring attitude can be seen in her interaction with children. She does not view the principal as the head disciplinarian, whom children should fear, but as someone who will listen to the children:

> I don't think there is fear when I talk to a child with a problem. There are times when I need to clarify my expectations for the child. My comments are not as a disciplinarian: I want the child to know what he owes himself in terms of behavior. If a child drops from an "A" to a "D," I want him to know that I care about him; we try to work out a strategy together.

This principal has a unique approach for integrating new students into the school environment. The new student begins to feel that someone cares for him or her when he or she receives a printed invitation to have lunch with the principal:

> Children are given the invitation on Monday for lunch with the principal on a specified day. We eat together at a separate table in the lunchroom. Our luncheon discussion allows me to learn the name of the students and some background information about each one of them. I make a point the next day to meet each child in the hall or in his classroom and to address him by his name.

Contacts between the school and community are being mandated today by school boards and state legislatures. Lightel has established strong relationships with the community, not because the relationships are mandated, but because she feels they are vital for the children. These relationships include informal discussions with small groups of parents, parent directed minicourses for the students, and retirees doing volunteer work with the children.

What should the relationship be between the teacher and principal? "We [principal and teacher] are only going to help a student if we work together. The teacher is going to have problems. I'm going to share my problems with you [teacher] and ask for your help; at the same time, you can share some of your problems with me and ask for my help." Lightel is aware that not all principals have a reciprocal, helping relationship with their faculties. She feels that if a teacher cannot find this sharing/helping relationship with the principal, that he or she must find it somewhere else in the school:

> My very blunt feeling is if you don't hear the "vibes" from a principal, that he is there to support you, then you have to look to another teacher for the colleagueship that you need. If a new teacher listens to the conversations in the halls and teachers' lounge, it doesn't take long to identify those teachers who are willing to help their inexperienced colleagues.

As you read the biography of Ferguson Meadows notice that his counseling is not limited by one approach or philosophy. As you read his biography, think about the following:

- Meadows feels that the school and community should develop close relationships. What are your thoughts about the way he attempts to establish these relationships?
- Meadows feels that he could help you as a teacher. How could you make use of his skills?
- Do you agree that students, parents, and teachers should share the counseling role with school counselor? Contrast your views with those of Ferguson Meadows.

We can predict what you will think: "Ferguson Meadows was not the counselor in *my* school. The only time a student saw the counselor was

Ferguson Meadows
SCHOOL COUNSELOR

The vision of the school counselor as someone who spends his day sitting at a desk studying IQ or personality tests does not match the behavior of Ferguson Meadows. This counselor spends his day with teachers, students, and parents on their "turf," i.e., in the classroom, teachers' lounge, and community.

Ferguson envisions a school/community environment where all persons care about and help counsel one another. In order to create this environment, he tries to build a cadre of care givers (students, teachers, and parents) who develop and use counseling-type skills. He summarizes his views about people learning to counsel one another:

> It seems to me that one of the reactions that we had in the 1960s was something like, "Well, we now have more money

for education, so let's hire a counselor for every school. These experts will solve the social and academic problems in the schools." We didn't realize in the 1960s that a handful of people would have little impact on a school with 200 or 2000 students. We couldn't service that many children; now we're trying to develop the untapped resources found in every school: students, teachers, parents, custodians, secretaries.

Students learn counseling-type skills through a series of seminars with Ferguson that include topics such as interviewing techniques, identifying the problem, and when to refer situations to the counselor. Since Ferguson does not limit these sessions only to the "good" students, he finds that those students who have had difficulty with school often obtain insight into their own situations as they talk about other students who have problems similar to their own. Ferguson has found that most teachers want to develop noninstructional skills, such as the ability to lead values-clarification and magic-circle groups. Afterward the teachers inform Ferguson that they are better able to deal with situations that they had formally referred to the school counselor or psychologist.

Ferguson feels that both counselors and teachers need to make contacts in the community. Those contacts, he feels, will help break down the barrier that often exists between school and community. This community connection can begin with a simple procedure, the home visit:

The home visit should bring positive information to the home, not just the typical information about a problem in school or the need for counseling. I'm trying to help the kids and their families. A counselor does not just deal with kids in a vacuum; he must deal with the family system.

Although home visits typically have a formal structure, i.e., a specified meeting time where preplanned topics are discussed, Ferguson feels that counselors should also have unplanned, informal visits in the community. These informal contacts may occur in the supermarket, at the community park, at church, etc.:

Let me tell you what frequently happens. I'm walking in the community and I see a student with his parents. Often the student will introduce me to his parents. When I have the need to invite these parents in for a conference or to request that they share their skills with

the students, I find that those parents with whom I have had this informal contact feel much more comfortable about me and the school.

The beginning teacher, Ferguson feels, should learn about the role of the counselor during his undergraduate preparation. Visit the schools and knock on the counselor's door. Ask him directly how he plans to work with the children and staff. He also recommends that college faculty include a counselor as part of their teacher-education team. Who should be a teacher?

You may be the most brilliant student, but you won't make it in the schools if you don't have a "feel" for students. I think you need to find this out early. Teacher-education programs should introduce the students to children early in their programs rather than waiting until their junior or senior years: this is a hell of a time to find out that teaching and children aren't for you.

when he was in trouble." This counselor talks about prevention, a community of helpers, and a colleagueship with teachers. An impossible dream? Contact the counseling department at your university and ask them to describe the roles for which their students are being trained. Are the roles similar to Meadows'? Visit counselors on the "firing line" in the schools; observe and interview them about their roles.

Secretary

The school secretary's role is viewed differently by the diverse people who are a part of the school:

- To the child she is the person who has the Band-Aids.
- To the parent she is the person who sends messages to the children.
- To the teacher she is the person who types dittos, keeps records, and handles the supplies.

Pat Hawkins
SECRETARY

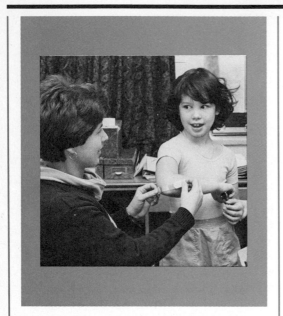

I am considered the secretary to the principal. The job is doing the typing for him plus work for the teachers: running off dittos and ordering materials. In addition, I'm the receptionist in the office and I do a little first aid with the kids. That's about it.

"That's about it" is an understatement, considering the responsibilities Pat Hawkins has been assigned and has assumed on her own. The assumed roles are the ones that tend to be most demanding on her, both from a physical and an emotional perspective.

The children in this school are aware that Hawkins is a person who is never too busy to listen to them: "The middle school kids will stop in just to talk. Sometimes the conversation is about their boyfriends or something that hap-pened in class that upset or pleased them."

Hawkins' close relationships with children are not limited to the middle school students:

There's a little girl who comes in here who is one of my favorites. She's six or seven. She is a very unhappy child because of some home problems, and I think she comes in to talk to me—just to talk. I think because she doesn't get enough attention at home that she tries to get it here from me.

School secretaries are often the first person a parent contacts through a school visit or a telephone conversation. Hawkins realizes that her behavior may affect the parents' attitude about the school. Therefore, she tries to be very responsive to the parents' questions and requests.

When asked, "How can a beginning teacher learn about the responsibilities of the secretary," Pat Hawkins responded, "Come into the office and talk." This secretary demonstrated her insight into people with her suggestion that "the best way to meet the secretary as a person is make sure that she is invited to school-related social functions outside of the school." In other words, she is suggesting that the barrier between faculty and staff be broken. The breaking of the barrier will enable the entire school family to know one another better both on a professional and personal level.

Pat Hawkins began the interview by stating that she is "the secretary to the principal." From her comments and our observation, we concluded that Hawkins is also the secretary to the teachers, children, and parents—a large responsibility for one person.

- To the principal she is the glue that holds the various components of the school in one piece.

Wiley classified the tasks assigned and assumed by a typical school secretary.[21] After you read his classification system, you will be aware that the secretary's role is not limited to taking telephone messages or running the ditto machine.

- *Editorial and research.* Preparing reports, outlining speeches, collecting information, preparing statistics.
- *Public relations.* Handling news releases, distributing newsletters.
- *Bookkeeping and finance.* Receiving fees, budget, and payroll.
- *Student records.* Maintaining enrollment records and transcripts.
- *Instructional supplies.* Handling purchasing and distributing textbooks and paper.
- *Secretarial.* Arranging appointments and handling staff.
- *Receptionist.* Guiding visitors and receiving new students.
- *Typing.* Typing letters, memos, lists, etc.
- *Communication.* Handling phone calls.
- *Office and maintenance supplies.* Preparing purchase orders and handling stock.
- *Staff personnel.* Handling records of application, transfer, etc.
- *Machine operation.* Typing and training staff to use machines.
- *General office.* Sorting mail, keeping bulletin board, and handling keys.

Pat Hawkins, whose biography appears on the opposite page, fills these multiple roles. This school secretary has established a warm tone for the school with her smile and her desire to help *all* persons. As you read this biography ask yourself the following:

- How should Hawkins communicate her complex role to children, teachers, and parents?
- Why would you include or not include the school secretary in a discussion of a particular child's behavior.
- What types of verbal and nonverbal behaviors enable Hawkins to inform all those who come in contact with her that she cares about them?
- As a teacher, how will you interact with your school secretary?

Summary   The school of the 1980s is a complex social system. Perhaps you would like to have been an educator 50 or 100 years ago, when the system seemed simple, only you and your students. But we cannot turn back the clock. In order to be a competent educator today you must acquire, in addition to the pedagogical skills, an ability to do the following:

1. Manage a team that may include volunteers and paid teacher assistants;
2. Decide when and how you want to use the services of the counselor and school psychologist;
3. Develop a knowledgeable sensitivity for the support staff in the school: secretary, custodian, and security guard;
4. Understand how the decisions of the board of education affect your day-to-day work in the school;
5. Make use of the skills of the educational leaders of the school system: the principal and the superintendent.

We hope that the biographies presented in this chapter have helped to immunize you against a disease that is common among educators: tunnel vision. This ailment limits one's perspective of the school to an imaginary tunnel that runs from the school's parking lot to the classroom. A person inflicted with this tunnel vision does not have the ability either to see or to use the entire school environment. To further immunize yourself, we suggest that you complete the Encounters suggested below.

1. Obtain a copy of a current teacher's contract from the teacher's bargaining organization. Compare the contract of the 1980s with the one presented in this chapter. What are the implications of the changes in the teacher's role for you as a beginning teacher?

2. Visit a nearby school. List all the roles in this school. Try to fantasize what it would have been like to have taught in a school in the eighteenth century, when it was expected that you alone would assume all the roles found in a modern school. Share your fantasies with your colleagues and instructor.

3. Conduct an oral history with retired teachers who are in their seventies and eighties. Ask them to describe their responsibilities as teachers and then compare them with the responsibilities of a modern teacher.

4. Obtain the names and backgrounds of members of boards of education in your area. As you examine the backgrounds of the members, do you feel they are capable of "guarding the integrity of the various minority groups"?

5. Attend a school board meeting. If possible, talk with a board member after the meeting. Look for signs of cooperation or tension. Do the board and the superintendent seem to work well together? In what types of activities does the board take direct action? How does the board affect the daily operations of the school?

6. Spend an hour or two with a school custodian. What sort of contact does the custodian have with children? What attitude does the custodian have toward the school? Does this tell you anything about the school environment?

7. Interview three volunteers in the school. Why are they there? What special talents do they bring to the classroom? What are their responsibilities? Observe them working with children. What sort of relationship exists between the child and the volunteer?

8. Spend some time with a school principal in an urban, a rural, and a suburban school. Chart the differences you observe in areas such as these: time spent disciplining students, type of discipline used, nondisciplinary types of contacts with students, contacts with teachers, attitudes displayed by the principal, and general atmosphere of the school.

9. Volunteer to spend a morning helping a busy school secretary. How does the secretary handle jobs such as public relations, helping students and teachers, and keeping the school running smoothly?

Notes

1. Johana Lemlech and Merele B. Marks, *The American Teacher: 1776-1976* (Bloomington, Ind.: Phi Delta Kappa Educational Foundation, 1976), p. 22.

2. David E. Dix, "Along the Way," *Kent-Ravenna (Ohio) Record Courier*, July 28, 1977, p. 12.

3. Larry Cuban, *The Urban School Superintendency: A Century and Half of Change* (Bloomington, Ind.: Phi Delta Kappa Educational Foundation, 1976), p. 9.

4. George Counts, *American Education: Its Men, Ideas, and Institutions* (New York: Arno Press, 1969), p. 83–84.

5. *Ibid.,* p. 97.

6. Jesse H. Newlon, *Educational Administrator as Social Policy* (New York: Scribner's, 1934), p. 125.

7. Cuban, *The Urban School Superintendency,* p. 12.

8. Neal Gross, *Who Runs Our Schools?* (New York: Wiley, 1958), p. 59.

9. Joseph Wint, "Contrasting Solutions for School Violence," *Phi Delta Kappan, 54* (November 1975), 175–76.

10. Henry C. Black III, *Parent Volunteer Programs in Early Childhood Education* (Hamden, Conn.: Linnet, 1976), p. 12.

11. Eva Schindler–Reinman, and Ronald Lippitt, *The Volunteer Community* (Washington, D.C.: Center for a Voluntary Society, 1971), p. 34.

12. Arthur Pearl and Frank Riessman, *New Careers for the Poor* (New York: Free Press, 1965).

13. *Ibid.,* p. 57.

14. George R. Kaplan, *From Aide to Teacher: The Story of the Career Opportunities Program* (Washington, D.C.: U.S. Department of Health, Education and Welfare, 1977).

15. *Ibid.,* p. 24.

16. *Ibid.,* p. 3.

17. R. E. Campbell, L. L. Cunningham, and R. F. McPhee, *The Organization and Control of American Schools* (Columbus, Ohio: Merrill, 1965), p. 303.

18. *Ibid.,* p. 303.

19. David B. Tyack, *The One Best System: A History of American Urban Education* (Cambridge, Mass.: Harvard University Press, 1974), pp. 255–56.

20. Edward C. Roeber, *The School Counselor* (Washington, D.C.: Center for Applied Research in Education, 1963).

21. Eldon L. Wiley, "A Secretarial Staff Adequacy Formula for Elementary Schools," *Educational Technology, 16* (January 1976), 59–60.

For More Information

JOURNALS

Carey, Maggie, and Hamm, Russell. "Dysfunction in School Administration," *NASSP Bulletin, 62* (1978), 1–4.

Creekmore, Edward L. "How Big Cities Train for School Security: A Nationwide Survey," *Security World, 11* (1974), 28–29, 46.

Jackson, Philip W. "Lonely at the Top: Observations on the Genesis of Administrative Isolation," *School Review, 85* (1977), 425–432.

Koehler, Michael D. "Schools Without 'Lowerarchies': Are They Possible?" *Clearing House, 52* (1979), 434–435.

Lolli, Anthony, Jr. "Implementing the Role of the School Psychologist," *Psychology in the Schools, 17* (1980), 70–74.

Maguire, John W. "The Beginning Secondary Principal: Any Path Won't Do," *Education, 98* (1978), 311–315.

Mann, William D. "Work with Your School Secretary," *NASSP Bulletin, 64* (1980), 87–90.

Mooney, Joseph P. "The School Community Relations Triangle," *NASSP Bulletin, 64* (1980), 63–69.

Neill, Shirley Boes. "Violence and Vandalism: Dimensions and Correctives," *Phi Delta Kappan, 59* (1978), 302–307.

Newman, Ian M. "School Health Services, Health Education and the School Environment. Do They Fit Together?" *Journal of School Health, 50* (1980), 173–174.

Podemski, Richard S., and Childres, John H., Jr. "The Counselor as Change Agent: An Organizational Analysis," *School Counselor, 27* (1980), 168–174.

Reed, John A. "Keys to Becoming a School Administrator," *Thrust for Educational Leadership, 7* (1977), 21–22.

Schiff, Martin. "The Principal as a Personnel Leader," *Educational Horizons, 56* (1978), 121–125.

Schiff, Martin. "School Service Personnel," *NJEA Review, 47* (1974), 24–25.

Siden, David M. "Vandalism: How Classified Personnel Might be Able to Help in Shaping Student Attitudes Toward School Property," *Security World, 15* (1978), 101–102.

BOOKS

Ashby, Lloyd W. *The Effective School Board Member.* Danville, Ill.: Interstate Printers and Publishers, 1968.

Bardon, Jack I., and Bennett, Virginia C. *School Psychology.* Englewood Cliffs, N.J.: Prentice-Hall, 1974.

Blumberg, Arthur and Greenfield, William. *The Effective Principal: Perspectives on School Leadership.* Boston: Allyn and Bacon, 1980.

Cohen, Louis Arthur. *The Administration of Non-instructional Personnel in Public Schools.* Chicago: Research Corporation of the Association of School Business Officials, 1964.

Dykes, Archie R. *School Board and Superintendent: Their Effective Working Relationships.* Danville, Ill.: Interstate Printers and Publishers, 1965.

Fawcett, Claude W. *School Personnel Systems.* Lexington, Mass.: Lexington Books, 1979.

Florentine, Helen Goodale. *The Preparation and the Role of Nurses in School Health Programs: Guidelines for the Use of Administrators, Educators, and Students.* New York: National League for Nursing, 1962.

Weldy, Gilbert R. *Principals: What They Do and Who They Are.* Reston, Va.: National Association of Secondary School Principals, 1979.

MOVIES

The Audio-Visual Supervisor (IFB, 19 min., 1959). Discusses the responsibilities of a school audio-visual supervisor. These responsibilities include proper caring for the materials, the use of student assistants, and helping in curriculum development.

The Evaluation by the School Psychologist (Instructional Media Services, 20 min., 1977). Explains the process of a student evaluation by the School Psychologist. Traces the steps from the teacher referral to the acquisition of remedial strategies.

The Five Facing Ten: School Boards in Crisis (IDEA, 26 min., 1970). A school
  board deals with upset parents concerning busing, an explosion in a school,
  and a teachers' strike. The board learns to anticipate such problems in hopes of
  avoiding potential crises.

What They Want to Produce, Not What We Want to Become (EDC Film Library, 60
  min.,). Students, teachers, and principals discuss the problems of the school.
  The principal also explains the reasons why he runs the school the way he
  does.

Chapter 8

Chapter 8

THE PARENT AS PARTNER

When we began our careers as public school teachers more than a decade ago, the issue of "community" was largely ignored both in teacher-education programs and in the public schools. In the intervening years, however, the issue of community has so grown in importance that we now find it difficult to limit our discussion to a single chapter. In our opinion the topics discussed in this chapter—topics that we were unprepared to deal with in our early teaching experience—are absolutely critical if one hopes to become a competent teacher. These topics were chosen as a result of reliving our own early years as teachers and analyzing the current issues involving school–community relations.

Parent as Educator

From a historical perspective, parents have only recently abandoned their roles as "teachers" to the school. The first compulsory education law was passed in 1852. Prior to the passage of these laws, parents were responsible for teaching their children language, reading, crafts, vocational skills, sex education, moral education, mathematics, parenting skills, and so forth. The curriculum we commonly find in an American school district in the 1980s mirrors what was taught by parents prior to the onset of compulsory schooling, but the parents were able to teach without bachelors or masters degrees, and certification.

The rediscovery of the critical importance of the home learning environment, and specifically the importance of the parent as teacher, oc-

curred in the early 1960s. The research of J. McVicker Hunt and that of
Earl Schaefer indicated that a child's success in school is probably related
to the quality of his interaction with his parents.[1] This quality is not
dependent upon expensive toys and clothes but upon the quality of the
social interaction between parent and child. This research led to the
design and implementation of many parent–child programs featuring the
parent as teacher. Common to most of these programs are the following
beliefs:

- Parents are (or can be) effective teachers.
- Parents need encouragement and guidance in order to develop and use
  their teaching skills.
- Parents can use the informal environment of the home and community
  to teach their children; they do not need expensive toys and learning
  materials.

Earl Schaefer, a pioneer in the parent-education movement, summarized
the issue of parent as educator:

> If a mother said, "I'm a parent educator," rather than a housewife, she would
> feel much better about her role. As educators, parents try to promote shared
> activities, shared experiences—accentuated by language. You go to the gro-
> cery store and you talk about things that are happening. You cook and talk.
> You look at a book and talk. You talk at meals. Education works into life.[2]

Interviews with the developers of three parent-education programs
may give you additional insight into how parents can be helped in their
efforts to become competent teachers.

PARENT-EDUCATION FOLLOW-THROUGH PROGRAM

Ira Gordon's program is built around the assumption that some parents
have the ability to help others develop or improve their parenting and
teaching skills. The parents who function as trainers are usually from the
same social and community background as the parents whom they are
training. Gordon's assumption is unique: a parent does not have to be
middle-class and college educated in order to become an expert parent
and teacher.[3] Our first interview is with Pat Olmsted, a close colleague of
the late Ira Gordon and the project director of the Parent-Education
Follow-Through Model.

RICHARD GOLDMAN: Why did you, Ira Gordon, and the other developers of
the Parent-Education Follow-Through Model become interested in
using the parent as a teacher and the home as a learning environment?
PAT OLMSTED: We feel that the parent is probably the most important
teacher that the child ever has. This is not only true in the preschool
years but for all the childhood years. We feel that it would make a
stronger environment for the child and increase the likelihood of his
being successful in life if both the home and the school work together.

R. G.: In your program you bring the school to the home and the home to the school. Could you describe how you go in both directions?

P. O.: Our basic vehicle for getting into the home or for bringing school into the home is by the use of a paraprofessional whom we call a "parent educator." Parent educators, who play a major role in our program, spend half of their time in the school and the other half making home visits. Because they are involved in the school environment, the parent educators can communicate to the parents a number of things happening in the school, such as curriculum developments and new innovations in the classroom. Their major purpose, however, is to work on Home Learning Activities* with the parent and to stress particular kinds of teaching behavior which the parent should use with the child. The parent educators very often have or have had a child in the same school program. They are largely from the same neighborhoods and have the same cultural background as the parents they are visiting.

R. G.: Why have you chosen your parent educators from within the school community, rather than bring in middle-class volunteers from outside the community as some programs do?

P. O.: We felt that it was important in terms of gaining rapport with the home to use parent educators who have similar characteristics to the population that we were visiting. We also believe that by employing people from within the school community we can increase the degree of community involvement in our program. Finally, since the parent educators are paid employees in our program, we feel that we are introduc-

*See p. 233.

ing them to a career in education. At present there are no clear data to show that middle-class home visitors have advantages over ours. There doesn't seem to be any really clear-cut evidence that one or the other is superior.

R. G.: Why does your program focus on the parent rather than the child?

P.O.: We feel that it's crucial to work with the mother, or with the mother and child as opposed to just the child, because one of the things that we are after in our program is to change the nature of the interaction between the parents and the children—not only the parent and the particular child that we're working with, but the parent and all of her children. If the parent educator works only with the child, you don't have the opportunity to impact on the mother's behavior.

R. G.: Are you saying that if a mother learns a specific skill, that she can then use this skill with older and younger children?

P. O.: Right. In fact, we have data from two of our communities which show that the parents in our program tend to interact more with all of their children.

R. G.: You have described why you involve parents. Please describe some of the other major components of the Parent-Education Follow-Through Program.

P. O.: In addition to our parent educators who work in both the home and classroom, we also put a heavy stress on parent volunteers working in the schools.

R. G.: In other words, your model is not limited to the parent educators?

P. O.: No, not at all. We're concerned with parent involvement in all possible ways. Another key feature of our model is the Policy Advisory Committee [PAC]. We're working very hard with our communities to develop these PACs and to help them become truly involved in the decision-making aspects of the school program. One kind of data that we gather consists of analyzing the minutes of the PAC meetings to see what types of decisions are made by the parents. In short, we're concerned with parents at the decision-making level (PAC), as volunteers in the classroom, as paid employees in the program (parent educators), and as teachers of their own children.*

R. G.: In other words your Follow-Through Model has an educational, political, and an economic perspective?

P. O.: Right! The educational perspective is not limited to the children or to the parents' acquisition of teaching skills. We also encourage our parent educators to continue their own education. Over 20 of our paraprofessionals have completed their college training and are now teachers in the same school system.

*What a major commitment to parents! Do you share Olmsted's recommendation that parents should be involved at all levels? Can a teacher who lacks outside financial support use all the levels of parental involvement that are in the Parent-Education Follow-Through Program? If you had to choose one level of parental involvement, which level would you choose? Explain why?

R. G.: So they have gone up the "career ladder"?*

P. O.: Right, this is a very important part of our program.

R. G.: Ira Gordon has had the Parent-Education Follow-Through Program since 1968. What have been some of the major changes in the program since its founding?

P. O.: In the beginning we did a lot of classroom observation because we felt that it was very important to look at the interaction between the teacher and the child and between the parent educator and the child. But as we began to view our model more closely, we realized that our real area of interest was the home. We then designed observation systems which enabled us to study the interactions between the parent and child.

R. G.: Any other changes?

P. O.: We were very excited about the theory of Piaget and tried to relate many of our Home Learning Activities to his theory. Later, we decided that we should encourage each community to design Home Learning Activities which matched the educational goals established by that community.

R. G.: In other words, you now accept any curriculum that is used by the local school system where you are working?

P. O.: Yes! We're very different from most of the other Follow-Through models in that respect, because we do not ask that the communities use any particular curriculum. They may use any curriculum their district has said is appropriate for their school, and then our program just fits on top of it.† The Home Learning Activities in our different communities vary greatly, depending upon the particular approach to reading or math that is used in that community.

R. G.: Are there any other changes in your program?

P. O.: I'd like to add one more. Several of the school districts with whom we work have undergone the desegregation process. I think that the desegregation process went more smoothly in the schools that we were in because we had already been involved with integrated home visiting: black educators visiting white parents or white parent educators visiting black parents. Consequently, this made the procedure go more smoothly in some of our communities.‡

R. G.: Could you outline the major teaching skills that the parent educators try to stress?

---

*See the section on the teacher assistant in Chapter 7, "Those Who Make the School Work," for a detailed discussion of the "career ladder."

†Is Olmstead saying that how the parent interacts with the child is more important than the curriculum? See her list of parent-teaching skills later in this chapter. Do you feel that "how" something is taught is more important than "what" is taught? You will be asking yourself this question throughout your career.

‡As a teacher in a school, what will you try to do to increase the interaction among parents (and students) from various backgrounds? Or should this be your responsibility? Perhaps you feel that you were hired to teach and not to become involved in human relations.

P. O.: We decided that what we really wanted to focus on was the interaction process between the parent and the child, not the outcome of the particular activity. In other words, we don't really care whether the activity going on in the home is a reading activity, a math activity, or something else. What we're concerned about is *how* the parent teaches this activity to the child and the kinds of behaviors that occur. So we surveyed the literature on both classroom instruction and parent–child interaction and tried to develop a list of teaching behaviors that seemed related to success for the child.

These behaviors include things like getting the child to ask questions; asking questions that have more than one answer; asking questions that have more than a one-word answer; giving the child time to think about the problem; praising him when he does a good job; telling him when his answer is wrong, but doing so in a loving way or in a positive way; telling the child what you are going to do and why; encouraging the child to evaluate his answer with evidence rather than guessing.*

R. G.: Describe what might go into a Home Learning Activity.

P. O.: A Home Learning Activity includes the following components: why the task is being done; what materials will be needed; how to go about it; how to do the procedure; and then extensions, which we call "what else" or "what then." A typical activity might be something like having the child go to the grocery store with the mother where they talk about why certain foods are kept in refrigerated cases, why some are packaged in boxes, others in cans, others in bottles. We are very concerned that the learning task be part of an ordinary activity like shopping, cooking, or cleaning. That way the parent minimizes the loss of time from her daily routine. [Figure 8.1 provides an example of a Home Learning Activity developed at one of the Follow-Through sites.]

R. G.: An article by Stephen and Joan Baratz accuses people involved in programs similar to yours of being a part of an institutionalized racist system.[4] I'm sure that you and Gordon have been asked about this periodically. What tends to be your reaction to that kind of question?

P. O.: Our reaction is that we're concerned that the children going through our program be successful in life, and by *successful* we mean a variety of things: being happy, being productive, and so forth. Even though many of the behaviors that we're concerned with reflect middle-class white values, we feel that these behaviors are the ones that the child has to be able to deal with in order to succeed. When people say, why don't you teach street language in your classrooms, our

---

*A complex list of teaching behaviors! Olmsted wants parents to acquire these, even though some teachers do not have these skills. Can parents learn these skills? Remember that both Olmsted and Levenstein found that parents with less than a high school education tend to teach as well as do those persons with a college education and specialized training in education.

NATURE WALK

DTB: Before starting an activity, give the learner time to familiarize him- or herself with the materials.

OBJECTIVE: (Why?) The learner will go on a nature walk to help develop an awareness of the outdoor environment and will classify what learner sees.

MATERIALS: (What?) A booklet of blank paper with pages labeled "Insects," "Flowers," "Birds," etc.

PROCEDURE: (HOW?)
1. Show the learner the pages of the booklet and talk about each group. Then go for a walk and watch for the items you talked about.

2. Rules of the walk:
   a. Walk slowly and quietly with ears and eyes alert.
   b. Point out interesting things to be seen and heard.
   c. Spend some time sitting silently, listening and watching a specific bird or insect.

3. Return to the house and draw or cut out pictures of the things you saw on your walk and put (paste) them in the booklet.

Encourage the child to make a collection of live specimens and learn more about them. A lovely thing to share at school.

Figure 8.1. Sample of a Home Learning Activity. *DTB* is an acronym for desirable teaching behavior, one of the ten primary teaching strategies to be emphasized during an activity

response is that street language is not a way to make it in the world today. Street language is not a way to be successful. We feel that it's fine to have street language, but what we're concerned with is helping the child learn the kind of language that he needs in order to get a job, to keep a job, to make it in the world.

R. G.: But you're not going to punish the child for other languages?

P. O.: No. Our communities are very diverse, so our children should have a variety of language models in the classroom. That is one of the advantages of having paraprofessionals who come from the same neighborhood as our children.

R. G.: How could your model be adapted to grades 4 through 8, or even 4 through high school?

P. O.: Some adaptations of our models are going on now in our communities. In one community they have started middle school and high school home visits. The primary purpose of these visits is to maintain the basic system of communication between the home and the school. What begins to change is the content of what happens during the home visits. We find that with the parents of older children the topics for the

home visits include drugs, alcohol, communication, stages of development that the child is going through, and the curriculum in the school.

R. G.: Would you have Home Learning Activities for a parent of a ninth
grader?

P. O.: Yes. But they would have a different format and would include
tasks that an adolescent could do with his family.

R. G.: Can you summarize the major findings from your project and
discuss their implications for a typical elementary school teacher who
is not involved in such a project?

P. O.: We know that the teaching behaviors that the mother uses with the
"target" child are also being used with other children in the family.
That means we're having an impact on interaction patterns of the entire family. These changes should have a long-lasting effect.

We have also found that the parent educators' home visits have an
impact on children's school achievement. This tells a teacher that she
is not the sole person responsible for the child's success in school. I
think one of the problems that has come with the accountability movement is that the schools are beginning to feel more and more responsible for 100 percent of what the child does in the school; this feeling is a
mistake. Studies have shown that factors outside the school (mainly
the home) are responsible for at least 50 percent of the child's achievement. The home has to be just as accountable as the school is for the
child's success in school. As the school systems realize that a positive
home–school partnership must exist (it is not a luxury), achievement
scores will rise dramatically.

R. G.: How else can teachers build a positive relationship with the home?

P. O.: I think there are a number of ways that you can have parent involvement without home visitors, without paraprofessionals, and without a great deal of money. One example here in Chapel Hill involves a
parent newsletter. It does involve some money, but it's really a very
small amount considering the cost of home visits. In these, the teacher
may include a small learning activity for the parent and child to do together over the weekend or during the week. In this way, you do
acquaint parents with the kinds of things the children are doing, and
they begin to learn along with the children.*

Another of our communities encourages parents to make home
visits to one another.† The visiting parents do not assume all of the responsibilities of the parent educator, but they can disseminate infor-

*Volunteer your help to a teacher; ask whether you can help with the design and writing
of a classroom–parent newsletter. You will learn about the classroom's curriculum, formats
for newsletters, and experience a positive relationship with parents.
†This is a good idea for teachers who do not have the time to go into the community. The
parent visitors must experience training from the teacher before making the visits. What
should be involved in the preparation of the parent visitors?

mation about the curriculum, encourage volunteer work, and share in certain activities.

R. G.: You mention that teachers should encourage parents to volunteer in the classroom.

P. O.: Right. There is very little cost involved in terms of money. The main cost involved is in terms of teacher time. However, once the teacher has successfully oriented the parents to their classroom duties, they will begin to see the payoff.

R. G.: What kind of advice do you have for someone who is just beginning a career in teaching?

P. O.: The teacher should always see the parents as important teachers of their children. If the teacher understands this and begins to involve a few parents in the classroom right from the start, it will gradually blossom until most of the parents are involved. I think beginning teachers are very often overwhelmed by the system, and I understand why. It's a very overwhelming system. But I know that many parents are willing to become involved and to assist the teacher in a variety of ways. Once started, the teacher will begin to see this parent help as sort of a support system and a very important one in terms of the payoff to the teacher, the child, and the parent.

MOTHER–CHILD HOME PROGRAM

Phyllis Levenstein, executive director of the Verbal Interaction Project, designed a program for children (ages two to four) and their mothers that focuses on the development of the child's language abilities, the improvement of the child's IQ, and the acquisition of teaching skills by the parent.

RICHARD GOLDMAN: Why did you become interested in using the home as a learning environment and the parent as "teacher in the home"?

PHYLLIS LEVENSTEIN: The family is the link between society and the child and provides the main social life for the child prior to school. Parents are the child's first teachers, the main channel for transmitting the values and expectations of society, so it seemed pretty obvious to me that they should be a very integral part of the child's education. Low-income parents in particular are too busy with income-related problems to give their children the verbal and other kinds of interaction needed to prepare them for school. These were the main reasons for starting with the parent.

In referring to parents, "she" is probably better than "he" because, unfortunately, a lot of children are not raised in two-parent families. It dawned on me and maybe one or two other people that the mother's role could involve cognitive as well as social and emotional development.

Now, why the home? The most obvious reason is that the home is the major spot for both the mother and child. They are both likely to feel more comfortable at home. The mother feels that she is the hostess and somewhat in control of the situation when someone comes into her home. It is also very convenient for her. In anonymous evaluations of our program, mothers would say over and over, we don't have to get dressed and go anywhere in the morning. If the child has a cold, he can be at home.

R. G.: Could you talk about some of the possible problems a home-based program may have?

P. L.: One of the possible problems might be imposing the program on a mother who really does not want it. Another might be the violation of family confidences by talking about them outside of the home. Finally, there is the possibility of imposing on the family values and practices which they really don't want.

R. G.: Doesn't it take a lot of sensitivity to be aware of possible infringements on the family?

P. L.: Yes, it does. To give you a very small example, in our own program no mother's last name is ever mentioned in the weekly Toy Demonstrator's supervisory conference. We have worked out various safeguards for protecting the right of a parent to say "no" to us. One of the problems with low-income mothers, in particular, is that they don't feel free to say "no" outright. They will tell us "no" in indirect ways that we have to be sensitive to.*

R. G.: Could you give an overview of your program?

P. L.: It's a voluntary, home-based, early education program, that is aimed at increasing and improving the mothers' interactive behavior and, thereby, enhancing the child's development and his readiness for school learning.† The program has one-half hour home sessions that occur twice a week for seven months in each of the two program years, beginning when the child is around age two. So that is a total of 46 home visits each year, a total of 92 home sessions over two years.

A "toy demonstrator" visits the mother and child together. Without any direct teaching, the toy demonstrator models for the mother interactive techniques that she can use when playing with her child. The modeling is done around colorful, progressively complex toys and books which are selected here to stimulate interactive behavior. We call them Verbal Interaction Stimulus Materials, or VISM, and they are given to the child as presents. The child receives one toy or book for

---

*Levenstein does not elaborate on the indirect ways of saying "no." What behaviors do you think they may include? Ask teachers who are sensitive to parents to inform you of the ways parents say "no."

†Some critics of education argue that we should not prepare young children for a school environment that will take away their individuality and creativity. What are your reactions to these critics?

each week of the program. The toy demonstrators are either paid or volunteer women who don't have to have any previous work experience or formal training in education. In practice, the volunteers tend to be middle-income, college-educated women. The paid toy demonstrators are usually low-income, high school–educated mothers who were former participants in the program. All of them learn their skills from a program coordinator who is on our staff. The toy demonstrators learn their skills first in an initial eight-session workshop and then in weekly group meetings throughout the program.

The curriculum for the children is structured but flexible enough for individualization. It consists of fun-oriented guide sheets which are written around each VISM and show the toy demonstrator how she can use that particular week's toy or book. The core of the guide sheet is a list of concepts to be taught—labels, colors, shapes, sizes, numbers, and so on—that are made concrete by examples that are focused around the toy or book. The mother also receives a copy of the guide sheet at the end of the first session each week and is given a folder to keep it in. It is up to her whether or not she ever looks at it again. This is essentially the program.

R. G.: Explain how modeling is used by the toy demonstrator.

P. L.: The Toy Demonstrator models, i.e., simply shows, the techniques that the parent *may* use. There is absolutely no formal teaching of the parent. It's part of the toy demonstrators's role to draw the mother in as much and as soon as possible. The amount that the mother involves herself varies from person to person. A very shy mother may never get involved, whereas a very active mother may practically take over right from the beginning.

R. G.: You mentioned that some of the toy demonstrators were once parents in the program. Can you compare their performance with that of the middle-class parents who are toy demonstrators?

P. L.: They are different in some ways. For one thing, the middle-income women who come as volunteers have almost always had a college education and that means lots of practice in writing; the college-educated women find it much easier to keep records. The former participants in the program need more help with the writing. We've also done an analysis to see whether our three types of toy demonstrators have had similar effects on the children. The three types include the middle-class women volunteers, former parent participants in the program, and members of our senior staff. We were very surprised and pleased to find out that the three groups of toy demonstrators had equal effects on the IQ growth of the kids.*

R. G.: Baratz and Baratz accused those persons who work with the low-income families of being part of a system of institutionalized racism.[5] What is your reaction to that?

P. L.: We're color-blind. Our program is not geared to any particular ethnic or racial group.

R. G.: What about class? Is there a class bias?

P. L.: Obviously, we don't feel that we are being "classist." All we are doing is offering mothers techniques to prepare a kid for school learning that they may take or leave. That's one of the reasons why I am now careful to emphasize the word "voluntary" in describing the program. In addition to the obvious things—like asking, "Do you want it or don't you want it?"—we try to be extremely sensitive to the nonverbal cues that the mother gives us. Our philosophy is to preserve every family's personal and ethnic subculture but, at the same time, to have the mainstream culture available to it in language, in materials, in attitudes, or anything else in case they want to avail themselves of it. I think we have a kind of social obligation to prepare children to have choices. If they don't want to use those choices, that's up to them.

R. G.: You choose children at age two and work with them until age four. Why two to four rather than three or four to six?

---

*Compare Levenstein's finding about the quality of performance of the low-income toy demonstrators with the performance of the home visitors in the North Carolina Follow-Through Model described in the interview with Olmsted.

P. L.: Well, our philosophy is that children are emerging from the sensory motor stage of development at age two. Language and everything else in development are just bursting out. There is a sort of revolution taking place in the child. Therefore, it seems to be the most appropriate age to begin. As it happens, we are experimenting this year with a downward extension to age one. I don't have a really good rationale for extending it to age one, except the possibility that empirically it might be more effective. We feel that we might help to prepare the child for language and complex concepts that he will face later.

R. G.: Can you think of any processes in your program that can be adapted by elementary school teachers?

P. L.: Within the classroom, I suggest reversing the usual attitude about children being silent.* We need more talking in the classroom between children and between the children and the teachers. The other thing is that I think it might be useful for teachers to show concrete examples of the complex concepts that they are teaching.

R. G.: Do you see teachers playing some role similar to the toy demonstrator in their classrooms?

P. L.: I don't think so. It's very explicit in our program that toy demonstrators model for parents but do not teach them. I think it would be too much, too difficult and time consuming, to expect teachers to fill both roles, that is, to switch from being a teacher in the classroom to being a model in the home.

R. G.: How can the teacher reach the parent?

P. L.: There are a couple of things, I think, that might be taken as lessons from our program. One is the importance of reaching out and having home visits with parents. I mean, just get acquainted once or twice a year. Have a visit with parents so that the parent and teacher get to know each other and so that there is a bridge between the school and the home for the child. Another strategy is giving some positive feedback to parents about their child. It might be a nice idea if teachers would occasionally write home and say, "Johnny did this great thing today." I don't think that teachers are aware themselves how distant they are from the parents and particularly from fathers.

R. G.: As a third-grade teacher (or a seventh- or eighth-grade teacher) should I know about how two-, three-, and four-year-olds interact with their parents?

P. L.: Yes, I think you should, because this relates so much to the equipment which the child brings to school. I also think it's extremely important for teachers to know that parents are more important than they [the teachers] are. Also, the teacher should know that parents are under a lot of pressures. They are well motivated (most parents want

---

*Levenstein feels that language is the core of the learning process. As you visit classrooms and homes, observe for those experiences that encourage language development in children.

their children to be well educated), but they are harried in one way or another, whether they are middle-class parents or low-income parents. Teachers sometimes forget this.

R. G.: Can you summarize the results of your program?

P. L.:   Our goals aim toward stimulating mothers, increasing the mother's interaction with her child, and preparing the child for the school experience. As a group, our children are maintaining most of the IQs in third grade that they achieved in this program at age four. There is one other interesting bit of data that we have: Younger kids who follow their older brothers and sisters into the program have an average IQ of eight points higher than their older siblings.* It's a very gratifying thing, because it means the mothers are doing what we want them to do.

HOME AND SCHOOL INSTITUTE

The aim of this program, according to Dorothy Rich, is to develop programs and materials to help families teach their children in ways that do not duplicate the school and to help professionals work more effectively with parents and the community.

RICHARD GOLDMAN: You were an early pioneer in the work with parents. When did you begin your involvement with parents?

DOROTHY RICH: I began to work with parents in the early 1960s when it was radical to think that parents were a key to their children's success. In 1964 I started a column for the *Washington Post* titled "Home and School." A year later I started to put together programs for parents on how they could help their children at home: Success for Children courses.

Before the outpouring of research in the late 1960s and 1970s on parent–child interaction, it was clear to me that something determines and predicts children's success in school. This intuition was correct: Parents are a—or perhaps *the*—key element in the success of their children.

R. G.: When I began my work in teacher preparation in the early 1960s, the issue of parental involvement was never discussed.

D. R.: Parents weren't mentioned in any teacher training at all. It was as though the whole world outside of school did not exist, in terms of education. As I began working with groups of parents, I saw the need for organizing programs that would enable educators and the other "helping professions" to reach families. My interest has always been on the parent–teacher relationship in the regular school grades.

---

*These data mean that low-income mothers care about and can affect the development of their children. How will you respond now to those who state that "those people" (low-income) do not care about their children?

In 1971 I started a volunteer program for teachers called School and Family Involvement. In 1972 we officially incorporated as the Home and School Institute to bring both the parent-trainee program and the professional-trainee program under one umbrella. The basic idea then, as it is now, was to create a real working partnership between the family and what are called institutional support systems. Even though we are officially called the Home and School Institute, we are really broader in that we now work with schools and other human-service agencies, including hospitals, to design staff-training programs and special programs for families, the bottom line of which is the development and the achievement of the child. We are now adapting our strategies for families of handicapped children and for bilingual families.

The program that people seem to associate us with most, because it's such a tangible and workable thing to lay their hands on, is what we call home-style learning recipes. [Figure 8.2 gives an example of a recipe that is useful for children in the elementary grades.] Our first publications, "Reading, Writing and Thinking Success for Children Begin at Home," were directed at the parent. We are very basic-skill–oriented and have been since the mid-1960s. We believe that children need to apply their skills in the home environment and in the community. This application reinforces rather than duplicates the work of the school. This has been a key ingredient in everything we do.

LET 'EM EAT SHAPES

WHY

To recognize basic shapes such as squares, rectangles, triangles, circles. To learn to match shapes for reading and math practice.

MATERIALS

Bread, peanut butter or other spread, knife (plastic or dull edged)

HOW TO

Cut bread into different shapes. Ask child to choose a pair of identical shapes (two triangles, two rectangles). When child finds the pair of shapes, ask youngster to put spread on one piece. Child matches the second shape on top to make a sandwich. Allow time to eat the shapes.

TIME

5 to 10 minutes to prepare with time to eat as needed

EVALUATION

Can child find sets of similar shapes and match them?

ADAPTATIONS

Children can cut the shapes themselves or use cookie cutters to cut more intricate shapes.

Figure 8.2. An example of a home-style learning recipe.

From D. Rich, *The Three R's: Teaming Families and Schools for Student Achievement* (Washington, D.C.: Home and School Institute, 1978). Copyright © 1978 by Home and School Institute.

R. G.: Could you give some examples of the recipes and how they differ from what happens in the school?

D. R.: HSI has developed an educational method called home learning recipes. The recipes are short activities which provide clear instructions on how to use everyday objects found in the home or the neighborhood to develop children's basic skills. For example, recipes may call for the use of sales receipts or toolboxes or cooking utensils in the home. In the community, recipes may call for the use of such places as supermarkets and gas stations. The best recipes are those that take little time, use resources already on hand, and promote feelings of accomplishment and togetherness for children and parents.

Let me describe the stages we went through in the development of the recipes. My own research indicated reading achievement went up significantly with the use of the recipes. Then I asked, "How can we replicate this in a school system?" As a next step, we designed Project HELP (Home Educational Learning Program) with the Benton Harbor public schools. Third, we began using this program as a design in our courses, including Home and School Curriculum Development in the Home and School Institute master's program at Trinity College. Data thus far from projects show that the recipe method is markedly effective for older as well as younger children.

The HSI Families Learning Together curriculum, our most recent program, builds children's skills and adult knowledge simultaneously. The recipes are designed for children in kindergarten through sixth grade and for adults of any age. As an outgrowth of the Families Learning Together project, HSI has prepared kits for individual families containing home learning recipes to develop children's reading and math capabilities, build adult basic knowledge in such areas as nutrition and safety, and give adults tips on how to be better parents.

Our main goal is to involve anybody who is in the home (brother, sister, aunt, uncle), any person who can spend a few minutes a day using the resources of the home to help a child apply the skills he has learned in the school. Every home has a bathroom, a kitchen, some sort of family area that can be used to teach basic skills.

How do you use a bathroom to teach math? One of the ways is to have plastic containers of different shapes. Throw those into the bathtub with the child and as the child is bathing, start asking questions like, "How many of those pints will it take to make a quart?" Guess, hypothesize, and then try it out using the liquid that is in the tub. In this way, the learning activity is part of daily life. We encourage the making of lists for such tasks as brushing teeth and picking up clothes.

In the bedroom we do a lot of reading. We encourage parents to attach words to clothing, for example, "What's this—a shirt, a blouse, a shoe?" Also, we do games with words for body parts and for clothes.

In the kitchen we do a lot with groceries. For youngsters who cannot yet read, we ask them to remove items from the grocery bag and put them together in categories. This teaches classification, a skill that is necessary for reading but which people don't think about as school-related. If a child can write, he can help his parent prepare a grocery list.

At the grocery store parents, use recipe activities to involve their kids in the shopping. When the children are very young, they can help find the items: "Find the package with the blue and yellow label." When they get older, they find an item that costs the least for the most amount. We have a sequential design of activities that goes from easier to harder for children as they move through the grades.

R. G.: It sounds as though a primary goal of the recipes is to help parents use the materials that already exist in the home.

D. R.: Absolutely. . . . These recipes are completely cost effective in that you are using what you already have in the home, only you are recognizing the educational importance of it.

Today, there are many working and single parents; their first thought about parent involvement may well be, "Can't the schools do it? We're so tired when we come home." That's why at HSI we are always looking for activities that work within the rhythm of the day. There are certain things every family has to do, such as eat, shop, and sleep.

R. G.: You seem very involved with the relationships within the family.

D. R.: Yes. Perhaps this is a function that I should say more about. We are always looking for activities that help people relate more effectively. I think it's very important that parents feel involved as a constructive part of their child's education. Much research data deal with how parent–child interactions affect the child's school achievement. We have found that by increasing this interaction there is a long-term improvement on the total family environment.

R. G.: Who are the primary audiences for your program?

D. R.: Clearly, one target audience is the child. Our goal is to build the child's basic competencies and thereby improve his school success. The parents or other adult caregivers in the family are another target audience. We strengthen their abilities and their self-confidence. We also attempt to provide staff training and support systems for the various institutions that serve families (social agencies, schools, hospitals, etc.) so that their staffs will have strategies and materials that they can share with their clients.

R. G.: Doesn't your work with parents go well beyond the learning recipes, to helping them with a broad spectrum of parental duties?

D. R.: Right. It's a chance for them to enhance their total parenting role. We have found that the recipes are a good starting point, since they are immediately acceptable to everybody, rich and poor alike. The responses to doing the activities demonstrates that the activities make both parent and child feel good. Once parents develop the teaching competency, they often want to improve other aspects of the family life. For example, many parents want to learn about the health care system in order to improve the quality of care their children receive, so we help them. We try to help them understand the school system in order to make it work better for them. We also help with areas like personal home management, although we do not intrude into the private affairs of the family.*

---

*As a teacher, should you limit your goals specifically to education, or should you be concerned with helping the families improve their quality of life in all areas?

R. G.: How do you work with the parents?

D. R.: Most of our work with parents involves identifying a group of parents, e.g., parents of Title I children or parents of handicapped children. Parents are involved, for example, in an HSI training program called "Home – The Learning Place." The idea of this program is that parents work in combination with teachers, not just parent to parent.* We are trying to build the bridge between parent and teacher, between home and school. Together parents and teachers design activities that are shared throughout the city, through PTA meetings with other Title I parents.

We have programs for middle-class parents too. During the late 1960s and early 1970s, many middle-class parents identified their parenting needs with such questions as: "How do I communicate with my child? How do I manage my child?" While HSI is very much interested in communication, we go a step further and recommend communicating through activities. You don't do it just with words, through counselling techniques. Now we are finding a growing middle-class audience suddenly confronted with their own children who are having trouble with reading and writing.

R. G.: Related to the class issue, Baratz and Baratz accused programs like yours of being racist.[6] What are you doing with the parents as far as imposing values on them?

D. R.: I have often had more difficulty cutting across the defenses of the middle-class than with the poor. I have always talked in terms of "payroll" English, of everyone having the basic skills and attitudes needed to function effectively in the world whether they are black, blue, or green. It was the economically disadvantaged parents who first said, "We need this; what we want to know is how we ourselves can help our children."

The recipe approach and our other programs have parents, teachers, social workers, etc. designing many of their own activities which they know will work.

We provide a format and a stimulus, but each person can adapt the approach to fit his own personal situation. I have found that parents often have better success with a recipe they have designed themselves than with one that was designed by my professional staff. The reason for this is simple and basic. Parents have a commitment and involvement to their own ideas and to their own children.

R. G.: You mentioned that you are working with parents of handicapped children.†

*An interesting idea! Would you want parents to be involved in your teacher-preparation courses? What would be advantages/disadvantages of including the parents?

†See Chapter 6 for a description of Public Law 94-142. This law mandates the use of the least restrictive environment for handicapped children. Do you feel Rich's work can be beneficial in reaching this goal for the handicapped?

D. R.: Yes. They often feel helpless and guilty. We have found that the building of confidence is a must for teachers and parents of all children, but especially for handicapped children. So we provide them with a variety of different ways for working with their children. For example, we set up a family center in a school where people can just walk through and see how easy it is to use our recipes. (You know there is unused space in school buildings all over the country that could be used for parents.) This model is also called "Home—The Learning Place." Basically, the room is made to look like an ordinary home. Parents can come through on their own and pick up what they want in the way of information and materials for use with their children. The emphasis is to correlate the recipes with basic skills and to encourage parents to use these with their children.

Do you want to hear about how our work with parents and teachers helped to lessen the problems associated with desegration of schools?

R. G.: Of course.

D. R.: We were asked by a school system that recently completed the desegregation process to help build a positive relationship between parents and teachers. This district had recently employed group-dynamics consultants who worked with small groups of black and white parents and teachers. The focus of these groups was to *discuss* how improved racial relationships could develop. The discussions led nowhere. We came in with a concrete goal: the designing of learning recipes. As the black and white parents and teachers worked together on a task, they found that they shared aspirations for their children. We found a mutual respect cutting across race (black and white) and role (parent and teacher). Our task-oriented strategy proved to be very effective.*

R. G.: I have found that telling teachers the truth ("You cannot do the job alone even if you are the greatest teacher in the world working in the greatest school in the world") generally gets them to accept the idea of parental partnership. I tell them, "It is a part of your professional work to get involved with the parents and the other community resources. It's integral, not something extraneous that happens after school hours." This is a very difficult point to get across because this has not been a standard operating procedure in education up to now.

What advice do you have for the teacher, especially the beginning teacher, about school–community relationships?

D. R.: First, don't assume that you can do it all yourself. You can't! Even

---

*Olmsted has described how her parent program contributed to a successful school desegregation process. Compare their approaches. Why do you think a "product"-oriented approach (as used by Rich and Olmsted) may be more effective than a human-relations approach?

if you work 24 hours a day, you don't have kids 24 hours a day. The family is the critical determining influence, and if you are going to make changes in the kids, you are going to have to work with families and also with other community institutions. Teachers should try to use the home as the first link in a network of services that includes the school and the other social agencies.

We are always looking for easy yet effective strategies. One example is the 60-second call that goes something like this: "Hello, Mrs. Jones, I am _____, Johnny's new first-grade teacher. I just wanted to let you know who I am and that I am available to you. Please be sure to visit with us on Parents' Night." The parent will hang up with the feeling that the teacher really cares about her child. We even encourage teachers to give parents their home phone numbers, since we have found that it is not abused by the parents.

We also encourage every class to have a family bulletin board that features news and pictures of a different family each week. Children bring in pictures of their families and write or tell about them. This type of "homework" assignment encourages interaction between the child and his family.

The field trips that we encourage are the kinds that, once again, link the school with the family. I think that going to the zoo should be cast out of almost every school program. But if you can find a factory or an office of a class parent that allows the kids to visit and see the kind of work that parents do, then these are meaningful field trips.

Finally, we try to show teachers how they can quickly write what we call "a state of the class message" or a quick newsletter. Obviously, we hope every school will have a newsletter, and this is becoming more common. But, we also try to encourage the teachers to send home a couple of paragraphs every other week on what the individual classes are doing.

It should be emphasized that HSI programs are designed to be used not only by parents and teachers, but by the broadest cross-section of the community: by all persons directly or indirectly concerned with caring for children. For example, this includes household workers, grandparents, even neighbors. We need to take advantage of the education and the "educators" that are part of our lives everyday.

Olmsted, Levenstein, and Rich have diverse approaches for teaching a common goal: the success of all children in school. A common element inherent in each of the programs is the need for parents to be involved in their children's development. Your task, as you begin your career, is not to select one approach over the other, but to adapt the ideas from each of the programs that match the goals of your parents and the larger school community.

TEACHERS' INTERACTIONS WITH PARENTS

A colleague of ours who teaches fifth grade told us about a recent telephone conversation that she had with a parent whose child, after having experienced considerable difficulty in school, began to demonstrate progress. The teacher, aware that the child had rarely experienced adult praise, decided to call the parent and inform her of her child's improvement. The parent's first reaction after hearing, "This is Ms. Smith, Bobby's teacher; I want to tell you—" was to inform the teacher that she had her permission to use any punishment she thought necessary with Bobby. Was this a case of the mother not listening? It is more likely that this parent had developed certain expectations based on the fact that contacts from the school had always dealt with the child's problems, not his progress. After a few minutes our colleague was able to relay her message: "Bobby has been trying and is showing some progress." It is hoped that, as the idea of an active partnership between parents and educators gains momentum, a partnership that has as its common goal the full development of the child's potential, this type of negative teacher–parent interaction will become less frequent.

Another obstacle to teacher–parent communication is caused by the excessive use of jargon by some professional educators. Listen as a principal or teacher explains a new program (or even an old one!) to parents; too often excessive jargon insures *against* the message getting through. The following memo, sent by a principal to some parents, was intended to inform the parents of the school's new educational program. What do you think the memo says?

> Our faculty is concerned with the whole child, his learning style and ability to adapt to a complex environment. The core curriculum is based on a continuum of behavioral objectives; each objective is assessed through the use of a criterion-referenced test. Your child is placed in a cross-aged, multi-cultural group where self-actualization is a primary goal.

This principal obviously has a communications problem. Some critics even argue that professional educators deliberately use jargon with parents in order to minimize the parents' involvement with the school. Parental involvement, according to this argument, is seen as a threat by insecure, incompetent teachers. In the next section two experts discuss how the behaviors of professional educators can lead to a lack of parental involvement in the schools.

Parents' Political Involvement in Education

Partly as a result of unsatisfactory teacher–parent relationships and partly out of a desire to renew their role as "parent educators," parents have begun organizing in recent years. Evidence of this desire to form a partnership with professional educators can be found in documents like the Parents' Bill of Rights, which was adopted by the Parents' Union of Public Schools:

PARENTS' BILL OF RIGHTS

EVERY PARENT HAS THE RIGHT TO:
1. BE TREATED WITH COURTESY by all members of the school staff.
2. INSPECT HIS OR HER CHILD'S CUMULATIVE RECORD and remove or correct any false or misleading statements in conformity with current guidelines established by the state and federal governments.
3. VISIT SCHOOLS AND CLASSES after notifying the principal and in accordance with guidelines which establish the rights of parents, while protecting the rights of teachers.
4. BE INFORMED OF ACADEMIC REQUIREMENTS of any school program.
5. BE INFORMED OF SCHOOL POLICIES AND ADMINISTRATIVE DECISIONS.
6. BE INFORMED OF APPROVED PROCEDURES FOR SEEKING CHANGES in school policies and for appealing administrative decisions.
7. BE INFORMED OF ALL PROGRAMS in special education.
8. APPEAL THE PLACEMENT, in accordance with established guidelines, of his or her child in a special-education class.
9. Expect that every attempt will be made by school personnel to insure the RECEIPT BY PARENTS OF IMPORTANT NEWS AND MESSAGES FROM SCHOOL.
10. Participate in meaningful PARENT–TEACHER CONFERENCES to discuss his or her child's progress and welfare.
11. REASONABLE PROTECTION for his or her child from physical harm while under school authority.
12. Organize and participate in organizations for PARENTS ONLY.
13. ASSISTANCE FROM SCHOOL PERSONNEL to further the progress and improvement of his or her child, which includes, but is not limited to, counseling, tutorial and remedial programs, as well as information about academic and psychological services within and without the school district.
14. A FULL DAY OF EDUCATION for his or her child within the legally defined number of hours and days.
15. Participate in PLANNING AND SCHEDULING whenever SHIFTS are necessary.
16. TO BE INFORMED of the procedures, data and information required to properly select and assign administrators, principals and faculty.
17. TO BE INFORMED of the services and data that enable administrators and principals to properly carry out their functions, powers and duties.
18. ASSIST in the interviewing and selection for principals.
19. Participate in FACULTY EVALUATION under agreed upon guidelines approved by the Board, recognizing that the responsibility for final evaluation rests with the principal.
20. BE RESPECTED AS AN INDIVIDUAL, regardless of race, creed, national origin, economic status, sex or age.
21. A GRIEVANCE PROCEDURE with the RIGHT OF JUDICIAL APPEAL.[7]

The Parents' Bill of Rights does not mention the traditional school roles of parents: pouring tea at PTA meetings, lunchroom aide, classroom mother (why not the father?). The Bill of Rights does mention such politically sensitive issues as participation in scheduling, selection of principals, and participation in faculty evaluation. As both parents and professional educators, we read the Bill of Rights from two different perspectives. As parents we feel that we have the right and obligation to participate in our children's education as described in the Bill of Rights. As professional educators, however, our first reaction is to say in protest, "Many of the items mentioned in the Bill of Rights are the prerogative of the professional educator. Does the public tell the law or medical professional how to perform or who can or cannot enter the profession? We don't feel the public should have this type of input into the schools."

One recent study that sheds some light on the question of the proper relationship between parents and educators was that of Cynthia Wallat and Richard Goldman, which looked at success and failure of innovative programs in the public schools.[8] Of those programs that were evaluated as being "successful," all shared the component of having major involvement by parents in the design, implementation, and evaluation of the program. In other words, the successful programs adopted the intent of the Parents' Bill of Rights.

To simplify a very complex issue, we feel that parents and educators must develop a partnership that has as its major goal the success of children. Two states, Florida and California, have legislated that parents must have policy and political input into the administration of the public schools. The California Early Childhood Act (6445.01) states:

> Parent participation shall be included in a manner which: a) involves parents in the formal education of their children directly in the classroom and through the decision making process of the California Public School System; b) maximizes the opportunity for teachers and parents to cooperatively develop the learning process and its subject matter. This opportunity shall be a continuous permanent process.

Many parents lack the skills (but not the ability to learn the skills) that are needed to implement the California law. Parents may need training to develop the skills that are necessary to participate as full partners according to the mandate of the law: being participants in the classroom, participants in the decision-making process, and partners in the selection of subject matter and related learning processes.

In most instances, the training that parents need and receive is not from professional educators in the school but from national parent organizations such as the National Committee for Citizens in Education and the Center for the Study of Parent Involvement. These organizations publish newsletters and booklets and sponsor regional/national workshops for parents. Topics at a recent national conference conducted by the Center for the Study of Parent Involvement included, among others, "Parent Involvement: An Inalienable Right," "Parent Rights: A Time for

Enforcement," "What Keeps Us Involved, or Putting Up with Being Put Down," and "The Need for Strengthening Advocates of Parents' and Children's Rights."

Increasingly, parents are organizing at national, regional, and local levels. The issue for professional educators is easy to state but difficult to solve. "Should we join with parents in an unselfish coalition for the benefit of children, or should we oppose their entry into the affairs of our profession?" This dilemma, which is common to all the professions, is examined in the following discussions with Terrel Bell, Secretary of the United States Department of Education, and Crystal Kuykendall, former director of the Citizens Training Institutes sponsored by the National Committee for Citizens in Education.

Kuykendall and Bell both advocate parental involvement in education, but they disagree on the nature of this involvement. Whereas Bell focuses on parental assistance for existing school programs, Kuykendall argues for parental involvement in policy decisions regarding curriculum, staffing, and financial matters. As you read their comments, try to formulate your own opinion regarding how much and what kind of parental involvement you advocate.

We mentioned earlier that some school critics believe that educators deliberately minimize parental involvement in education through the excessive use of jargon. Kuykendall, a proponent of this argument states:

> Educators talk down to parents; they make them feel inferior: "You people know nothing about education." School personnel tell parents, "If you want to help, you must do it on our terms." Ninety-nine percent of the parents want to work with the schools. They don't because, of the way they are talked to and treated.

Bell agrees with Kuykendall that not enough has been done by the schools to encourage parent participation but, unlike Kuykendall, does not feel that educators have conspired to exclude parents:

> Professional educators have had much pressure on them during the last decade: unionization, desegregation, equality of educational opportunity, mainstreaming. These pressures have taken so much time of the professionals that they have neglected this realm of parent and community. I don't think it was an overt effort on their part to exclude parents. As we enter the 1980s, I think that educators will turn more to community groups and parents.

Volunteerism, and especially volunteerism in the school, may be a hallmark of American democracy. Bell feels that the school volunteer movement

> . . . is and will be a major force for community involvement in the schools. Over the past few years, this movement has been one of the most promising directions that we've had in American education. I see the school volunteer movement growing, and I feel the movement should be encouraged.

A contrasting view on the importance of the school volunteer movement is presented by Kuykendall:

> We are past the stage when we can say that we have community involvement because the parents bought the uniforms for the band. Or that we have involvement because the parents served as school volunteers. This is not involvement; it is token involvement that an administrator points to when he wants to impress you that parents are involved in the school. Many parents do not see this volunteerism as involvement, but they do it because it is the only thing that they are allowed to do. Parents want to do more.

According to Kuykendall, the "wanting to do more," includes the active participation in the decision-making process of the schools. Two routes for parental involvement in the decision-making process were developed in the 1960s: Parent Advisory Councils (PACs) in Head Start, Follow-Through, and Title I programs, and community control of the schools, as occurred in Intermediate School 201 in New York City. Again, our two advocates for parents do not share the same opinion on these two approaches to community involvement. On the issue of PACs Bell states:

> I think they are fine on an ad hoc basis. Permanent, standing committees of this type start to usurp the responsibilities of the school board. I recommend the use of ad hoc committees which have specific goals and a specified duration for their existence. Again, I caution against committees that run over several years. They get their own establishment into place; all of this can cause difficulty.

Kuykendall supports the goal of the PACs but feels that

> . . . they exist in name only. The quality of the PAC's operation is dependent on each school's administrator. Rarely have I seen a principal who wants to share his budget and other decision-making processes with the parents.

When asked to discuss what real citizen participation is, Kuykendall responded that she would like to see PACs expanded to community boards of education where "real decision making would take place." Real decision making includes decisions on

> ... how the money is being spent, making sure the curriculum correlates with what the children will be doing in the future, and the hiring and firing of teachers and administrators.

In responding to the issue of community boards of education, Bell stated:

> I feel the parent involvement should be advisory. I don't feel that there should be control elements there. We have our decision-making system—the board of education—which is mandated by law. We must be cautious about layering decision-making bodies. This layering could lead to a decision-making paralysis.

Prior to reading this chapter, and particularly this section, your response to an educator who stated, "In our school we have much parental involvement," may have been a variation of, "Isn't that nice." We hope that you will now, in your most sincere and polite voice, respond to the educator: Please define what you mean by parental involvement.

The Community as a Resource

In Chapter 3 we discussed the use of anthropological observation techniques. An anthropologist analyzing the effect of the eight-foot fence that surrounds many schools might infer that outsiders are not allowed in and that insiders are not allowed out—and both inferences may be correct! If exclusion is the purpose, it certainly conflicts with the educational philosophy of John Dewey who felt that the school should be an extension of the community. School life and real life, according to Dewey, should be as similar as possible; after all, the purpose of schooling is to prepare children for effective participation in community affairs. In short, there should be as little discontinuity as possible between life in schools and life in the surrounding community. In this section we will see what one of today's most well-known educators has to say about using the community as a resource.

Mario Fantini, dean of the School of Education at the University of Massachussets, is nationally known as an expert in the area of educational alternatives. In order to use alternative methods, delivery systems, and personnel, Fantini feels that educators must make use of the rich resources that can be found in every community in the United States. Instead of paraphrasing his ideas, we will allow him to "speak" to you directly.

Mario Fantini
COMMUNITY AS A RESOURCE

We can't expect the school to do it all: basic academic skills, career education, sex education, moral development, driver education. We must share the responsibility for the education of our children among all parts of society. Today we must look at the process of education in much broader terms than just what goes on in the classroom. The limited boundaries of the school are inappropriate for the goal of quality education. These are the reasons why we must move toward community education. The family and the larger community become the crucial components in the support of the schools.

Allow me to begin by talking about the importance of the family. The parents are the first teachers. Language, values, and approaches to learning are developed in the home with the parents as the primary teachers. Teachers must establish with the parent the idea that "we are both teachers; you work primarily in the home, and I work in the school. As teachers we must come together as frequently as possible to share and reinforce one another."

The parent's teaching need not be limited to the home. As a teacher you can begin to utilize the skills of the parents in the classroom. Try this: make an inventory of your parents' talents: art, music, technical skills, and so forth. Begin to invite them to enrich your classroom environment when possible, reverse the movement, and arrange for your students to visit the parents in their locations where they use their skills: factories, homes, research centers. Children will begin to see that parents are teachers, that they have worth and are respected by the school personnel.

Persons from the community, along with the parents, can also be utilized to build this continuity between school and community: Retired grandparents can be tutors; college students can listen to young children read; high school students from child-development classes can interact with the kindergarten children.

Beginning teachers have a unique problem. Since they want to do everything well, they try to have all aspects of their program operating from day one in the highest gear: individualization, learning centers, peer tutoring, parental involvement. Very quickly, they get in over their heads and retrench their total program with the statement, "I'll do this when I get more experience."

They rarely find the time to return to their original goals and techniques. The beginning teacher should think about various levels of parental involvement, begin with the lowest level, and progress with additional experience. A good place to begin is to learn about the community: Walk around the community and meet the grocer, doctor, merchant, sanitation worker. You'll be surprised what happens when you say,

"Hi, I'm a new teacher in the community and I want to learn about you and the total community." After making these initial contacts, you can begin to ask "Would you be able to speak to my class (or have my class visit you) to discuss what you do?" I think you will establish a rapport with the community. With additional experience in the classroom and with the community, you will have the competencies to organize parent discussion groups, train parents as tutors, and design learning activities for the students in the community. Be patient. Start slowly. But your contact with the community must be continuous.

Parents are your best resource in the community, although you need not limit your community involvement to parents. Libraries, museums, medical and legal centers, factories, and recreation centers offer a rich variety of resources which you can utilize for your students. For example, a library is more than a collection of books: It has a staff with numerous skills; programs designed around literature, records, and puppets; and some libraries lend paintings and sculpture (hang a Picasso in your classroom!). A medical school is a unique resource. Ask medical students to visit your class to discuss health education, sex education, drug education. Frequently, parents are more comfortable if these critical issues are discussed by doctors rather than teachers. An employee in a shoe factory can talk about the design, manufacture, and marketing of shoes. A representative from an insurance company can explain his practical approach to math. A banker can discuss finances or the use of computers. The list of possible resources is endless; it is only limited by your imagination.

Allow me to conclude my comments with a few general statements. You, as the teacher, are in the best position to orchestrate the resources in the community. These resources will enrich the development of your students. This relationship among the school, home, and community shows the students that there is a continuity between the school and its surrounding environment. Learning can and should be a rich, dynamic experience.

Summary   Although schools provide consciously planned learning environments staffed by professionally trained teachers, they should not be viewed as the only or necessarily the primary setting in which learning occurs. In this chapter we have attempted to show you, through a series of interviews with prominant educators, how children's learning and development can be continued beyond the school setting. Particular attention was paid to the home as a primary learning environment and to the parents as "teachers in the home."

Although our experts agreed on the need to establish a broad and coordinated educational network, one that encompasses home, school, and the surrounding community, they did not always agree on how this network should operate. As is true throughout this text, we have tried to confront you with various alternatives that you can choose from in developing your own teaching philosophy. The encounters that follow should help you to understand better and evaluate the contents of this chapter.

Encounters

1. Ask a neighbor, friend, or relative who has school-age children whether you can visit in the home and observe the informal learning environment. Listed below are some focuses for data collection:
   a. Write a list of topics discussed between parents and children. Who initiated each topic? Was eye contact established? Did parents listen to the child's comments and questions?
   b. How does the parent use the material in the home for learning activities (e.g., count the diapers, read a recipe, compare sizes of the plates on the table, talk about a television program)?
2. Develop a short interview survey that focuses on the parents' awareness and desire to be "parent-educators." The following are possible questions that you might include:
   a. How do you think parents could help children in your child's school?
   b. I have heard that you are an excellent _____. Would you be willing to share your skill with the students in the school?
3. Visit and observe parent-education programs in your area. These programs can probably be found by contacting neighboring universities, health and welfare agencies, children's hospitals, etc.
4. From your involvement with the issues related to parental involvement in the schools, develop a Bill of Rights for parents, one for teachers, and a third for students. Place the three lists side by side: Identify those items from each Bill of Rights that conflict with items in the other two. Decide how you will deal with the conflicts. Share your ideas with your colleagues and instructor.
5. Borrow a list of courses offered at a nearby middle school. Next to each course offering, write possible community resources that could be used.
6. Whereas Olmsted's parent educators are generally community residents who work with neighboring parents, many of Levenstein's "toy demonstrators" are college graduates, middle-class volunteers from outside the community who work directly with the children. Comment on the advantages and disadvantages of each approach.
7. Compare the views of Olmsted, Levenstein, and Rich regarding the role of the parent as teacher. How do they compare regarding the following?
   a. The relationship or levels of involvement between parents and school.
   b. The skills that parents are expected to acquire.
   c. The materials that parents are to use.
   d. The one who is to train the parents.
   e. The environment(s) that parents are to use.
8. Olmsted recommends that parents be involved in all levels of the school program, from one-to-one child interaction to school policy decisions. Can a teacher who lacks outside financial support make use of all the levels of parental involvement found in the North Carolina model? If you had to choose one level of parental involvement, what would it be? Why?
9. List each form of parental involvement recommended by Olmsted, and beside each one estimate the time and money it would cost you, the teacher, each week.

Given this cost, what type of parental involvement would you try to initiate during your first, second, and third year of teaching?

10. Rich and Olmsted stress the parents' role in teaching cognitive skills to their children. Do you think there should be additional goals in a home-based program?

Notes

1. Hunt, J. McVicker, "Parent and Child Centers: Their Basis in the Behavioral and Educational Sciences," *American Journal of Orthopsychiatry, 41* (January 1971), 13–42; Schaefer, Earl, "Parents as Educators: Evidence from Cross-Sectional, Longitudinal and Intervention Research," *Young Children, 27* (1972), 227–29.
2. Schaefer, Earl, *Newsweek*, May 22, 1972, p. 30.
3. Gordon, I., and Breivogel, W., *Building Effective Home-School Relationships* (Boston: Allyn and Bacon, 1976).
4. Baratz, Stephen S., and Baratz, Joan C., "Early Childhood Intervention: The Social Science Base of Institutional Racism," *Harvard Educational Review, 40* (February 1970), 29–50.
5. *Ibid.*
6. *Ibid.*
7. Happy Fernandez, *Parents Organizing to Improve Schools* (Columbia, Md.: National Committee for Citizens in Education, 1976), pp. 48–49.
8. C. Wallat and R. Goldman, *Home/School/Community Interacting* (Columbus, Ohio: Merrill, 1979).

For More Information

JOURNALS

Atkeson, Beverly M., and Forehand, Rex. "Parents as Behavior Change Agents with School-Related Problems," *Education and Urban Society, 10* (1978), 521–538.

Baumann, Jean. "Teachers are Important People Too," *Momentum, 10* (1979), 10.

Bricker, Diane, and Caruso, Valerie. "Family Involvement, A Critical Component of Early Intervention," *Exceptional Children, 46* (1979), 108–116.

Huggins, Allen L. "This Small School System Mobilized Community, Staff, and Kids to Boost Student Competency Test Scores," *American School Board Journal, 167* (1980), 23–24.

Kappelman, Murray M., and Ackerman, Paul. "Between Parent and School," *Exceptional Parent, I* (1977), 15–17.

Keller, Marti. "Parents: A Resource for Day Care," *Day Care and Early Education, 6* (1979), 44–47.

Kennison, Pat. "Parent Volunteers: Crucial Helpers," *Thrust for Education Leadership 6* (1977).

Kimmel, Carol. "Parent Power. A Plus for Education," *Educational Leadership, 34* (1976), 24–25.

Larrick, Nancy. "From 'Hands Off' to 'Parents, We Need You'," *Childhood Education, 52* (1976), 134–137.

Lattimore, Louis. "Parent Involvement in the Classroom: Good Grief," *Thrust for Education Leadership, 6* (1977), 9–11.

Laubenthal, Nadine. "What Did You Do in School Today?" *Teacher, 97* (1979), 80–82.

BOOKS

Bell, Terrell H. *Active Parent Concern: A New Home Guide to Help Your Child in School.* Englewood Cliffs, N.J.: Prentice-Hall, 1976.

Brandt, Ronald S., ed. *Partners: Parents and Schools.* Alexandria, Virginia: Association for Supervision and Curriculum Development, 1979.

Croft, Doreen J. *Parents and Teachers: A Resource Book for Home, School, and Community Relations.* Belmont, Calif.: Wadsworth Publishing Co., 1979.

Gordon, Ira, and Breivogel, William. *Building Effective Home-School Relationships.* Boston: Allyn & Bacon, 1976.

Gordon, Thomas. *P.E.T. Parent Effectiveness Training* New York: New-American Library, 1975.

Kindred, Leslie W., Bagin, Don, and Gallagher, Donald R. *The School and Community Relations.* Englewood Cliffs, N.J.: Prentice-Hall, Inc. 1976.

Nedler, Shari E., and McAfee, Oralie D. *Working With Parents.* Belmont, California.: Wadsworth Publishing Co., 1979.

Wallat, Cynthia, and Goldman, Richard. *Home/School/Community Interaction.* Columbus, Ohio: Charles E. Merrill Publishing Company, 1979.

MOVIES

Crowded Out (NEA, 29 min., 1967). Overcrowding in the schools forces a teacher to resign because she can no longer give individual attention to her students. Parent-teacher conflicts and discipline problems also arise.

A Film on Early Intervention (Instructional Media Services, 30 min., 1979). Focuses on the need for early intervention strategies of handicapped in the first five years of development. Home based, center based, and parent involvement programs are shown using actual settings.

Inside Out (Jack Robertson, 56 min., 1971). Demonstrates the various resources available from the community that can be provided to urban high school students. This is exemplified by the Franklin Parkway Program.

No Little Hope (Center for Urban Education, 28 min.). New York City parents state that parents, the community, media, and the schools must be considered before fully understanding the process of education.

Teachers, Parents, and Children: Growth Through Cooperation (Sterling Educational Films, 16 min., 1974). Expresses the importance of parent-teacher cooperation for the child's emotional development. Three elements of this development are discussed—safety, endorsement, and mutual respect.

Chapter 9

Chapter 9

TEACHERS AND SCHOOL LAW

Historically, teachers and administrators have had powers in determining the regulations and procedures that govern a child's school experience. This power was virtually unchallenged until the mid 1950s and early 1960s. Since that time students and their parents have demanded, through the judicial process, justification from teachers and administrators for a myriad of educational actions, touching nearly every aspect of the American educational system. These challenges from a litigation-conscious society have had a profound impact on schools. Today it is a rare school district that does not have either a contractual agreement with a local law firm or a full-time attorney to interpret court rulings and state and federal mandates related to school policies and procedures. School law has become so complex that few educators are fully cognizant of the status of laws governing their own schools and classrooms.

This chapter is designed to help you become aware of some of the precedent-setting legal decisions that will affect you as an educator. Unless you develop and maintain a rudimentary knowledge of school law, you will not be able to deal effectively with situations like those contained in the following quiz. Take a moment to test your knowledge of these situations and, if you miss or are uncertain about more than one, read the brief discussions that follow.[1]

1. *Situation:* A fight erupts between two students in your classroom, and during the struggle a desk and tape recorder are broken. You send the two offenders to the principal's office and immediately phone their parents to come pick them up.

Question: Can teachers, even with the principal's support, suspend a student without observing due process procedures?

Yes _____   No _____   Sometimes _____

Comments _____

_____

_____

2. *Situation:* You see a student cheating on an exam and confront him about it. In the ensuing exchange he swears at you and, in return, you send him to the school office where you intend to use your paddle on him.
   Question: Is it legal for a teacher to paddle or otherwise physically punish a child?

Yes _____   No _____   Sometimes _____

Comments _____

_____

_____

3. On the basis of continuing misconduct throughout the school year, you have decided that one of your academically average students should not be promoted.
   Question: Can a teacher legally lower a student's grade because of persistent misconduct?

Yes _____   No _____   Sometimes _____

Comments _____

_____

_____

4. *Situation:* One of your students refuses to stand and recite the Pledge of Allegiance with the rest of the class despite your repeated urging.
   Question: Are teachers within their rights to insist that all stu-

dents participate in patriotic recitations such as the Pledge of Allegiance?

Yes _____ No _____ Sometimes _____

Comments _____

_____

_____

5. *Situation:* As part of a social studies lesson dealing with Thanksgiving you ask the class to join in a nondenominational prayer to be followed by a Bible reading.
   Question: Are teachers within their rights in conducting nondenominational prayers and in reading from the Bible?

Yes _____ No _____ Sometimes _____

Comments _____

_____

_____

6. *Situation:* You are a member of the board of education in a large urban community where 72.8 percent of the students are black. In an attempt to comply with a desegregation order, you and the other board members decide that the best course of action is to arrange for cross-district busing with a neighboring school district that is predominantly white.
   Question: Must all schools within racially imbalanced school systems maintain the same racial balance?

Yes _____ No _____ Sometimes _____

Comments _____

_____

_____

7. *Situation:* The parents of a child who was to have been in your kindergarten program asked your advice about the following letter they have just received:

Dear Mr. and Mrs. _____:

I have tested David and concluded that a public kindergarten is not the most appropriate learning environment for him since he tested "untrainable." I recommend that you work with David at home (I'll send you some games and activities) or send him to the special school. I'm aware that the special school is private and expensive but it is also very good. If I can be of additional help, please contact me.

Sincerely,

B. E.
School Psychologist

Question: Can public schools exclude students whom they believe to be unteachable?

Yes _____   No _____   Sometimes _____

Comments _____

_____

_____

8. *Situation:* Carol, an exceptional athlete, asks you (the coach) if she can try out for the boys' volleyball team since there isn't a girls' team. You advise her that league rules prohibit girls from participating in the boys' league.
Question: Must public schools provide equal access to all school programs, both academic and extracurricular, for both boys and girls?

Yes _____   No _____   Sometimes _____

Comments _____

_____

_____

9. *Situation:* The father of a child who slipped and broke her arm on a recent field trip calls to inform you that he is suing you, the principal, and the school district for negligence. The fact that he signed a permission slip releasing you and the school from responsibility for possible accidents doesn't deter him.
Question: Are teachers and schools automatically relieved of liability for negligence when parents sign permission slips to that effect?

Yes _____ No _____ Sometimes _____

Comment _____

_____

_____

10. *Situation:* You receive notice that you and several other teachers along with the local school board are being sued by a former student (now 18) who claims he was allowed to graduate with only a second-grade reading level. He is now having difficulty finding employment.
Question: Can a teacher or a school be held accountable for a student's failure to learn?

Yes _____ No _____ Sometimes _____

Comments _____

_____

_____

11. *Situation:* During a parent–teacher conference you recommend to a mother that her child be placed in a special remedial class. The shocked mother asks to see her child's cumulative records but you inform her that school policy limits the examination of student records to school personnel.
Question: Do parents have a legal right to examine their children's school personnel.

Yes _____ No _____ Sometimes _____

Comments _____

_____

_____

The remainder of this chapter is devoted to brief discussions of each of these questions (discussions that you should amplify through additional readings such as those provided at the end of the chapter). A note of caution: Court cases involving school-related legal issues are decided each day in courts throughout the country; therefore, teachers must pay continuous attention to the media in order to stay current on educational legal issues.

Can a Teacher, Even with the Principal's Support, Suspend a Student without Observing Due Process Procedures?

In the case, *Goss* v. *Lopez* (419 U.S. 565, 1972), the Supreme Court concluded that public education is a property right and, as such, it cannot be denied a student without due process proceedings. Due process in the case involving the two fighting students should have included a hearing where the students, after hearing the school's evidence, would have an opportunity to present their side of the story. In cases involving long suspension or expulsion, the courts recommend the following procedure: (a) notice of hearing, (b) providing students with the right to counsel, (c) providing student's counsel an opportunity to cross-examine witnesses, and (d) presenting the student's parents with a summary of the findings and recommendations.

Is It Legal for a Teacher to Paddle or Otherwise Physically Punish a Child?

The legal guideline on corporal punishment in schools was established in British Common Law. In brief, the common-law principle is that teachers and administrators may use whatever force they feel is necessary for the training and education of the child.

"But surely," you are probably thinking; "the Eighth Amendment's prohibition against cruel and unusual punishment applies to students as well as to criminals?" According to a 1977 Supreme Court case, *Ingram* v. *Wright* (97 Supreme Court 1401, 1977), it does not. In this case, students at Drew Junior High School in Dade County, Florida, testified that school administrators armed with paddles, brass knuckles, and belts had engaged in unnecessarily vicious beatings that resulted in serious injuries ranging from bleeding hematoma to a badly disfigured hand. The Supreme Court agreed to review the case on two grounds: (a) that the punishment used was cruel and unusual in contradiction of the Eighth Amendment and (b) that due process laws require that students be given some form of prior notice and hearing before being subjected to corporal punishment.

In a close five to four decision the Supreme Court ruled that the cruel-and-unusual-punishment clause did not apply outside the criminal process; that because schools are essentially "open" institutions where students are not denied the support of family, friends, and teachers, the student has little need for the protection of the Eighth Amendment. Likewise, the due process argument was dismissed as unnecessary in this case since existing state laws (a) require that teachers and principals confer before administering corporal punishment to a student and (b) permit the

civil and criminal prosecution of teachers and administrators who unreasonably harm a student.

In short, federal laws and court decisions do not at this time prohibit the use of corporal punishment in the schools. Consequently, individual states and school districts are free to pass laws either forbidding or authorizing such punishment. At present, two states (Massachusetts and New Jersey) and numerous school districts have laws or regulations that prohibit paddling and other forms of corporal punishment. However, as long as the public continues to view lack of discipline as the leading problem in American education, it is probable that many states and districts will continue to arm school personnel with the legal right to impose corporal punishment. Whether or not they elect to use this right is another matter.

Can a Teacher Legally Lower a Student's Grade Because of Persistent Misconduct?

Generally, the courts have taken the position that social behavior and academic performance should be separated for evaluative purposes. Since schools must have procedures for dealing with negative behavior, grades should be used solely for the purpose of evaluating academic performance. Consequently, should you hear yourself saying to a student, "I'll lower your [academic] grade if you continue to misbehave," reconsider your comment based on the legal implications of the comment.

Are Teachers Within Their Rights to Insist That All Students Participate in Patriotic Recitations Such as the Pledge of Allegiance?

According to the courts, a teacher is incorrect in telling all students that they must recite the Pledge of Allegiance. In the case of *West Virginia State Board of Education* v. *Barnette* (319 U.S. 624, 1943) the Supreme Court ruled that the religious freedom of the Jehovah's Witness children was violated by the school district that demanded a salute to the flag. The court also included reasons of conscience as an argument for abstaining from participation in the Pledge (*Banks* v. *Board of Public Instruction of Dade County, Florida,* 314 F. Supp. 285 S.D. Fla., 1970). Teachers who force a nonparticipating child to stand "out of respect for others" or to leave the room are engaging in a form of illegal punishment: The nonparticipants cannot be punished unless they disturb the room with loud comments.

Are Teachers Within Their Rights in Conducting Nondenominational Prayers and in Reading from the Bible?

The years 1962 and 1963 brought two landmark Supreme Court decisions concerning prayer and Bible reading in public schools. In the 1962 *Engel*

v. *Vitale* (370 U.S. 421, 1962) case the high court ruled that the daily recitation in the New York public schools of the denominationally neutral prayer composed by the Board of Regents was unconstitutional because it violated the Establishment Clause (which denies the government any legislative power concerning religion) of the First Amendment. Justice Black, in delivering the opinion of the court, wrote:

> There can be no doubt that New York's state prayer program officially establishes the religious beliefs embodied in the Regent's prayer. . . . Neither the fact that the prayer may be denominationally neutral nor the fact that its observance on the part of the students is voluntary can serve to free it from the limitations of the Establishment Clause, as it might from the Free Exercise Clause, of the First Amendment, both of which are operative against the States by virtue of the Fourteenth Amendment.

A more far-reaching decision was handed down by the court the following year in the case of *Abington School District* v. *Schempp* (374 U.S. 203, 1963). In reaching their decision the court considered the suits brought by both Edward Schempp and Madalyn Murray. Edward Schempp was a Unitarian who objected to the daily Bible reading in the Pennsylvania Schools as dictated by the state laws of Pennsylvania. At Abington Senior High, the school his children attended, ten verses of the Bible were read each morning without comment, and the Lord's Prayer was recited in unison. Schempp believed that a literal reading of the Bible could be misleading and, therefore, that the daily readings should be abolished. Although students were not forced to participate, Schempp believed that asking to have his children excused would cause them inconvenience and embarrassment.

Greater publicity was given to the suit brought by Madalyn Murray for her son, William J. Murray III, because Murray was an atheist who apparently felt nothing but contempt for religion. This is indicated in a letter to *Life* magazine:

> We find the Bible to be nauseating, historically inaccurate, replete with the ravings of madmen. We find God to be sadistic, brutal, and a representation of hatred, vengeance. We find the Lord's Prayer to be that muttered by worms groveling for meager existence in a traumatic, paranoid world.[2]

Mrs. Murray's suit involved a practice of the Baltimore Schools that required the daily reading, without comment, of a chapter from the Bible and/or recitation of the Lord's Prayer. At Murray's insistence the school policy had been altered to allow children with written permission from their parents to be excused from these practices.

The Supreme Court, joining the two cases and rendering a single decision, determined that in both cases the religious activities taking place in the schools were unconstitutional in that they violated both the Establishment Clause and the Free Exercise Clause of the First Amendment. The court also rejected "the contention that the Establishment

Clause forbids only governmental preference of one religion over another."

The Court's decision, as delivered by Justice Clark, emphasized the importance of governmental neutrality in the area of religion:

> . . . it is no defense to urge that the religious practices here may be relatively minor encroachments on the First Amendment. The breach of neutrality that is today a trickling stream may all too soon become a raging torrent and, in the words of Madison, "it is proper to take alarm at the first experiment of our liberties. . . ."

Another much-discussed issue in this case involved the will of the majority. It was argued that if the majority of persons affected wished to see these practices continued, what right had the courts to rule otherwise? Justice Clark responded to this by saying that the Constitution "has never meant that a majority could use the machinery of the state to practice its beliefs." Such a contention was effectively answered by Justice Jackson for the Court in *West Virginia State Board of Education* v. *Barnette* (319 U.S. 624, 1943):

> The very purpose of a Bill of Rights was to withdraw certain subjects from the vicissitudes of political controversy, to place them beyond the reach of majorities and officials and to establish them as legal principles to be applied by the courts. One's right to . . . freedom of worship . . . and other fundamental rights may not be submitted to a vote; they depend on the outcome of no elections.

The Supreme Court's decision did not have the effect of totally barring religion from the classroom. It did not prohibit nondevotional Bible reading (i.e., studying the Bible as a part of the regular curriculum), observance of religious holidays, or studying the cultural impact of various religions. This point was emphasized in Justice Brennan's concurring opinion:

> The holding of the Court today plainly does not foreclose teaching about the Holy Scriptures or about the differences between religious sects in classes in literature or history. Indeed, whether or not the Bible is involved, it would be impossible to teach meaningfully many subjects in the social sciences or the humanities without some mention of religion.

One option does exist for the classroom teacher related to prayer. A Massachusetts federal court upheld a state law that allowed a daily period for meditation or silent prayer that does not exceed one minute. The court felt that the law was constitutional since each student had a choice of silent prayer, meditation, or thinking on any topic that interests the student.

One final note: Some of you may have attended public schools after 1963 where Bible reading occurred on a daily basis. If so, your school was violating the Constitution in what amounts to civil disobedience. Those school districts that violate the Constitution feel that morality, as expressed through Bible reading, transcends the Constitution.

An Ethical Issue: **What will you do if you are employed in a public school district that mandates Bible reading and prayer as part of the opening exercises?**

Must all Schools within Racially Imbalanced School Systems Maintain the Same Racial Balance?

In the 1954 *Brown* v. *Board of Education* (347, U.S. 483, 1954) case, the Supreme Court made its landmark ruling against segregated schooling, stating:

> We conclude that in the field of public education the doctrine of "separate but equal" has no place. Separate educational facilities are inherently unequal. Therefore, we hold that the plaintiffs and others similarly situated for whom the actions have been brought are, by reason of the segregation complained of, deprived of the equal protection of the laws guaranteed by the Fourteenth Amendment.

The Supreme Court did not dictate the procedures for desegregating the schools; the primary responsibility for the desegregation process remained with the local school authorities, under the supervision of the local courts. The judges on the Supreme Court reasoned that the local officials were in closer touch with the realities and the unique needs of each local district; therefore, local authorities rather than the Supreme Court assumed responsibility for this difficult process. In the court's language:

271

The Death of "Separate but Equal"

HISTORICAL FLASHBACK

The doctrine of "separate but equal," which was used for more than 50 years to maintain a system of segregated public schools, derived its legal foundation from an 1896 Supreme Court decision involving the use of separate railroad cars for whites and nonwhites (*Plessey* v. *Ferguson,* 163 U.S. 537, 1896). In that case the high court had ruled that segregation was permissible if the facilities provided were of equal quality. Using this case as its legal foundation, there were by 1954 seventeen states, as well as the District of Columbia, that required segregation in their public schools, and four states that permitted it under certain conditions.

Reactions to the Supreme Court's 1954 reversal of its earlier decision were varied. In some places desegregation plans were carried out with little opposition (e.g., Newcastle, Delaware, and Oak Ridge, Tennessee). In some cities, e.g., Baltimore and Washington, D.C., there were brief strikes, but desegregation continued without violence. In other places the situation became so volatile that schools were temporarily closed.

In Little Rock, Arkansas, a situation arose that led to yet another Supreme Court decision. The school board and superintendent of schools had developed a desegregation plan that was to commence in the fall of 1957 and to be completed by 1963. The plan, though not popular, had been discussed with many citizens' groups, and it was believed that it could be implemented with a minimum of dissension. However, on September 2, 1957, Governor Faubus sent in the Arkansas National Guard to prevent black students from entering Central High School, the first school to be desegregated. President Eisenhower responded with federal troops to force the admittance of black students to the previously all white school. Because of the tensions created by this situation, the Little Rock school board petitioned the courts for the right to postpone their desegregation plan.

The case (*Cooper* v. *Aaron,* 358 U.S. 1, 1958) ultimately reached the Supreme Court, which ruled against postponement stating, "[Law] and order are not here to be preserved by depriving the Negro children of their constitutional rights." The court went on to chastise the Arkansas legislature, and particularly Governor Faubus, in the following statement:

No state legislator or executive judicial officer can war against the Constitution without violating his undertaking to support it. Chief Justice Marshall spoke for a unamious Court in saying that: "If the legislatures of the several states may, at will, annul the judgments of the courts of the United States, and destroy the rights acquired under those judgments, the Constitution itself becomes a solemn mockery. . . ." (*United States* v. *Peters,* 5 Cranch 115, 136.) A governor who asserts a power to nullify a federal court order is similarly restrained.

Resistance to desegregation was not limited to open attacks on desegregation programs. Throughout the South, white citizens' councils were formed for the purpose of pressuring blacks who openly supported desegregation. "The slogan of these councils was 'No job, no credit, no loan' — for Negroes unwilling to submit to segregation."[3] The lives of many blacks actively involved in the NAACP were threatened, and Rev. G. W. Lee, a NAACP leader in Mississippi, was killed by a shotgun blast.

Full implementation of these constitutional principles may require solution of varied local school problems. School authorities have primary responsibility for elucidating, assessing, and solving these problems; courts will have to consider whether the actions of school authorities constitute good faith implementation of the governing constitutional principles. Because of their proximity to local conditions and the possible need for further hearings, the courts which originally heard these cases can best perform this judicial appraisal.

As each school district developed its own plan for desegregation, numerous court cases appeared. One case that affected desegregation decisions throughout the United States was *Swann* v. *Charlotte-Mecklenberg Board of Education* (402, U.S. 1, 1971). To the question, "Must each school be racially balanced," Justice Burger wrote: "The constitutional command to desegregate schools does not mean that every school in every system must always reflect the racial composition of the school system as a whole." In effect, schools within a given system can maintain different racial balances if it can be proved that school assignments are in no way a result of discriminatory actions, whether in housing, political districting, or any other way.

In order to desegregate the Detroit Public Schools (69.8 percent black, 30.2 percent white) a plan of cross-district busing to neighboring suburban districts (81 percent white, 19 percent black) was proposed but eventually denied by the Supreme Court. The court ruled that since the unconstitutional procedures were developed within Detroit, the city had to devise its own remedies. However, this type of cross-district busing may be legal if previous school boundaries were tampered with in order to avoid racial integration. In short, the courts have ruled that no rigid rules can be prescribed regarding busing since local conditions differ.

The United States Supreme Court decision in the case of *Brown* v. *the Board of Education* has perhaps spawned more violence and bitterness than any other single court case. Such violence has persisted in places such as Boston and Louisville in response to the issue of busing. But the picture is far from bleak. The progress over the past years toward an educational system that is open and equal for all has been tremendous. Perhaps the next decades will bring the dream to full fruition.

Can Public Schools Exclude Students Whom They Believe to Be Uneducable?

In 1972 a group of 13 parents together with the Pennsylvania Association for Retarded Children (PARC) challenged the right of public schools to exclude children who had been labeled as "uneducable" or "untrainable." Before that time more than 1 million children who had been given these labels were being denied a free public education. In this case, the *Pennsylvania Association for Retarded Children* v. *the Commonwealth of Pennsylvania* (343 F. Supp. 279, E.D. Pa., 1972), the plaintiffs sought to establish three primary points:

1. Mentally retarded children can learn if an appropriate educational program is provided.
2. "Education" must be viewed more broadly than the traditional academic program.
3. Early educational experience is essential to maximize educational potential.[4]

This case was settled out of court in favor of PARC. Guidelines were established for implementing a comprehensive program for educating mentally retarded students within Pennsylvania's public school system.

A similar case, but one that was more comprehensive because it applied to all handicapped persons, was *Mills* v. *the Board of Education of the District of Columbia* (348 F. Supp. 866, D.D.C., 1972). In this case the court ruled, on the basis of constitutional principles, that the public schools must provide appropriate educational services for all handicapped persons.

Various state actions like these culminated in 1975 in landmark federal legislation, Public Law 94-142, which mandated free public education for all handicapped children by 1980. The major provisions of this bill guarantee:

1. *An individualized educational plan (IEP)* based upon comprehensive, nondiscriminative evaluation procedures for each handicapped child seeking a public school education. The bill states that "[evaluation] procedures . . . will be selected and administered so as not to be racially or culturally discriminatory."[5]
2. *Access to the "least restrictive" educational environment* for each handicapped child. This concept of "least restrictive" environment has led to a controversial practice referred to as "mainstreaming," i.e., the placement of handicapped children in regular classrooms. While the bill does not require that all handicapped children be placed in regular classrooms, it does call for this practice whenever feasible, with or without the consent of the handicapped child's parents. The practice of

mainstreaming has created much controversy, and its educational value for both handicapped and nonhandicapped students will be closely studied and hotly debated for years to come.

3. *Access to their children's records and to due process procedures* for parents of handicapped children. Besides having access to all records concerning their child's evaluation, placement, and progress and the right to obtain an independent evaluation if they so desire, parents also have the right to an impartial hearing where they can present complaints concerning their child's program.

Public Law 94-142 will not resolve every problem relating to educational opportunities for handicapped children. It is, however, an important step toward meeting their individual needs and helping them gain acceptance in a society that has not fully come to terms with its own fears and misconceptions about them.

Must Public Schools Provide Equal Access to All School Programs, Both Academic and Extracurricular, for Both Boys and Girls?

In *Brenden* v. *Independent School District* (742, 477 F 2d. 1292, 8th Cir., 1973), a case similar to the quiz situation at the beginning of the chapter, the court ruled unconstitutional a school system's rule prohibiting qualified female athletes from participating in its athletic league. Peggy Brenden's civil rights had been violated when she was discriminated against "on the basis of sex and sex alone." One of the keys to the case was the fact that her school provided no alternative athletic programs for female students. The Brenden case did not state that all schools must have an athletic program for female students; it did imply that if a program for male students existed, a similar program must be operated for females.

Undoubtedly, the most far-reaching attempt to rid the schools of practices that discriminate against females and reinforce outdated stereotypes of what females can and cannot do was the passage by Congress in 1972, of Title IX of the Education Amendments, which states:

> No person in the United States . . . shall, on the basis of sex, be excluded from participation in, be denied the benefits of, or be subjected to discrimination under any education program or activity receiving federal financial assistance.

Because virtually every school in this country receives some type of federal aid, the impact of Title IX has been far-reaching. It is important to note that Title IX applies to nearly all aspects of a school's program if federal funds are received for *any* program; it is not limited to those particular programs or activities that are being funded.

Specifically, Title IX applies to the following three areas of school operation:

1. *Admission and recruitment of students.* The admissions requirements of Title IX apply only to secondary vocational schools, public undergraduate colleges, and both public and private graduate and professional schools. Excluded from its reach are all public elementary schools and nonvocational high schools and all private undergraduate colleges. Public single-sex elementary and nonvocational secondary schools are permissible only if they are provided for students of both sexes and have comparable facilities, programs, services, and standards.

   For those schools whose admissions and recruitment practices are covered by Title IX, the following discriminatory practices are prohibited:
   a. The separate ranking of students according to sex
   b. The use of sex-related quotas
   c. Asking preadmission questions concerning marital status
   d. Excluding or discriminating against a person because of pregnancy, childbirth, etc.
   e. Recruiting primarily at single-sex schools.[6]

2. *Treatment of students.* Title IX prohibits many discriminatory practices that have been common for years in the public schools, particularly at the secondary level. Under its guidelines schools may no longer require that certain classes (e.g., home economics) be taken by all female students and others (e.g., shop) be taken by all the male students. The school may, however, require that all students of both sexes take a given course, e.g., either home economics or shop.

   Just as a school may not require a course on the basis of sex, neither may it deny admission to a course on that basis. Therefore, a girl must be allowed to enroll in auto mechanics if she chooses, just as the boy must be allowed to enroll in home economics. (Single-sex classes are allowed only for that part of a course that deals exclusively with human sexuality.)

   The practices employed by school guidance counselors must also be revised insofar as they direct students into single-sex classes or sex-related career choices. Schools are also directed to end job referral practices by which students of only one sex are recommended for particular jobs.

   Physical education courses may not be divided according to sex, although students within a given class may be separated for participation in contact sports (specified as wrestling, boxing, rugby, ice hockey, football, and basketball). Physical education classes may, however, be grouped by ability if the same standards are applied to both boys and girls and if high-ability groups are not given preferential treatment in the use of facilities, equipment, etc.

3. *School employment practices and policies.* Title IX prohibits sexual dis-

You and Title IX

Until recently the subordinate role of women in our society was given relatively little consideration. It was a generally accepted fact that "the woman's place is in the home," and if a woman did work outside the home, hers was simply a supplemental income, and, therefore, a lower salary was acceptable. This old cliché is, of course, highly inaccurate, for many single women must support themselves, and many others with children are the sole support of their families. Married women who work outside the home have been further burdened by the assumption that even if they do work, they must also manage to run a home and raise their children, often with little or no help from their husbands. Because such assumptions have pervaded our society, it is not surprising that women today are disproportionately represented in low-status, low-paying jobs.

As this chapter has attempted to show, however, things are beginning to change. Under the impetus of recent court cases and legislation such as Title IX, what will tomorrow's schools look like? Will boys and girls populate the same courses and the same extracurricular activities? Will girls and boys aspire equally to careers as doctors and nurses? In all probability, persons preparing to teach in the 1980s must be prepared to work in and defend such schools. If you become a teacher in a conservative community that supports traditional roles for males and females, how will you explain Title IX to the parents?

crimination against any school employee whether professional or nonprofessional. The following areas are included: employment criteria, recruitment, compensation, job classification and structure, fringe benefits, marital or parental status, advertising, and preemployment inquiries.

Enforcement of Title IX is the responsibility of the funding agencies through compliance actions initiated by them. If an investigation indicates the existence of ongoing discriminatory practices, the offending school faces the loss of federal funds. However, prior to such loss of funding, a hearing will be held, and if either party so desires, a judicial review of the case is available after the hearing.

Are Teachers and Schools Automatically Relieved of Liability for Negligence If Parents Sign Permission Slips to That Effect?

The answer to this question is "No!" Teachers must always supply adequate supervision to students both within the school and outside it on school-related business. The key issue, of course, is how the court defines "adequate supervision."

In the case of *Sheehan* v. *St. Peter's Catholic School* (188 N.W. 2d. 868, Minn., 1971) the jury found that a teacher was negligent when she left her group of students unsupervised on the athletic field. During this unsupervised period, a student was hit in the eye with a pebble. The jury concluded that it was "reasonable" to foresee that an unsupervised student might be hurt on an athletic field and ruled in favor of the student and her parents.

From the above case you may have concluded that students must always be supervised by a teacher. This is not necessarily true. On a trip to a museum with a group of twelve- to fifteen-year-old students, one teacher allowed the students to view the exhibits in small groups without any direct supervision. In this case, one of the students was beaten up by several boys who were not students in the school. The court concluded in the case of *Mancha* v. *Field Museum of Natural History* (283 N.E. 2d 899, Ill., 1972) that the possibility of a student being attacked in a museum was minimal. In addition, the court felt that a ruling in favor of the child would discourage teachers from planning educational trips outside the school environment.

In short, it is difficult to foresee precisely how the courts will define "reasonable supervision." In the absence of any definitive rulings, however, we do offer the following advice, cutting across many legal situations:

- Always instruct students on the proper use of the facilities: e.g., the swings on the playground or the equipment in the shop. Such advance instruction will serve the double purpose of reducing accidents and protecting you against claims of negligence.
- Be more careful in your supervision as the danger of an accident increases.
- Be aware that young students (usually defined as seven years old or younger) are usually not blamed for contributory negligence. This means, in brief, that young students who cause their own injury due to carelessness can still sue you and the school for negligence.
- "Assumption of risk" is recognized as a defense against liability when students voluntarily engage in activities (such as sports) that have higher possibilities for injury than participation in a less physical activity (e.g., a math class).

Finally, you should be aware that you can purchase insurance coverage through various professional educational organizations.

Can a Teacher or a School Be Held Accountable for a Student's Failure to Learn?

While it appears that a teacher will not be held "accountable" in malpractice suits, students may feel the effects of accountability. As of June

1977, 24 states had instituted accountability tests for students. A "no pass" on the accountability tests may lead to failure of a grade level or an inability to graduate. The State of Florida began its testing program in the Spring of 1977 for third, fifth, eighth, and eleventh graders. The test items focused on "survival skills," i.e., basic skills in math and communication that are essential in life situations, such as:

• Making correct change
• Reading maps
• Figuring out interest and sales tax
• Filling out credit application forms
• Making out a check
• Following cooking instructions
• Figuring out the best buy among similar products of different size
• Computing an electric bill and rent
• Reading a department store catalog
• Figuring out how much you save when you buy something at x percent off

Numerous arguments exist for and against such student-accountability tests. On the "pro" side we hear, for example, "If a student can't do these very basic skills, then a high school diploma is worthless," or "Application of the basic skills to real life situations is the bottom line for learning." On the "con" side, civil rights advocates argue that such tests may violate civil rights laws if a disproportionately high percentage of minority students fails the tests. Opponents further argue that such tests could be considered a method for resegregating the public schools based on test-score data. Should such test data indicate that minority schools were less effective than racially balanced schools in teaching basic competency skills, then the school system that used such tests would be in the embarrassing position of having compiled evidence against itself.

An Ethical Issue: Your team leader insists that you spend two months preparing your students for the accountability test. You disagree since you feel that your students need more time in science, social studies, and language arts. What will you do?

Do Parents Have a Legal Right to Examine Their Children's Records?

It is interesting to note that prior to 1974 the records of school children were open to government investigators (e.g., the CIA and the FBI) and other nonschool personnel but not the children's parents. In 1974

Congress passed the Family Educational Rights and Privacy Act, which mandated the following:

- Parents or guardians have the right to inspect their child's records
- Protection of the confidentiality of student records is guaranteed
- Procedures are established through which parents can challenge questionable information.

Today, the parent in the quiz scenerio could successfully challenge the school policy of closed records to parents. There are numerous implications of the Family Educational Rights and Privacy Act for you as a beginning teacher. First, you must be aware of those persons who are allowed to have access to your students' records. Second, your ancedotal comments should include data (e.g., specific behaviors) to support the inferences you make about the student. And finally, you should learn to view the parent as a partner who will join you in making decisions about his or her child.

An Ethical Issue: Your principal informs you that the school has a double record-keeping system: one set of records that can be read by parents and another set (the *real* set) that is kept in the principal's office. You realize that this record-keeping system violates the intent of the Family Educational Rights and Privacy Act. What will you do?

Summary

This chapter has dealt with some precedent-setting legal decisions that have had a profound effect upon present-day schools. But it must be remembered that we have seen only the tip of the iceberg: Legal decisions are being made every day that will directly affect you as a teacher. Therefore, it is in your best interests as a professional educator to keep abreast of these legal developments and to understand how they influence you and your students as well as the larger society.

1. Develop a case study of all legal cases of a school district during the past year. Your sources can include newspaper articles, an interview with the school board's lawyer, and a review of the school board's minutes. Based on the knowledge you acquired in this chapter, try to predict the outcomes of each case.
2. Compile a legal file on school-related issues in your area. The categories in the file can include the issues discussed in this chapter (e.g., discipline, prayer in school, review of records).
3. Write a handbook for teachers beginning their teaching careers on the topic of "law and the teacher."
4. Audit a course in your college on school law (courses are offered in law schools and schools of education).
5. Interview a parent who has been involved in a school-related law suit. Try to understand both sides of the issue(s) involved. Predict what you think will be the decision of the court.
6. Examine the paddling and suspension policies of three nearby school districts. Contrast the policies among the districts. When you understand the court decision related to the topics, decide whether the districts' policies are within the spirit of the law.
7. Talk to a student who has been suspended. Try to ascertain whether the procedures used by the school district follow the procedures recommended by the courts.

Notes

1. The major categories used in this chapter are based on those in David Schimmel and Louis Fischer, *The Rights of Parents in the Education of Their Children* (Columbia, Md.: National Committee for Citizens in Education, 1977).
2. Madalyn Murray, Letter to *Life,* April 12, 1963, p. 63.
3. Herbert Hill and Jack Greenberg, *Citizen's Guide to Desegregation: A Study of Social and Legal Change in American Life* (Boston: Beacon Press, 1955), p. 128.
4. Bill R. Gearheart and Mel W. Weishahn, *The Handicapped Child in the Regular Classroom* (St. Louis: Mosby, 1976), p. 14.
5. Michael L. Kabler, "Public Law 94-142 and School Psychology: Challenges and Opportunities," *The School Psychology Digest, 6* (Winter 1977), 22–23.
6. Norma Raffel, *Title IX: How It Affects Elementary and Secondary Education,* Report No. 803, Equal Rights for Women in Education Project, Ford Foundation Grant, (Denver, Colo.: Education Commission of the State, February 1976), p. 3.

For More   JOURNALS
Information Clem, Judith. "School District Liability for Negligent Supervision of the Califor-
               nia Student," *Journal of Juvenile Law, 3* (1979), 120–134.
             Cole, Robert. "Title IX: A Long Dazed Journey into Rights," *Phi Delta Kappan, 57*
               (1976), 575–577, 586.
             Drowatzky, John N. "Liability: You Could be Sued," *Journal of Physical Educa-
               tion and Recreation, 49* (1978), 17–18.
             Fischer, Louis, and Sorensen, Gail Paulus. "Censorship, Schooling, and the Law,"
               High School Journal, 62 (1979), 320–326.
             Flygare, Thomas J. "Recent Court Decisions Could Greatly Increase Cost of
               Special Education Programs," *Phi Delta Kappan, 62* (1980), 210–211.
             Forgione, Pascal D. Jr. "Early Childhood Policy-Making, Inputs, Processes, and
               Legislative Outputs," *Education and Urban Society, 12* (1980) 227–239.
             Goldschmidt, Steven M. "Teacher Accountability: Liability for Personal Injuries
               to Students Resulting from Inadequate Supervision, Instruction, and the Ad-
               ministration of Discipline," *Teacher Education and Special Education, 1*
               (1977), 76–90.
             Hazard, William R. "A Tort is Not a Piece of Cake: Teachers' Legal Responsi-
               bilities," *Music Educators Journal, 65* (1979), 26–33, 62–65.
             Hazard, William R. "How Three Laws Are Changing the Picture," *Today's Educa-
               tion:* Social Studies Edition, *69* (1980), 49–52.
             Lewis, Jean B. "Freedom of Speech and Expression in the Public Schools: A Closer
               Look at Teachers' Rights," *High School Journal, 63* (1980), 49–52.
             Nolte, M. Chester. "The Legal Heat on Teachers—How to Avoid It," *Learning, 6*
               (1978), 86–89, 93.
             Patterson, Arlene H. "Professional Malpractice: Small Cloud, but Growing
               Bigger," *Phi Delta Kappan, 62* (1980), 193–196.
             Pincus, John. "The Serrano Case: Policy for Education or for Public Finance?"
               Phi Delta Kappan, 59 (1977), 173–179.
             Van der Smissen, Betty. "Minimizing Legal Liability Risks," *Journal of Experi-
               mental Education, 2* (1979), 35–41.
             Zirkel, Perry A. "A Quiz on Recent Court Decisions Concerning Student Con-
               duct," *Phi Delta Kappan, 62* (1980), 206–208.

             BOOKS

             Coons, John E., and Sugarman, Stephen D. *Education by Choice: The Case for
               Family Control.* Berkeley: University of California Press, 1978.
             Fischer, Louis, and Schimmel, David. *The Civil Rights of Teachers.* New York:
               Harper & Row, 1973.
             Hudgins, H. C., and Vacca, Richard S. *Law and Education: Contemporary Issues
               and Court Decisions.* Charlottesville, Va.: Michie Co., 1979.
             Learner, Susan. *P.L. 94-1422: Related Federal Legislation for Handicapped Chil-
               dren and Implications for Coordination.* Washington, D.C.: National Education
               Association, 1978.
             McCune, Shirley, and Matthews, Martha. *The Context of Title IX: Outline and
               Participants' Materials for Generic Session One.* Washington, D.C.: U.S. Office
               of Education, Dept. of Health, Education and Welfare, 1978.
             Patterson, LeRoy James, Rossmiller, Richard H., and Volz, Marlin M. *The Law
               and Public School Operation.* New York: Harper and Row, 1978.

Sadker, Myra. *A Student Guide to Title IX.* Washington, D.C.: Department of Health, Education and Welfare, 1976.

Valente, William D. *Law in the Schools.* Columbus, Ohio: Charles E. Merrill Publishing Company, 1980.

White, Charles J., ed. *Teaching Teachers About Law.* Chicago: Special Committee on Youth Education for Citizenship, American Bar Association, 1976.

Your Legal Rights and Responsibilities: A Guide for Public School Students. Washington, D.C.: Office of Human Development Services, Department of Health, Education, and Welfare. Available from Consumer Information Center, Dept. 652F, Pueblo, Colorado 81009.

MOVIES

The Bill of Rights in Action: DeFacto Segregation (BFA Educational Media, 22 min., 1972). Shows the differences of opinion that develop in a community over the integration of their school system. This is an open-ended film, used to stimulate discussion.

In the Mainstream (CBS; Carousel, 14 min., 1979). Examines some of the successes and failures of Public Law 94-142, on placing handicapped children in the least restrictive environment. Some ramifications previously unseen by lawmakers, educators, and parents are presented.

Is the Teacher Liable? (Educators and Executive Ins., 16 min.). Presents several liability issues which face the teacher in the classroom, office, playground and after school activities, connected with the school.

Legal Liability of Teachers for School Accidents (Barbre, 30 min., 1960). A discussion of the legal liability of school teachers for school accidents.

One Step at a Time (Informatics, 25 min., 1972). Shows how the Department of Education in Michigan dealt with the issue of accountability within its school system. Six steps are outlined to achieve this goal with the educators and community working together.

Chapter 10

Chapter 10

WHO CONTROLS THE SCHOOLS?

Have you ever wondered who selects the textbooks for a particular course or grade level? Who determines the boundaries of the school district? Who really decides which person applying for a teaching position will get the job? Have you ever wondered who determines the school calendar, and have you wondered about their reasons? Who determines the forms of school discipline to use, and who decides whether dress codes should be written and enforced? Who determines the requirements for the successful completion of a particular course, and who decides which students will be promoted to the next grade? Have you ever wondered who determines the salary schedule for teachers as well as the "fringe" benefits? Who determines what can and what cannot be taught in the school curriculum (e.g., whether the school curriculum will contain sex education)? Who determines how teachers will be evaluated? And who in the world determined the teacher certification requirements?

We could probably go on for many pages with questions like these. In essence these questions ask, "Who really controls our schools?" As recently as 20 years ago these questions were seldom asked. Teachers, students, and the general public assumed that there were few, if any, alternatives and just accepted schools the way they were. Today, however, this is not the case. Teachers, administrators, the general public, and even students are asking who makes these decisions and why they are made. In addition, there are many individuals and groups attempting to gain a greater voice in determining what takes place in our schools. The purpose of this chapter is to look at the various roles that professional educators, federal and state governments, and formal and informal groups

have in controlling the schools. It is hoped that by studying this aspect of schools you will gain a better understanding of the "politics" of education.

A quick response to the question of who controls the schools would be "the people." That is, in a democratic society citizens have a general expectation that they will indeed be involved in some manner in the decision-making process within the educational system. Often, this involvement is in the form of consent. If strong feelings for or against a particular issue do not exist, the issue is generally accepted by the public. If a decision is made that is adverse to the general feelings of the public, however, some type of action is often taken. This action may be in the form of voting against an elected official who supported the decision, or it might take the form of individual's becoming directly involved in the decision-making process by running for office, attending meetings, or supporting lobbyists for a particular idea. The field of education is extremely broad at this time, and decisions are being made at all levels, ranging from the federal to the local school district to the individual classroom. When we speak of *control* we mean that an individual or group is influencing the actual outcome of the decision-making process. Control in education is usually determined by one of two methods. It can be achieved by actual participation, in which there is direct and unmediated involvement, or by representation, whereby the point of view of individuals or groups is represented by someone who is acting on their behalf.

In this chapter we will discuss the formal control exercised by educational agencies at the local, state, and federal levels. However, since there are many other groups that exert considerable influence in the decision-making process of the schools, we will also look at two types of informal control: that exercised by teachers' groups and that by citizens' groups.

Formal Control: Organization of Public Schools

Public schools in the United States are cooperatively controlled by a unique mix of local, state, and federal branches of government. This cooperation is quite different from that seen in educational systems in most other countries, where primary "control" of the schools is delegated to the federal branch of government. In the United States, since our founding fathers made no mention of education when they drafted the Constitution, the Tenth Amendment has become extremely important in the determination of governmental control of schools. The Tenth Amendment states that "powers not delegated to the United States by the Constitution, not prohibited by it to the states, are reserved to the states respectively, or to the people." Interpretations of this amendment have given the legal responsibility for our educational system to the states. Consequently, each state, except for Hawaii, has turned over large parts of the governance of schools to local governments. This has resulted in large amounts of local input in the development and interpretation of educational policy. Hawaii is an exception in that the entire state is organized as one school district and is administered by the state board of education. The federal government has not completely removed itself from the control of schools, however. Over the years the federal government has assumed the role of supporting innovative programs by providing additional funding for schools who adopt federally sponsored programs.

In the following sections we will discuss some of the universals that are part of the formal control of public schools. You will need to do additional research in order to understand fully how the schools are formally organized in your state and community.

LOCAL SCHOOL DISTRICT CONTROL

The most common form of local control is exercised by the individual school district. It is through the local district that citizens exercise formal control of the school's activities. The number of school districts in the United States has been steadily dropping. For example, in 1960 there were more than 40,000 school districts, as compared to the fewer than 16,000 that exist today. This decline in number has been the result of the consolidating of small districts, thus enabling them to provide a broader range of curricular, instructional, and support activities. Individual school districts range in geographical area and population from such large city systems as New York, Chicago, and Los Angeles, with thousands of students, to small, rural school districts such as Baugo Township in Northern Indiana, which covers only 24 square miles and has only a few hundred students.

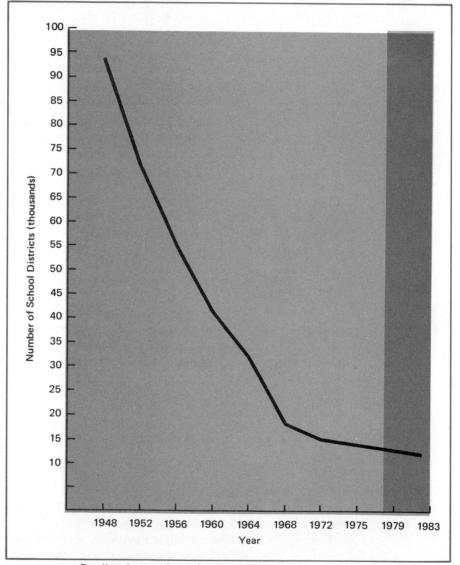

Figure 10.1. Decline in number of school districts.

From Mary A. Golladay, *The Condition of Education: A Statistical Report on the Condition of Education in the United States,* 1977 ed., vol. 3, Part 1 (Washington, D.C.: U.S. Department of Health, Education and Welfare/National Center for Education Statistics), p. 169.

Functions of the Local School District

The local school district is the governmental agency charged with the major responsibility for managing and operating the local schools. They exist, however, within the framework provided by the state. In fact, states have a right to modify or even reorganize school districts, but in most cases they have been unwilling to take any drastic action that would lessen input at the local level. Local school districts are governed by an appointed or elected school board that serves as the school's legal agent. The school board oversees all aspects of school districts' activities.* Specifically, the local board of education, under the auspices of the state, has the following major functions:

1. To establish sound educational policies for an effective school administration
2. To make current and long-range plans for the development and improvement of the educational programs and policies
3. To appraise and evaluate policies made by the board and executed by the school administrators
4. To select a professional, competent superintendent of schools, and appoint qualified professional and nonprofessional staff members
5. To examine and approve the annual educational budget
6. To provide needed funds and facilities
7. To fix salaries and determine conditions of employment
8. To consider and approve major educational programs and policies

*See Chapter 7 for a profile of a school board member and additional discussion of the role.

9. To interpret the needs, problems, and plans of the schools and enlist community support
10. To cooperate in carrying out the state and county educational regulations and policies in the local district.[1]

At the local school-district level the school board oversees and manages the operation of the school. It *does not* execute plans or policies. That is the responsibility of the administration, teachers, and staff who are hired and paid by the school board.

ROLE OF STATE GOVERNMENTS IN THE CONTROL OF SCHOOLS

The state is the governmental branch that is primarily responsible for providing a free education to its citizens. In the past, most states have delegated large portions of this responsibility to local school districts, but the current trend in virtually all of the 50 states is toward greater state control of public education. This change has been slow in coming because of strong feelings that local citizens should have a direct voice in decisions related to the schooling of their children. Despite the strong support for local control, three factors have spurred increased involvement in education at the state level.

School Finance

One of the most obvious factors leading to increased state control involves the rapidly growing cost of operating local school districts. Government figures show that 1950 school expenditures have increased from 3.4 percent of the Gross National Product (GNP) to 7.9 percent of the GNP. This higher cost has made it increasingly more difficult for local districts to support educational programs. The result has been that affluent communities have been able to finance their schools at a much higher rate than have poorer communities. To alleviate this problem many state legislatures have begun enacting tax equalization laws that have significantly increased per pupil expenditures in less affluent communities. Tied to this additional support have been additional regulations as to how state funds may be expended by the local school district.

Accountability

In Chapter 5 we discussed the legislation passed in many states, requiring students to pass minimum competency tests before they can graduate from high school. The responsibility for supervising this action has often been assumed by the state. Because of such minimum competency requirements, states are beginning to require more uniformity across the state regarding what is taught in schools and how achievement is tested. The accountability movement has thereby increased the amount of state control over the schools.

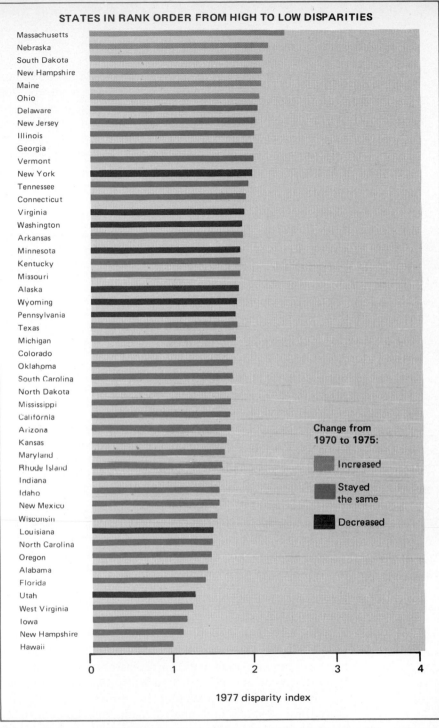

Figure 10.2. Gross National Product (GNP) related to total expenditures for education, health, and defense.

From Mary A. Golladay, *The Condition of Education: A Statistical Report on the Condition of Education in the United States,* 1977 ed., vol. 3, Part 1 (Washington, D.C.: U.S. Department of Health, Education, and Welfare/National Center for Education Statistics), p. 154.

Teacher Organizations

Another factor in the growth of state control in education has been the effective political lobbying of teacher organizations. As early as 1973, teacher groups were identified as the strongest of all state legislative lobbying groups.[2] Teachers' organizations, like all labor organizations, have discovered that there is strength in numbers, and they have directed much energy, therefore, to implementing changes at the state level rather than to attempting to solve all their problems within the framework of the local districts.

State Level Organization for Education

It is the state legislature that is responsible for the formulation of educational policy at the state level. Through the state executive branch the governor can also exert control over the schools. This control is usually provided in the form of general policies that are enacted into state law. Most states have an elected, or in some cases appointed, chief state school officer (state superintendent) and state board of education that oversees the implementation of state policies. It is the Department of Education that provides the professional assistance to local school districts in carrying out state policies. The following are five areas of control that are exerted by most states:

1. Levy taxes to support the schools.
2. License teachers and other school-related personnel.
3. Set standards for required student attendance, transportation, etc.
4. Outline a minimum curriculum that must be taught (in some cases states provide approved textbook lists that local districts must adopt).
5. Regulate the nature and size of local school districts.

FEDERAL GOVERNMENT CONTROL OF EDUCATION

The federal government has less involvement in the control of local schools than either the state or local districts. However, although the Constitution does not outline a specific educational role, the federal government always assumed a supporting role. For example, Congress declared in the Ordinance of 1785 that in the Northwest Territory (Indiana, Illinois, Michigan, Ohio, Wisconsin, and Minnesota) "there should be reserved the lot No. 16 of every township, for the maintenance of public schools, within said township." This ordinance provided that blocks of land were set aside for the establishment of public schools before the settlement of the land. This ordinance became a model for many of the states that were subsequently admitted to the United States. In all, more than 30 states had land set aside for schools through federal grants, totaling more than 80 million acres.

As early as 1867 Congress created the first Department of Education, headed by a commission appointed by the President. The purpose of the department was

. . . to collect such statistics and facts as shall show the condition and progress of education in the several States and Territories, [and] to diffuse such information respecting the organization and management of schools and school systems, and methods of teaching, as shall aid the people of the United States in the establishment and maintenance of efficient school systems, and otherwise promote the cause of education throughout the country.[3]

Later, the department was changed to the Office of Education, and over the years it was incorporated into a number of other federal agencies, including the Department of the Interior and the Federal Security Agency. In 1953 the Office of Education became a part of the new Department of Health, Education, and Welfare. In the late 1970s President Carter proposed that a Department of Education be organized in order to consolidate the federally sponsored educational programs that are scattered about in many diverse agencies of the government. In 1979 legislation mandating the new Department of Education passed both houses of Congress.

FUNCTIONS OF THE FEDERAL GOVERNMENT

The functions of the federal government in controlling the schools can be divided into four major areas. The first is to provide interpretation of the United States Constitution through the Supreme Court. The profound impact that the courts have had on education can be seen in cases such as *Brown* v. *Topeka Board of Education* and others discussed in Chapter 9. A second function assumed by the federal government has been to conduct research and disseminate findings through the Department of Education. This department conducts surveys and funds educational research studies across the country. This information is made available to states and local school districts to assist in educational planning. Members of Congress and their educational committees and staffs also use this information when formulating new legislation. The third area includes the administration of federal educational programs. These numerous programs include Title I of the Elementary and Secondary Education Act, which provides funds to aid in the education of children from low-income families, and the Higher Education Act, which provides assistance to college libraries and funds loans for college and university students. Finally, the federal government has taken an active role in providing federal funds to support specialized educational programs. Some of the programs sponsored by the federal government include:

- Military service academies:
  - U.S. Military Academy, West Point, New York
  - U.S. Naval Academy, Annapolis, Maryland
  - U.S. Air Force Academy, Colorado Springs, Colorado
  - U.S. Merchant Marine Academy, Kingsport, New York
  - U.S. Coast Guard Academy, New London, Connecticut
- Elementary and secondary schools on Armed Forces bases
- Elementary and secondary schools on Indian reservations
- Elementary and secondary schools in U.S. Territories: Guam and Virgin Islands
- Gallaudet College for the Deaf, Washington, D.C.
- Howard University, Washington, D.C.
- East-West Institute, University of Hawaii, Honolulu
- U.S. Department of Justice: FBI National Academy, Policy Training Schools

Informal Control: Teachers' Organizations

There are many ways in which an individual teacher exercises control over the educational process. Simply closing the door and going ahead with a new project not authorized by a higher authority is one of the most frequently used methods of teacher control. Teachers also exercise their power when they initiate school- or system-wide projects, choose textbooks and other instructional materials, seek curriculum revision, and so forth. However, teachers in recent years have discovered that their most potent power lies in unification. As a result, the two teachers' organizations now functioning in the United States, the National Education Association (NEA) and the American Federation of Teachers (AFT), have become a powerful force in American educational and political life.

Teachers' organizations were slow in gaining the power they now exert. The NEA, begun in 1857 as the National Teacher Association, was originally comprised of teachers and administrators; administrators are still eligible for NEA membership. The AFT was begun in 1916 as an organization existing solely for teachers; this stipulation still remains in effect. In the beginning, both organizations were considered to be primarily "coffee and doughnut" organizations: Educational problems and issues were discussed, but activism was not yet a part of the picture. Both organizations remained in this rather passive role until the 1960s, when rather abrupt changes began to occur.

The AFT was the first to depart from the old stereotypes. Using methods employed by the AFL-CIO, of which it is an affiliate, the AFT won representation rights in school districts throughout the country, most notably in New York City. It quickly gained the right of collective bargaining in many districts, thus giving teachers a share of the decision-making power in the schools. As teachers met opposition from school boards they began to threaten strikes, and by the mid-1960s teacher strikes were becoming increasingly common. The NEA, lacking the support of a large labor organization, was slow to follow suit, but in 1968, after losing representation rights in some major school districts, NEA authorized its first strike. Today, the NEA and the AFT not only promote the advancement of education by providing assistance to members; they also work as effective lobbyists to encourage the passage of legislation designed to improve education at both state and national levels.

COMPARING THE NEA AND THE AFT

Today the NEA and the AFT remain rivals but do occasionally form a coalition for the purpose of obtaining passage of major legislation or accomplishing mutually desirable goals. In fact, there have been rumors for more than 15 years that a merger is pending, although in actuality no progress toward this end has been made.

NEA remains by far the larger organization, with 1.7 million members as compared to AFT's membership of 500,000. Of course, the NEA membership is boosted somewhat by the administrative and supervisory members. NEA remains independent, while AFT is still affiliated with AFL-CIO. AFT has used this affiliation to its advantage in strike situations inasmuch as all members of labor organizations affiliated with the AFL-CIO must honor their picket lines. In many cases this has prevented the delivery to the schools of food and materials, further disrupting any attempts to continue the educational process. The leadership of the AFT has claimed that such practices limit the number and duration of teacher strikes.

Both the NEA and the AFT are well financed. Income for both organizations consists of dues, interest from bank deposits and investments, fees, receipts from advertising, sale of publications and services, and gifts or bequests. The largest source of income is from dues, which range on a per member basis from $120 to $250 per year.

NEA–AFT FACT COMPARISON SHEET

NEA	AFT

Historical Origins

In 1875 a small group of educators met in Philadelphia to establish the National Teachers Association. This group was the forerunner of what is today known as the National Education Association (NEA). | The American Federation of Teachers (AFT) was founded in 1916 and affiliated itself with the American Federation of Labor. This group stayed small, and membership was limited to small groups located in urban centers until the early 1960s.

Purpose

The purpose of the NEA, as stated by its charter, is to elevate the character and advance the interests of the profession of teaching and to promote the cause of education in the United States. | The primary purpose of the AFT is to promote collective bargaining for teachers and other education workers, to secure adequate funding for school programs, and to promote academic freedom and professional autonomy to enhance academic excellence.

Membership

NEA is the largest teachers' association in the United States with more than 1.7 million members. Included in the NEA are more than 29 different departments and affiliated organizations. Throughout the country, NEA has more than 8000 affiliates. The members include teachers as well as administrative and supervisory personnel. The NEA was originally comprised of only school administrators. | AFT is the second largest teachers' organization in the United States with more than 500,000 members from approximately 2000 affiliates. AFT is an affiliate of the AFL-CIO. John Dewey took out the first membership in the AFT in 1916 and remained an active member all his life. He believed that it was important that there be an organization made up exclusively of teachers. To this day, only teachers are allowed to join the AFT.

Policy Making

The NEA employs more than 1500 full-time people. The NEA consists of an elaborate organization, with offices at the national and state levels. The local concerns of the membership are dealt with by full-time uniserve directors. | The AFT is governed by a convention of delegates. Every two years the convention elects a president and 30 vice presidents who constitute the National Executive Committee. An executive board consisting of five members and the president are selected from the National Executive Committee.

Affiliations

The NEA works closely with the Coalition of American Public Employees (CAPE), which includes fire, police, municipal, and other public employees. | The AFT is affiliated with the AFL-CIO, which operates on a principle of reciprocal support. That is, the AFT gets the support of other unions' 14 million members when an important piece of legislation is up for consideration.

NEA	AFT
Political Clout	
The NEA is a very powerful political organization. Traditionally, its power has been at the state level, but it is rapidly becoming a powerful lobby in Congress as well. Recently, the NEA has begun to endorse political candidates who support educational measures. Political activities are coordinated by the Political Action Committee for Education (NEA-PAC). In a recent election year, the NEA sent 172 delegates to the Democratic convention and 55 delegates to the Republican convention.	The AFT's political strength is in Washington, D.C., and local districts. The Committee of Political Education (COPE) coordinates AFT political activities. The AFT, like the NEA, endorses political candidates, monitors voting records of politicians, and analyzes the positions of new candidates. Both organizations contribute to campaign funds, but their greatest strength lies in organizing their memberships to campaign for candidates. The AFT participates primarily through the Democratic Party.
Budget	
NEA has an annual budget of approximately $48 million and a professional staff of approximately 280.	AFT has an annual budget of approximately $16 million and a professional staff of 66.

The general goal of improving the professional role of the teacher as well as education in general is shared by the NEA and the AFT, although the organizations do differ in terms of more specific goals. The primary purpose of the NEA is to "elevate the character and advance the interest of the professional teacher and to promote the cause of popular education in the United States." While the AFT would not dispute the importance of this goal, it places greater emphasis on social, economic, and professional reform in the field of education. The *NEA-AFT* Comparison Sheet provides a quick portrayal of the underlying differences between the NEA and the AFT.

COLLECTIVE BARGAINING

In recent years, more and more teachers have won the right to collective bargaining, most commonly through local affiliates of the NEA or AFT. In collective bargaining, representatives of management (the school board and administration) sit down with representatives of the employees (the teachers) and through compromise develop a master contract that outlines the personnel policies and conditions of employment under which teachers will function for a specific period of time (usually from one to three years). Once the bargaining unit reaches consensus, the master contract must be approved by both teachers and the school board. The following section identifies those issues most commonly negotiated in public school bargaining.

Salary

By far the most hotly debated issue in school negotiations is the salary and fringe-benefits package. Teachers believe that while school boards frequently discuss the problem of keeping good teachers in the profession, they do little in the way of providing financial rewards for teachers. Despite more stringent certification requirements, teachers have remained among the lowest-paid professionals, a problem intensified by the inflation rate of recent years. In addition to salary increases, teachers have also requested benefits such as improved insurance benefits, more liberal sick leave, personal leave and sabbaticals, duty-free time for association officers, sick-leave banks, and tax-sheltered annuity programs.

School boards have often felt that while teachers do deserve salary increases, their demands have been out of line. School boards are faced with the problems of budgeting monies to meet state and federal mandates in areas such as vocational education and special-education programs. They are also plagued by constantly spiralling costs for items such as building maintenance and purchase of educational materials. In addition to this, school boards are being pressured by taxpayers to hold expenditures down in order to prevent tax increases.

Due Process

The American Association of School Administrators ranks due process as the second major cause of teacher strikes in the United States. "Due process" most commonly refers to the procedures used to terminate a teacher's contract. In most school districts, such procedures have been established for tenured faculty or for those with continuing contracts, but frequently such protection does not exist for new faculty. Therefore, a first- or second-year teacher may have a contract terminated without being informed about the reasons that such action was taken and, in some cases, without enough notice being given to find another job.

Working Conditions

The negotiation of specified working conditions has also become more common in recent years. Some considerations, such as duty-free lunch periods, came more slowly to elementary teachers, but today are enjoyed by most teachers at all grade levels. Other items that fall into this category include improved teacher lounges, relieving teachers of some clerical tasks, establishing limits on required attendance at after-school functions (such as open houses and PTA meetings), and lower student–teacher ratios.

Other Issues

Other issues that are frequently negotiated within the collective-bargaining process include removal or transfer of a teacher-organization leader, greater teacher involvement in curriculum decisions, and a voice

Albert Shanker
PROFILE OF A TEACHER LEADER

Albert Shanker, President of the American Federation of Teachers, represents dynamic and sometimes controversial leadership. From rather humble beginnings, Albert Shanker has emerged as one of the most powerful labor-union representatives to date. As the President of the AFT he has exhibited a tenacity for work, with a normal work week that reportedly consists of 98 hours. For his efforts, Albert Shanker is well paid, drawing a salary that is reported to be more than $75,000 per year. He defends his salary by stating that a major problem with union leadership is that the most effective leaders are often offered school administrative positions with high salaries. Associates, as well as opponents, describe Albert Shanker as a tough, articulate, and extremely competent individual.

Albert Shanker was brought up by working-class parents who were strong union supporters. He graduated with honors from the University of Illinois as a philosophy major, after which he completed a master's degree and the course requirements for a Ph.D. in mathematics and philosophy at Columbia. Shanker then began working as a substitute teacher of mathematics in New York City, where he found himself bewildered by the details of classroom management. He tells how excited he was when he learned that the principal was finally going to visit him. At last he was going to get some help and advice. Instead, he was reprimanded for having pieces of paper strewn about the floor. Another favorite Shanker story concerns a principal who regularly observed the gym teacher—believe it or not—from his fourth-story office, using binoculars.

Situations such as these, coupled with the fact he was making $42 per week, led Shanker to resign in 1959 to become a full-time teacher-union organizer. He was quite successful in this role and was able to convince many antiunion teachers to join. Most notable among these converts was Edith Gerber, who had been firmly opposed to unionization. Shanker not only convinced her to join, but to marry him as well!

Shanker's teaching experiences convinced him that teachers needed to join together, but it was not until he was negotiating with the New York City School Board, that he became convinced that strikes were a necessary tool to be used in order to negotiate contracts successfully. Bernard Bard reports the incident that changed Shanker as follows:

> Back in the salad days of the teachers' union movement in New York before it ever struck, City Hall refused to come across with higher pay, claiming the cupboard was empty. But later that same year, it found millions to clear the streets when New York was hit by a hurricane and then a heavy snowfall. Shanker asked then Mayor Robert R. Wagner how the city found money for these unbudgeted items, but had nothing for the teachers. "Al, those were disasters," the Mayor answered.
> Shanker says: "That's when we decided to become a disaster."[4]

The rest is history. Shanker organized the New York City teachers and led one of the first major big city strikes. The teachers won many benefits, including a salary scale that places them among the highest-paid teachers in the country, and Shanker went on to become the national president of the AFT.

Using the strike as a bargaining tool is now common in rural and suburban areas as well as in large city school districts. Throughout his career, Shanker has remained a major teacher advocate, speaking out forcefully for the right of teachers to demand competitive salaries and strike if their demands are not met. Shanker explains the crux of his argument in the following statement:

> There is no inconsistency in teachers wanting the right to make money to have a home, a car, and a vacation—to have a share in the productivity of our society. Nobody says the doctor who earns $100,000 isn't interested in medicine or isn't interested in patients. . . . I think this is part of the brainwashing that teachers have gone through. If you indicate you have your own economic needs, then people believe you don't love children, or that you're not committed to Latin or social studies. Now, that's a lot of hogwash, it has hurt all of us. . . .[5]

in how to deal with the lack of community or state financial support of the schools.

A comprehensive listing of all issues discussed in contract negotiations is, of course, impossible because of the diversity among individual school districts. Those discussed here do, however, cause the greatest concern and conflict. There are no easy answers for teachers and administrators in a collective-bargaining situation, and when an impasse occurs, the result has often been a strike, the teachers' ultimate weapon in what all too often becomes a struggle for control.

WORK STOPPAGES

Teacher control has not been achieved without some sacrifice on the part of classroom teachers. School boards have not easily given in to the demands of teachers, and in several cases they have used the courts to prosecute teachers involved in work stoppages. The following article describes one situation in which teachers were prosecuted for striking.[6]

Bridgeport, Connecticut, Teachers Set Record for Mass Jailing

Bridgeport, Conn.——The night before he went to jail with his wife, Carol, also a teacher, Bridgeport Education Association member Jim Tiernan told cheering colleagues, "I'll take off my watch, I'll take off my belt, and I'll take off my tie—but I'll be damned if I'll take off my dignity!"

Pride and determination like this enabled Bridgeport's 1,200 teachers to hold together during the 13 days they shut down their city's 37 schools and gave themselves, 23,000 students, and the local community a lesson in labor negotiations. They also set a record for mass teacher jailings in Connecticut.

Over 20 percent of the city's teachers, some 273 of them, ended up behind 10-foot chain-link fences at Camp Hartell, an Army National Guard Camp located 70 miles away in Windsor Locks, near Hartford.

Last used to shelter troops who helped dig out Connecticut during last winter's great blizzard, Camp Hartell is no stranger to teachers, having housed some 90 striking Federation teachers from New Haven three years ago. Incidentally, while the smaller Bridgeport Federation of Teachers supported the strike, not one BFT member was ever jailed; their case was legally separated. During one BFT rally outside Camp Hartell's gates, a marcher yelled to imprisoned BEA members, "We're right behind you!" Shouted back a teacher from inside the fence, "Why aren't you in here with us?"

Bridgeport's teachers were joined not only by teachers and association leaders throughout the state of Connecticut, but also by supporters in New Jersey, New York, and the New England States.

NEA President John Ryan strongly supported Bridgeport's teachers in a rally outside Camp Hartell's gates. On separate occasions, Ryan and NEA Secretary-Treasurer McGarigal entered the camp to personalize NEA's support.

The strike, which ran September 6–24, is over now, but not forgotten. BEA and individual teachers face fines of $930,000, including a $61,000 bill for room and board at Camp Hartell. BEA was fined $10,000 a day, and individual teachers $350 a day, for refusing to obey a back-to-work order. Teachers are appealing to the Connecticut Supreme Court.

STRIKE INCREASES SALARY

After weeks of bitterness, both the teacher-negotiators (who were driven from the camp to the state labor office in Hartford for bargaining) and the school board settled, leaving a few minor issues to be decided by Connecticut's labor commissioner.

The two-year contract (the school board originally demanded one running four years) provides average salary increases of 6 percent this year and 7.5 percent next year, including annual increments of 2.6 percent. The starting salary of $9,450 rises to $9,771 this year and goes to $10,250 next year. During both contract years, teachers on the maximum steps, who don't receive increments, will get a $200 bonus if they've put in 16 to 20 years, and $350 for 20 or more years' experience. Maximum salaries for a B.A. go from last year's $15,820 to $16,358 this year and $17,160 next year. Teachers with master's degrees at the first step who made $10,055 last year would make $10,397 this year and

$10,906 next year. Those with M.A. plus 15 years experience go from last year's $18,675 to $19,310 this year and $22,256 next year.

The school board also agreed to add nine specialists in art, reading, and music during the second year, a major teacher demand since the number of specialists has dropped from 35 to 12.

Rosalyn Schoonmaker, interviewed during the strike at the BEA Crisis Center, said, "I saw a physical ed teacher once a month. I never saw a music teacher. An art teacher appeared maybe three times a year."

Agreed Sybil Allen, another BEA elementary teacher, "We don't have an art teacher. A physical education teacher comes once every six weeks—unless that day falls on a holiday, then it's another six weeks."

One reason Bridgeport's teachers were so united: Mayor John Mandanici, presiding over a $5 million surplus, recently upped his salary 50 percent until, at $42,000 he is Connecticut's highest paid mayor.

The school board was widely believed to be controlled by the mayor. Ironically, Mandanici's own daughter, a schoolteacher, was cited for contempt. The strike was settled the day before she was scheduled for sentencing.

TEACHER SOLIDARITY

Generally, it is safe to say, more people want to get out of prison than in. But Bridgeport's teachers were an exception. In their solidarity, they were eager to join jailed colleagues.

Only the "Bridgeport 13"—BEA's executive committee and negotiating team—were taken to an actual prison.

If the court hoped to frighten teachers into accepting a school board–forced contract, it miscalculated. Teachers were angry that their leaders were sent to maximum security prisons, men to the New Haven Correctional Center, and women to the Niantic Correctional Center, where they underwent handcuffing, delousing, and other physical indignities. The "Bridgeport 13" were soon transferred to minimum security Camp Hartell to join other teachers.

Historically, the teaching profession has been considered a place for obedient civil servants. In addition to professional duties, the role of the teacher was to show respect for the community, to maintain a strong moral character that would serve as a model for students, and, in general, to remain a passive individual. Today, this image has changed drastically. With the help of strong national organizations, the power of collective bargaining, and the threat of work stoppages, teachers have become a powerful and aggressive group.

Little more than 15 years ago, most teachers felt that strikes were inconsistent with their roles as professional educators. Such thinking has largely disappeared among teachers, although many are still reluctant to strike because it disrupts the educational process. Nevertheless, work stoppages have been frequently used to force solutions to all sorts of educational problems, primarily because such action so often provides successful results for teachers. During work stoppages, citizens, parents, and even industry have pressured school boards and administrators to get the school reopened, often resulting in teachers' demands being met. In some situations, school boards have given in to demands that they had previously labled "impossible," thus lessening their credibility with teachers during subsequent contract negotiations.

Although we think of work stoppages among teachers as being a totally recent phenomenon, we can find a few examples of teacher militancy beginning as early as 1666, when Ezekiel Cheever, a teacher in Charlestown, Massachusetts, decided that he had had enough of the situation as it stood. When Ezekiel's pay was withheld by the town elders, he had the audacity to do what a "mild-mannered" teacher was never expected to do: He confronted the elders at a town meeting. He made public the fact that he had not been paid, and he provided information that the school was falling apart and that supplies were almost nonexistent. He persuaded the elders to guarantee payment of his salary, to promise that he would not be replaced, and to make speedy repairs to the school building. In a *Phi Delta Kappan* article, Marshall Donley, Jr., describes two other examples of early teacher militancy.

In the 1790's, also in Massachusetts, school master Caleb Bingham, usually a timid man, had reached the end of his tether. The town fathers had not paid

him for months. Instead, he and other teachers were handed "town orders"—
papers redeemable at the bank with a considerable discount. When Bingham
received his next town order, he advertised it in the newspaper—in effect
publicizing the fiscal state of the community. This public insult led to a town
meeting, to which Bingham was summoned. Called on for his apology,
Bingham instead said, "I have a family and need the money. I have done my
part of the engagement faithfully, and have no apology to make to those who
have failed to do theirs. All I can do is to promise that if the town will punctu-
ally pay my salary in the future, I will never advertise their orders for sale
again." Reportedly the town officers responded to the forthright behavior, paid
his current salary in cash, and promised to meet the payroll in the months to
come.

In 1802, Thomas Peugh, a teacher in a settlement north of Cincinnati,
"refused to unlock the school and hold classes until such time as the school
committee formally committed to paper a stipulation giving him at least one
afternoon per month off so that he might move to his new lodging." It was—as
far as we know—the first teacher strike in the new nation.[7]

The Supreme Court and Striking Teachers

The courts have increasingly become a part of teacher work stoppages as
school boards have sought back-to-work orders and teachers have
claimed violations of their civil rights. One such case that was taken all
the way to the Supreme Court began in a small, rural town in Central
Wisconsin.

As school began in the 1973–74 school year, the teachers in the Hortonville, Wisconsin, school district were without a master contract. Negotiations had been going on for some time, but by late winter of 1974 the
negotiators had reached an impasse. On March 18, 1974, the teachers
went on strike. Strikes by public employees were illegal in the state of
Wisconsin, and the superintendent of the schools sent letters to this effect
to all the striking teachers, inviting them to go back to work. During the
course of this long and intensive strike, the school stayed open; the administration hired substitute teachers to fill the vacancies left by striking
teachers. Letters were finally sent to the striking teachers stating that
the board had decided to fire any teachers not honoring their contract. Of
the 83 teachers who were out on strike, only one returned to work; the
others were duly replaced by substitutes.

These teachers, represented by the Hortonville Educational Association, an affiliate of NEA, filed suit in state court alleging that due process
had been denied them, and that they had been fired illegally (several of
the teachers did have tenure in the school district). The striking teachers
took their suit to several state courts; the decisions were appealed, and
the case finally went to the United States Supreme Court. On June 17,
1976, in a six-to-three decision, the Supreme Court ruled that the school
district legally had the power to fire the striking teachers. Chief Justice

Warren Burger, who wrote the majority opinion, stated that the "sole issue in this case is whether the due process clause of the 14th Amendment prohibits the school board from making a decision to dismiss teachers, admittedly engaged in a strike, and persistently refusing to return to their duties."[8]

This decision was extremely important in that it gives school boards, under certain circumstances, the right to fire striking teachers. Had the Wisconsin Supreme Court opinion that firing was illegal been upheld, significant ramifications for collective bargaining in education would have been felt.

Informal Control: Citizen's Groups

This country's educational system was founded upon citizen involvement. From colonial times, citizens formed the schools, financed the schools, and hired people to staff the schools. Almost every existing public school in the United States is built upon this legacy and is controlled by a board of education made up of local citizens. However, citizen control is not limited to the formal structure of the school board. With the advent of extensive federal funding of the schools in the 1960s, a vehicle for citizen participation has developed through a structure that has numerous names: community advisory committee, parent advisory committee, etc. The control mandated to these groups ranges from an advisory role to a role that includes control over budget, program, hiring, and firing. This new mechanism is different from the responsibilities mandated to the school board or assumed by the traditional parent–teacher organizations.

Another type of citizen control involves citizens' reactions to specific issues, such as sex education, moral education, and textbook adoption. If a group of citizens become irate over a critical issue, they can challenge the control of the school's formal power structure through the ballot, picketing, and various forms of confrontation.

In this section, we want you to join us in the examination of citizen control as demonstrated by two case studies. One examines a textbook controversy that led to physical confrontation and the destruction of property. The other case study examines how parents are beginning to share control of the school through community advisory committees.

Perhaps at this point you think that the discussion should return to the classroom; after all, your primary reason for selecting teaching as a career was to work with children, not to become involved in political debates. However, the classroom is a part of the larger, complex social system, which includes numerous groups. You will find it difficult to hide from the other elements of the social system. It is crucial that you learn about control, your responsibility regarding control, and possible positions that you can take within the issue of community control.

KANAWHA COUNTY: THE TEXTBOOK CONTROVERSY

Kanawha County has become a classic example of the type of control that citizens' groups can exert in the realm of public education. Kanawha County is one of the largest counties in West Virginia, with approximately 229,000 residents. Roughly two-thirds of this number live in urban areas (primarily in and around Charleston, the state capital); the remaining one-third of the population live in rural areas.

The beginning of the Kanawha County story is quite unremarkable. In a process similar to that used by thousands of American schools every year, a group of Kanawha County teachers scrutinized new textbooks and supplemental materials in preparation for the adoption of updated materials. Contrary to what had occurred in past years, however, this particular study group was made up solely of educators, receiving no input from parents or representatives of the community. The controversy did not erupt until the materials had been selected, presented to the school board, and put on display at the public library. At this point parents began to express concern, labeling the selected textbooks, and particularly the supplemental materials, as "dirty, anti-Christian, and anti-American." Concerned citizens expressed their displeasure to the school board who indicated that the books would be adopted, although none would be purchased until the board had a chance to study them in more depth. During this time lag several fundamentalist churches became involved in criticizing the materials and subsequently formed several pressure groups. Although many citizens had never seen the materials, emotions were high and over 1000 people attended the meeting at which the board's decision was to be announced. Despite the vocal concern expressed by those in attendance, the school board endorsed the adoption of the textbooks selected by the study group. Negative reaction was virtually inevitable, but few expected the violence of that reaction.

During the summer months the new materials were collected and displayed in churches. Offensive passages were duplicated and circulated through informal channels. Parents threatened to organize their own schools if the new materials were implemented. In the fall, the schools were picketed, and a boycott kept 20 percent of the county's 45,000 students away from school. As the boycott began to lose momentum, pickets moved from the schools to local coal mines. When 3500 miners went out on wildcat strikes, the fever of controversy spread not only throughout the county but into neighboring counties as well. Pickets appeared in front of industries and stores. The growing tension eventually erupted into violence: Two men were shot; teachers' car windows were smashed; television crews covering the controversy were accosted and their equipment destroyed. Schools were closed in both Kanawha County and in neighboring areas. A televised school board meeting, which was intended to provide a forum for airing opposing points of view, turned into a brawl in which a board member was attacked and the superintendent was struck.

Eventually, the school board was forced to reevaluate its position. A new textbook review committee was formed, including local citizens. New guidelines were developed, and the controversial materials were removed from the schools. The citizens had prevailed, but at what cost? The coal companies estimated their loss of revenues at more than $2 million, and more than $300,000 in damages had been done to the schools as the result of vandalism. The cost in terms of teachers' income and loss of education to the students has not been calculated. And, of course, the damage done in terms of school–community relations cannot be easily repaired. It was indeed an expensive lesson in the importance of citizen participation in the educational process.

COMMUNITY ADVISORY COMMITTEES*

There are many reasons offered for citizen involvement in the schools. Since it is the public that pays the taxes to support the schools, proponents of citizen involvement believe the public's involvement is crucial to the financial security of the school system. Others see community participation as vital in the promotion and expansion of any school program providing a degree of built-in accountability. Another rationale for encouraging community participation is that it represents a renewal of grassroots democracy. According to this reasoning, community participation would improve education, bolster ethnic and racial identity of children, and consolidate political power. While school policy making is seen as a part of more general neighborhood participation, Barbara Hatton sees school involvement as an avenue to improve the state of minority communities.[9] Previous experiences with community advisory committees in the late 1960s and 1970s have shown that there are many negative viewpoints that must be overcome before an advisory committee can become a viable, functioning body.

Early advisory committees were established with the intent of serving an advisory function that was peripheral to the decision-making structure of the schools. Those who held power (administrators, teacher organizations, school boards, and in some cases PTA groups) were often cautious and reluctant to share that power with other community members. Such experiences convinced the participants that their role was only token and that they were expected to rubber-stamp existing programs.

*The name and title of community groups vary in different communities and programs. They function under labels like Parent Advisory Committees, Community Councils, and Parent Advisory Committees. In some communities the Parent–Teachers Association (or Parent–Teachers Organization) assumes this advisory role. Regardless of the title, the community group activity implies an "active" and "real" community involvement in the control (governance) of schools.

Marilyn Gittell best summarizes this state of affairs by observing that "those who held power in existing institutions resisted any participatory role for citizens which would interfere with their power. They used the terminology of participation, but their definition excluded delegation of power."[10]

F. S. Coombs and R. L. Merritt suggest that there is an undercurrent of resistance, often not publicly stated, present in our school organizations and political system, one that assumes that the average citizen is simply not competent enough to make sound educational-policy decisions. That is, the average citizen does not have enough information or background to see how a particular decision fits into broader educational context. Furthermore, Coombs and Merritt suggest that those who resist community advisory committees feel that if the information were made available to the average citizen, he or she would not take the time or make the effort to synthesize that information in order to be an effective decision maker."[11] To demonstrate such contrasting viewpoints N. I. Fainstein and S. S. Fainstein surveyed community leaders and found that they not only felt competent to become involved in educational-policy decision making, but they also wanted to be involved. More than half of those surveyed (52 percent) favored decision-making powers residing in the community, while another 30 percent felt the community should be involved in an advisory capacity; only 8 percent were opposed to community control.[12]

Statistical data are just beginning to be published regarding the impact of community advisory councils. Thus far, the primary factor, student achievement, has shown little change in programs with community input, although there are so many confounding factors that one must be wary of these findings. Research done by Bruce Joyce involving one of the early federally sponsored educational programs, the Urban/Rural School Development Program, which required community advisory committees, showed that involvement of a council helped to reduce alienation between community and teachers. Other conclusions cited by Joyce are the following:

1. Over the program as a whole, a relative equality of community and professional input was achieved. Councils took from one to two years to get organized, but, once organized, they did an effective job of translating local needs. The greater the level of equality achieved, the more active were the teacher education programs that were generated.
2. The effect of participation seems to have been to reduce alienation and to increase feelings of efficiency among community members and professionals alike.
3. The more the participants were involved in the planning process, the greater were their feelings of integrativeness toward other groups, and the greater their perception of project impact on their local situation.

4. It appears possible for teachers and community members to assess local needs and generate them into programmatic efforts.
5. Many projects managed to capture and focus the energy of community members and professionals in important problems in their areas. Urban/Rural appeared to fill a void where community members and others were seeking participation and had previously lacked the channels for it. From findings in the comparison sites of Georgia, Michigan, and California, it appears that many community members throughout the United States would like to participate increasingly in educational decision making and are willing to put time into that enterprise. The more they desire this, the more favorable they are toward approaching the hard problems of creating vital schools and supportive staff development programs.
6. Urban projects, on the whole, will be more expensive than rural projects and generally will provide less output for the dollar. This differential, we believe, is the price of the complexity of an urban society.[13]

As we look at the past experiences of those school systems in which community advisory committees have been used, there are some generalizations that do appear significant. The most successful community committees were those that achieved a high degree of parity between committee members and school personnel. Successful committees tend to be those that have clearly specified roles and authorities. Committees will accept some decision making by school personnel, if the decision areas are clearly defined at the outset. Past experience shows that if community committees do not feel that they have an important role, equality with school personnel, and a well-defined decision-making role, the committee will be very ineffective. The one variable that appears to be most important is the establishment of parity.

Summary   We have attempted to address the question of who controls the schools by looking first at three categories of formal control. This formal control is exercised by legally chartered federal, state, and local groups. This type of control is the oldest and is traditionally identified as the central source of control. In order not to mislead you, we discussed other types of effective and powerful groups that exercise less formal control. The two examples cited were the teachers' professional organizations and organized community groups. There are, of course, others, but these provide a real contrast to the traditional legislative control bodies.

We will close this chapter with an attempt to answer our original question: Who controls the schools? Effective control represents a balance among many groups: legislators, administrators, teachers, and citizens. You can and should be aware of the impact you can have in this balance.

The schools are controlled by a variety of groups that reflect individual leadership styles and personalities. The ideal situation is for all groups to have input into the decision-making structure of the schools. The exclusion of any one group or the total domination by any one group can (and, we feel, *will*) lead to conflict (e.g., teacher strikes or community rebellions). A balance in the decision-making authority lends itself to harmonious support for schools and teachers in the community. In this time of conflict and dissent, it is important that teachers be aware of educational politics in order to practice effective involvement.

You can do a great deal as an individual teacher to become involved in the governance of the schools. The teacher assumes many roles and each of them can have an impact on the schools. The teacher is a professional who can have impact through involvement in professional organizations; a voter who can have impact through involvement in community activities and politics; a community member (and often a parent) who can exert influence by serving as an informal spokesperson for the schools in community activities. Our primary point is that control of the school's activities and policies is something that can be influenced by you, the classroom teacher—especially if *you* know how it works.

Encounters

1. Attend a local school board meeting. Observe the nature of the topics that are addressed by the board. How do these topics correspond to the ten major functions of local school boards listed in this chapter?
2. How are school board members selected in your local schools (elected or appointed)? Report to the class concerning the selection process.
3. Interview local school board members and determine why they wanted to serve on a school board. In particular, determine whether there were controversial issues that compelled them to get involved?
4. Review the educational policies from your state educational agency. Identify specifically the areas of education they control. How does that compare to the list presented in this chapter?
5. Identify the present Secretary of Education. What are this person's goals for federal involvement in local schools? Determine the local support for these policies from the perspectives of the teachers' associations, school board members, administrators, and the public at large.
6. Assume that you have just taken a teaching position and have been asked to join a professional organization. Would you select the NEA or the AFT, or would you choose not to join either one? Be prepared to support your position to peers. (This is a real dilemma many new teachers have to face.)
7. Assume the local education association has just called a strike in your school district. The reason for the strike is to call attention to the need for higher salaries. Would you support the strike by participating on the picket lines? Why or why not? Would you continue to strike even if it meant going to jail?
8. Survey administrators from a local school district and determine to what degree they feel the community is involved in the schools.
9. Survey community members from a local school district and determine to what degree they feel the community is involved in the schools.
10. Explain the agreements or disparity you found in items 8 and 9.

Notes

1. Oliver S. Ikenberry, *American Educational Foundations* (Columbus, Ohio: Merrill, 1974), pp. 349–50.
2. J. Alan Aufderheide, "The Place of Educational Interest Groups in State Educational Policy-Making Systems." Dissertation, Ohio State University, 1973.
3. Thirty-ninth Congress, 2nd session, Approved by President Andrew Johnson, March 2, 1867.
4. Bernard Bard, "Albert Shanker: A Portrait in Power," *Phi Delta Kappan, 56* (March 1975), 468.
5. *Ibid.,* p. 472.
6. Barbara Lawless, "Bridgeport, Connecticut Teachers Set Record for Mass Jailing," *NEA Reporter, 17* (November 1978), 5.
7. Marshall O. Donley, Jr., "The American School Teacher: From Obedient Servant to Militant Professional," *Phi Delta Kappan, 58* (September 1976), 112.

8. Thomas J. Flygare, "Supreme Court Upholds Board's Right to Fire Striking Teachers," *Phi Delta Kappan, 58* (October 1976), 206.

9. Barbara R. Hatton, "Community Control in Retrospect: A Review of Strategies for Community Participation in Education," in *Community Participation in Education,* ed. Carl A. Grant (Boston: Allyn and Bacon, 1979), pp. 2–20.

10. Marilyn Gittell, "Institutionalizing Community Participation in Education," in *Community Participation in Education,* ed. Carl A. Grant (Boston: Allyn and Bacon, 1979), p. 47.

11. F. S. Coombs and R. L. Merritt, "The Public's Role in Educational Policy-Making: An International View," *Education and Urban Society, 9* (February 1977), 167–196.

12. N. I. Fainstein and S. S. Fainstein, "The Future of Community Control," *American Political Science Review, 70* (1976), 905–923.

13. Bruce Joyce, "The Urban/Rural School Development Program: What It Was and What It Attempted," in *Involvement: A Study of Shared Governance of Teacher Education,* ed. Bruce Joyce (Syracuse: National Dissemination Center, 1978), pp. 9–10.

For More Information

JOURNALS

Anselma, Sandra. "Parent Involvement in the Schools," *Clearing House, 50* (1977), 297–299.

Black, Theodore M. "The Political Role of Educators," *Educational Leadership, 34* (1976), 122–125.

Byrne, Tim C. "Who Gets What, When, How," *Education Canada, 18* (1978), 34–41, 45.

Hogler, Raymond L. "Collective Bargaining in Education and the Student," *Labor Law Journal, 27* (1976), 712–720.

Ianni, Francis, A. J. "A Positive Note on Schools and Discipline," *Educational Leadership, 37* (1980), 457–458.

Jenkins, Gladys Gardner, "For Parents Particularly" (111), *Childhood Education, 55* (1979), 213–214.

Judah, Marvin, and West, Philip T. "Planning for Citizen Participation in Public Schools," *Catalyst for Change, 8* (1979), 24–27.

Koehler, Michael D. "Schools Without 'Lowerarchies': Are they Possible?" *Clearing House, 52* (1979), 34–35.

LaNoue, George R. "Is the Federal Government Controlling Education? The Federal Tailors," *Education and Urban Society, 9* (1977), 197–214.

Male, George A. "Forces Seeking to Control Education," *Education and Urban Society, 9* (1977), 127–134.

Patterson, Arlene H. "Professional Malpractice: Small Cloud, but Growing Bigger." *Phi Delta Kappan, 62* (1980), 193–196.

"Teachers' Stronger Voice in School Management." *U.S.A. Today, 108* (1979), 9.

Williamson, John, and Moorman, Hunter. "The Immediate Future of the Federal Role: A Framework for the Debate," *Educational Research Quarterly, 1* (1977), 54–69.

BOOKS

Bishop, Leslie J. *Collective Negotiation in Curriculum and Instruction: Questions and Answers.* Washington, D.C.: National Education Association Publications, 1967.

Browder, Lesley H., Jr. *Who's Afraid of Educational Accountability?* Denver, Colorado: Cooperative Accountability Project, 1975.

Campbell, Roald F., Cunningham, Luvern L., McPhee, Roderick F., and Nystrand, Ray. *The Organization and Control of American Schools.* 2nd ed. Columbus, Ohio: Charles E. Merrill Publishing Company, 1970.

Donley, Marshall. *Power to the Teacher.* Bloomington, Ind.: Indiana University Press, 1976.

Fantini, Mario, and Gittell, Marilyn. *Decentralization: Achieving Reform.* New York: Frederick A. Praeger, 1973.

Fischer, Louis, and Schimmel, David. *The Civil Rights of Teachers.* New York: Harper & Row, 1973.

Guthrie, James W., and Craig, Patricia A. *Teachers and Politics.* Bloomington, Ind.: Phi Delta Kappan Educational Foundation, 1973.

Koerner, James. *Who Controls American Education?* Boston: Beacon Press, 1968.

Meyers, Donald A. *Teacher Power: Professionalism and Collective Bargaining.* Lexington, Mass.: D.C. Heath, 1973.

Wirt, Frederick M., and Kirst, Michael W. *The Political Web of American Schools.* Boston: Little, Brown, 1972.

MOVIES

The Bill of Rights in Action: DeFacto Segregation (BFA Educational Media, 22 min., 1972). Shows the differences of opinion that develop in a community over the integration of their school system. This is an open-minded film used to stimulate discussion.

A Chance to Learn (NBC Educational Enterprises Code #006C1, 17 min.). A discussion by Daniel Moynihan and Charles Hamilton on control of the school systems. Who makes the controlling decisions?

Community Control (Boston Newsreel, 50 Min.). Black and Puerto Rican communities are fighting the bureaucracy and a striking teacher's union to control their own schools.

The Five Facing Ten: School Boards in Crisis (IDEA, 26 min., 1970). A school board deals with upset parents concerning busing, an explosion in a school, and a teachers strike. The board learns to anticipate such problems in hopes of avoiding potential crises.

Inside Out (Jack Robertson, 56 min., 1971). Demonstrates the various resources available from the community that can be provided to urban high school students. This is exemplified by the Franklin Parkway Program.

Just A Simple Misunderstanding (Holt, Rinehart and Winston, 11 min., 1970). How should a teacher handle a situation in which a student quotes a teacher out of context and the parents become upset because the child has acquired some ideas which are in direct conflict with their values?

No Little Hope (Center for Urban Education, 28 min.). New York City parents state that parents, the community, media, and the schools must be considered before fully understanding the process of education.

Point of Decision (Ohio State University, 17 min., 1958). A discussion about administrative behavior and group action in the search of answers to questions like" "How are school policies decided?" "Who actually makes these decisions?" "At what point is a decision really reached?"

A Whisper of Dissent (IDEA, 35 min., 1969). The complex problems and emotions involved in collective bargaining are shown in this film. Teachers, principals, and government figures express their views on this topic.

Chapter 11

Chapter 11

IS TEACHING FOR YOU?

"What a silly question! Teaching has been my career choice since I was a young child. My 'training' began with a babysitting position at age 11 and continued with a series of teaching-related jobs: camp counselor, recreation worker, Sunday School teacher."

"Is teaching for me? I'm not sure. This book has encouraged me to observe in classrooms, visit homes, attend board meetings, study textbooks, and interview teachers. I'm not yet ready to answer the question. I do have a better understanding of what teaching is and what it isn't."

"I was forced into education by my parents. They told me, 'You'd better graduate from the university with a profession.' I don't think teaching is the profession I'm looking for."

Do any of these statements express your feelings regarding teaching as a career? The information that has been provided in the preceeding chapters and the accompanying activities should help you as you begin to develop a definitive answer to the question, "Is teaching for me?" You might expect that we would perceive this book to be successful only if you decide to choose a career in education. On the contrary, we anticipate that many readers will look for another profession after having observed and participated in the complex systems surrounding the classroom: community, home, school board, administration, state department of education, parent advisory committee. In this chapter you will be supplied with additional data to consider in making that decision regarding your career in education.

We will focus on a series of issues that are often discussed by those considering teaching as a possible career. In debate fashion, we present the two extreme responses to any given issue. You should keep in mind that the information presented, for both the "pro" and the "con," is based on accurate data. Your task, as the referee in the debate, is to examine the data presented from both sides and to develop alternative inferences that may be congruent or in conflict with the inferences presented by the "pro" and "con" sides.

Is Teaching an Emotionally Rewarding Profession?

YES!

Joseph Masling and George Stern identify the "nuturant" role as one of the ten critical roles of the classroom teacher:

> Teachers with this orientation are characterized by a pervasive feeling of affection for children and a desire to assist and support them. They are warm and loving in their relationships with children, devote themselves freely to their pupils' problems, and derive their greatest satisfactions from the reciprocal affection and gratitude of the children.[1]

What other professional environment allows an adult to have a relationship with children that is as supportive as that of the teacher? The joy and sadness, success and failure of the children are seen and felt by the classroom teacher each moment of the school day. What could be more emotionally satisfying than to see a five-year-old read his or her first words, the nine-year-old begin to develop a positive self-concept, the fifteen-year-old cope well with the pressures of adolescence? In what other profession can you see the immediate effects of your work: the child who replicates a scientific feat of Galileo or discovers the answer to a complex (or even a not-so-complex!) question? For a person who desires a career that continually offers emotional rewards, teaching is a natural selection.

NO!

Emotionally rewarding? No! Emotionally draining? Yes! How can one consider teaching to be rewarding when in a recent study on school violence presented to a Senate Subcommittee to Investigate Juvenile Delinquency the following data were reported: Between 1970 and 1973, "Homicides increased by 18.5 percent; rapes and attempted rapes increased by 40.1 percent; robberies increased by 36.7 percent; assaults on students increased by 85.3 percent; burglaries of school buildings increased by 11.8

percent; drug and alcohol offenses on school property increased by 37.5 percent."[2]

In addition to the negative effects of violence on the teacher's emotional well being, day-to-day responsibilities also take their emotional toll on the teacher. R. H. Nelson and M. S. Thompson studied the reasons why teachers leave the profession shortly after their entrance into this career. Many teachers, in spite of negotiated contracts, have excessive teaching loads and assignments beyond the regular teaching responsibility. Teachers state that they receive inadequate supervision, especially during the first critical years in the profession. Other teachers feel that their preparation for teaching was inadequate; prior to student teaching they had little or no direct contact with classrooms. In this period of budgetary crises in school districts throughout the United States, many teachers are finding it impossible to function given inadequate materials and support services. Another subgroup of teachers quit because of the emotional frustration of children not receiving what they morally and legally deserve.[3] Teaching is not an emotionally rewarding profession.

Summary

You have studied the "pros" and "cons," and you have had numerous contacts with teachers, pupils, classrooms, and homes. What is your response to this issue? If you are one of the majority of beginning teachers who chose teaching because of its helping attributes, you must continue to search for *your* personal answer to this first issue. How will you continue to investigate this issue?

Is Teaching Financially Rewarding?

YES!

The average teacher's salary in 1953 was $3825; this figure increased dramatically by 1980 to $15,200. Significant increases occurred in the beginning teacher's salary. To cite one example, the beginning teacher's yearly salary in the school district of Pittsburgh increased from $5000 in 1964 to $10,000 in 1978. Other financial rewards are received more indirectly through fringe benefits: health, dental, and life insurance; tuition payments for faculty's graduate study; access to low-interest loans; and discount travel through professional organizations. While a teacher does not become wealthy, there is adequate compensation for his or her efforts.

NO!

Although between 1968 and 1976, the average teacher's salary in the United States increased by $5000, or 41 percent (an impressive figure), in real income (the increase as balanced by inflation during the period), teachers have received a $90 per year increase, or 1.2 percent, which is not much to shout about, especially when one considers that the years cited coincide with the dramatic increase in collective bargaining by teachers' organizations. In fact, Richard Musemech and Sam Adams report that a variety of increases and decreases in teachers' purchasing power have occurred, depending upon the state. The largest increase in purchasing power was in Mississippi (+19.2 percent), the state with the lowest average salary in 1967; the largest decreases in purchasing power were in Florida (−12.7 percent), with Indiana and Vermont close behind (−9.2 percent and −9.1 percent, respectively).[4] The salary situation is so bad that it is possible for a beginning teacher with a family to be eligible for food stamps and other government-related welfare programs. No one has ever argued that a teacher will become wealthy, but to be on the lower fringes of the middle-class is unacceptable!

Summary

The above "pros" and "cons" seem to coincide in terms of the data related to economic benefits, but their inferences are divergent. Interview teachers who have taught for 15 to 20 years. Have their incomes increased in real dollars? Examine the salary records of the school districts in your area by visiting the offices of the teachers' professional organizations. Ask the staff of the professional organizations to describe salary patterns from the past to the present and predictions for the future. More importantly look at your own lifestyle. As you examine present salaries and projections for the future, do you feel the financial compensation will satisfy your needs and the needs of a possible family? Summarize your analysis of present and future salaries as they match your lifestyle.

Are There Teaching Positions for Recent Graduates of Teacher Preparation Programs?

YES!

During a given year, there tends to be approximately 285,000 teaching vacancies because of separation from active employment by teachers. Until 1970 the United States needed 78,000 teachers a year to fill newly created teaching positions.[5] While the newly created positions are now at a zero growth rate in most parts of the United States, it is evident from the above data that there continues to be a need for teachers, especially competent teachers. Even in this period of decreasing student enrollments, certain teacher roles are experiencing growth. Among the growth areas are special education, reading, physical education (for women), agriculture, business education, chemistry, physics, and industrial arts. Students who develop multiple specialties (e.g., special education and early childhood) find themselves to be more employable. Researchers of one study predict that those areas for which there is now an overabundance of applicants (high school English and mathematics) will in future years experience a paucity of certified persons for these positions, since enrollments in these programs are currently so small. The *Journal of Teacher Education* has recently predicted that "barring major changes in the estimated 6–8 percent rate at which teachers leave the profession and changes in pupil–teacher ratio, a shortage of qualified teachers may arise in the mid-1980's if the new supply keeps decreasing."[6]

Musemech and Adams predict that a teacher shortage will exist in the 1980s.[7] This prediction is based primarily on the large decrease in teacher candidates in colleges and universities (one university reported a decrease of teacher preparation candidates from 2100 in 1967 to 1000 in 1977) and the anticipated birthrate increase from 14.7 per 1000 in 1976 to 17.1 per 1000 in 1985 (a population increase of 900,000).

No one argues that the United States will experience the need for teachers that occurred in the early 1960s. What is rarely mentioned by those who present the "doomsday" data related to present and future employment needs in education is that there is and will be (and will always be) a need for well-prepared, competent teachers.

NO!

We do admit that the oversupply of teachers in some teaching areas is less severe than in others. Those foggy romantics who state that we always need competent teachers in all areas of instruction, even those areas that are severely overcrowded, are being unfair to the prospective students of education. Listed below are the data that support our view:

1. The birth rate continues to remain constant. Even if there is an increase in the 1980s, the newborn babies will not attend school for four or five years after their birth.
2. More schools are closing than are being built. During 1975 seven schools in one district of Seattle, Washington, were scheduled to be closed.[8]
3. Teachers generally, and female teachers particularly, are remaining with their positions. The employment picture may contribute to this pattern, along with likelihood that many female teachers do not leave their positions for child bearing and child rearing.[9]

During the next decade, you will continue to see those who have prepared themselves for careers in education in such diverse roles as the popcorn vendor at the baseball game and the insurance salesman in your living room.

Summary

Whom should you believe? Perhaps you should do your own survey. Contact school personnel offices in your region: Do they need teachers? If so, in what specialties? Contact friends who are recent graduates of programs in education. Are they employed in education? What percentage? In what fields are they teaching? Have any found employment outside your region? What regions are in the greatest need of teachers?

Is Teaching an Esteemed Profession?

YES!

If one examines the tasks that teachers assume (transmitter of culture, values clarifier, instructor of the basic skills, career educator, counselor), one must assume that the teacher is both a professional and esteemed by the society. While teaching does not carry the highest status as measured in public opinion polls, it does rank thirty-fifth out of 90 vocations and ranks higher than journalism and social work.[10] While all professions are beginning to open for women, teaching is the occupation with the highest status among those occupations largely populated by women.

Teaching today is closer to full professional status than were medicine and dentistry just 100 years ago. Often the roles of these two professions, for which Americans give the highest salaries, were performed by barbers. Teaching is beginning to develop its own knowledge base and a larger degree of autonomy, which will allow it to enter the category of "profession" in the future.

NO!

Teaching is neither esteemed nor a profession. Sociologists like Amitai Etzioni have tried to develop a framework for deciding whether a particular vocation is a profession.[11] The first element of a profession is that it has an extensive "knowledge" base: ideas and concepts that are unique to the profession. The knowledge base for teaching is not unique to this vocation but borrowed from sociology, psychology, and numerous other knowledge bases. Most professionals (e.g., lawyers and doctors) have extensive periods of internship during or immediately after their training. Student teaching can barely qualify as an "extensive" experience; in many states a student teaching experience of five weeks satisfies the internship requirement. The knowledge base acquired during this short and often unplanned experience does not develop the professionalism of the perspective teacher.

A second element of a profession is "autonomy," the ability to decide upon one's fees, working conditions, hours of employment, and support services needed. We can forget this element as far as the teacher is concerned. Autonomy is not even a part of the teacher's vocabulary.

Teaching is not a profession. Is it esteemed by society? Just ask your neighbor.

Summary

Is teaching esteemed? A profession? Interview persons who are in professions other than teaching; what is their opinion of teaching as a profession? When you are asked by a new acquaintance of your future career goals, what is the person's reaction when you inform them that you plan to become a teacher? From their verbal and nonverbal responses, do you feel they have esteem for teaching? If you find that the public does not have a high esteem for teaching, will the public's opinion affect your decision to become a teacher?

Does Teaching Offer the Teacher Opportunities for a High Level of Responsibility?

YES!

Jackson reported that teachers in elementary school classrooms have as many as 1000 interpersonal interchanges each day.[12] Admittedly, some of the interpersonal contacts include such mundane acts as collecting milk money and patrolling the playground. In contrast, the majority of teacher roles include high levels of responsibility:

- *Teacher as diagnostician.* Every day the teacher makes judgments regarding each child's social and academic strengths and weaknesses. In many classrooms this diagnosis is completed on an informal basis; in others, on a formal basis. With the implementation of Public Law 94-142, teachers must develop a diagnostic analysis and instructional plan (IEP) for each handicapped child. Many experts predict that IEPs will be mandated for all children in the future.

- *Teacher as instructional designer.* All teachers receive a minimum of texts, paper, pencils, and chalk. It is dependent on the teacher's creativity how these and other materials are mixed into learning activities for the students. Even with the most structured set of objectives, teachers have the opportunity to design the instruction to match the activities.

- *Teacher as counselor.* In Chapter 7, Ferguson Meadows (the elementary school counselor) presents an argument for the inclusion of teachers in the counseling team. Teachers throughout the United States are experts in counseling-related techniques, such as Magic Circle, values clarification, and reality therapy.

Other teacher responsibilities of importance include building a positive relationship with parents, participating with an assessment team that consists of other helping professionals (psychologist, social worker, psychiatrist, and community worker), and working with teacher teams to design curriculum.

If a problem does exist for teachers in the area of responsibilities, it is that teachers have too many areas of high responsibility. It is difficult to carry out these high level responsibilities adequately because of the restraints imposed by time and lack of physical and material resources.

NO!

Margaret Lay and John Dopyera identify the major responsibilities of teachers of young children: More than 30 percent of the responsibilities fit into the category of the mundane; of the remaining tasks, very few are at a high level of responsibility.[13] Among the most mundane tasks, and typically the tasks that consume most of the teacher's time and energy are the following:

- Maintaining accurate attendance records
- Preparing equipment for use
- Collecting scrap materials
- Supervising children's toileting
- Serving and supervising snacks and lunches
- Helping children with dressing
- Taking care of ill or injured children
- Maintaining physical orderliness in the classroom
- Taking care of or supervising care of classroom pets and plants
- Arranging displays on walls, tables, and bulletin boards.

Those who plan to teach at the middle or high school levels may have sighed with relief: "I could never be a babysitter for young children." We recommend that you change your sigh to a groan. With a few variations for grade levels, all teachers assume the mundane tasks listed above. The middle school teacher may not supervise toileting, but the teacher may be assigned the task of patrolling the bathroom for cigarette smokers. The high school teacher may not "help children with dressing," but he or she may have to enforce a school-mandated dress code.

Does teaching offer the teacher opportunities for a high level of responsibility? No. Should it? Yes, if the teacher is to do what he or she as well as society asks of the profession.

Summary

You have observed teachers and students in a variety of environments. What are your conclusions, after having become an expert on classrooms, regarding the issue of teacher responsibility? Do teachers feel they have positions of responsibility? Has the level of responsibility changed over the years? What are the prospects for the future? Does teaching have the same level of responsibility as other helping professions: psychology, social work, counseling?

Is the Preparation for Teaching Adequate for the Demands of the Position?

YES!

The critics of teacher-preparation programs base their arguments on a series of myths. In this section, we present the myths most commonly perpetuated and follow each myth with the accurate data on the situation.

Myth: The student teacher is placed in a conflict situation during student teaching. The cooperating teacher is concerned with the practical; the university supervisor, with the theoretical.

Reality: In a national survey, it was found student teachers perceive that their cooperating teacher and university supervisor share similar views on education.[14]

Myth: Professors of education have had very little experience in public and private classroom teaching.

Reality: Over 90 percent of the professors of education have had classroom teaching experience; they average eight years of experience.[15]

Myth: Professional education courses are "Mickey Mouse" and have no usefulness in the real-life of the classroom.

Reality: More than two-thirds of a national sample of teacher-education graduates reported that they were "very satisfied" with their professional-education courses.[16]

Myth: The major proportion of a teacher candidate's university courses are in education; a small part of the program is in the liberal arts.

Reality: From a national survey of teacher-preparation programs, it was calculated that 54 percent of the credits were in liberal arts and 46 percent in education; of the 46 percent, one-third of the credits are in clinical experiences.[17]

Myth: There is little or no relationship between clinical and course-based experiences.

Reality: Teacher-education graduates generally agree that there is a satisfactory articulation between the clinical and course-based experiences.[18]

Myth: A major problem with teacher preparation is that students in these programs have very few contacts with classrooms and pupils.

Reality: Seventy-five percent of the teacher-preparation programs surveyed reported that they have a large clinical program; many of the clinical experiences begin in the student's freshman year.[19]

Myth: Students in teacher-preparation programs have little or no contact with poor and/or minority children.

Reality: Two-thirds of the teacher-education programs report that students can elect to or are required to work with poor and/or minority children.[20]

Myth: Recent graduates of teacher-preparation programs feel inadequate to meet the needs of their first teaching position.

Reality: Graduating students believe they are adequately prepared to begin teaching in their area of specialization and believe they are capable enough to organize and manage a classroom.[21]

NO!

The inadequacies of the teacher's preparation is not limited to one facet of the training; all aspects have glaring weaknesses. In a national study of undergraduate teacher-education programs, it was found that enrollment criteria in more than 80 percent of the programs were based on the student's decision to enter rather than stringent criteria established by the programs in education.[22] Could you imagine a medical school or an engineering department operating on the same admission's criteria as those in education? We would have many misdiagnosed patients and untold number of bridges collapsing! Related to the problem of admissions is the provincialism of a typical group of students in an education program: 83 percent of the students attend a college or university in their home state; more than two-thirds of the students attend a school within 100 miles of their homes; and only 4 percent of the teacher candidates can speak a second language.[23]

There is a movement in teacher-education programs (87 percent of the programs reporting) to specify the objectives desired of the students when they complete the program.[24] While much debate exists about the advantages/disadvantages of those so-called competency-based programs, we will not enter into *that* debate. What is appalling is the fact that of the large majority of programs that specify objectives for the participants, only 5 percent of the programs have a preassessment technique to measure those skills that are lacking or have been achieved previously by the individual student. Individualization of teacher education is impossible without this preassessment. Is it acceptable to individualize instruction for children but not that for the adults who are preparing to become teachers?

Professors of education, those same persons who do not use preassessment instruments with their students, teach with technology of the eighteenth and nineteenth centuries and avoid the technologies of the twentieth century. Very few teacher-education programs use the videotape recorder (home use of the VTR may be more common than that in the university!); simulation, a technique that is cost effective and can mirror the experiences of the school community (this technique is used in the space program and by developers of public policy among others); or microteaching, a technique developed by and for education but one that experienced an early death before there had been sufficient field testing.

Student teaching, the experience that continually rates high in value by those preparing to become teachers, has problems. We will avoid the minor problems (such as the cooperating teacher receiving an average of only $35 for this most critical experience, the lack of training in supervision by the cooperating teacher, or too little classroom experience gotten too late) and focus on the major problem with the student teaching experience: the lack of interaction among the student teacher, the cooperating teacher and the university supervisor. On the average, the typical student teacher is observed by and has conferences with the university supervisor six times during this most important experience. Often, the observations are cursory at best, lasting but a few minutes. Enough has been said on supervision—or more correctly stated, the lack of supervision.

What are the outcomes of the teacher-preparation experience? Wayne Hoy and Richard Rees summarize the effect of student teaching on the student preparing to become a secondary teacher:

> Secondary school teachers become substantially more bureaucratic in orientation as a result of student teaching. Apparently the school bureaucracy quickly begins to impress upon student teachers the value of conformity, impersonality, tradition, subordination, and bureaucratic loyalty. Regardless of the talk of change and innovation which often occurs in professional education courses, it seems that secondary schools in general begin almost immediately to mold neophytes into roles devised to maintain stability.[25]

Another major outcome relates to the desired clients of the student who completes a teacher-preparation course. The medical doctor is trained to treat those with physical problems; the lawyer's clients have problems related to the law. In contrast, the typical graduate of a teacher-preparation program desires clients with the smallest risks: middle-class students in suburban and rural areas.[26] Why do these recent graduates want to avoid those students who are in need of the greatest help: urban and rural poor, racial and cultural minorities? Is it because of the type of person who chooses or is accepted into a teacher-education program? Is it the types of experience the student has or does not have in his or her professional courses? Is it because of the lack of supervision the student receives from the university supervisor? Whatever the cause of the problem, the issue is clear: preparation for teaching is inadequate.

Summary

Use the arguments raised in this presentation as a basis for analyzing your teacher education program. If your analysis satisfies your expectations, dive in and begin your movement toward the goal of becoming a competent teacher. On the other hand, if you discover what you feel are program deficiences, what can you do to fill in the missing gaps (e.g., volunteer work in schools or communities, meetings with teacher-education faculty)?

Summary   It is hoped that this chapter has provoked some thinking on your part about teaching and whether or not it is for you. Because this chapter presents many contrasting arguments regarding the teaching profession it is difficult for us to provide the same type of summary that we have in other chapters. Consequently, we have decided to let the encounters provide the structure for you to write your own summary to this chapter. We believe this type of summarization is important and strongly encourage you to address the encounters as though your career depends upon your answers—because in a very real sense it does.

Is teaching for you? Relax, the final response need not be supplied now. We do have a suggestion for an activity that may enable you to become a bit more definite regarding this very important personal and professional question. The activity uses a problem-solving technique called force-field analysis. Your task, based on your experiences with this book and others related to your decision regarding teaching as a future career, is to list in Column A all of those forces supporting your desire to become a teacher and in Column B all those forces against your entrance into this profession. The forces selected, for both Columns A and B, will come from your numerous experiences in this book, and from those child/school related experiences you have had over the years.

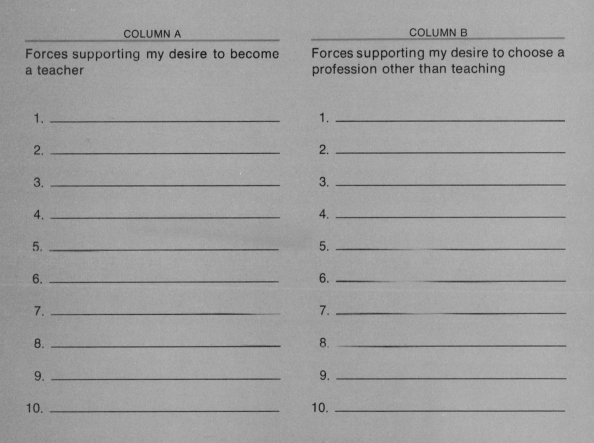

COLUMN A	COLUMN B
Forces supporting my desire to become a teacher	Forces supporting my desire to choose a profession other than teaching
1. _____	1. _____
2. _____	2. _____
3. _____	3. _____
4. _____	4. _____
5. _____	5. _____
6. _____	6. _____
7. _____	7. _____
8. _____	8. _____
9. _____	9. _____
10. _____	10. _____

Which column contains the stronger forces? Is it possible to reduce the forces in Column B (e.g., salaries for teachers are low, but I can change my lifestyle and still live adequately on the salary). Become a peer counselor for a colleague who is going through the same decision-making process. As you interact with your colleague, try to do the following:

- reduce the forces in B;
- increase the forces in A;

• if the balance toward teaching as a profession cannot be made, talk with your colleague about other career areas for which the person's skills and needs have a better match (and recommend that your colleague visit your college or university's placement and/or guidance office).

For many readers, the decision regarding a career in teaching need not be made for two or three more years. During this period of time, they should continue their active involvement with schools and their communities. For others, the decision was made prior to their involvement with this book: Teaching as a career has been a long-sought goal, a goal that has been reinforced during their involvement with the information and activities presented in this book. For those of you who have made the definite decision that teaching is not for you, you have not failed: In fact, you may be a great success. Better to discover now that teaching is not for you rather than three or four years in the future.

Notes

1. Joseph Masling and George Stern, "Changes in Motives as a Result of Teaching," *Theory into Practice, 2* (February 1963), 97.
2. Shirley B. Neill, "Violence and Vandalism: Dimensions and Correctives," *Phi Delta Kappan, 60* (January 1978), 305.
3. R. H. Nelson and M. S. Thompson, "Why Teachers Quit," *Education Digest, 29* (September 1963), 12–16.
4. Richard A. Musemeche and Sam Adams, "The Rise and Fall of Teachers' Salaries: A Nine Region Survey," *Phi Delta Kappan, 58* (February 1977), 479–81.
5. Ellis Evans, *Transition to Teaching* (New York: Holt, Rinehart and Winston, 1976), p. 14.
6. "Topics 'n Trends," *Journal of Teacher Education, 29* (September–October 1978), 3.
7. Richard A. Musemeche and Sam Adams, "The Coming Teacher Shortage," *Phi Delta Kappan, 60* (January 1978), 691–93.
8. Evans, *Transition to Teaching,* p. 14.
9. *Ibid.,* p. 15.
10. Dan C. Lortie, "The Balance of Control and Autonomy in Elementary School Teaching," in *The Semi-Professions and Their Organization,* ed. Amitai Etzioni (New York: The Free Press, 1969), pp. 1–53.
11. Amitai Etzioni, ed., *The Semi-Professions and Their Organization* (New York: The Free Press, 1969), pp. v–xviii.
12. Philip W. Jackson, *Life in Classrooms* (New York: Holt, Rinehart and Winston, 1968).
13. Margaret Z. Lay and John D. Dopyera, *Becoming a Teacher of the Young Child* (Lexington, Mass.: D.C. Heath, 1977), p. 47.
14. Sam Yarger, Kenneth Howey, and Bruce Joyce, "Reflections on Preservice Preparation: Impressions from the National Survey, Part II: Students and Faculty," *Journal of Teacher Education, 28* (November–December 1977), 35.
15. *Ibid.,* p. 36.
16. Sam Yarger and Bruce Joyce, "Going Beyond the Data: Reconstructing

Teacher Education," *Journal of Teacher Education, 28* (November–December 1977), 21.

17. Kenneth Howey, Sam Yarger, and Bruce Joyce, "Reflections on Preservice Preparation: Impressions from the National Survey, Part III: Institutions and Programs," *Journal of Teacher Education, 29* (January–February 1978), 39.
18. *Ibid.,* 39.
19. *Ibid.,* 36.
20. *Ibid.,* 40.
21. *Ibid.,* 39.
22. *Ibid.,* 39.
23. Yarger, Howey, and Joyce, "Reflections, Part II," p. 35.
24. Yarger, Howey, and Joyce, "Reflections, Part III," p. 39.
25. Wayne K. Hoy and Richard Rees, "The Bureaucratic Socialization of Student Teachers," *Journal of Teacher Education, 28* (January–February 1977), 25.
26. Yarger, Howey, and Joyce, "Reflections, Part II," 34–37.

For More Information

JOURNALS

Bloch, Alfred M. "The Battered Teacher," *Today's Education, 66* (1977), 58–62.
Dunathon, Arni T. "Teacher Shortage: Big Problems for Small Schools," *Phi Delta Kappan, 62* (1980), 205–206.
Elsworth, Gerald R., and Coulter, Frank. "Relationships Between Professional Self Perception and Commitment to Teaching," *Australian Journal of Education, 22* (1978), 25–37.
Hendrickson, Barbara. "Teacher Burnout: How to Recognize It; What to Do About It," *Learning, 7* (1979), 37–39.
Payne, Charles, "Teacher Pride," *Teacher Educator, 11* (1975), 17–24.
Renshaw, Domeena C. "Teachers are Human Too," *Pointer, 20* (1976), 3–6.
Shackmuth, Thomas J. "Creating Job Satisfaction in a Static Teacher Market," *Clearing House, 52* (1979), 229–232.
Stevenson, George S., and Milt, Harry. "Ten Tips to Reduce Teacher Tension," *Today's Education, 62* (1975), 52–54.
Stevenson, George S., "Teachers, Children, and School," *Outlook, 18* (1975), 9–17.

BOOKS

Ashton-Warner, Sylvia. *Teacher.* New York: Simon & Schuster, 1963.
Ginott, Haim. *Teacher and Child.* New York: Macmillan, 1972.
Herndon, James. *How to Survive in Your Native Land.* New York: Simon & Schuster, 1971.
Herndon, James. *The Way It Spozed to Be.* New York.: Simon & Schuster, 1967.
Hight, Gilbert. *The Immortal Profession.* New York: Weybright & Talley, 1976.
Jersild, Arthur. *When Teachers Face Themselves.* New York: Teachers College Press, 1955.
Morris, Van Cleve, et al. *Becoming an Educator.* Boston: Houghton Mifflin, 1963.
Ryan, Kevin, ed. *Don't Smile Until Christmas: Accounts of the First Year of Teaching.* Chicago: University of Chicago Press, 1970.

Ryan, Kevin, et al. *Biting the Apple: Accounts of First Year Teachers.* New York: Longman, 1980.

Sterling, Philip, ed. *The Real Teachers: Conversations After the Bell.* New York: Random House, 1972.

MOVIES

A Class of Your Own: Instructional Technique (MLA, 25 min., 1965). Discusses the importance of planning ahead, so the lesson will flow smoothly. Also shows that planned questions and media use are valuable.

Crowded Out (NEA, 29 min., 1967). Overcrowding in the schools forces a teacher to resign because she can no longer give individual attention to her students. Parent-teacher conflicts and discipline problems also arise.

Is the Teacher Liable? (Educators and Executive Inc., 16 min.). Presents several liability issues which face the teacher in the classroom, office, playground, and after school activities connected with the school.

Just a Simple Misunderstanding (Holt, Rinehart and Winston, 11 min., 1970). How should a teacher handle a situation in which a student quotes a teacher out of context and the parents become upset because the child has acquired some ideas which are in direct conflict with their values?

One Step at a Time (Informatics, 25 min., 1972). Shows how the Department of Education in Michigan dealt with the issue of accountability within its school system. Six steps are outlined to achieve this goal with the educators and community working together.

Teachers? (Franciscan Communications Center, 13 min., 1957). A satire of four teaching styles used to make the point that the sight and sound of teachers should add up to effective and rewarding teaching.

To Sir, With Love (Columbia Cinematheque, 105 min.). Stars Sidney Poitier as a teacher in London's rough East End. The students are treated as adults and eventually show favorable results.

You and Your Classroom (Bailey Films, 10 min., 1959). Typical problems of behavior in the elementary classroom are enacted in fourteen individual problem scenes.

Chapter 12

Chapter 12

CAREERS IN EDUCATION

"Do I want to be a teacher?" In Chapter 11 you began to address this important career question seriously. This chapter carries the decision-making process one step further in offering you an opportunity to learn about additional careers in the general field of education. Those who have definitely decided on a teaching career may want to investigate a specialty, such as special education. Those who are unsure or who have definitely decided against a career as a classroom teacher may discover an interest in some other segment of the educational process. A major purpose of this chapter is to show that there are a variety of ways in which one can help children discover their full potential.

As we continue to explore alternative educational careers, you will become increasingly aware of the complexity inherent in the process of selecting a career. As you consider a teaching career, you must consider your preference of the age-level of students, the content to be taught, and the location of the school. Still more issues arise as you look at both the instructional and noninstructional roles within a school that were introduced through this book as well as through your field experiences in numerous schools. To further complicate the decision-making process, an educational career is not limited to schools; it can occur in numerous institutions and organizations outside the well-defined walls of a school. The purpose of this chapter is to introduce you to a variety of careers in the education arena. Keep in mind that it is only intended to serve as

TABLE 12.1 Selected Educational Careers

In-School, Teaching	In-School, Nonteaching	Teaching, Nonschool	Community, Youth and Family Services	Higher Education	School Support	Government Agencies
Day care Public and Private school: Elementary Middle High school Content Specialties: Reading Math Science Social studies Language arts Home economics Driver education Physical education Foreign language Career education Vocational education Resource teacher Special education teacher Adult basic education teacher Team leader Department chairperson Substitute teacher	Social Worker Nurse Speech therapist Counselor School psychologist Librarian Media specialist Coordinator of programs (e.g. volunteers) Principal	Teacher in a: Museum Hospital Planetarium Zoo Parent educator Teacher with a tutoring service Youth development center teacher	Community center director Scout director Coordinator of community action programs Social worker Educational psychologist County extension agent 4-H director Religious leader	Teacher education Educational researcher Educational author Educational consultant Educational evaluator	School lawyer School architect Director of buildings and grounds Educational journalist Educational consultant Instructional supervisor Business manager Labor negotiator Dietician Staff: professional organizational Superintendent Director of personnel School board member	Federal agencies: Program directors Program specialists Commissioner of education State agencies: Department of Instruction Staff

a starting point for your own exploration into the area of educational careers.

Selected Educational Careers, or "What Do I Want to Do When I Grow Up?"

When the average person on the street considers careers in education, thoughts immediately turn to classroom teachers, building administrators, and superintendents. Few individuals consider alternative education careers, even though there are dozens of alternative educational careers in both in- and out-of-school settings. Throughout this text we have focused primarily upon "in-school teaching" positions, such as that of the elementary school teacher. However, "in-school, nonteaching" careers, such as principal, school social worker, and media specialist, may be another career category you should seriously consider. Teaching in non-school settings—museums and hospitals, for example—is emerging as another viable education-career opportunity. Other alternative education careers include such diverse occupations as scout-education director, university professor, school architect, and government-service education. Table 12.1 identifies seven categories of alternative education careers and cites examples of careers that would fit into each category. In the following sections we will explore each category in greater detail.

An In-School, Instructional Role with Children

During the period of the 1970s, we witnessed a rapid decline in the number of individuals who sought and received teacher certification. The Association for School, College, and University Teaching reported a 28 percent drop in the number of candidates completing student teaching in 42 states that were surveyed. Fewer and fewer college freshmen have been enrolling in education courses, and often the reason cited is the difficulty in finding teaching positions. These events have led to a teacher shortage in many parts of the country. This point is clarified by Robert Alfonso, a former dean of the College of Education at Kent State University: "There was a terrible oversupply of teachers at one time. But that isn't true anymore." To back this statement, Alfonso points out that during the early 1970s Kent State certified more than 2000 teachers each year, while today, fewer than 700 receive teacher certification. The situation at Kent State is similar to that of many universities around the country. Areas showing the greatest need for classroom teachers are the following:

- Secondary education (particularly science, math, and, increasingly, English)
- Vocational education (industrial arts, business, and vocational education)
- Special education (all areas)

Although the shortage of elementary-education teachers is not as severe, many educators are predicting that they will also become difficult to recruit in the next few years. Throughout the past decade a trend has developed in that teachers who have an intradisciplinary background (teachers who can teach in more than one area) have been the first ones to be hired. For the moment we will assume that your answer to the career-decision question is "Yes." Your problem solving does not end with your short response. The next level of decision-making involves selecting the appropriate type of school: public, private, day care, elementary, middle, secondary, or vocational. Once you have selected the type of school, you must examine the content specializations found in most schools: reading, math, science, social studies, language arts, home economics, driver education, physical education, foreign languages, career education, vocational education, and special education.

While most professional employees involved with instruction may be categorized as "classroom teacher," numerous other categories of instructional personnel have developed during the past two decades. For example, the resource teacher often works with individual and small groups of students who have unique strengths and weaknesses—the gifted, the learning disabled, the slow learner. Teachers are increasingly recognized for their teaching and leadership abilities and appointed (by the administration or a vote of their colleagues) to roles titled team leader, grade coordinator, and department head. In most instances, these leaders have teaching responsibilities as well as management responsibilities in the areas of curriculum planning, scheduling, and supervision.

If you plan to assume one of the in-school instructional roles described above, you should respond positively to the questions below:

- Do I want to see the effects (and often immediate effects) of my work with students?
- Do I like to work with groups of students?
- Do I enjoy being involved with the "total" child, that is, with his or her academic *and* emotional needs?
- Do I want to work in an environment where most of my personal contacts are with students and not with colleagues?

As problem solvers, we tend to place our thoughts regarding a decision on a scale of pluses and minuses. The pluses and minuses for "Do I want an in-school instructional role with children?" include:

PLUS	MINUS
You have considerable academic freedom within your classroom.	Your day is controlled by others.
You can see the success of your efforts.	You tend to have limited contacts with other adults.
You can influence critical issues in the life of a child.	You tend to be involved in a "pressure-cooker" situation, day in and day out.
You have the feeling that what you do makes a difference.	Decisions regarding your school life emanate from the top to the bottom (you tend to be placed nearer the bottom).

Throughout this text we have placed a heavy emphasis upon traditional, in-school instructional roles. In order to extend our perspective we sought out Melinda Benedetti, a preschool hearing-impaired teacher, and asked her to discuss her role and how she chose it. As you read this case study, try to determine (a) the primary reason Benedetti went into preschool hearing-impaired instruction, and (b) why she is so successful in her chosen career.

The salary range for special-education teachers is the same as that of the classroom teacher, ranging from $10,000 to $23,000 for nine months. Although a four-year degree is enough to certify a person to teach hearing-impaired classes, there is a critical need to continue one's education through attendance at conferences and workshops, as well as by taking graduate courses.

An In-School, Noninstructional Role

If you were to play a word-association game with the word *school,* a common response would be *teacher,* not *social worker, nurse, speech therapist, counselor, psychologist, librarian, coordinator of special programs* (e.g., volunteer program), or *school administrator.* This list of roles includes representatives of relatively new educational careers that are commonly found in today's schools. We discussed many of these roles in depth in Chapter 7. In order to be effective, these people must develop an expertise in their own area and understand the role of the classroom teacher and how the school works. The primary characteristic of this category of educational careers is the support of the classroom teacher, each contributing part of a broad range of responsibilities. The social worker, the school nurse, and others must have a realistic understanding of the world in which teachers and children function. By assisting periodically in the classroom, by listening to the needs of the teacher, and by building a

Melinda Benedetti
A SPECIAL TEACHER

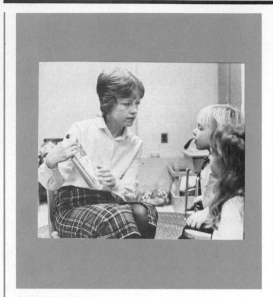

Melinda Benedetti is a special teacher who works with special children. For more than ten years Benedetti has served as a preschool teacher of deaf children. With greater attention being given to children with physical and learning disabilities, more and more educators are training for careers in special education to meet the special needs of these special children.

Benedetti is very enthusiastic about her nontraditional teaching role:

> I feel that the profession's greatest rewards result from the fact that most of the time you start with children who have no language when they come to school at three years of age, and by the time they leave the preschool program they have quite an extensive vocabulary. I also find the delight of the parents when their hearing-impaired child says his or her first words to be very exciting. The job is totally consuming because you are giving yourself all day. You're talking to the kids; you're reinforcing; you're working, working; and

by the end of the day, you're very tired. The rewards, however, far exceed the negative factors.

A benefit that Benedetti enjoys in her teaching position is that she can organize her school day to meet the needs of the students:

> In a typical day I will work with ten to twelve preschoolers. I have presently set up three small group sessions. The first group, which meets for one hour each day, is made up of three-year-olds; the second group, the four-year-olds, stay two hours and 45 minutes a day; and the third group, comprised of five-year-olds, comes for approximately four hours per day. As you can see, the length of time each child spends at school is primarily related to the child's age attention span.

In order to become a teacher of preschool deaf children Benedetti had to obtain a four-year degree with a major in education for the hearing-impaired students ranging from preschool to high school. During her training Benedetti had more than 150 hours of classroom experience in teaching hearing-impaired children before her student teaching, a fact that she believes to be very important, because it was during that time she became convinced that this was the career she wanted. Even more important, however, was the volunteer work she did before she ever enrolled in the hearing-impaired education program:

> As a high school student I visited many different types of programs for kids. I visited a crippled children's home, a program for hearing-impaired children, a program for retarded children, and an orphanage. At that time I became very

interested in teaching hearing-impaired children and tentatively decided that this is what I wanted to do.

We asked Benedetti what personal characteristics a person needed to be a successful teacher of the hearing impaired. She quickly replied:

I think that you have to enjoy people; you have to be a very pleasant person yourself. Hearing-impaired children are so visually oriented that they can tell a lot about people just by looking at them. They can tell when you're angry, when you're upset; you don't even need to show it, because they seem to have a sixth sense about that. They seem to feel tension or feel it when you are upset or when you're mad, so you need to be a person who enjoys working with people, is pleasant, and is hard-working too. You've got to feel that I'm here to do a job and I've really got to put everything I have into that job while I'm here. Most importantly, you have to love what you are doing.

Ms. Benedetti stressed during our in-terview that the teacher of the hearing impaired has to have many skills in order to be successful. Not only must one be an expert in the instruction of hearing-impaired students, but a working understanding of regular classroom instruction is also needed, since many of the hearing-impaired students are mainstreamed into regular classrooms during the school day, To make the mainstreaming work, the hearing-impaired teacher must be able to team with the regular teacher in the planning of assignments and setting of expectations. It is also important to remember that in addition to teaching hearing-impaired students, the teacher also has to train parents:

There is a lot of personal contact between myself and parents; in fact, they often refer to me by my first name. They often come in with very private problems concerning what is happening at home that may be affecting a hearing-impaired child's life or attitude at school.

team that includes the teacher as the key component, noninstructional staff can improve the quality of school instruction.

In-school, noninstructional career opportunities have significantly increased in numbers over the past 20 years; Table 12.2 provides a compari-

TABLE 12.2 **Full-Time Employment in Education, by Occupation and Sex, 1974.**

Number of Full-Time Staff	Principals	Assistant Principals	Elementary School Teachers	Secondary School Teachers	Guidance Counselors/ Psychologists	Librarians/ AV Personnel	Teachers Aides	Clerical/ Secretarial Personnel
Male staff								
Number	61,535	29,805	165,303	480,621	35,858	6,623	9,567	5,236
Percent of occupational group	87.3	80.5	16.7	54.3	50.5	12.7	4.6	2.4
Female staff								
Number	8,920	7,201	821,652	404,657	35,141	45,410	196,010	209,820
Percent of occupational group	12.7	19.5	83.3	45.7	49.5	87.3	95.4	97.6
Total full-time staff	**70,455**	**37,006**	**986,955**	**885,278**	**70,999**	**52,033**	**205,577**	**215,056**

Adapted from Mary Golladay, *The Condition of Education: A Statistical Report on the Condition of Education in the United States,* 1977 ed., Vol. 3, Part 1 (Washington, D.C.: U.S. Department of Health, Education, and Welfare/National Center for Education Statistics), p. 165.

son of the number of individuals in selected in-school, noninstructional roles with that of elementary and secondary level classroom teachers. Classroom experience is helpful with some of the in-school, noninstructional careers and is required in others. Moreover, most require graduate-level training. Consequently, many teachers take graduate courses and gradually work their way into noninstructional careers after they have completed that training. Salaries in this occupational category are generally based on the teacher pay scale, although an additional pay increment is provided to compensate for the additional training that is required. As you consider an in-school, noninstructional career you should consider the following advantages and disadvantages:

PLUS	MINUS
Together with other professionals, in-school, nonteaching personnel can help the "whole" child. For example, the speech therapist working in a speech clinic outside the school must make a concerted effort to coordinate his or her work with that of other professionals. If the school is the speech therapist's clinic, she or he can develop a better overall strategy for the student's needs.	In order to qualify for most careers in this category graduate training is required.
School-related problems of children are often the focus of those in the "helping" professions who are not teachers. The professionals can often have the most immediate impact on the child by working within the school environment.	In-school, nonteaching personnel often have to serve in more than one building, which results in mixed loyalties.
Because many education professionals work with problems, children who seek help in a clinic are often looked upon as "deviant." Since everyone attends school, the involvement with these professionals as a part of the school routine often prevents this assumption of deviancy.	Parents, teachers, and students often do not understand the role of noninstructional personnel.

A Teaching Role, Outside the Formal School

We mentioned the word association that usually occurs between *school* and *teacher*. When *school* is mentioned, it is usually assumed to be a building with classrooms, desks, learning materials, teachers who teach, and children who learn. This word association breaks down when one realizes that teaching also occurs in many institutions that have little in common with the school, such as museums, hospitals, zoos, and planetariums. Museums, especially museums for children, frequently have education departments. The teachers in these departments interact with children on an informal basis — in the traditional-looking classes that are housed in the museum. Much learning also takes place by children in hospitals. Often the learning is related to the child's hospitalization: learning about what will happen in the foreign (and usually frightening) environment. If the hospital stay is an extended one, the child will learn his or her formal school-related subjects with a teacher who is on the hospital staff or who is employed by the public school and is assigned to the hospital. "Teachers" are also used in various capacities in planetariums, zoos, and other nonschool educational settings.

Adult education is another area with increasing education-career opportunities. Community agencies, large industries, and the military have extensive in-service education programs for their employees. Teachers, in increasing numbers, are needed in these nonschool settings, since these large organizations recognize that quality in-service training affects the level of efficiency of their employees. The following compares some of the pluses and minuses of teaching in nonschool settings.

PLUS	MINUS
The bureaucracy, when compared to the bureaucracy of the school, is less imposing and more flexible.	In times of budget crunches, education will be the first area to be cut.
Since you will have a minority role among the employees, you will be looked upon as an expert.	As an outsider and a minority (an educator in a nonschool setting), you will have difficulty influencing policy decisions in the institutions.
Since teaching roles in nonschool settings began their rapid development less than a decade ago, you (rather than those before you) can establish policies, expectations, and traditions.	You will have a difficult time advancing within the institution since very few roles related to education are likely to exist in the organization.

Community Youth And Family Services

At this time, you might be asking, "Although I don't want to be a teacher (school or nonschool), I do want to work with children and youth; do professional roles exist for me?" While the student spends a considerable part of each day in the school, evenings and weekends are "reserved" for the student's involvement in other institutions. When involved in these institutions, the young person sheds the role of "student" and frequently assumes the role of "participant": a participant in a community center, scouting, religious organizations, or social and vocational groups, such as 4-H. Numerous professionals are involved with the youth as they participate in these organizations. The professionals' college training may be from one of many fields: education, social work, health and recreation, theology, or agriculture. Jeffery W. McCombie's position provides an example of this type of alternative career.

After completing his bachelor's degree in education, McCombie was employed as the educational services director for Talus Rock Girl Scout Council. In this position he was responsible for the development and implementation of training programs for approximately 800 adult volunteers and employed staff who worked with the Girl Scout organization in a five-county area. This group included scout leaders, assistant leaders, trainers, day-camp directors, day-camp staff, troop consultants, camp rangers, resident-camp directors, and camp staff.

Individuals working in community youth and family services positions often assume a broad range of administrative, supervisory, and curriculum-planning responsibilities. This certainly was the case with Jeffery McCombie. As the education director for the Girl Scout Council, his administrative duties required that he keep current on camp-related legislation so that he was certain that scout camps under his direction were in compliance with all federal and state regulations. He had to plan and supervise budgets totaling more than $100,000 per year. As the supervisor of the training program, he organized a variety of one-day workshops, served as advisor in the development of program materials, and edited a bimonthly newsletter. His educational background was also extremely valuable in his position because he was responsible for developing self-study materials for adult volunteers and materials about wildlife for Brownie and Girl Scout troops. You can see that careers such as McCombie's in the Community, Youth, and Family Services area are both challenging and demanding. As you begin to explore careers in this area, consider these advantages and disadvantages:

PLUS	MINUS
The professional can often develop goals for the participants	Hours of work are often in the evenings and on the weekends.

PLUS	MINUS
rather than using (without questioning) the goals sent down through the bureaucracy.	
The participants' environment can change from day to day (as contrasted to the more confining atmosphere of the school).	The goals for the participants tend to be more diverse than those associated with schools.
The participants are not required to attend. Therefore, they will be better motivated than most students in a school.	Funding for programs is not predictable and varies from year to year.

Careers in Higher Education

It may seem a little ridiculous to consider a career in higher education when you are worried about trying to complete a bachelor's degree. However, many teacher educators, educational researchers, authors, and evaluators make that decision during their four-year college experience. While the school and the classroom tend to be the hub of the educational system, an important spoke in that wheel are the professionals in higher education who are concerned about the schools. Although the roles are diverse, a familiar role to all teachers is that of teacher educators, the professionals involved in the preservice and graduate training of teachers. Their areas of expertise range from teaching methods and curriculum to the history of education to techniques for conducting research and evaluation of school programs.

There are many kinds of institutions in which a person can work in the area of higher education. These institutions include community colleges, technical colleges, liberal arts colleges, municipal colleges, and universities. In all, there are more than 2200 institutions of higher education in the United States. Approximately 63 percent of these institutions are in the private sector; however, two-thirds of all students are enrolled in public institutions. Whether one is teaching methods courses, doing educational research, or evaluating programs, a solid understanding of what takes place in the classroom is essential if one is to be successful in a career in higher education. The greatest drawback to higher education careers is that most require individuals entering the profession to have bachelor's, master's, and Ph.D. degrees. This means a minimum of eight years of education after high school. If a career in higher education is of interest to you, keep in mind the following issues:

PLUS	MINUS
You are working with those in the process of becoming teachers at their most critical stage of development.	Many persons feel that you are in an "ivory tower" and, therefore, have little understanding of the critical needs in education.
You have access to a variety of schools. Your observations enable you to have a broad perspective on what education is (and is not).	You often must be a critic of institutions with which you identify as a professional.

Deciding Whether One Is Interested in School-Support Careers

Throughout this text we have discussed how complex schools have become. This has resulted in the emergence of a large cadre of school-support professions. The school-support personnel tend not to be on the "front line" with students and teachers. Working behind the scenes, they often affect the lives of all persons involved with the schools. For example, we discussed in Chapter 9 how the courts have become deeply involved with education. All school districts have a lawyer on staff, either full- or part-time. If the lawyer is involved in a case regarding alleged negligence on the playground, he or she must be familiar with the policies and operations of the playground facility. The school architect, usually hired for the duration of a school's design and building, must have intimate knowledge of all aspects of the school's goals and procedures. Positions that did not exist two decades ago but are of importance today include the school board's labor negotiator and the paid staff of the teachers' organizations. While some persons may challenge the conclusion that persons in such adversary positions support the school, we feel that both roles are important.

There are also school-support roles that have no contractual ties to the school system. Among these roles are the education journalist and the professional staff of education organizations (e.g., the National Council of Teachers of Mathematics or the National Association for the Education of Young Children). The journalist informs the public of the current educational issues critical to the community. The staff of professional organizations shares research findings and current trends with school professionals via workshops, conferences, and journals. Keep the following issues in mind as you investigate professional roles that support the schools:

PLUS	MINUS
Salaries for these positions tend to be higher than for those employed in the schools.	Specialized training is often required for these positions.

PLUS	MINUS
Persons in these roles tend not to be constrained by the school's bureaucracy.	Since these positions lack direct day-to-day involvement with students and teachers, one has difficulty measuring one's impact on the system.

Government-Agency Careers

Unlike many European countries, education in the United States is primarily the responsibility of the local community. However, there has been a trend in the past three decades for the federal and state agencies concerned with education to increase their influence over educational programs and policies in local communities. Most careers in the area of government agencies fall under the jurisdiction of one of the 50 state departments of education or under the federal Department of Education.

Occupational roles in state departments of education fall into five categories: operational, regulatory, service, developmental, and public support and cooperation. Operational careers deal with the implementation of state instructional programs, e.g., director of special schools for blind and deaf. Regulatory roles center upon the enforcement of state regulations, such as certification of classroom teachers and supervision of the spending of state funds. State departments of education have been assuming greater service responsibilities in providing consultant services, research information, and legal advice to school districts. Curriculum developers and planners have been employed to develop state-wide curricula. The focus of those persons involved in public service is to improve communication between the public and the state legislature and governor.

Since President Carter signed legislation in 1979 approving a cabinet-level Department of Education, education-related programs have been consolidated. The new federal Department of Education employs more than 17,000 people. Liaison persons — those responsible for linking federal, state, and local efforts — are often titled program directors or program specialists. They assist the local community in implementing policies and programs that emanate from the state and federal levels. To help you develop a better understanding of the nature of a career in a governmental educational agency, we talked with Eleanora Ridgley, an educational program specialist with the Department of Education.

As a program specialist Ridgley is responsible for monitoring and offering technical assistance to school districts and universities that receive federal monies to implement innovative educational programs. She is responsible for assisting in the implementation of programs as well as for ascertaining their compliance with established federal guidelines.

Her job requires a great deal of travel, since she is required to visit each of her ten projects at least twice a year. In addition to site visitations, Ridgley assists in determining the school districts and universities that will receive federal funds, reviews progress reports, and participates in planning program guidelines and policies.

A highpoint of this educational career, according to Ridgley, is the opportunity it gives her to help determine educational policies on a national level and to encourage the implementation of these policies in local schools. A less attractive feature of the job, however, is the bureaucratic "red tape" for which Washington is famous.

There are two common ways for an individual to enter the Department of Education. First, an individual may enter as a trainee. Trainees, who normally have at least a bachelor's degree (not necessarily in education) go through a rigorous training program. Other individuals enter the Department of Education after they have obtained teaching and/or administrative experience in schools. Ridgley explains that local school experience is often extremely valuable:

I think experience certainly plays a large part in being able to be an effective program specialist because you're dealing with school programs, human resources, principals, teachers, and other support personnel. I was a classroom teacher for fifteen years and an administrator for eight years. Since I must continuously deal with people in the schools, my school experience allows me to better understand the problems that the educators in the schools must address.

We asked Ridgley to outline the personal characteristics she felt were most important if one is to be a successful education-program specialist:

In order to work with people, understand people, and be effective in the monitoring and technical assistance mode, you must have a fondness for people. You just can't function effectively with people if you don't like people! You must have a desire to serve, patience, and a willingness to explore. Finally, I think the skills of listening, interpreting nonverbal communication, and observing are critical if one is to provide effective technical assistance.

During our discussion, Ridgley explained that she was not aware of alternative educational careers when she began teaching:

I went to undergraduate school, started teaching, and obtained a master's degree. During this time I never considered a job outside the school system until I was offered an opportunity to serve as an IPA* recipient for two years in a program at the Office of Education. My advice to people who are looking at education as a possible field would be to explore all of the areas of education. You can be involved in research and in government programs at the state and federal levels. Based on my 20 years of observing teachers, I would say that there are many who apparently were not given that advice because they were unsuitable for teaching-learning classroom experiences; however, many could have been great in some other area, such as writing, research, or technical support.

Salaries in the Department of Education depend upon rank, years of experience, and educational background; they can range from $12,000 to $50,000.†

PLUS	MINUS
You obtain a broad perspective on the needs and problems in education.	You become a bureaucrat and may get lost in the maze of red tape.
You have some control on the "purse strings," which gives you some leverage with local school systems.	Your distance from the students and teachers tends to let you lose sight of their needs.
You can help those school systems that have the greatest need.	You are looked upon as a outsider who is trying to force change on a school district.

*Title IV of the Intergovernmental Personnel Act of 1970 (5 U.S.C. 3371–3376).

†For more information about a career in the Department of Education, write to Department of Education, 400 Maryland Avenue, S.W., Office of Education, Washington, D.C. 20202.

TABLE 12.3 A Comparison of Education-Related Careers

	Preparation Required	Experiences	Salary Range	Role Description	Job Possibilities
In-school, teaching	Bachelor's Degree * Specialization* Student Teaching*	Vounteer work with children† Camp counselor† Babysitter†	$10–26,000 for nine months	Instructional responsibilities completed by certified classroom teacher in formal school organization.	Improvement over 1970s in all areas. Better possibilities in rural areas and Sun Belt. Needs exist in special education, mathematics, science, and vocational education.
In-school, nonteaching	Bachelor's (except for nurses)* Specialization* Postbachelors and Masters–Counselor, Psychologist, Principal*	Extensive experiences with children† Teaching experience†	$10–35,000	Educational support provided in emotional, physical, and cognitive areas. Responsibilities carried out within formal school organization.	Among the best rapid-growth areas in the last decade.
Teaching, nonschool	Bachelor's Degree* Area of specialization outside education*	Teaching experience† Acquire specialized content knowledge*	$8–20,000	Conveying specialized school-related knowledge in formal organization outside school.	An emerging area for jobs in 1980s.
Community, youth, and family services	Bachelor's Degree* Specialized training outside education*†	Teaching experience† Volunteer work with groups†	$8–35,000	Conveying specialized knowledge usually not related to school curriculum, with emphasis on the psychomotor and affective areas.	An emerging area because of increased leisure time. Long-term employment not guaranteed because of problems with funding sources.

	Preparation Required	Experiences	Salary Range	Role Description	Job Possibilities
Higher education	Master's Degree* Doctorate†	Teaching experience with children* Experience with school organizations†	$12–42,000	Expert in specific school-related area. Some offer direct service (e.g., teacher preparation); others offer indirect service (e.g., educational researcher)	The shrinking job market of the 1970s will improve in the 1980s.
School support	Bachelor's Degree* Specialized training*	Teaching experience†	$15–75,000	Concern with all aspects of education; do not have direct involvement with teaching/learning process.	Many positions in area are new since the 1960s. With the demands currently being placed on schools by the public, additional support staff needed.
Government agencies	Bachelor's Degree* Master's and doctorate†	Teaching experience†	$15–50,000	Individuals responsible for developing and implementing policy and programs mandated by legislative bodies	Legislatures have mandated that specified groups receive improved education (e.g., handicapped and the disadvantaged). These mandates have opened additional occupational possibilities in government agencies.

*Required
†Recommended

Summary   We have tried to provide an overview of a variety of alternative educational careers. You will need to review these possibilities as well as many others before you settle upon a career choice. You will find it useful to turn to Table 12.3 as you plan your career. We hope the table and the preceding narrative have made you aware of new careers in the area of education. We have tried to provide you with a brief synopsis of several types of jobs, including background experiences required, salary range, role description, and job possibilities after you graduate. If you have not yet made a choice, do not feel discouraged: It will take much time and consideration. What is important is that you are thinking about the many alternatives that are available and are constantly gathering information that will assist you in making an intelligent decision. Careers not discussed in this chapter, as well as others that do not even exist yet, can have an effect on your plans. Your career is just that, a plan. A plan should be adapted, added to, and changed. The plan gives you a framework that will assist you as you develop professionally.

Welcome to the field of education! We hope the excitement that you now have will continue until your retirement in the twenty-first century.

Encounters

1. There are just too many career possibilities to give equal time to each one. In this chapter we identified seven categories of career choices. Rank each category with your personal preference.

YOUR PREFERENCE	CAREER CATEGORY
_____	In-school; teaching
_____	In-school; nonteaching
_____	Teaching; nonschool
_____	Community, youth, and family services
_____	Higher education
_____	School support
_____	Government agencies

2. Does your preparation (e.g., university studies, volunteer work, paid work experiences) match well with your top three career categories? If not, what additional experiences will you need?

3. Outline the pluses and minuses (advantages and disadvantages) of your first career category choice. Repeat for your first and second choices.

PLUS	MINUS

4. An important factor in selecting a career is observing a person presently in that position. List the careers in which you are interested. Are there any possible careers that you have not observed? If so, make arrangements to observe and interview a person in those roles.

5. Will your work roles be preparatory "training" for your career goal? Will you need additional academic training? Outline briefly the work and educational experiences that you believe would be ideal preparation for your career choice.

6. Before you can make career choices, you will need additional information. List people and agencies from whom you can acquire additional information about your career choice. Examples might include your college advisor, the college placement office, and professional organizations.
7. College placement centers have records of organizations that interview and employ education majors. Make arrangements for a representative of the college placement office to come to your class and discuss career possibilities.
8. Are you willing to take a risk? Outline guesses about your career aspirations a decade from now. Two decades from now. (You will be in the twenty-first century.)

For More Information

JOURNALS

Adams, Polly K., and Taylor, Michael K. "Volunteer Help in the Classroom," *Education Unlimited, 2* (1980), 26–27.

Barrett, Marjie C., and McKelvey, Jane. "Stresses and Strains on the Child Care Worker: Typologies for Assessment," *Child Welfare, 59* (1980), 277–286.

Dreskin, Wendy. "Where Have All the Preschools Gone?" *Instructor, 89* (1980) 26–27.

Furcron, Margaret. "Setting Up a Tutoring Program," *Journal of Developmental and Remedial Education, 3* (1980), 27–29.

Kraft, Daniel W. "New Approaches to the Substitute Teacher Problem," *NASSP Bulletin, 64* (1980), 79–86.

Lolli, Anthony, Jr. "Implementing the Role of the School Psychologist," *Psychology in the Schools, 17* (1980), 70–74.

Arnstein, Allen C. "Teacher Surplus? Trends in Education's Supply and Demand," *Educational Horizons, 57* (1979), 112–118.

Podemski, Richard S., and Childres, John H., Jr. "The Counselor as Change Agent: An Organizational Analysis," *School Counselor, 27* (1980), 168–174.

Schiff, Martin. "The Principal as a Personnel Leader," *Educational Horizons, 56* (1978), 121–125.

Schiff, Martin. "A School Guard Who is Taken for Granted: The School Nurse," *NJEA Review, 53* (1980), 20–21.

Scurfield, Raymond Monsour. "Educational Preparation for Social Work Administrators: A Survey," *Journal of Education for Social Work, 16* (1980), 49–56.

Zehring, John William. "How to Get Another Teaching Job and What to Do if You Can't," *Learning,* (1978), 44, 46–51.

BOOKS

Brill, Naomi I. *Working With People: The Helping Process.* Philadelphia: Lippincott, 1978.

Feldman, Beverly N. *Jobs: Careers Serving Children and Youth.* Los Angeles: Till Press, 1978.

Fine, Janet. *Opportunities in Teaching Careers.* Skokie, Ill.: VGM Career Horizons, 1977.

Greenburg, Polly. *Day Care: Do-It-Yourself Staff Growth Program.* Washington, D.C.: The Growth Program, 1975.

Melaragno, Ralph J. *Tutoring With Students: A Handbook for Establishing Tutorial Programs in Schools.* Englewood Cliffs, N.J.: Educational Technology Publications, 1976.

Student National Education Association. *Interview Skills for Teachers, Training Manual.* Washington, D.C.: Student National Education Association, 1976.

Tripodi, Tony, ed. *Social Workers at Work: An Introduction to Social Work Practice.* Itasca, Ill.: F.E. Peacock Publishers, 1972.

U.S. Department of Labor, Bureau of Labor Statistics. *Occupational Outlook Handbook, 1980-1981 Edition.* Washington, D.C.: U.S. Government Printing Office, 1980.

United States. Women's Bureau. *Training For Child Care Work, Project Fresh Start: A CETA Program Model.* Worcester, Mass.: U.S. Dept. of Labor, Women's Bureau, 1979.

Weldy, Gilbert, R. *Principals: What They Do and Who They Are.* Reston, Va.: National Association of Secondary School Principals, 1979.

EPILOGUE

The world of schools includes children, teachers, parents, administrations, psychologists, and coaches — and the list goes on and on. Is there a place for you in this exciting, rewarding, and often trying world? We hope this book has helped you take a positive step toward answering that crucial question. We would like every one of you to capitalize on your idealism in making schools better places for learning to occur, in terms of both intellectual and human development. But we also want you to enter the profession with a strong background in the realities of what you will face. Teaching will not be easy. You will know success, but you will also know failure. You will feel joy, but also despair. Parents will entrust you with what is most precious to them, but they will hold you accountable for their child's growth and happiness.

Our society has made the role of the teacher one of utmost importance. We now spend more money educating our children than we spend for national defense, and the bulk of this expenditure goes for the salaries of more than 2 million elementary and secondary teachers.

If you choose education as your career, you may teach or you may go into one of the myriad of educationally-related occupations. Whatever your choice, we hope that you approach your career with determination, humor, and a passionate desire to make a positive difference in the lives of children.

GLOSSARY

Ability Level The optimal level at which a student can function in any given content area. Ability levels vary greatly from one student to another.

Acceleration A method sometimes used as part of a special program for the gifted. It may include any or all of the following: early school entrance, grade skipping, advance placement in college, credit courses taken in high school, and early graduation.

Accountability The theory that teachers and school systems may be held responsible for improvements in student achievement and that such improvements are measurable through tests.

Accreditation An evaluative process used to indicate the quality of programs within a school system or institution of higher education. Such evaluations are conducted by an association of professional educators.

Achievement Test A test designed to measure a student's knowledge and skill in a given subject area.

Affective Domain That part of human existence that involves feelings, emotions, attitudes and values. In teaching it centers on areas such as fostering positive feelings about learning and high self-esteem.

Aide (See PARAPROFESSIONAL.)

Alternative School Any school, public or private, that offers educational programs significantly different from traditional educational concepts and practices (for example, free schools, open schools, and storefront schools).

Arbitration In collective bargaining, a process whereby both parties may submit their dispute to an impartial third person, who recommends a course of action that is usually a compromise. If the parties are required to accept the decision, the process is called binding arbitration.

Assessment Any method, e.g., tests or observation, for measuring how a school, a teacher, or a student is functioning in a particular situation or area of concern.

Authoritarian In teaching, this refers to a person who stresses strict obedience and rigid control and who discourages input from students.

Back To Basics A movement among some parents and educators who favor a return to the educational "basics." Some interpret this to mean focusing on factual knowledge, some as a return to what they feel is more acceptable student behavior, and some as a return to emphasis on basic skills, particularly in the areas of reading and mathematics.

Basic Skill A skill that is fundamental to the mastery of a school subject.

Behavior Disorder A disorder in which children exhibit extreme behaviors that someone has labeled as unacceptable. These behaviors take such forms as aggression or withdrawal.

Behavior Modification A method for changing a person's mode of conduct that stresses the use of positive reinforcement to encourage desirable behavior. This method focuses on positive results rather than on the underlying causes of the original undesirable behavior.

Behavioral Objectives The aims or objectives of education stated as actual performance criteria or as observable descriptions of measurable behavior.

Career Education Comprehensive educational program that focuses on individual career development from childhood through the adult years.

Certification The process through which state departments of education designate who may legally be employed as teachers and the act of issuing certificates to such qualified persons.

Child-Centered Curriculum A program for educating children in which the needs and interests of the students are the primary concern. Determining the needs of children, however, remains a highly controversial area.

Child Find The massive national effort mandated by Public Law 94-142 to identify all handicapped children living in the United States.

Cognitive Domain Those things that have to do with thought, knowledge, and perception. In the classroom this involves skills such as classifying, analyzing, imagining and creating.

Collective Bargaining An attempt by representatives of both the employees and the employer to reach an agreement on wages and working conditions.

Community Education Educational plans or programs that involve parents, teachers, children, and other members of the local community in the learning process.

Compensatory Education Educational programs designed to lessen the academic problems commonly associated with students considered to be disadvantaged (usually a socioeconomic distinction). Such programs are usually funded at either a state or federal level.

Competency-Based Teacher Education (CBTE) Teacher education programs in which specific skills and behaviors are outlined. All prospective teachers must demonstrate these skills and behaviors as a condition for certification.

Computer-Assisted Instruction (CAI) Instruction in which a computer is used to supplement the teacher's instruction; the computer does not replace the teacher.

Computer-Managed Instruction (CMI) Usually an individualized instructional program in which a computer is used as a record-keeping device to store information regarding student progress.

Consultant (educational) An expert in some specialized area of education, whose advice is sought in improving education offerings, facilities, etc.

Core Curriculum A plan for developing unified studies based upon the common needs of the learners and organized without restriction by subject matter.

Corporal Punishment Disciplinary action in which one person (usually the teacher) inflicts physical pain on another person (usually the student). In the public schools of today, corporal punishment most commonly implies paddling.

Criterion-Referenced Evaluation Used to determine mastery of a particular skill. The level of mastery deemed acceptable is the criterion by which the student's performance is judged.

Curriculum (academic)
1. A systematic group of courses required for graduation or certification.
2. A general plan of the content or specific materials of instruction that the school should offer the student.
3. Everything that occurs, planned as well as unplanned, in the classroom.

Decentralization A process in which some higher, central authority assigns certain functions to subordinate positions.

Departmentalization An organizational structure based on division into specific areas of knowledge. Such a structure is typically found in secondary schools and colleges, and is also used to some extent in the upper elementary grades.

Desegregation Process of integrating a previously segregated facility or system. In education, it usually refers to changing a school system from one that separates races into one in which schools and classes are racially mixed in a nondiscriminatory pattern.

Diagnosis In teaching, this refers to the process of searching out the specific strengths and weaknesses of a student and finding specific reasons for a student's failure to master a skill or concept.

Diagnostic-Prescriptive Teaching A method of teaching in which the work of an individual child is analyzed in order to diagnose learning problems and prescribe activities to help overcome those problems. Pre- and post-tests are used to assess the student's progress.

Differentiated Staffing School staffing patterns in which teachers are assigned varying roles with differing responsibilities. Such patterns are most common in schools that use team teaching.

Disadvantaged Child A child who has an impoverished range of experience and whose physical needs are often met at a mere subsistence level. Such a child is often deprived of toys, verbal interaction, written materials in the home, and often adequate food and medical attention.

Discovery Learning An instructional approach in which direct exploration and interaction lead the student to discover a concept without having it explained by the teacher.

Due Process The exercise of official power to protect individual rights. Due process is now used in situations such as student suspension from school, disputed adequacy of special education programs, and termination of teaching contracts.

Educable Mentally Retarded For educational purposes, this label is usually applied to children with mildly impaired intellectual functioning.

Enrichment A method sometimes used as part of a special program for the gifted in which individualized modifications within the regular class are designed to permit the very capable student to progress at his or her own pace and to pursue individual interests.

Evaluation The process of judging, measuring, and/or testing, to determine the degree to which performance reflects prespecified criteria.

Exceptional Child A child who deviates markedly from the developmental norms of a particular age group (intellectually, physically, socially, or emotionally).

Extracurricular Activities Planned learning experiences, usually provided outside a classroom setting, but under school guidance. Common examples include athletic programs, student government, and various clubs (debate, glee, auto, etc.)

Family Educational Rights and Privacy Act Passed by Congress in 1974, this act gives parents the right to inspect their child's school records, protects the confidentiality of student records, and establishes procedures through which parents can challenge the information contained in student records.

Flexible Scheduling A method of scheduling class periods that allows for their shortening or lengthening to fit the time requirements of a variety of activities.

Formal Learning Any training or education that is given in an orderly, planned and systematic manner.

Free School A school with an unstructured curriculum and a relationship of equality and informality between teachers and students.

Gifted Child A child who is far more educable than most children or whose performance is consistently outstanding in some worthwhile type of human endeavor (e.g. intellectual, physical, or artistic performance).

Hardware Originally used to refer to the mechanical or electronic devices used in computer technology. The term is also currently used to refer to the technological equipment that serves as media for educational purposes, such as videotape recorder, computer terminals, and film projectors.

Head Start A federally funded preschool program designed to provide compensatory experience for children from low-income families.

Hearing Impaired A label used in referring to children with a hearing loss significant enough to affect learning. This term encompasses the entire range of hearing loss, from mildly hard-of-hearing to profoundly deaf.

Heterogeneous Grouping Instructional groups with a high degree of dissimilarity in terms of ability and intellectual performance.

Hidden Curriculum The unplanned informal learning experiences that occur as a natural by-product of school life. Such experiences normally reinforce existing social values. For example, competitive grading systems and spelling bees reinforce the competitive values underlying the free-enterprise system.

Homebound Instruction Individual instruction in the child's home under the tutelage of an itinerant teacher.

Homogeneous Grouping Instructional groups having a relatively high degree of similarity regarding certain factors that affect learning, such as ability and intellectual performance.

Individualized Education Program (IEP) A detailed plan for educating a handicapped child that must meet the specific needs of that child. IEPs must be developed jointly by a representative of the school administration, the teacher, the parents and when appropriate, the student. Annual IEPs for all handicapped children have been mandated by Public Law 94-142.

Individualized Instruction Instruction that is tailored to the needs of individual students and situations. It is normally characterized by such features as clear learning objectives, detailed student assessments, learner-selected objectives, frequent feedback, mastery learning, etc.

Informal Learning Learning acquired by oneself through reading, real-life experience, etc.

Innovation (Educational) The introduction of a new idea, method, or device into school operations. Recent innovations include practices such as computer-assisted education.

In-service A plan for providing practicing educators with ongoing training or current knowledge related to their educational role. Such training may include workshops, seminars, or the showing of films. These may be conducted during or after regular school hours, either at the school or at some outside site.

Instructional Resources Anything used for instructional purposes. Although the term is generally confined to materials specifically designed for educational purposes, such as films, worksheets, audio-visual materials, educational toys, etc., almost any physical object can be adapted to instructional ends in the hands of a creative teacher.

Intelligence The use of mental processes to solve problems. Because of disagreement among psychologists about what constitutes intelligence, it is sometimes defined as being what is measured by an intelligence test.

Intelligence Quotient (IQ) A measure for expressing the level of mental development in relation to chronological age. It is obtained by dividing the mental age (as measured by a general intelligence test) by the chronological age and multiplying by 100. For example, if a child's mental age is 12 and the chronological age is 10, the IQ would be 120: $(12 \times 100)/10 = 120$.

Interaction Analysis Any of several methods for analyzing communication patterns (verbal and/or nonverbal). Often, an interaction analysis will be done for a specific classroom.

Learning Disability A "category" of exceptionality that is educational rather than psychological or medical. Children with learning disabilities are considered to be essentially "normal" but have problems or weaknesses in specific areas, such as perceptual handicaps, dyslexia, or minimal brain dysfunction.

Least Restrictive Alternative Public Law 94-142 has mandated that handicapped children be educated in the educational setting that offers the least restrictive alternative. This means that, whenever possible, these children should be educated with nonhandicapped students and that special classrooms or schools be used only when the severity of the handicap precludes an adequate education in the regular classroom.

Magnet School A public school with some type of unique educational program designed to attract students. Such schools are frequently associated with attempts at voluntary desegregation.

Mainstreaming The process of integrating children with special educational needs into regular (mainstream) classrooms for at least part of each school day.

Mastery Learning School of thought which rests on the assumption that mastery of a topic is theoretically possible for all children, given sufficient time and optimum quality of instruction.

Microteaching A scaled-down, controlled teaching encounter used to provide introductory teaching experience, in-service training, or a controlled environment for research. Normally it involves no more than eight students, lasts only about five minutes, and focuses on a specific teaching skill, such as introducing a lesson, lesson closure, or questioning techniques.

Minimum Competence Standards Formal statements of the lowest student achievement that will be deemed acceptable for graduation.

Multicultural Education Special programs provided to minority students to enable them to make the transition into classrooms that are culturally different from their own background.

Nongraded School A school in which grade labels are not applied to the students and in which instruction is given on an individual basis or in groups formed on the basis of subject matter mastery rather than by chronological age.

Normal College The name formerly given to teacher-training institutions.

Open Classroom The open classroom represents the antithesis of the traditional classroom. There is a spirit of openness that is evident in the architecture of the buildings and classrooms, and in the use of materials and time. Students move naturally in the school environments, working on individualized and personalized instructional programs. Emphasis of instruction is on the development of the individual child within the context of general norms.

Paraprofessional   Someone who assists the teacher by assuming a variety of roles. These may include supervising students, evaluating some aspects of students' work, assisting in a lab or materials center, doing clerical chores, etc.

Parochial School   A school conducted by some church or religious group, usually without tax support.

Peer Group   Usually interpreted as people who are similar in developmental level, age, or experience.

Process-oriented Curriculum   A curriculum that stresses the process skills normally associated with the scientific method, e.g., observation, measurement, classification, prediction, communication, and inference.

Programmed Instruction   Instruction provided from a workbook, textbook, mechanical, or electronic device, in which the content has been carefully sequenced into small, easily mastered elements, with each element building upon the preceding ones and with feedback (answers) provided at each step. Such instruction allows each student to progress at his own rate.

Project Follow-Through   A federally funded program for children in grades K-3. Each community is encouraged to adopt a curriculum approach which matches the needs of the children in the community.

Psychomotor Domain   Those areas of learning that involve physical movement and coordination.

Public Law 94-142   This law, entitled "The Education for All Handicapped Children Act," was enacted in 1975 and affirms the right of every handicapped child, regardless of the severity of the handicap, to a free, appropriate education.

Release Time   Time granted by schools to

their teachers to attend conferences and workshops or to pursue particular school projects during regular school hours. May also be used to refer to time granted to students for the purpose of attending religious classes.

Remedial Instruction   Instruction specifically designed to help students overcome some diagnosed learning deficiency.

Role Playing   An instructional technique in which a student spontaneously acts out a situation or condition, such as a job interview in a secondary vocational education course.

School Board   The local agency responsible for conducting the business of the local public education system. Although usually elected, school board members are sometimes appointed. School boards determine regulations and policy for the school system, but hire administrative personnel (e.g., superintendents) to implement their policies.

School Without Walls   An educational innovation popularized in the late 1960s and early 1970s, in which self-contained classrooms were eliminated in favor of large, open areas that were used for large numbers of children. Such schools also often embrace such ideas as team teaching, flexible scheduling, and multiage grouping.

Self-Contained Classroom   The traditional organized arrangement for elementary schools in which a given class, teacher, and materials are contained within one room.

Sex Discrimination   The denial of certain rights or privileges to some individuals on the basis of their sex.

Spiral Curriculum   An instructional program that begins with very basic concepts and "spirals" upward through increasingly difficult and more complex levels.

Standardized Tests   Commercially prepared tests, such as achievement tests, aptitude tests, and intelligence tests, that have been checked for reliability and for which norms have been established.

Storefront School Classes held in an available store, usually in the inner city.

Student–Teacher Ratio An index of the number of students per teacher in a classroom, in a school, or in an entire school system. For example, two teachers handling 45 students in an open space classroom represent a student–teacher ratio of 22.5 to 1 (45:2).

Supplementary Materials Materials used to enrich the primary instructional resources or for providing additional practice. In most classrooms a basic text is the primary instructional tool, with newspapers, workbooks, hand-out sheets, films, etc. being used as supplementary or enrichment devices.

Survival Skills Often linked to the accountability and back-to-basics movements, these skills include the ability to perform activities such as balancing a checkbook, figuring one's taxes, completing a job application, and computing the unit price for comparison shopping.

Team Teaching An instructional approach in which teachers work as a team to plan for and instruct a large group of students. Ideally, this allows each teacher to contribute his or her special talents to the entire group.

Tenure A system of employment in which teachers, having served a probationary period, retain their position indefinitely under protection by statute or rule of the school board.

Trainable Mentally Retarded For educational purposes, this label usually refers to children with moderately impaired intellectual functioning.

Upward Bound A program designed to generate the skills and motivation needed for educational success in and beyond high school among students from low-income backgrounds.

Visually Handicapped A term generally applied to children whose vision is impaired to such an extent that it requires educational modifications and adaptations. Some visually-impaired children can use printed material with special devices, while others must use materials other than print (i.e. braille or taped material).

Voucher System A plan in which parents would receive a voucher for each school-age child that could be used at the school of their choice. The school would exchange the voucher for operating funds.

Film Distributor Addresses

Anti-Defamation League of B'nai B'rith
315 Lexington Ave.
N.Y., N.Y. 10016

BFA Educational Media
Div. of Columbia Broadcasting System, Inc.
221 Michigan Ave.
P.O. Box 1795
Santa Monica, CA 90406

Baily Films (see BFA Educational)

Barbre, Thomas J., Productions
2130 S. Bellaire St.
Denver, CO 80223

Benchmark Films
145 Scarborough Rd.
Briarcliff Manor, N.Y. 10510

Carousel Films
1501 Broadway, Suite 1503
N.Y., N.Y. 10036

Center for Urban Education
105 Madison Ave.
N.Y., N.Y. 10016

Columbia Pictures
711 5th Ave.
N.Y., N.Y. 10022

Coronet, Div. of Esquire, Inc.
65 E. South Water St.
Chicago, IL 60601

EBEC: Encyclopedia Britannica Educational
    Corp.
425 N. Michigan Ave.
Chicago, IL 60611

EDC: Education Development Center, Inc.
55 Chapel St.
Newton, MA 02160

Films Incorporated
1144 Wilmette Ave.
Wilmette, IL 60091

Franciscan Communications Center
Telekinetics
1229 S. Santee St.
Los Angeles, CA 90015

Holt, Rinehart and Winston
383 Madison Ave.
N.Y., N.Y. 10017

IDEA: Institute for Development of Educa-
    tional Activities, Inc.
P.O. Box 446
Melbourne, FL. 32901

IMS: Instructional Media Services
128 E. Pittsburgh St.
Greensburg, PA 15601

Indiana University Audiovisual Center
Bloomington, IN 47401

International Film Bureau, Inc.
332 S. Michigan Ave.
Chicago, Il 60604

MLA: Modern Learning Aids
P.O. Box 1712
Rochester, N.Y. 14603

McGraw-Hill Films
1221 Avenue of the Americas
N.Y., N.Y. 10020

Media Five
3211 Cahvenga Boulevard West
Hollywood, CA 90068

Kent State University Audiovisual Center
Kent, OH 44242

Media Guild
118 S. Acacia
Box 881
Solana Beach, CA 92075

NBC Educational Enterprises
30 Rockefeller Plaza
N.Y., N.Y. 10020

National Education Association
1201 Sixteenth Street, NW
Washington, D.C. 20036

National Film Board of Canada
1251 Avenue of the Americas, 16th floor
N.Y., N.Y. 10020

Ohio State University
159 W. 19th Ave.
Columbus, OH 43210

Sterling Educational Films, Inc.
241 E. 34th St.
N.Y., N.Y. 10016

Time-Life Multimedia
Time-Life Building
N.Y., N.Y. 10020

University of California
Extension Media Center
2223 Fulton St.
Berkeley, CA 94720

INDEX